Nick Lloyd is Lecturer in Defence Studies at King's College London, based at the Joint Services Command and Staff College in Shrivenham, Wiltshire. He is the author of *Loos 1915* (2006) and holds a PhD from the University of Birmingham.

'A brilliant piece of almost forensic revisionist history.'
— **Denis Judd, author of** *Empire: The British Imperial Experience from 1765 to the Present.*

'Nick Lloyd's study of the massacre at Jallianwala Bagh is a stirring tale well told.'
— **Kaushik Roy, author of** *The Oxford Companion to Modern Warfare in India.*

THE
AMRITSAR MASSACRE

The Untold Story of
One Fateful Day

Nick Lloyd

I.B. TAURIS

LONDON · NEW YORK

The analysis, opinions and conclusions expressed or implied in this book are those of the author and do not necessarily represent the views of the JSCSC, the UK MOD or any other government agency.

Published in 2011 by I.B.Tauris & Co Ltd
6 Salem Road, London W2 4BU
175 Fifth Avenue, New York NY 10010
www.ibtauris.com

Distributed in the United States and Canada Exclusively by Palgrave Macmillan
175 Fifth Avenue, New York NY 10010

ISBN: 978 1 84885 723 0

A full CIP record for this book is available from the British Library
A full CIP record is available from the Library of Congress

Library of Congress Catalog Card Number: available

Typeset in Adobe Garamond Pro by MPS Limited, a Macmillan Company
Printed and bound in Sweden by ScandBook AB

Dedicated to the memory of George Macdonald Fraser
(1925–2008)

Contents

List of Illustrations

List of Maps

Abbreviations

CID	Criminal Investigation Department
CSAS	Centre for South Asian Studies, University of Cambridge
CWMG	Collected Works of Mahatma Gandhi
GOC	General Officer Commanding
ICS	Indian Civil Service
IOC	India Office Collections, British Library, London
IWM	Imperial War Museum, London
LHCMA	Liddell Hart Centre for Military Archives, King's College London
NAI	National Archives of India, New Delhi
NCO	Non-Commissioned Officer
NWFP	North-West Frontier Province
OC	Officer Commanding
PSA	Punjab State Archives, Chandigarh
RAF	Royal Air Force
TNA	The National Archives of the UK, Kew

Acknowledgements

T he *Amritsar Massacre: The Untold Story of One Fateful Day* was written between 2006 and 2010 in Cranwell and Cheltenham, UK. It has always been an ambition to write a book about India and I would like to thank the following for their support and help. First, to Dr Mark Hilborne, Dr Ben Jones and Dr Bettina Renz, who became my friends during my time at RAF Cranwell, where much of the groundwork for this project was laid. Many thanks to Professor Clive Dewey for reading the manuscript and suggesting a number of additions, as well as being an invaluable sounding board for my ideas. For various other favours and encouragement, thanks to Matt Brosnan, Professor David French, Dr Nathan Greenfield, Stuart Hallifax, Dr David Omissi, Peter Robinson, Jonathan Walker and all at I.B. Tauris.

Thanks to my colleagues in the Defence Studies Department, King's College London, at the Joint Services Command and Staff College, Shrivenham, particularly Dr Guy Finch, Dr Ashley Jackson, Dr Saul Kelly and Mr Srinath Raghaven. The staff of the following institutions deserve praise for their valuable assistance: the Bodleian Library, Oxford; the British Library, London; the Centre for South Asian Studies, Cambridge; the RAF College Library, RAF Cranwell; the library at the Joint Services Command & Staff College, Shrivenham; the Imperial War Museum Department of Documents; the Maughan Library, London; the National Archives in Kew; the National Archives of India in New Delhi; and the Punjab State Archives in Chandigarh. Some of the ideas presented in this book have appeared in three journals, *BBC History Magazine*, *Small Wars & Insurgencies* and *South Asia*.

The research for this book was based on two visits to India in 2007 and 2009. My trip to India in October 2007 would not have been possible without the help and support of the Sandhu family. Many thanks to Prabhdev Singh and Mridula Chettri Singh for looking after me during my time in Delhi, and thanks to all the families in Chandigarh, particularly Jogi, Ghulam and

Brahm. I would also like to record the professional help of the following: Jaya Ravindran, whose efficiency and assistance during my time in the Research Room of the National Archives of India was beyond praise; and Parminder Kaur Sandhu of the Punjab State Archives, Chandigarh, was extremely helpful and guided me through their holdings over tea and lively conversation. I was able to visit India again in September and October 2009 owing to a British Academy research grant, when I was able to locate some final documents and visit the Amritsar District Record Room. On this trip I received a great deal of help from the following: Swarn Singh Kahlon; Kahan Singh Pannu (Deputy Commissioner, Amritsar); Dr Mahesh Rangarajan; Professor Balvinder Singh; Dr Karamjeet Singh (Deputy Commissioner, Gurdaspur); Praveen K. Sinha; Professor Ian Talbot; and all the staff at the Amritsar District Record Room. Thanks also to Rattan Bhandari and all those I met at Mrs Bhandari's Guesthouse in Amritsar. Finally, thanks to my friends and family, and of course, Louise.

NL
Cheltenham

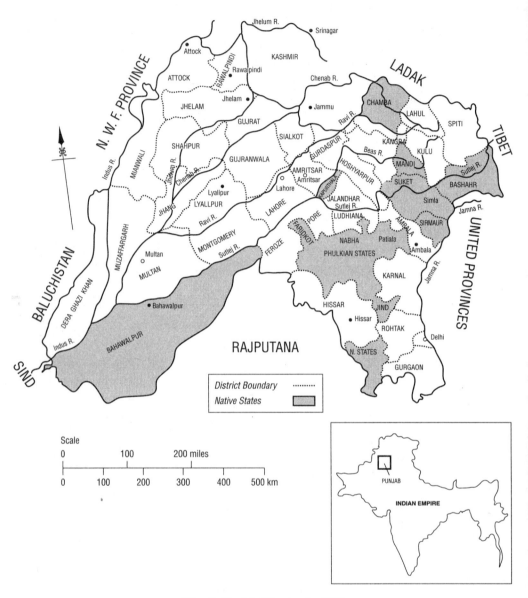

Map 1. Punjab Districts in 1911

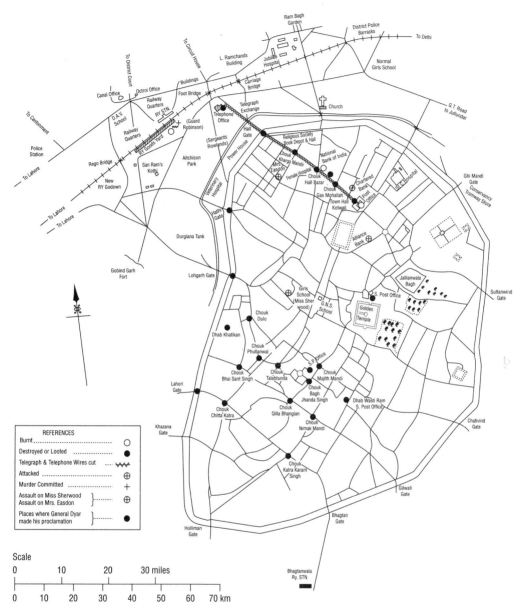

Map 2. Amritsar city, from the official inquiry

Tragedies and horrors and disasters do occur in the history of men, and it is useless to pretend that they do not. In the history of India they have not been wanting; and as in the case of the Mutiny, there have been instances where the racial element was introduced and where there were deeds of blackness and shame. But that is no reason for ignoring them. Pass over them the sponge of forgiveness; blot them out with the finger of mercy and reconciliation. But do not pretend that they did not take place, and do not, for the sake of a false and mawkish sentiment, forfeit your chance of honouring that which is worthy of honour. All these events are wayside marks in the onward stride of time. God Almighty placed them there; and if some of the stepping-stones over which the English and the Indian people in this country have marched to a better understanding, and a truer union, have been slippery with human blood, do not ignore or cast them away. Rather let us wipe them clear of their stains, and preserve them intact for the teaching of those that come after.

Lord Curzon,
Viceroy of India,
at the opening of the Mutiny Telegraph Memorial, Delhi,
19 April 1902

Preface

Massacre at the Jallianwala Bagh

While I was searching for my brother, I saw, the Bagh was like a battlefield. There were corpses scattered everywhere in heaps, and the wounded were crying out for water.

Lala Karam Chand[1]

Amritsar, Northern India, 11 April 1919

Brigadier-General Reginald Dyer confidently made his way up the steps and into the foyer of the railway station. Dyer, known as 'Rex' to his friends, was tired and stiff from the journey but he tried not to show it. He had come from Jullunder, a dusty garrison town about 90 kilometres to the east, driving for several hours in darkness along the Grand Trunk Road and arriving just after 9 p.m. Dyer was not terribly impressed with what he found. The atmosphere in the railway station was not unlike that of a siege; a mixture of suppressed panic, nervousness and fear. The station had become the headquarters of the administration after it had lost control of the old walled city the previous afternoon. As most stations did in India, it occupied a strategic position between the old city and the European settlement, the cantonment, which lay further to the north.

The party that was there to greet Dyer was led by the Deputy Commissioner, Miles Irving. By his side was the Deputy Superintendent of Police, Mr Reginald Plomer. Irving was a mild-mannered man, perhaps ill-suited to the grave situation that he was faced with at Amritsar, and obviously relieved that a senior commander was now on hand to restore order. After shaking hands, Irving invited Dyer into his headquarters where they could talk.

Following Irving and Plomer, Dyer made his way through the station to a hastily converted railway carriage that lay next to the main platform and then, sitting down, Irving gloomily explained what had happened. Upon receiving orders for the arrest and deportation of two local nationalist leaders, men whom the civil authorities believed had been inciting sedition and disloyalty for many years, Irving had summoned them to his residence in the civil lines yesterday morning. The two men, Drs Kitchlew and Satyapal, were then taken into custody and driven to Dharamsala, further to the north, where they were detained.

It was at this point, Irving said, that things had begun to go badly wrong. Although he was convinced that the violence was the result of a pre-planned conspiracy – he had been warning the government about it for some time – the arrests only sparked the violence that they had wanted to prevent. Within an hour news of the deportation began to spread through the city, causing people to spill out onto the streets and form into larger and larger groups, demanding the release of the two men. Irving issued orders that any crowds should be prevented from getting into the civil lines and sent troops to the bridges over the railway line to head them off. He arrived shortly afterwards. 'They were very noisy,' Irving recounted, 'a furious crowd, you could hear the roar of them up the long road; they were an absolutely mad crowd, spitting with rage and swearing.'[2] Irving sounded terrified. He was sure that they were in danger of being overwhelmed. Several shots were fired and they backed off. Although no one was sure exactly what happened next, it seems that mobs then stormed back into the city and attacked various buildings, banks mainly, but also post and telegraph offices. They knew that five Europeans had been murdered and at least three others had been seriously assaulted, including a female missionary, Marcia Sherwood. The situation was incredibly serious. They were threatened, Irving claimed, 'with the greatest calamity since the mutiny'.[3]

☙

Dyer was 54 years of age and commander of 45 Brigade at Jullunder.[4] A tall, well-built man, Dyer looked like a soldier, with clipped, greying hair and a stiff, smart moustache. He was a hard-working officer of middling ability, full of courage and 'dash', but some would have accused him of lacking more cerebral qualities. One of those who knew him while he was at the Staff College in Camberley, said that 'he does not know what fear means, and is happiest when crawling over a Burmese stockade with a revolver hanging from his teeth'.[5] Although Dyer was not stupid (he had spent many years patenting designs for infantry range-finding devices), he was a man of few subtleties, someone who knew what he believed in and would act upon those beliefs if he saw fit. He was a man accustomed to giving orders and to being obeyed.

In March 1918 Dyer had been given command of a brigade at Jullunder and took to his position like a man making up for lost time. His promotion to Brigadier-General marked a considerable achievement for someone who was not known for any sparkling promise and had not seen much active service during the Great War, apart from a brief spell in Eastern Persia. More worryingly, he was man in physical decline. The strain of operations in Persia had a harmful effect on his health. When heat exhaustion was combined with a bad fall from his horse in April 1917, which 'squashed the life' out of him,[6] Dyer's health became increasingly fragile. By the end of the war he was in constant pain and a lethargic, troubled figure. A chain-smoker, he was always with a cigarette between his fingers or fumbling for one that he either kept stuffed in envelopes or loose in the large pockets of his uniform.[7]

Irving seemed to be on the verge of collapse, rather bluntly telling Dyer that he could not deal with the situation any longer, that it was beyond all civil control and that it was up to him to take matters into his own hands. For Dyer the situation was very simple. 'Roughly speaking,' he would later claim, 'I understood the position to be that civil law was at an end and that military law would have to take its place for the time being.'[8] Dyer was not a man to spurn such an invitation and he immediately took action. He did not think there were sufficient facilities at the railway station so he decided to transfer his headquarters elsewhere. The place eventually selected was the Ram Bagh, a large park to the north of the city walls, which was well liked by his men.[9] Before this could be arranged, however, he led a small party through the eerie, deserted streets of the old town, down Hall Bazaar, past the still smouldering remains of the National Bank, which had been burnt and looted by mobs the previous day, towards the *kotwali* (police station). Once there he met the Chief Inspector of Police, Muhammad Ashraf Khan, and brought him back to his headquarters so he could explain what the situation was and who had been responsible for these 'dastardly acts' as Dyer would later call them. He also withdrew some men from the picquets, which he believed were too strong, and reorganised them into 'a larger striking force'.[10]

At ten o'clock the following morning Dyer led a strong party through the city: 120 British and 310 Indian troops, supported by two armoured cars. The reaction of the people they met on the way was hardly encouraging. Many shouted at them or spat on the ground as they passed. Dyer met a mob at the

Sultanwind Gate, which he managed to disperse peacefully, although he did consider opening fire.[11] He arrived back at the Ram Bagh at 2 p.m., exhausted from his foray into the city, but pleased that they had been able to make some arrests. His mood, however, was darkened by the news coming in from other parts of the Punjab, which may have been patchy and unclear, but was decidedly unnerving. Telegraph wires and railway lines were being torn up all over the province and large mobs were moving through the main towns and cities. At that moment Dyer could not be sure whether the reports and rumours he was hearing were true or just lies spread by those intent on confusing him. At 10 p.m., after hearing that a Mission Hospital near Atari was being attacked, a party of British troops were sent there. It seemed that the disturbances were spreading, out of the towns and into the rural areas, imperilling British control over the Punjab and placing Europeans who lived in more isolated areas in danger.

❧

The thirteenth of April dawned, as always with the *muezzin* calling the faithful to prayer and the holy verses of the Sikhs being sung at the Golden Temple. The old city of Amritsar was the most congested part of the province, a dense and confusing nest of buildings, many of which were two storeys high and built close together, which darkened the streets below. Water supply was always a difficulty in Amritsar, so at dawn the women of the city would make their way to the wells to bathe, before it got too hot and the streets came to life.[12] Usually it would not take long before the streets were full of pilgrims and the shops were open for business, but that day they remained closed, as they had done for the last two days. Many people remained in their homes, perhaps afraid of British reprisals, others fearing the possibility of outsiders coming into the city looking for loot.

For the British, breakfasting anxiously after another uneasy night, the morning brought no relief, only a greater sense of urgency in their attempts to restore normality. At 9 a.m. Dyer again returned to the city, leading a small party through the streets, reading out a proclamation that had been drafted the previous afternoon. No resident was allowed to leave the city without a pass and no person was to go into the streets after 8 p.m. or they would be liable to be shot. No procession would be permitted in the streets and any gatherings of four men would 'be looked upon and treated as an unlawful assembly and dispersed by force of arms if necessary'.[13] Moving through the city and reading the order was time-consuming and exhausting, which became even more so as the temperature rose during the morning. Preceded by the beat of a drum, the proclamation was read three times both in Urdu and Punjabi at 19 locations throughout the city. As the column made its painfully slow way down Hall Bazaar, more and more residents began to emerge from their homes and come out onto the streets to find out what was happening. One of those in the column estimated that around 400 to 500 people gathered in each location. As they went deeper into the city Dyer noticed that the crowds began to increase, particularly groups of young men standing around street corners; bored, sullen and hostile. There were also more and more people standing on the rooftops, peering down at the streets below, interested in what was happening. Some laughed at the soldiers and others jeered. One or two of the more aggressive men spat at Dyer or shouted at him, attacking the government and hailing Mahatma Gandhi or Dr Kitchlew.[14] Dyer's men did not meet with any violence or stone throwing, but to those soldiers in the column it often seemed that the population was so hostile that violence could have broken out at any moment. It was, therefore, with some relief that around 1.30 p.m. Dyer finally called a halt to the proclamation, turned his columns around and returned to the Ram Bagh.[15]

The afternoon was a slow one for the authorities. The heat was intense and unyielding, with temperatures soaring to over 40° Celsius. April was a hot month in India, a month when the sun comes up early and beats down upon the parched ground for the rest of the day, causing lethargy and tiredness, which was almost unbearable for those British officials who had had little sleep since 10 April. Dyer spent it at the Ram Bagh, smoking furiously, trying to find out what else he could about the situation elsewhere in the Punjab, studiously reading over the reports that came telling him of more unrest and disorder further to the north. But despite his best efforts to prevent any large gatherings from taking place, things were happening in the city. By the afternoon more and more people were moving into a piece of wasteground known as the Jallianwala Bagh. Some were shouting for the men who had been arrested, some were denouncing the British Government, but others were in the Bagh because it had been used for many years as an unofficial meeting place in the city; an open space near to the Golden Temple where people of all ages would gather. When Dyer heard news of this gathering, he went off to disperse it.

❧

The Bagh was not really a garden at all – as its name would suggest – but a large stretch of dusty wasteground, about six or seven acres in size, walled in on three sides by the backs of houses with a low wall at the far side. There were several trees, a well and a small tomb (*samadhi*). That day a grand meeting had been organised by the local branch of Mahatma Gandhi's civil disobedience movement, the *Satyagraha Sabha*. The committee, now without its two leaders who were in British custody, decided that they would meet and read out a letter from one of those who had been arrested and pass further resolutions against government, condemning the actions of the police on 10 April. It was said that an eminent local pleader, Lala Kanhyalal Bhatia, would speak.

The meeting had been going on for about three hours, with eight speakers having delivered orations to the crowd, denouncing the British Government and urging the adoption of passive resistance to tyranny, when Dyer's detachment arrived: 25 Baluchis and 25 Gurkhas armed with .303 Lee Enfield rifles, and 40 Gurkhas armed only with *kukris* (curved knives). Quietly, they formed up on either side of the entrance, lying down or kneeling; their rifles pointed at the huge mass of people before them. As soon as he was satisfied that they were ready, barely 30 seconds after entering the Bagh, Dyer gave the order to open fire. The firing had a devastating effect on those who were in the Bagh. When fire was opened, the crowd immediately panicked and stampeded to the narrow exits in a desperate attempt to escape.[16] There seems to have been a cry (perhaps from one of the speakers) that the troops were only firing blanks, but this illusion did not last long when it became obvious that people were being hit and falling to the ground.[17] Although several retired Jat and Sikh officers who were in the crowd tried to get people to lie down, and hence avoid the worst of the rifle fire, this was not notably successful and panic ensued.

From the piece of raised ground where Dyer's party stood the view was one of horror. John Rehill apparently retraced his steps from the Bagh because he could not stand to watch the slaughter; later suffering from bouts of depression, never speaking about the incident and taking solace in bottles of whisky and gin.[18] A resident of Amritsar, Ghulam Mohammed, was hit by two bullets; one sliced through his cheek and lodged in his lower jaw, another struck him on the back of the right arm, passing through his armpit before stopping in his right shoulder. Wazir Ali was also wounded twice that afternoon. He was hit in the right eye and also shot in the chest with the bullet passing through him. Another resident, Seth Lakhmi Chand, tried to escape by running for an exit by the well, but by the time he reached it, it was impassable and blocked by large numbers of bodies. He tried to find another way out, but before he could do so he was hit in the right ankle by a bullet. He fell to the ground and lost consciousness.[19] It was not just the sight of hundreds of people being hit by bullets that was disturbing. The grating sound of rifle fire, combined with the screams and cries of the crowd, made for a horrid cacophony that echoed around the Bagh and into the surrounding streets. People in Amritsar could still recall the roar that was produced when Dyer's 50 rifles opened fire many years later.

The shooting continued for up to ten minutes; its intensity waxing and waning as Dyer directed. For him, the key areas of concern were the two narrow exits that lay on either side of the Bagh. It was here that large numbers of people were massing, panicking and clambering on top of one another. He personally directed fire onto these points and also made sure that all those who tried to scale the rear wall were fired upon.[20] One of those watching the scene was a local businessman, Girdhari Lal. He gazed in horror at the gunfire that was being directed at people trying to reach these exits, resulting in piles of dead and wounded, many of whom each received numerous bullet wounds.[21] There was precious little shelter. Although many people ran to the exits or behind the *samadhi* – perhaps the best cover available – for many the only other means of escape was the well near the northeastern wall. But this soon turned into a death trap, with many people either jumping or falling in only to drown in the tepid, polluted water at the bottom. Another possible escape route was at the other side of the garden next to the Hansli Gate. Lala Karam Chand, an assistant accountant from Patiala, was one of those who tried to get out this way. As soon as fire was opened, he ran towards this exit, but:

> The end of the passage was blocked by a wall as high as my chest, and so people could not get out quickly, but only one by one. When I got into the passage, I saw that people were being shot down behind me. I tried to crunch down and saw that the trap door of the Hansli was broken. So, in the crush, I managed to get down into it, one leg at a time. I got into the water up to my thigh at the place where the lid over it was broken. Three other men slipped in.[22]

Lala Karam Chand had been one of the fortunate few to take cover in a drain next to the Hansli Gate. Like the well, the drain gradually filled with people as the firing continued, but Chand managed to remain safe; bullets ricocheting off the walls or thudding into the piles of dead and wounded only yards from where he was.

After several minutes the rifles were becoming hot and clouds of dust were in the air, parching the throats of those in the Bagh. Dyer continued to direct the fire to the end, pointing out suitable 'targets' and making sure that there could be no one left there that could pose a threat to his men. There were heaps of bodies, particularly near the gates, some of which were in piles of 10 to 12 feet high. The few survivors still in the Bagh were either lying prone on the ground, clinging onto the walls of the well or sheltering behind the bricks of the *samadhi*. Hundreds of people had been trampled upon in the rush to leave the killing zone, but some had managed to escape from the Bagh by clambering over the rear wall or climbing through the small exits at either side. From there they filtered into the surrounding streets; shocked, shaken and amazed by what they had witnessed. Finally, Dyer decided that he had done enough and barked the order to cease-fire. Gradually the sounds of rifle fire ebbed away. Dyer ordered his men out and they promptly marched off. Within an hour they were back at the Ram Bagh.

ℰℒ

As soon as it was safe locals emerged from the surrounding bazaars and crept silently through the streets, hoping that the military would not return. Some carried bodies away while others administered first aid to the wounded. Approximately 1,650 rounds of ammunition had been fired into that confined space with devastating results. One of those who entered the Bagh only minutes after the firing had ceased was Lala Nathu Ram, a contractor from one of the bazaars. 'We saw a very large heap of the dead and wounded near the exits, and all along the southern wall of the Bagh. All the exits were blocked by a very large number of the dead and wounded.' Ram frantically began to search for his brother, desperately turning over the dead until he found him, lying under three or four bodies near a small section of raised ground.[23] It would later be claimed that the well, on the left hand side of the Bagh, held up to 120 dead.[24] There were also scattered bodies in nearby streets where people had collapsed from their wounds, leaving little trails of drying blood through the bazaars.

The following morning, 14 April, the skies above Amritsar would be darkened by the cremations of those who had died in the Jallianwala Bagh. The city was stunned, totally shocked by what had happened. There were so many questions on everyone's lips: what had happened? Why had the British fired upon them without warning? Why had they killed so many people? What did it all mean?

Introduction

I first visited the Jallianwala Bagh in October 2007. As you enter the Bagh, you leave behind the loud chaos of the adjoining streets, packed as always with tourists, hawkers, auto-rickshaws and pilgrims. Many of them are undoubtedly on their way to the Golden Temple – the holiest place in Sikhism – that lies only a few hundred yards beyond. Moving up its narrow entrance, bordered on both sides by three-storey houses, you enter a quieter, greener world. A notice at the entrance informs you that it is 'saturated with the blood of about two thousand Indian patriots who were martyred in a non-violent struggle to free India from British domination' and is 'thus an everlasting symbol of non-violent and peaceful struggle for freedom of [the] Indian people and the tyranny of the British'. But now the Jallianwala Bagh is a tranquil place. Visitors humbly wander around its pathways, inevitably ending up at the far side where a large brick monument, representing the flame of liberty, now stands. The monument is the heart of the Jallianwala Bagh, but perhaps the most poignant aspect are the bullet holes, which can clearly be seen on sections of wall and upon two small buildings, the martyr's well and the *samadhi*. Schoolchildren eagerly poke the bullet holes with their fingers, helpfully marked by wooden frames, and tourists sit in groups on the grass eating their lunch, and trying to gain some shade from the searing heat of the Indian sun. Indeed, the Bagh is so pleasant that it is sometimes hard to imagine the scenes of horror and carnage that took place here 90 years ago.

During the spring of 1919, British India witnessed the largest and most sustained series of violent disturbances since the Mutiny of 1857. Responding to the introduction of unpopular new legislation (the Rowlatt Bills) and suffering from the economic and human costs of the First World War, the Indian nationalist movement was able to mobilise popular support and organise an unprecedented series of strikes (*hartals*) and demonstrations. These began at Delhi on 30 March and reached their peak at Amritsar and Lahore, as well as various smaller localities in the Punjab, between 10 and 14 April. Although supposedly following Mahatma Gandhi's doctrine of non-violent civil disobedience (*satyagraha*), the demonstrations were marked by rioting, arson and, in a number of cases, murder. And it was at Amritsar where the worst of the violence would take place and where the bloodiest response would be. The Jallianwala Bagh was the scene for what was perhaps the single most infamous incident in the entire history of British rule in India; a brutal massacre within such dubious historical company as Peterloo, Sharpeville, My Lai, Bloody Sunday and Tiananmen Square. The official Government of India investigation into the incident concluded that 379 people had been killed and up to 1,200 had been wounded on 13 April.[1]

The Amritsar Massacre was an act of stunning brutality. To the primary voice of educated Indian opinion, the Indian National Congress, the massacre was 'a calculated piece of inhumanity towards utterly innocent and unarmed men, including children, and [was] unparalleled for its ferocity in the history of modern British administration'.[2] As the historian, Derek Sayer, has explained, 'no previous use of military force, in the United Kingdom or colonies, against an unarmed and peaceable crowd had resulted in a remotely comparable loss of life'.[3] The firing at the Bagh had a thousand aftershocks and is commonly accepted as marking a turning point in the struggle for India's freedom; a fatal parting of the ways between British and Indian that would never be mended.[4] Although he had once been an admirer of the British Empire, the political and social campaigner, Mahatma Gandhi, was moved to express his complete estrangement from 'the present Government' by the 'wanton cruelty' and 'inhumanity' shown by Dyer and others in the Punjab.[5] Amritsar polarised British and Indian opinion and created a sore that still has the power to cause controversy and embarrassment over 60 years since British power in India finally came to an end. During a visit in 2005 the then Foreign Secretary, Jack Straw, expressed his shame and sorrow for the 'slaughter of innocents' at the Jallianwala Bagh.[6]

The Amritsar massacre has become, in some ways, a necessary myth in Indian nationalism, providing legitimacy to those who would inherit the Raj, while at the same time undermining those attempts to portray British rule in a sympathetic and progressive light. It came with a stellar cast of heroes and villains, and a long list of 'martyrs' who – it was claimed – died to free India from imperial rule. Furthermore, it was not just the events in Amritsar that have become part of this story. The way that the disorders elsewhere in India were dealt with – from Ahmedabad to Lahore and Delhi – and the subsequent period of martial law, which came into force two days after the massacre, have been widely seen as yet more proof of British disdain for Indian opinion and a willingness to resort to violence. Indeed, although Brigadier-General Dyer has borne the brunt of nationalist anger, a great deal of criticism has also been levelled at the Lieutenant-Governor of the Punjab, Sir Michael O'Dwyer, who, it is alleged, was guilty of ruling the province with an 'iron fist'.[7] The two are sometimes even confused and, on occasion, conflated into one super villain.[8] According to many historians, O'Dwyer was notoriously reactionary, deeply opposed to Indian political developments, and who oversaw the restoration of order in the Punjab with a brutality and vindictiveness that had not been seen in India for over 60 years. The Jallianwala Bagh may be the most notorious incident of this period, but it was not the only time that the authorities resorted to violence and coercion to maintain their position, and dark tales of oppression, bloodshed and 'imperial terrorism' have become enshrined in Indian history, recounted by generations of teachers and still employed to tarnish the reputation of the British Raj.[9]

℘

Since 1920 at least 14 books and a handful of articles have been written on the Amritsar Massacre.[10] The biographies of the key actors, from Brigadier-General Dyer to Mahatma Gandhi, also discuss the incident at length.[11] Although the factual details have generally been accepted, their interpretation has been fiercely contested and there has been extensive discussion of two main questions: why Dyer fired and whether he was justified in doing so. Views have been polarised, often reflecting the ideological position of the writer, with Indian nationalists criticising Dyer for his brutality, but those sympathetic to the Raj, such as Ian Colvin and Arthur Swinson, defending Dyer and claiming that by firing he saved India from a repeat of 1857, and that his actions were necessary and justified.[12] As perhaps is to be expected, most writers have taken a dim view of Dyer. Although disagreeing on his exact motives, all stress both the extreme violence of the shooting and the innocence of those in the Jallianwala Bagh.[13]

In 2005 Nigel Collett published *The Butcher of Amritsar*, the first biography of Dyer since 1929. Collett argued that understanding the massacre was dependent upon appreciating Dyer's difficult and complex personality. He believed that Dyer fired in the Jallianwala Bagh 'not because he was callous or bloodthirsty', but because he interpreted the violence in Amritsar and the gathering of the assembly in the Bagh as a 'challenge to his way of life and everything he thought it stood for'. He believed that he was facing a violent revolt, perhaps a repeat of 1857, and that he must fire to 'save' India and the

European community.[14] Collett's detailed reconstruction of Dyer's life and character has added important clarification to his personality, but has continued to perpetuate two major problems with so many works on this event: first, the failure to present the massacre within its *proper historical context*, and second, the repetition of *numerous inaccuracies and misconceptions* based on nationalist criticism.

Regarding the first problem, the 'Dyer Affair' dominates the historiography and has assumed an importance that is perhaps overstated; the incident was the exception *not* the rule. Although the question of why Dyer fired (and whether he was justified or not) is an important one, to understand what the massacre meant and whether it was part of policy of 'imperial terrorism' (as has so often been claimed), it is necessary to take a step back and appreciate events from a wider perspective. Although there has been some work by Indian historians on the violence elsewhere,[15] attention has traditionally been focused on events in Amritsar and on the choices available to Dyer.[16] But it is only by understanding the full scale of the violence in 1919, how disorders in different places related to each other, how other officers in similar positions of responsibility as Dyer acted, and how this related to the ways in which the Raj was governed, can the Jallianwala Bagh be truly understood.

This book is the first comprehensive account of the disorders of 1919 to be written. Although in certain respects the Jallianwala Bagh massacre lies at the heart of this book (and is discussed in detail), extensive coverage is extended to the disturbances elsewhere in India, as well as the later period of martial law. It also discusses the attitude of the British authorities to the growth of nationalist and communal discontent in India in the opening years of the twentieth century and the various methods that were employed to channel this energy down avenues that were more amenable to government. From reading many accounts of this period, one could believe that the British responded to the growing calls for power-sharing and more representative government with only repression and 'imperial terrorism', but this was not the case. In 1917, when this account begins, the Secretary of State for India, Edwin Montagu, undertook a wide-ranging and comprehensive review of the governance of the Indian Empire with a view to introducing representative institutions to the subcontinent that, it was hoped, would stabilise British rule and allow nationalist elements to be brought within government. The background to the Jallianwala Bagh was not one of ruthless imperial control, but of a fluid situation in which the British Raj was introducing a variety of reforms that increased the participation of Indians in the administration and placed a greater emphasis on nationalist opinion.

Turning to the second problem with much of literature – the repetition of numerous fallacies – it is necessary to avoid the exaggerations and bias of previous accounts. These have often been written from (or heavily influenced by) the perspective of Indian nationalists, whose understanding of Amritsar was determined by their dim view of British imperialism. For many writers, looking at Amritsar was a way of not only portraying the British authorities as brutal, unthinking oppressors, but also about reinforcing the legitimacy of the Indian 'freedom struggle' and the centrality of 'non-violence' and 'truth' within it. As a result, our understanding of the British response to disorder has not received the proper examination it deserves and has often been reduced to crude caricatures of Indian-hating *sahibs* (European 'masters'). This unsatisfactory and selective approach has allowed a whole host of inaccuracies to take root that continue to bedevil our understanding and prevent us from taking a more realistic, and arguably, fairer view of the events in question. Although this is by no means an exhaustive list, some of the most common assumptions about this period can be found below:

- The Punjab lay under the 'iron rule' of its 'barbaric' ruler, Sir Michael O'Dwyer.
- The Rowlatt *Satyagraha* was, by and large, a peaceful and non-violent movement.
- The police and military were heavy-handed and punitive when dealing with crowds, often firing without sufficient justification.
- The people of Amritsar were provoked by the authorities so that they could be suppressed.
- The meeting in the Jallianwala Bagh was planned by British intelligence.
- The crowd that gathered was innocent and peaceful.
- Dyer either used machine-guns on the crowd or would have done so had he been able to get his armoured cars into position.
- He fired until his ammunition ran out.
- Aeroplanes were used to indiscriminately 'carpet bomb' Indian towns.
- The Indian population were subjected to a variety of demeaning and insulting punishments.
- Hundreds of people were arrested by the authorities and jailed without evidence.
- The British tried to cover up the massacre and that the official inquiry into the disorders was nothing more than a whitewash.

As will be shown, many of these myths are ill-founded. Some are complete fabrications; others are gross over-exaggerations, but they still hold a remarkable power over our understanding of these events and have done much to demonise and distort our view of the British authorities.[17]

Given the importance of Amritsar in the history of modern India, it is particularly regrettable that historians have been content to repeat these myths without question or comment. It seems that because Amritsar is so central to our understanding of India's 'freedom struggle' and the idea of non-violence, historians have shied away from examining many aspects of the events of 1919 in detail for fear of undermining this tradition. But critical analysis is urgently required. This account offers a new history of this contentious period and challenges much of the conventional wisdom. First, it argues that the traditional emphasis on the peaceful and non-violent nature of Gandhi's protest movement has obscured the great amount of violence and brutality that it produced and which was directed against the European population. Second, the British response to this unrest was proportionate and reasonable. When the authorities resorted to firing upon crowds, it was, in the vast majority of cases, a last resort and was not conducted in order to 'terrorise' the civilian population. The situation in 1919 was dangerous and required the introduction of martial law, which was administered fairly and responsibly, although there were rare instances of abuse. The much maligned Sir Michael O'Dwyer also needs re-evaluating. His stewardship of the Punjab through the war, and his handling of the disturbances of 1919, was masterly and showed his professionalism and skill, which had been gleaned from years of service in India. Finally, this account argues that the Jallianwala Bagh massacre, so often seen as the epitome of cold-blooded imperial ruthlessness, was in fact nothing of the sort.

✌

In order to gain a more detailed understanding of this contentious period it is necessary to strip away years of assumptions and accumulated historical baggage and re-evaluate the original archive material. The most important source is the papers relating to the official Government of India inquiry into the unrest.[18] This committee, known after its President Lord William Hunter, was composed of seven other members (four British and three Indian) and heard evidence from a wide range of witnesses (including Dyer) for 46 days between October and December 1919. The committee was able to gather an immense amount of source material, including statements, interviews and reports, which are of considerable use to the historian. Much of this has never been analysed before. Of the seven volumes of evidence compiled by Lord Hunter's committee, only one was directly concerned with the events in

Amritsar, the remaining six covered the disturbances elsewhere. Although this mass of material provides important insights into a range of issues, including the nature of British rule in India and the role of the administration, most of it has remained overlooked. Nevertheless, in order to fully understand the violence at Amritsar and its relationship to the disorders elsewhere, this forgotten source material must be used. This is the only account of the violence of 1919 that draws from *all seven volumes* of evidence compiled by the Hunter Inquiry.

The Hunter Committee published its report in May 1920, and was subsequently accepted by the Government of India. It concluded that although the disturbances had been of a serious nature and had caused the Punjab Government the 'gravest anxiety', there was no evidence for a pre-existing conspiracy aimed at overthrowing British rule.[19] It censured Dyer on two counts, first, because he had not given the crowd sufficient warning before opening fire, and second, because he had continued to fire whilst the crowd was attempting to flee. As well as criticising Dyer's actions in the Jallianwala Bagh, his conduct during the subsequent period of martial law was also attacked, particularly his notorious 'crawling order', whereby Indians who wanted to pass through a street where an English missionary had been assaulted would have to do so on all fours.[20] Unfortunately, the committee could not agree upon its findings and split along racial lines, with the three Indian members breaking off to write their own, so-called, Minority Report. This claimed that the riots were no more than spontaneous demonstrations of hostility towards the introduction of repressive legislation and that the actions of the authorities were both brutal and counter-productive.[21]

The Hunter Report has received criticism from all sides and its reputation remains cloudy. To nationalists, it was always an official whitewash that may have criticised Dyer, but exonerated others who had been involved in quelling the disorders, particularly Sir Michael O'Dwyer.[22] For loyalists, it always represented a gross betrayal of British officials, with Hunter receiving much personal criticism for his lack of familiarity with Indian politics or languages.[23] However, the fact that Hunter received criticism from all sides is perhaps an indication that he did get some things right. Given the controversy of its subject and the political sensitivity of such an inquiry, Lord Hunter was in a difficult position with no hope of satisfying everyone. This was particularly the case after the publication of the Indian National Congress's investigation two months before his own, which meant that he was not able to frame the debate in the way that London had wanted.

On 16 October 1919 the Congress began to gather evidence for what would become the *Report of the Commissioners Appointed by the Punjab*

Sub-Committee of the Indian National Congress, which was published in two
volumes on 25 March 1920. The Congress Inquiry aimed to give a 'voice to
the victims of the repression' and was written by a team of investigators that
included Gandhi.[24] As might have been expected, the report was deeply critical of the British authorities, chronicling a story of political repression and
harsh imperial rule, and detailing the abuses that had occurred under martial
law. It concluded with an 18-point indictment of the government, including the administration of Sir Michael O'Dwyer ('by reason of the cruel and
compulsory methods'), the Jallianwala Bagh massacre ('a calculated piece of
inhumanity') and the measures taken under martial law ('unnecessary, cruel,
oppressive'). It petitioned for the punishment of those officers who had acted
brutally, including Dyer and O'Dwyer, and also asked for the recall of the
Viceroy.[25]

The Congress Punjab Inquiry is an extremely useful source and like the
Hunter Committee it gathered a mass of statements – some 800 pages of text –
that were published in the second volume of the report.[26] Apart from the testimonies dealing with Amritsar, the vast majority of these have never been
used before. This report (and the evidence that it compiled) should, however,
be used with caution. Though nationalist historians have often relied heavily
upon its findings, it is not an entirely reliable source and even one of the investigators, M.R. Jayakar, complained of 'bad typing, incoherent and illegible
spelling, misspelt names, perplexing blanks, incoherent references, and con-
tradictory alterations'.[27] The fact that it was written (mainly) by Gandhi, who
had played such an important role in mobilising popular feeling against the
British, also calls into question its reliability. Although Gandhi defended the
report, claiming that it was prepared 'with a view to bringing out the truth
and nothing but the truth' and that there was 'not a single conscious exaggeration in it anywhere', this should be treated critically.[28] Whereas the Hunter
Report maintains a studious distance from the events and describes them in a
clear, sober style, the Congress Report is evidently the work of someone with
a deep emotional attachment to the Punjab and who is not afraid of using
romantic prose to exaggerate the importance of events.[29]

The evidence gathered by both the Hunter Inquiry and the Indian
National Congress, although limited in some respects, provides a mine of useful information and form the basis for any understanding of what occurred
in 1919. They can be consulted alongside a wealth of other source material
that is available on the disturbances, which is held at a variety of archives and
libraries in both the United Kingdom and India. The India Office Collections
in the British Library, London, holds much relevant material, including the

papers of a variety of British officials, ranging from the Viceroy and the Secretary of State for India, to minor members of the Indian Civil Service and Indian Army. Other collections are available in the Imperial War Museum and The National Archives in London. As well as sources in Britain, there is a mass of government reports and other official data available at the National Archives of India in New Delhi, and some subsidiary material in the Punjab State Archives in Chandigarh. It is hoped that by consulting a wider range of sources of previous histories of this period, a more reasoned and accurate portrayal of these important events can be written.

છ

This new account of the Amritsar Massacre aims to reassess many of the myths that have come to surround this period and provide a full analytical history of what became known as the 'Punjab Disturbances of 1919'. It places the shooting at the Jallianwala Bagh within its proper historical context, and discusses the wider issue of reform within the Indian Empire, beginning with the visit of the Secretary of State for India to the subcontinent in November 1917. The conclusions of *The Amritsar Massacre: The Untold Story of One Fateful Day* may surprise some readers, particularly its reappraisal of Dyer's motives, and its defence of Sir Michael O'Dwyer. It is not the purpose of this study to denigrate the victims, both Indian and British, of the violence in the Punjab in 1919, or to deny the tragedy and horror of the events that took place. It is not aimed at diminishing the place of Amritsar within Indian history, but it does present a more balanced view of the British response to the violence of 1919 than has been commonly accepted, and argues that to vilify the officials who were tasked with restoring order during such difficult times as nothing more than vindictive and brutal imperial oppressors is to misunderstand their motives and perpetuate an historical injustice. All nations, to a greater and lesser degree, require myths and stories that make sense of the past and give meaning and direction to future generations. This account looks again at what at first glance might seem to be a familiar incident, and in reassessing what we really know about it, tries to separate myth from reality. Only then can nations truly understand the events of the past and attempt to move on from them.

PART ONE
BEGINNINGS

CHAPTER 1

The Raj in an Age of Change

I told him that in my opinion the root cause of the whole trouble was the profound distrust, which may or may not be justified, shown by the civil servants of the Indian and the Indian of the civil servant.

Edwin Montagu[1]

Edwin Montagu landed in Bombay on 10 November 1917. The Secretary of State for India was, as he wrote in his diary, 'glad to get off the ship, for … although I found it so thoroughly equipped, it was tedious in the extreme'.[2] Montagu had spent the last three weeks travelling to India on the P&O liner, *Kaiser-I-Hind*, and apart from brief sojourns in Turin, Rome and Cairo, he had spent it on deck, studying the vexatious question of the reform of Britain's Indian Empire and trying to prepare himself for the weeks of intensive negotiation and discussion that would inevitably follow once he set foot on the subcontinent. But, for the moment at least, Montagu was free to enjoy the beauty and splendour of the landscape that greeted him. He would later recall with pleasure,

> The blue sea, the hills in the foreground, in the background, on the horizon, in the middle distance, of various degrees of blues and blacks and greys; the white buildings, the marvellous spacing, the silent, quiet crowds of foot passengers; the bright coloured garments of the women.

The city of Bombay was, he decided, 'one of the wonders of the world'.

Of all those who occupied his position, Edwin Montagu perhaps polarised opinion more than any other. A former Private Secretary to the Prime Minister (Herbert Henry Asquith), Montagu had been Financial Secretary to the Treasury and Minister of Munitions before becoming Secretary of State for India in June 1917.[3] Frequently described by his contemporaries as either nervous or fussy, Montagu was a deep-thinking man of decidedly liberal tendencies, whose time at the India Office was marked by controversy and fierce disagreement. A liberal by habit, Montagu was chronically afraid of conflict and deeply uncomfortable of anything that smacked of repression or punishment.[4]

Although an eloquent debater and hard worker, Montagu was not a charismatic man and had few friends. He was never able to convince Anglo-Indian opinion and the conservative wing of British political life that he would defend British interests in India with sufficient vigour. He was continually accused of being too close to a number of Indian politicians (particularly Mohandas Gandhi), and of not doing enough to support those who had to sustain the Raj in a period of acute difficulty. It also did not help that he was Jewish, and his career was dogged by anti-Semitism and distrust.

Montagu's seven months in India may have been something of a 'public relations gesture',[5] but his tour and the report that he would subsequently co-author with the Viceroy of India, Lord Chelmsford, marked a significant attempt to sketch out the future path along which the British Raj could operate. It was becoming clear that if the Raj was to have a future, then it would have to institute some kind of framework for increasing the participation of Indians in the decisions of government. In part this was a recognition of the unsettled international situation, for although the Great War had not touched India directly, the effects of over three years of bitter conflict between Britain, France and Russia, on the one hand, and the Central Powers of Germany, Austria-Hungary and Turkey on the other, had been felt throughout the subcontinent. The demands of recruitment, the economic dislocation and the mounting toll of dead and wounded began to erode the foundations upon which British power in India rested. The war had also given added fillip to the Home Rule and nationalist movements, which had by 1917 become increasingly difficult to ignore. The enormity of the task facing Montagu was not lost upon him. 'My visit to India means that we are going to do something big,' he wrote. 'I cannot go home and produce a little thing or nothing; it must be epoch-making, or it is a failure; it must be the keystone of the future history of India.'[6]

☙

The Raj may have been outwardly grand and monolithic, but as Montagu well knew, the reality was somewhat different. On contemporary maps India was an inverted pink triangle at the centre of the world where British rule stood firm, but internally it was a mess; a huge, unwieldy set of provinces that sat uneasily alongside hundreds of nominally independent princely states, covering lands and peoples of striking variety and complexity. The Indian subcontinent over which British rule was exercised lay between the jungles of Burma in the east to the mountains of the Hindu Kush in the west, bordered by the Himalayas and Tibet in the north and by the Arabian Sea and the Indian

Ocean to the south. India had a land mass of roughly 1.8 million square miles (approximately 4.66 million square kilometres) with a population – recorded in the census of 1921 – at over 318 million people, which included Hindus, Muslims, Buddhists, Christians, Jews, Parsees, Jains and a whole host of other ethnic and religious minorities. And if this was not complicated enough, these religious groupings were far from united, formed masses and, as 'old India hands' would often relate to newcomers, the caste Hindus of Bombay were a world away from the *bhadraloks* of Bengal, and the cultured Muslim elite of Lucknow were nothing like the peasants of the Punjab.[7]

Visitors to India, amazed by its colour and exoticism, would often marvel at how British control could be exercised over so many people and over such vast distances, and the system would often require some explanation. The Secretary of State for India, based in London, was ultimately responsible for the administration of India, and had to submit an annual account of Indian finances to the House of Parliament. He was assisted by two under-secretaries and by the Council of India. This comprised between 10 and 14 members, each of whom had considerable experience of Indian affairs and had spent at least ten years living in British India. In the subcontinent, the Governor-General, otherwise known as the Viceroy, was the head of the Government of India and was assisted by the Executive Council. This was composed of seven members who were each given one of the following portfolios: Home, Revenue, Finance, Legislative, Commerce and Industry, Education, and Army. Under this was the Indian Legislative Council, composed of the Executive Council plus up to 35 members nominated by the Governor-General and 25 other elected members.[8] The Legislative Council was empowered to discuss the financial statement of the Government of India and allowed to ask questions, but its resolutions were not binding and it always possessed an official majority. Its primary purpose was to allow for the discussion of government policy and bring to the attention of government any issues that were felt to be in the public interest.

The next level of power lay in the provinces. British India was divided into nine major and six minor provinces. The most important were the three presidencies of Madras, Bombay and Bengal. Each province was split into a number of administrative units, known as districts, which were overseen by a Collector or Deputy Commissioner, who was responsible for the administration of executive functions, including justice and taxation within that area. Further below them was a whole host of minor positions, occupied by both British and Indians, ranging from sub-divisional officers, magistrates and revenue officers, who ensured that the administration functioned effectively. And it was in these lower levels that the heart of the system lay; the world of the British official in India, where Briton and Indian met, which has been vividly chronicled in novels such as E.M. Forster's *A Passage to India* (1924) and Paul Scott's *Raj Quartet* (1966–75), and which remains essential to understanding the Raj.[9] It was a world of great pressure and often great loneliness, with some officials spending years in remote districts, fending off the dangers of disease and exhaustion, and trying to deal with vast amounts of work and the huge decisions that had to be taken every day. Certainly it was not a particularly easy life and beneath the veneer of tiffin, *memsahibs* (wives of British officials) and 'pig-sticking', lay the harsh reality of life in the Raj: a 'transient lifestyle' of homesickness, disease and alienation from both British and Indian societies.[10]

℃

To the untrained western eye, first impressions of India could be deceptive. Like Adela Quested in Forster's *A Passage to India*, the new arrival would often search for what was thought to be the 'real' India, the essential unchanging core of poverty, corruption and spirituality that was often said to make up the 'oriental'. But what may have initially seemed like a deeply conservative society, still in thrall to the terrifying visions of their ancient gods, the boundaries and regulations of the caste system or the time-honoured protocols due to the royal landowning elite, was in reality a society undergoing swift and significant change. The nineteenth century had seen remarkable developments in India as the ripples of the industrial revolution, that vast outpouring of power unleashed in the United Kingdom, washed upon India's shores. The industrial revolution and the ever-growing levels of global communication and exchange led to a quickening of pace that would intrude into every aspect of Indian life. The Suez Canal had opened in 1869 and dramatically reduced sailing times to the east, but it was the growing communication within India that would have even more profound effects upon the subcontinent.

It was not just the physical infrastructure of India that was changing during the second half of the nineteenth century, but the mental world in which the educated classes lived. One of the major changes ushered in by the British was the gradual spread of English education in an ever-expanding network of schools and colleges that started in the old presidencies of Bengal, Bombay and Madras, but soon reached into every corner of the subcontinent. By 1901 there were 23,000 college students and over 630,000 pupils in secondary schools in India; admittedly a fraction of the total population but a growing pool of educated Indians from whom the British could draw. A Western or English education soon became the passport to a position in the administration as one of the scores of Indians that the British depended upon to maintain their rule. And it was from these Western-educated Indians that new stirrings of dissent began to emerge, presenting the British with the decision of whether to encourage or repress them. In 1835 the famous English philanthropist, Thomas Babington Macaulay, had declared that it should be the aim of British rule to create a class of Indians to act as interpreters between the rulers and the mass of the population. It would be this group, Indians 'in blood and colour, but English in tastes, in opinion, in morals and in intellect', that was intended to safeguard British interests, but who were now becoming increasingly impossible to ignore.[11]

The crushing of the Mutiny in the opening months of 1858 may have banished the likelihood of any serious internal military threat to the stability of the Raj, but by the early years of the twentieth century, the British position in India was coming under increasing pressure, as more and more Indians, through various regional associations and in a vociferous nationalist press, pressed for a greater role in the administration of the country. Of these the most important was the Indian National Congress. Founded in 1885 by a former member of the ICS, Allan Octavian Hume, Congress was created to represent the interests of the Indian people and ensure that British policy in India was beneficial to them. Every year at Christmas a congress would be held in a city chosen in India and delegates from all over the country would come and discuss the key issues of the day.[12] Its first session was held in Bombay and was attended by 72 delegates. They agreed upon a set of resolutions, including a request for a Royal Commission to investigate the workings of the Indian administration, the reform of the Legislative Council and the admission of elected members, the need for simultaneous ICS examinations in both England and India, a decrease in military expenditure, and a protest at the recent annexation of Upper Burma.[13]

As might have been expected, Congress was an unpopular organisation within the corridors of power. Although there were some who welcomed it and believed that British policy should encourage the growth of educated Indian opinion, many others expressed a sincere dislike of it. Lord Curzon, Viceroy between 1899 and 1905, was one of those who regarded the Congress and its ilk as nothing more than an annoying nuisance that could be ignored. In a Parliamentary Debate on 28 March 1892, Curzon had stated that the politicians of the Congress Party were 'a microscopic minority of the total population' of India and expressed his hopes of presiding over its demise.[14] Men like Curzon argued that British rule should rest, as it always had done, on rural landlords and other local notables, men who were regarded as being the 'natural rulers' of the rural tracts of India. Curzon's criticisms of Congress as being unrepresentative of India's people were painfully correct and many leading Indian politicians were aware of it. They knew that they could only demand greater concessions from the Raj if they were representative of a much larger swathe of the population. Until they did so, their demands were likely to remain limited, constitutional and of little interest to the vast majority of Indians. But if they were to appeal to more and more people, then they knew that this would only serve to bring up the vast differences of interests and opinions that were held across India, thus potentially undermining their appeal. It was a dilemma that would run through the entire history of the freedom movement.

By 1907 Congress stated that its objective was 'the attainment by the people of India of a system of government similar to that enjoyed by the self-governing members of the British Empire'.[15] This goal was to be achieved through constitutional and legal measures, and the advocates of this, the 'moderates' as they were known, were led by Gopal Krishna Gokhale, a high-caste Hindu politician and teacher from the Bombay Presidency. Gokhale believed that India would eventually become a self-governing dominion within the British Empire, and argued that the only way this was to be achieved was through gradual and constitutional means. But Gokhale's moderate approach, one that kept politics within the hands of the elite, higher castes of the presidencies and within the realms of polite discussion, was coming under increasing pressure from those who were impatient and felt that Indian freedom could not be gained by goodwill or promises, but only by violent action. These 'extremists' were led by Bal Gangadhar Tilak – a forceful, passionate Indian nationalist – whose strategy was to advocate *swadeshi* (locally made goods) and the boycotting of all British cloth, and to uplift the people of India with passionate tales of their former heroes like the great Maratha king Shivaji who had defied the might of the Mughal Empire.[16]

ও

Curzon's departure in 1905 was the end of an era for the Raj; the closing of a period of self-confidence and assertion and the onset on a new series of problems for British rule. Curzon had seen his mission in India to improve the running and efficiency of the Indian Empire, to make it better able to serve India's peoples. During one of his final speeches, at Simla in September 1905, he had said that if he were asked to sum up his administration in a single word, he would say 'Efficiency'. 'That has been our gospel,' he enthused, 'the keynote of our administration.'[17] Nevertheless, as would become clear in the coming decades, Curzon's hopes for the continued stability of British rule in India would come under increasing pressure. Whereas he had hoped that by making sure the administration was run on the grounds of the greatest efficiency, British rule would be safe, this was no longer enough. Efficiency was no longer the gospel by which British administrations in India would run. Efficiency was to be replaced, to some degree, by sympathy and representation. In part this was due to the unforeseen effects of one of the last acts of Lord Curzon while he was in India, the partition of Bengal; a move that signalled the beginning of a new phase of violent resistance to British rule.

The partition of Bengal was an idea that had been mooted for a number of years. In 1904 Curzon decided in the interests of efficiency that it should finally go ahead. Bengal was to be split into two provinces: Bengal, and East Bengal and Assam. The partition was, in many ways, a sensible decision from an administrative point of view. Bengal was the most populous province in India, with 78 million inhabitants; a vast expanse of scattered habitation and jungle, home to poisonous snakes and tigers, and with large parts under water when the rains came.[18] Not only would it make Bengal more manageable and allow greater governmental influence, it also had a potentially beneficial economic rationale, which included the development of Assam and its seaport at Chittagong.[19] Plans for the partition of the province were also spurred on by the belief that it would secure the support of the Muslim population, which would now form a majority in East Bengal and Assam. It would allow them greater access and opportunity to government employment, which had previously been dominated by the high-caste Hindus of the region. The dominance of the Hindus in Bengal would be challenged and it was hoped that this would decrease the power and influence of the Congress Party, which drew much of its support from Bengal. As Curzon noted in February 1905, the Congress Party was dominated by Bengalis who were its 'best wire-pullers' and 'most frothy orators' and any measure that would 'dethrone Calcutta from its place as the centre of successful intrigue' was bound to be helpful to British interests.[20] It was also bound, as even Curzon suspected, to be bitterly resented.

Curzon did not remain in India long enough to see partition go ahead. In 1905 he resigned owing to a disagreement with the Commander-in-Chief in India, Lord Kitchener, over civilian control of the military. Perhaps it was just as well. The partition may have made sense for Curzon, but it was opposed by the Hindus, who were deeply concerned about this threat to their traditional dominance of the region, and cared passionately about the unity and coherence of Bengal. This was particularly worrying for those from East Bengal, who would now be a minority in a new province dominated by Muslims. Agitation began almost as soon as it was known that boundary changes had been sanctioned by the British Government.[21] The day partition came into force, 16 October, was celebrated throughout Bengal as a day of mourning.[22] Agitation initially took the form of protest meetings, resolutions and a boycott of English cloth, but anti-partition agitation soon spilled over into non-constitutional means. Inspired by the Japanese victory against Russia in the war of 1905, a war that proved Asians could defeat a major first-world power, a number of terrorist cells and secret societies were formed across Bengal. These organisations were committed to the overthrow of British rule by violent means.

The danger that Bengali terrorists posed to Europeans was vividly illustrated by the murder of two English ladies, Mrs and Miss Kennedy, at Muzaffarpur in April 1908. The Muzaffarpur murders may have been somewhat mistaken – the assassins had wanted to kill the Chief Presidency Magistrate of Calcutta, Mr D.H. Kingsford – but it marked an alarming rise in terrorism across India and was deeply shocking to the authorities. On 13 November 1909 Curzon's successor, Lord Minto, survived an assassination attempt and the following month, Mr A. Jackson, a district magistrate, was murdered.[23] Murders began to spread throughout the ranks of the administration. Members of the Criminal Investigation Department (CID) would occasionally be found on the streets of Calcutta, shot or stabbed, sending a chilly message to the rest of the services that anyone involved with government was a target in the unrest. Even more worrying was the realisation that Indian terrorism was not just confined to the subcontinent. Terrorist cells had sprung up in London. On 1 July 1909 Sir William Curzon Wyllie, political aide-de-camp at the India Office, was murdered in London by an Indian extremist.

❧

The way that India had been governed was changing. By 1907 it was felt that there could be no return to a Curzonian style of rule that had dismissed nationalist opinion and concentrated on governing 'in the interests of efficiency'. It was now deemed essential to move away from such an authoritarian style of government to something that was more responsive and flexible. The Viceroy at this time was Lord Minto, who always knew that his room for manoeuvre in India was more limited than his predecessors and was anxious to stabilise British rule for the long term. In a letter to the Secretary of State for India, John Morley, on 21 May 1907, Minto summed up his thoughts. 'I am always saying to you,' he wrote, 'the stability of our rule here will, in my opinion, depend largely on our capability of marching with the times in a rapidly changing political atmosphere.'[24]

As well as pacifying Bengal and Punjab (which had recently been un-settled), Morley and Minto were anxious to offer political concessions to 'moderate' nationalists in the hope that it would wean them away from the temptations of Tilak and the 'extremists', and weaken those who believed that concessions would only come by spreading violent disorder. In 1909 new political reforms, known as the Morley-Minto reforms, were introduced. Al-though these reforms were not strikingly radical and did not alter the fun-damental balance of power between British and Indian in the subcontinent, they were based on the realisation that the continued survival of the Raj de-pended upon the inclusion of educated Indians into the administration.[25] The reforms increased the level of representation in the Legislative Council and the powers of its members.[26] Two Indians were appointed to the Coun-cil of the Secretary of State and one Indian was invited to sit on both the Viceregal Council and the Governor's Executive Councils in the provinces. Of more importance perhaps was the formal recognition of separate represen-tation for the Muslims of India; they would choose their own members from their own electorate and the seats that were awarded would be 'weighted' by their 'importance' to the Raj.

The Indian National Congress may have claimed to represent all the peo-ple of India, but many of India's Western-educated Muslims were not content to accept this. Ever since 1857 Muslim elites had safeguarded their interests by being strictly loyal to the British, but by the beginning of the twentieth cen-tury, this was beginning to break down.[27] The resignation of the pro-Muslim Lieutenant-Governor of East Bengal, Sir Bampfylde Fuller, in 1906, and the rumours that the Government was increasingly anxious to appease Hindu anger over the partition of Bengal, did nothing to dispel the growing feeling within educated Islamic circles that the British did not pay sufficient heed to Muslim opinion. By 1909 the Muslims were becoming more and more vo-cal about their position in the Raj and had begun to organise themselves on political lines. The Muslim League had been founded in 1906 by a group of wealthy Muslims from Bombay, anxious about their position in response to the increasingly vociferous and politically aware Hindu majority. It played a crucial role in lobbying the administration to make these concessions and re-minding the British that the support of the Muslims of India could not be taken for granted. The award of separate electorates, therefore, was a prag-matic and logical political move that assuaged Muslim concern and ensured their loyal co-operation.

Bengal was repartitioned in 1912; a decision that not only made no sense given the administrative logic behind its original partition, which still applied, but it also alienated Muslim opinion, which had been supportive of the move. The Government of India had come to the conclusion that the only hope they had of weakening the terrorist threat and re-engaging with the 'moderates' was to give in on partition, but if this had been intended as a peace offer to the radicals of Bengal then it failed miserably. By mid-1912 terrorist attacks in Bengal were on the increase and were not simply linked to the arguments over partition. They began to take on a more nationalistic tone, and culminated in a number of well-known incidents such as the Delhi bomb plot.[28] On 23 December 1912 an assassination attempt took place against the Viceroy, Lord Hardinge, who was riding in a procession to mark the Delhi Durbar. A bomb was thrown at him and his wife, Lady Hardinge. Although an Indian attendant was killed, Lord and Lady Hardinge survived. An intensive police investigation eventually traced the plot to a revolutionary group in Bengal. The repartition of Bengal showed a Raj that was fearful, unsure of its own merits and willing to bow to public pressure.

At the same time that it was announced that Bengal would be repartitioned, it was also revealed that the capital of India would move from Calcutta to Delhi. This decision was motivated by a number of factors: a growing recognition of the importance of the 'martial races' of northern India to the survival of the Raj; a decision to move away from the nationalist movement in Bengal; and a belief that it would conciliate Muslim opinion, which had been disappointed over repartition. King George V laid the foundation stone for New Delhi in 1911 and over the following years a new capital was constructed on a vast scale. But this new capital, outwardly grand, self-confident and a fitting home for the Government of India, would not herald a revitalised age of imperial rule, but a memorial to it, lasting barely 36 years before its original owners left, never to return. But in 1912, when the southern approaches to Delhi were being turned into one vast building site, it seemed that this could mark a new start for the British in India, a renaissance for the Raj that would set the confident tone for another 100 years of British rule.

Clouds were on the horizon. Not in the east, but in the west where the increasing might of Imperial Germany was unbalancing the fragile balance of power in Europe, which had been at peace since the fall of Napoleon in 1815. Soon troops would be on the move, the German legions marching through Belgium and Northern France and the British Empire would become involved, playing a leading role in holding the German armies and then pushing them back. Though most of the destruction and damage that the war would unleash was concentrated in Europe, its effects were truly global and few parts of the world were immune to the demands of war for more men, more money, more equipment, more shells and more food. For India, like much of the world, the Great War changed everything. It would weaken imperial powers, strain the loyalties of those elites who buttressed the regime, and usher in new, radical ideas of self-determination and democracy; ideas that should they spread to India had the potential to challenge the basis of British rule. The first 'wind of change' was about to blow across the world. Montagu's visit to India was an attempt to control the direction in which these winds would blow. His success or failure would determine the future of British power in India.

CHAPTER 2

The Great War and Reform in India

Troubles never come in single spies but in battalions.

Lord Chelmsford[1]

Montagu's counterpart in India was the Viceroy, Lord Chelmsford, who had replaced Charles Hardinge in April 1916.[2] A Fellow of All Soul's College, Oxford, Chelmsford led a quiet, aristocratic life, captaining his university at cricket and being called to the Bar in 1893. He was elected to the London County Council in 1905, before being appointed successively the Governor of Queensland, the Governor of New South Wales and finally the Governor-General of Australia. Chelmsford was a calm and deep-thinking man; in many ways unsuited to taking decisive action against the increasing resistance to the Raj. He met Montagu during the winter of 1917 and although they were friendly, there was never a great deal of warmth between them. Montagu's views on Chelmsford were similar to those found in many contemporary accounts; Chelmsford had 'a fine, athletic figure, square shoulders, small hips, well-shaped head and a graceful forward inclination of the body'. He was 'thoroughly nice, but unfortunately cold, aloof, reserved'. Montagu would complain that Chelmsford was incapable of making a decision and, indeed, the Viceroy was not someone who would rush to do anything. After a game of tennis one afternoon, Montagu caught up with Chelmsford and talked over some ideas about the reforms with him. 'He took up the attitude,' Montagu recalled, 'which he always takes up of "I wish it were possible, but I am afraid." This really sums him up in almost everything – "I am afraid it is not."'[3]

Montagu's view that Chelmsford was a timid personality, dominated by his advisers and unable to pilot a firm course because of constant dithering and consultation, was a common accusation, but not totally fair. For his part, Chelmsford found Montagu to be fussy, nervous and, at times, completely unaware of the workings of the Government of India. Chelmsford did indeed place great emphasis on working through his Executive Council, not because he had no ideas of his own or because he was afraid, but because he felt that it was the only way that such a 'creaky and lumbering machine' could be run on sound lines.[4] Nevertheless, unlike Montagu, who was a seasoned political operator and understood the value of presenting a positive image, Chelmsford could never bring himself to do this and his administration was unloved. He found the rounds of officialdom tiresome and although he was scrupulously polite and personally likeable, he was never able to elicit a great deal of warmth and loyalty from his subordinates across India. Chelmsford's isolation, however, was to be rudely shaken by the arrival of Montagu, and the Viceroy would find the efforts to garner opinion across India and agree upon a new set of reform proposals to be too quick and decisive for his liking.

๛

The situation that Chelmsford inherited in 1916 was probably the most challenging and dangerous that had faced any new Viceroy since the Mutiny. The declaration of war in August 1914 may have been greeted in India with pleasing demonstrations of enthusiasm and loyalty for the British Crown, but the disappointments of the first two years of the war soon began to sap the energies of the Indian people and to galvanise the nationalist movement.[5] Matters were given greater urgency by the policy of Imperial Germany, which tried to widen the conflict and unsettle Britain's overseas dependencies in the hope that this would tie down manpower and other resources. Germany made a number of attempts to stir up unrest within India by supporting Indian revolutionaries, including those in Europe and America, and attempting to import arms and explosives into the country. Fortunately for the British, German-backed subversion in India was poorly organised and most of these plots were foiled by a combination of good police and intelligence work, inept planning, treachery and various strokes of luck.[6]

Perhaps the most romantic of these conspiracies was the so-called 'silk letter' case, which was foiled by British intelligence in 1916. This was a German-backed plot that was intended to destabilise India and ferment revolt in the Punjab. Tribesman from Afghanistan and the North-West Frontier Province (NWFP) would unite and push into India, which would be combined with a general Muslim rising throughout the country.[7] Letters written on yellow silk and hidden in coats worn by emissaries from Kabul (the 'silk letters') were despatched to various agents in India, urging them to revolt against the British and join an 'Army of God'. Unfortunately for them, word leaked about the plan and the leaders were arrested. A more serious movement was by the Ghadr party, which had been formed by Indian revolutionaries, mainly Sikhs, in the United States in 1913.[8] The Ghadr party aimed at the violent overthrow of British rule and when war broke out its members hoped to use this to their advantage and volunteers returned to the Punjab to ferment unrest, particularly amongst Sikh soldiers. Initially it seemed to work. Between October 1914 and September 1915 the Punjab was unsettled and, as the governor of the province wrote, 'all this time we felt we were living over a mine full of explosions', having to cope with a series of assassinations, bomb attacks, robberies and attempts to 'tamper' with Indian battalions.[9] Nevertheless, by August 1915 the Ghadr movement had been crushed by a combination of good intelligence and the withdrawal of certain political liberties, but the memory of Ghadr and its resistance would live on and the methods that had been employed to suppress it created unease in certain districts of the Punjab, contributing to a growing distrust of the British administration.

The danger that Indian revolutionaries posed to the fundamental stability of the Raj between 1914 and 1918 was always limited. Of more concern than a handful of terrorists and revolutionaries was the growth of a national consciousness within India. Indeed, the sensitivity of the Government of India to agitators and 'extremist' politicians increased markedly during the war and was one of the reasons why Montagu was travelling to the subcontinent. By 1918 the Indian National Congress was in an increasingly strong position, having transformed its organisation and become a much more effective voice for Indian aspirations.[10] The ever-growing newspaper circulation helped to spread new ideas and proved increasingly difficult for the British to control. Even in the Punjab, which was often regarded as a 'non-political' province, there were 276 newspapers in print by 1919, most of which were in Urdu, with a circulation of over 340,000 copies.[11] At a special session of Congress in August 1918, the Chairman of the Reception Committee, V.J. Patel, stated that Congress had now grown into a 'splendid Bodhi tree whose roots have reached down to the hearts of the nation, whose branches are the resting place of all patriotic thought, and whose shade is prophetic of the peace of the future' when India would become an equal member of the Empire. The so-called 'microscopic minority', Patel now claimed, had 'grown into the irresistible majority of Educated India with the uneducated masses ranged behind them in a serried phalanx'.[12]

There were two developments of particular importance during the war. The first occurred at Lucknow in 1916 when the Indian National Congress and the Muslim League agreed to work together to present a new package of constitutional reforms to the British Government. At Lucknow, the parties agreed that it was necessary to present a common position on the reform proposals; agreeing upon separate representation and fixing the percentage of representatives from each province that would be voted for solely by Muslims.[13] Although this rapprochement would not last for very long, it meant that for the first time the two parties were speaking on a united front and presenting a unified set of demands.

The second major development was the formation in 1916 of two Home Rule Leagues, the first in May by the great nationalist and journalist, B.G. Tilak, and the second in July, by Mrs Annie Besant, an Irish theosophist and socialist campaigner. The Home Rule Leagues were committed to securing self-government for India along the lines of the Dominions, such as Canada and South Africa, and marked an important development in the way in which political protest and agitation had been undertaken in India. Although the British had faced localised protest movements in earlier years – particularly in Bengal and the Punjab – the Home Rule agitation was the first that had a genuinely all-India approach, with branches spread across the subcontinent. Membership of these Home Rule Leagues grew rapidly. Tilak's rose from 1,000 in November 1916 to over 32,000 two years later. Likewise, by December 1917 Mrs Besant's movement had 27,000 members.[14]

What was Chelmsford to do with these groups? Essentially, he had to decide whether the Home Rule movement was 'seditious' and should be repressed, or whether it was advocating a legitimate political outcome and, therefore, must be tolerated. There was also the thorny issue of *how* Home Rule was advocated and whether by doing so, violence and disorder were the result. These issues came to a head in June 1917 when Annie Besant was interned by the Government of Madras for a number of articles that had been written in her newspaper, *New India*.[15] Besant had been prohibited from entering several provinces the year before, but the only strong action against her was taken by Madras. Besant's internment was widely supported by the British community in India, including a number of senior administrators, who felt that it was essential to prosecute those who crossed the line of criticism into sedition. Lord Chelmsford justified it on the grounds that 'while we have no wish to repress a movement moderately conducted on constitutional lines, we cannot tolerate a campaign of calumny and misrepresentation'.[16] The firm hand taken against Mrs Besant would, however, come under increasing pressure from a new occupant at the India Office, Edwin Montagu.

❧

Ever since his first tour of India in 1912, Montagu had been strongly of opinion that a new way of operating was required if the Raj was to survive into the twentieth century. He found the Government of India and its civil service to be too timid and conservative for his tastes, accusing them of hiding behind legislation and being distrustful of Indians. He believed that this lack of trust was at the root of the problem and must be tackled if progress was to be made. The Indian civil servant, Montagu claimed, 'rather than trust to his own authority and to the righteousness of his own cause, ties himself up and everybody else with what he calls safeguards – rules, regulations and statutes'.[17] He believed that it was unwise to ignore or discourage the small number of Western-educated elites in India, men who were calling for more power and responsibility, and it was necessary to engage with them in a coherent and constructive manner; 'for the amount of yeast necessary to leaven a loaf', he was fond of saying, 'is very small'.[18]

Both the Indian National Congress and the Muslim League were demanding that in recognition of India's war effort she should be rewarded with a number of reforms, including a statement on the future goal of British rule. A statement on the goals of British policy was something that would, by and large, be welcomed by British administrators in India, but there were other reasons why it was deemed essential. This declaration was a reflection of the need, at a particularly low point in the British war effort, to shore up support from 'moderate' elements of the Indian nationalist movement and curtail political agitation.[19] By June 1917 the war had not gone well for the British Empire. There had been a number of humbling defeats to the Ottoman Empire, first, in the agonising failure to open the Dardanelles Strait in 1915, and second, with the expeditionary operation to Mesopotamia in 1916. A report into this latter disaster was published on 26 June 1917. It was the result of an investigation into the circumstances surrounding the ill-advised drive to Baghdad (which had ended with the surrender of a British force at Kut on the Tigris River). According to Montagu, the Government of India was 'enormously lowered in the eyes of the people at home' by this report, which was damning of the British administration.[20]

Three days after the publication of the Mesopotamia report, the War Cabinet met to discuss the future of British rule in India.[21] After lengthy debates and various memorandums between Montagu, Curzon and others, the wording of the declaration was finalised. On 20 August 1917, Montagu announced to the House of Commons that:

> The policy of His Majesty's Government, with which the Government of India are in complete accord, is that of the increasing association of Indians in every

branch of the administration, and the gradual development of self-governing
institutions, with a view to the progressive realisation of responsible government in India as an integral part of the British Empire.[22]

The exact wording of the declaration was discussed extensively at the time
and has also been an area of historical enquiry ever since. Although the British
Government clearly felt that this declaration was a statement of considerable
weight, it was not intended to be a 'licence' for independence, but rather it en-
visaged a version of self-government for India that would be achieved through
progressive stages.[23] In order to assuage conservative unease, Montagu added
that

> this policy can only be achieved by successive stages. The British Government
> and the Government of India, on whom the responsibility lies for the wel-
> fare and advancement of the Indian peoples, must be the judges of the time
> and measure of each advance, and they must be guided by the co-operation
> received from those upon whom new opportunities of service will thus be
> conferred.

In line with this declaration was a reversal of the decision to intern
Mrs Besant. Montagu strongly petitioned Chelmsford to overrule the Government of Madras and order Besant's release. Although Madras remained
adamant, increasing pressure was brought to bear on its governor, John Sin-
clair, First Baron Pentland, to relent and let her go. Pentland ('thin, whiskered,
in tightly-button frock-coat, large gardenia-like flower in his buttonhole') was
an administrator of an earlier generation, 19 years older than Montagu. He
was committed to ensuring British superiority in the subcontinent and believed that unless constitutional development was kept firmly in check, there
was no hope for the empire.[24] But, however, stubbornly Pentland resisted,
he could not defy the will of both the Secretary of State for India and the
Viceroy. On 17 September, after satisfying the government on her future good
conduct, Annie Besant was released. The Government of India overruled a
provincial government and ordered the release of Besant for a number of reasons, including the fear of disorder if she remained in custody; a desire to avoid
making her into a martyr; a reluctance to deal harshly with an elderly woman
of European descent; and also a genuine distaste for political repression.[25]
But a major factor seems to have been the declaration of 20 August, which
was felt to be incompatible with the treatment of Mrs Besant. In Britain, the
Guardian spoke for liberal opinion when it noted that the internment was a
'strange anomaly' considering that 'Home Rule for India is precisely the goal
which Montagu now announced as that of the Government policy'.[26]

Needless to say, this new approach incensed many British administrators in India who regretted, as they saw it, a loss of prestige. When Pentland break-fasted with Montagu in December 1917, during the latter's trip to India, the subject of Annie Besant still rankled with him and he tried to bring Montagu around to his way of thinking. 'He assured me,' Montagu remembered, 'that all respect for the Government had gone; that people used to consider all officials, from the Viceroy downwards, as sort of gods not to be argued with or challenged. That had all disappeared; we were playing with fire; danger was written everywhere.' Montagu, of course, could not agree. 'I did not know what to say to him,' he wrote. 'It was almost oppressive. We shall simply have to ride over the Government of India.'[27] Pentland's discontent was widely shared, even in London. T.W. Holderness, working at the India Office, recorded that the release of Besant had created a situation amongst the European population that was 'quite as bad as the Ilbert Bill', the infamous bill of 1883 that would have allowed Indian judges to oversee cases involving Europeans.[28]

The decision to treat the Home Rule movement not as 'seditious' or 'revolutionary' and only to act when those advocating it actually broke existing laws marked an important change in British policy towards the Indian nation-alist movement. Although Chelmsford would deny it, the treatment of Annie Besant showed that the Government of India was no longer totally commit-ted to rallying 'moderate' politicians to its side and attempting to silence the 'extremist' wing of the national movement. Indian politicians, of whatever stamp, would now be appeased as much as possible. As time went by this ap-proach would become, as Peter Robb has noted, 'protected by precedent'.[29] It would guide the Government of India through the first non-co-operation campaign of 1920–2 when the consistent desire to avoid making Gandhi a 'martyr' put great strain on the patience of many Europeans in India, who were anxious to deal strongly with any threat and who were contemptuous of the restrained policies of Chelmsford's successor, Lord Reading. A turning point in the Raj was marked on 20 August 1917, which may not have imme-diately devolved power to local Indian elites, but it was only the beginning of a lengthy period of consultation. Montagu's visit to India was a major part of this process.

ल

By the spring of 1918 the months of hard work, endless discussions and rounds of meetings were coming to a conclusion. Montagu's trip to India and the consultation process that he began provided much of the groundwork for the report that he co-authored with Chelmsford, which was eventually published in June. The Montagu–Chelmsford Report would form the basis for the Government of India Act of 1919, which would substantially increase the participation of Indians in the administration in significant ways. The provinces were to be the arena for the 'progressive realisation of responsible government' in India. Montagu and his advisers, and Lord Chelmsford and the Government of India, had scrutinised a host of ideas about to move the Raj forward and had narrowed their search to a form of dualism.[30] This would mean 'reserving' the most important portfolios for the Executive Councils within the provinces, but 'transferring' the remaining subjects to non-official Indian ministers who would be chosen by the governor from elected members of the Legislative Council. Furthermore, the franchise was to be extended so that these councils would have elected majorities. Which subjects would be transferred and which would be reserved was, of course, the critical question, but for the moment at least there was agreement between Montagu and Chelmsford that strategically important policies – such as taxation, defence, communications and criminal law – would remain in British hands, while other less sensitive areas of responsibility would be transferred.[31] It was hoped that this would strengthen the position of the 'moderates', weaken the 'extremists' and preserve the essentials of British power in India.

The declaration of August 1917 and the Montagu–Chelmsford proposals were received well throughout India, but far from stemming calls for constitutional advance, they only increased the pressure on the Government of India and made those who were calling for reform redouble their efforts, becoming bolder as they did so. At a special session of the Indian National Congress, held in Bombay between 29 August and 1 September 1918, the reforms were widely discussed. Congress admitted that Montagu's and Chelmsford's efforts were appreciated, but then called their proposals 'disappointing and unsatisfactory', declaring that 'nothing less than self-government within the Empire can satisfy the Indian people' and disagreeing with the idea that it should be in the provinces where the first steps to representative institutions would be introduced. A number of modifications to the proposals were offered, including that the system of reserved and transferred subjects should be adopted at the centre and not just at the provinces, that the crucial portfolios of foreign affairs, army, navy and relations with Indian princes, should be transferred, and that at least half of the members of the Executive Council should be Indians.[32] The Congress delegates would surely have known that their modifications could not possibly be accepted by either Montagu or Chelmsford, who were taking a big enough gamble as it was, but probably felt that there was still capital to be gained from demanding more.

Montagu returned to London in May 1918 and spent the next 18 months working on the details of the reforms and trying to build up positive newspaper coverage for them in the British press.[33] Despite the grumblings of a section of the right-wing press, particularly the *Morning Post*, which always remained against constitutional change in India, the reform proposals were well received in Britain and helped to shore up support for the Government of India. Montagu may have been pleased at how the reforms proposals were being received in the clubs and offices of London, but before they could pass into law in December 1919, violence and unrest had erupted across northern India that left scores of dead and wounded, and bitter memories of bloodshed and oppression that would never be healed. Because for all his good intentions, Montagu had not foreseen the suddenness or violence of the disorders of 1919 and had not listened to those who urged caution and spoke of the dangers of disturbing the political balance across India. Montagu's position as Secretary of State for India would be gravely weakened; his dreams of a 'new epoch' in Indian history were to be realised, but not in the ways he had imagined.

CHAPTER 3

Gandhi and the Rowlatt
Satyagraha

It was a movement intended to replace methods of violence. It is a movement based entirely on truth.

Mohandas Gandhi[1]

Three years before Edwin Montagu had gazed wondrously at the blue hills surrounding Bombay on his way to sketch out a future for British rule in India, a short, frail man in a white *dhoti* (loincloth) had also stepped ashore. He too had stared with equal wonderment at the scene before his eyes because, although an Indian, he had not seen his homeland for 13 years. Mohandas Karamchand Gandhi did not enjoy the welcome that met the Secretary of State for India, with its fleets of dignitaries and official receptions, but a small crowd had gathered to see him and showered him with garlands and cheers. Unlike Montagu, however, Gandhi did not like Bombay. 'It looks,' he complained, 'as if it were the scum of London. I see here all the shortcomings of London, but find none of its amenities.'[2] In an interview with the *Bombay Chronicle* soon after he landed, Gandhi would not be drawn on political issues and revealed that the great Indian nationalist, G.K. Gokhale, had asked him to undertake a period of study and observation before he spoke on any of the great issues that confronted India at this moment. To this, Gandhi had agreed.[3]

Gandhi's return to India marked an important moment in his life, and as the slightly built man from Porbandar in Gujarat re-adjusted to his homeland after so many years away, he was focused on serving his country. His campaigns for racial equality for indentured labourers in South Africa meant that many Indian social campaigners and politicians had high hopes that he could achieve great things in the subcontinent. At a reception in Bombay for him and his wife, Kasturbai, when he was presented with the gift of a silver and gold casket (which he refused), Gandhi gave a short speech. A reporter from the *Bombay Chronicle* wrote that:

> The only idea behind his work was duty. He had only been able to do so far one *anna* of it and he had returned to his country after all these years to try his best to do what he could of the other 15 *annas* in the years that were left to him. He hoped for nothing and wished for nothing, beyond being able to fulfil the duty that lay before him. He entreated them all to accept whatever service he could give, and not to give him costly presents which he could not use, and which could be put to far better uses. He sincerely trusted that they would not misunderstand him; he was only expressing his innermost feelings.[4]

It would not be the first time that Gandhi would attempt to explain his actions and prevent them from being confused, and indeed he was a man who was often misunderstood. Many observers, both at the time and ever since, have been infuriated by him. In his evidence to the Hunter Committee, Mr J.P. Thompson, the Chief Secretary to the Government of Punjab, echoed a familiar British complaint when he said that 'Mr Gandhi is an enigma. It is very difficult to understand him.'[5] Indeed, it can be challenging to separate the 'real' Gandhi from his great reputation as the Mahatma (the Sanskrit word for 'great soul') and 'father' of India.[6] Gandhi's life was not just the struggle against the British Raj, but a battle with himself, as he tried to pursue a life that was based on non-violence, moral and religious purity and what he called 'truth'. During his life, Gandhi would, as he called it, 'experiment with truth' and he was not always consistent in his actions. At one time or another he confounded most of his closest friends and allies with his strategies for India's nationalist struggle and also with his 'fads' in respect to diets, medicines and other steps that he believed would contribute to India's moral and religious renewal. Contradiction was part of Gandhi's character. If he changed his mind, he would, cheerful as ever, admit it and move on; reassuring his friends that he had simply been fortunate enough to have received a greater understanding from God. In 1919 Gandhi would begin his greatest struggle so far.

༄

In India the signing of the armistice with Germany came as a profound relief for the British administration. The structure and efficiency of the Raj had buckled, but not broken, under the strain of war. By 1919, the Indian Civil Service, the key pillar of British rule was, according to one historian, 'depleted, disillusioned and fearful'. Recruitment had stopped in 1914 owing to the outbreak of hostilities and was slow to recover in the changed circumstances at the end of the war.[7] Indeed, almost as soon as toasts to the King-Emperor's health had been drunk and the bunting celebrating the end of the war had been taken down, a mood of profound disillusionment and gloom settled down upon India.[8] The report on India's 'moral and material progress' for 1919 described India's internal political situation – with monumental understatement – as 'a most interesting spectacle'.[9] Not only was India struggling to adjust to a new world order in which four empires (Imperial Germany, Tsarist Russia, Austro-Hungary and Ottoman Turkey) had collapsed, but it was also becoming aware of the radical new idea of 'self-determination' that was being touted by President Woodrow Wilson at the Paris Peace Conference. The war against Turkey was a particular sore point. India's Muslims had never been keen on fighting their co-religionists and when it became clear that the Allies were going to impose harsh peace terms on the defeated Ottoman Empire, groups of Indian Muslims began to form *Khalifat* (Islamic) committees to oppose this policy.

India's sacrifices in the Great War had fostered political expectation, at least among its Western-educated elites. One ardent nationalist, Jawaharlal Nehru, remembered how 'The dominant note all over India was one of waiting and expectation, full of hope and yet tinged with fear and anxiety.'[10] Therefore, it was with considerable disappointment when new legislation – the so-called Rowlatt Act – was ushered in by the Government of India in January 1919, which seemed to fly in the face of British promises of reform and for a new era of co-operation contained in Montagu's August declaration.[11] In some respects this was true, but there was always more to the Raj than just consultation and reform, and the Rowlatt Act symbolised its coercive side. The growth of nationalist consciousness and the increase in Indian terrorism had not gone unnoticed, and as well as trying to widen the administrative basis of the Government of India, there were calls to tighten up the powers available to combat anti-British 'agitation'. Indeed, one of the problems with reform was that it obviously allowed for a certain level of 'agitation', but that it was consequently more difficult to keep this in hand and to justify repressive measures.

The Rowlatt Act was intended to help the British maintain order in an unsettled period and was based on the findings of the 1918 Sedition Committee. It was headed by Mr Justice Rowlatt, a High Court Judge, and consisted of five other members.[12] On 10 December 1917, the committee was appointed to 'investigate and report on the nature and extent of the criminal conspiracies connected with the revolutionary movement in India' and to examine the ways in which they could be better dealt with. It concluded that in order to contain these conspiracies it was necessary 'to provide for the continuance after the expiry of the Defence of India Act (though in the contingent form and under important limitation) some of the powers which that measure introduced in a temporary form'.[13] The Defence of India Act had come into force in 1915 and contained similar provisions to the Defence of the Realm Act in the United Kingdom, granting the Government powers to detain political suspects without charge or trial and to deal with such cases without juries.

The Rowlatt Bills became law on 21 March 1919.[14] Among non-official Indian members of the Legislative Council there was considerable unease over the passing of the Bills. Several leading members including Madan Mohan Malaviya, B.D. Shukul and M.A. Jinnah resigned in protest.[15] Undeterred by this opposition the Government of India pressed ahead with Rowlatt's recommendations for various reasons: a desire to put them in place before peace was signed in Europe; to reassure conservatives who were concerned over the pace of reform in India; an underestimation of the likely reaction from Indian politicians; as well as a genuine belief that these measures were unavoidable, necessary and likely to be effective. Because it was felt that it would not be possible (or desirable) to use the Defence of India Act in peacetime, the Government effectively re-introduced the act in a slightly different form.[16] As a concession to nationalist opposition, the Rowlatt Act did contain important modifications. It would last for just three years and only be employed against 'anarchical and revolutionary movements'.[17]

The Rowlatt Bills may not have had much in common with the 'black bills' of nationalist myth, but they were ill-timed and poorly-explained. They were universally disliked by Indian politicians in the Imperial Legislative Council, but found their most fervent opponent in Mohandas Gandhi. Gandhi's views on the Rowlatt Bills are well known. He was deeply opposed to them, believing that they were 'evidence of a determined policy of repression', which had to be resisted at all costs.[18] Gandhi read the speeches on the Rowlatt Bills on 8 February and was 'much distressed', believing that something must be done in protest, possibly the non-payment of taxes. He wrote to a leading moderate, Madan Mohan Malaviya, and remarked that 'unless we do something really big they will not feel any respect for us'.[19] Gandhi spent the next few days discussing matters with his closest associates and friends. He now firmly believed that he would have to fight the 'greatest battle' of his life in opposing the Rowlatt Bills, but he remained unclear about his exact strategy for some time, being busy with his affairs in the *ashram*; a small, quasi-monastic community on the banks of the river Sabarmati in Ahmedabad, where he put into practice his ideas about 'truth', non-violence and purity.[20]

On 18 March Gandhi received news that the Rowlatt Bills were to become law. He somewhat melodramatically described in his autobiography,

> That night, I fell asleep while thinking over the questions. Towards the small hours of the morning I woke up somewhat earlier than usual. I was still in the twilight condition between sleep and consciousness when suddenly the idea broke upon me – it was as if in a dream.[21]

Gandhi decided that he would undertake a campaign of non-violent civil disobedience, what he called *satyagraha*. He telegraphed the Associated Press of India on 23 March and explained to them the background to, and purpose of, *satyagraha*. He wanted an 'effective public demonstration' to occur on the second Sunday after the publication of Bill No. 2 (6 April 1919), which would take the form of a 24-hour fast and a general *hartal*. A *hartal* was an Indian term, meaning the cessation of all work other than vital public services. He also explained that on 6 April public meetings should be held at which resolutions for the removal of the Bill would be made.[22] The *satyagraha* pledge was drafted at Gandhi's Sabarmati *ashram* on 24 February.[23] It committed its signatories to refuse to obey the Rowlatt Bills. The same day Gandhi also appealed to the Viceroy, Lord Chelmsford (through his Private Secretary), to 'reconsider' the Rowlatt Act. If this was not done, he would 'offer *satyagraha* and commit civil disobedience'.[24]

What was *satyagraha*? Gandhi described its 'root meaning' as 'holding on to truth'; hence, 'truth-force':

> I have also called it love-force or soul-force. In the application of satyagraha I discovered in the earliest stages that pursuit of truth did not admit of violence being inflicted on one's opponent, but that he must be weaned from error by patience and sympathy. For what appears as truth to the one may appear to be error to the other. And patience means self-suffering. So the doctrine came to mean vindication of truth, not by infliction of suffering on the opponent, but one's own self.[25]

Gandhi did admit, however, that people only had a 'hazy notion' of what *satyagraha* actually was. He believed that it was up to him to make sure that it was widely understood. Only then could it be truly successful. On 26 February, two days after he had drafted his pledge, Gandhi issued his instruction to would-be volunteers. He urged them to make sure they had read and understood the provisions of the Rowlatt Bills and that they must always adhere to the ideas of 'truth' and *ahimsa* (non-violence), never forcing people to sign and never misrepresenting the issues at stake. The idea of struggle and sacrifice was central to Gandhi's idea about what a *satyagrahi* should be. Volunteers must be 'prepared to bear every kind of suffering and to sacrifice, if necessary, both to his person and property'.[26]

Gandhi's role in organising the Rowlatt *Satyagraha* has been well documented. Although Gandhi's campaign lay outside of the established political groups in India, his attempt to spread his message of *satyagraha* across the vast subcontinent was aided by a number of existing organisations and networks, including the Home Rule Leagues. These provided an 'important grid of connections' for the spread of Gandhi's message, but inevitably the strength of this organisation was not the same across India, tending to be more useful in the 'northern, northwestern, and western regions and less so in Bengal, the Punjab, the centre, or the south'.[27] The main nationalist group within India at this time, the Indian National Congress, provided lukewarm support to Gandhi's *satyagraha*. Opinions within the Home Rule movement were split. Guy Horniman, editor of the *Bombay Chronicle*, strongly supported the campaign, but Mrs Besant, who had previously been the darling of the nationalist movement and who perhaps felt an understandable degree of jealousy at the Mahatma's swift rise, urged caution, citing the difficulty of maintaining unity and discipline and the likely effects of failure.[28] A group of non-official Indians from the Legislative Council, including the President of the Servants of India Society, Srinivasa Sastri, even issued a manifesto opposing the *satyagraha* movement, arguing that it was unsuitable, against the best interests of India, and impossible for ordinary citizens to follow.[29]

Undeterred, Gandhi undertook an extensive tour of India between March and the beginning of April, visiting Delhi, Lucknow, Allahabad, Bombay and Madras, and according to his own estimate, appearing before 30,000 people.[30] As H.F. Owen has noted, this tour was, in essence, a 'substitute for organization' in that it allowed him to communicate with his followers in the absence of a well-structured and coherent political organisation in which directions could be provided quickly.[31] In some ways Gandhi's tour was a failure. His health at this period was a particular worry. His punishing schedule, when combined with his irregular diet – he existed mainly on groundnut butter and lemons – prompted a debilitating bout of dysentery. Refusing food and medicine, Gandhi fell into a fever, and only went through an improvement after taking ice baths at his *ashram*. His weakness during this period had a serious effect on his ability, although not his desire, to direct the campaign. Most of his speeches were given by his secretary, Mahadev Desai, and those in Madras were delivered in Tamil by his hosts. It was also a considerable strain on his already-overtaxed body. He admitted in his autobiography that 'The incapacity to address meetings still abides. My entire frame would shake, and heavy throbbing would start on an attempt to speak standing for any length of time.'[32]

Whatever the merits (or otherwise) of the Rowlatt Bills, the feelings against them were heightened by much misunderstanding and confusion about what they actually were. One provincial governor thought that the Rowlatt Bills were 'a reasonable and practical measure to take the place of the Defence of India Act', but were the subject of 'the most unscrupulous campaign of malignant misrepresentation that India up to then had witnessed'.[33] Mr C.A. Barron, the Chief Commissioner at Delhi, blamed the vernacular press for reproducing the speeches made in the Legislative Council against the Rowlatt Bills in full, but not devoting much space to those which explained why they were important. The Rowlatt Bills also seem to have been confused with other laws that were being passed, including the Excess Profits Tax, Income Tax and the Patel Marriage Bill.[34] Given his aversion to the legislation, it was perhaps surprising why Gandhi did not take a great deal of time or effort to explain the provisions of the Rowlatt Bill. He seems to have assumed that this was well known across India, something that was clearly not the case. Although Gandhi had instructed volunteers to explain the Bills clearly to those wanting to take the *satyagraha* vow, he did not do this himself. During his tour of India in March, he rarely mentioned what was wrong with the Rowlatt Act, only that he was justified in taking firm action against it. For example, on 11 March he stated that it was important to understand the 'main features' of the Rowlatt Bills, but he made no attempt to do so.[35] He would later call the Bills an 'insult ... to the whole of India' and a representation of 'untruth', but he did not elaborate further, perhaps because he felt that it was not up to him to do so.[36]

This pattern continued throughout Gandhi's tour. On 26 March he spoke at Madura and said that it was not necessary for him to describe the 'effect' of the legislation, but that it was enough for him to say that it was 'of such a character that no self-respecting nation can accept it'.[37] Two days later, Gandhi spoke before an audience at Tuticorin. 'You all know or ought to know what the Rowlatt legislation is,' he stated, 'I therefore do not propose to occupy your time by going into the history of that legislation.'[38] Only on 30 March, by which time rioting had broken out in Delhi, did Gandhi make a vague reference to the Rowlatt Act and then it was only seen by the 'light' it threw upon the forthcoming government reforms.[39] Gandhi had published a number of pieces on the provisions of the Rowlatt Bills, but his unwillingness to discuss the details of the acts in person probably stemmed, in part, from his ill-health and his inability to stand and speak for long periods of time, but it may have also reflected a realisation that it would be easier to gain support if he remained vague on this matter. In many ways, however, the exact wording of the Rowlatt Bills was irrelevant to Gandhi. They were simply a representation of 'untruth' and 'symptoms' of a 'deep-seated disease'.[40] It was not really the Rowlatt Act that angered Gandhi as much as the way that it had been rushed through the Legislative Council in spite of Indian opposition. It was time for action.

☙

The first indication that Gandhi's call for *satyagraha* was having some effect was witnessed in the imperial capital of Delhi on 30 March.[41] Either ignoring or misunderstanding the date upon which Gandhi wanted to act (which had been pencilled in for 6 April), there was a widespread *hartal* in the city.[42] The Hunter Report noted that this was a 'very great success in the sense that shops both Muhammadan and Hindu were closed and business was brought to a standstill'.[43] Unfortunately, violence broke out when groups of youths went to the main railway station to force refreshment vendors to close their businesses and join the *hartal*. A contractor refused to do so, and in the ensuing scuffle, was hurt. Two men were arrested at the scene, but when news spread through the city that they had been detained by the police, increasing numbers began to gather outside the station, shouting for their release. Upon being told by the police that the men had not been charged and would be released, the crowd insisted upon seeing them. When they were not forthcoming, the situation began to slip out of control. Some in the crowd (which had gradually swelled in size during the morning) started throwing stones and brickbats at the police. Evidently fearing that an assault would be made on the station, the authorities decided to clear the crowd. The police and military engaged in two bouts of firing during the day, once outside the station and the second when they were endeavouring to push the crowd back through the nearby Queen's Gardens. Eight men were killed and two more died of wounds.

The violence in Delhi marked the first outbreak of disorder during the disturbances of 1919 and highlighted both the cautious British response as well as the danger and volatility of the situation. Gandhi received sketchy details a few days later. What he heard did not shake his determination to resist the authorities and he persisted in believing that Delhi had witnessed not a dangerous outbreak of disorder, but an indefensible 'slaughter of innocents'.[44] In truth, Gandhi's views were both hopelessly naive and completely wrong. The Chief Commissioner would later commend the police and infantry for their 'great restraint', and for those who gave the orders to fire with 'great firmness' in 'a very sudden and awkward situation', and he seems to have been right.[45] As with much of the evidence available on the disturbances of 1919, it is not possible to arrive at a complete understanding of the size and composition of the crowds that gathered during the day. It is clear, however, that the Indian and British officers who were tasked with restoring order on 30 March found it an extremely frightening and testing experience, and only employed lethal force when they had no other choice.

There are various estimates as to the size of the crowd that gathered outside the railway station – varying from 300 to 1,500 – but it was evidently large, intimidating and in no mood to go away.[46] Mr K.S. Laurie, a district railway engineer, believed that the crowd was 'as nasty as it could be' and a municipal commissioner, Islamullah Khan, who passed through the station at 2 p.m. found it 'very threatening' and 'very provocative'. In response to frantic calls for help, the nearest available military reserve, a picquet of 30 men from 1/Bedfords, were despatched, arriving there at around 1.40 p.m. The commanding officer, Second Lieutenant E.J.H. Shelford, found that the crowd was 'one seething mass, brandishing sticks and throwing stones'. Shelford met the senior official in charge, Mr M. Currie (Additional District Magistrate), who told him that they must clear the crowd as soon as possible. He split his force into two parties and worked with the police to push the mass of people back several hundred yards up Queen's Road.[47]

The attempt to clear the area around the station was difficult and the authorities had to resort to firing, which took place at around 2.30 p.m. As the police and military tried to force the crowd back, they came under 'a shower of stones and bricks'. All of the men under the command of Mr Jeffreys (Additional Superintendent of Police) were hit and he suffered a blow to the head, which could have been serious had he not be wearing his *topee* (helmet). When Mr Barron, the Chief Commissioner, arrived later that afternoon, he noticed that the area around the station was 'littered with bricks and stones'.[48] Testimony to the fierceness of this barrage was the amount of casualties in 1/Bedfords, half of whom sustained wounds. It is clear that at Delhi many in the crowd had *lathis* (sticks bound with iron rings) and were also making use of stones in the road, clumps of earth and other missiles they could get their hands on. In response to a request to fire from one of his officers, Mr Currie accented and 'a few irregular volleys' were fired by the police and military. As soon as the shots were fired the crowd retreated and the cease-fire was given. Two men were killed.[49]

The police and infantry moved forward, marching down on either side of the park towards the Town Hall, to where the crowd had retreated. The situation did, however, only get worse and Mr Jeffreys found a large mob on the western gate of the Town Hall, shouting and throwing bricks and stones. He rode up on his horse, but she became so frightened that he had to dismount. Fearing that his small picquet would be either rushed by the crowd or outflanked from the rear, he decided that he would have to fire. He had refused permission to fire at least once because he wanted to avoid bloodshed if at all possible, and was waiting for British troops to arrive, which he hoped would frighten the crowd. Unfortunately, they did not come up as quickly as he would have liked. Because the front row was 'simply thick with boys', he directed his men to fire to the right where there were more grown men. The firing did not have the desired effect and the crowd continued to advance upon his position. By this time a small party of British troops had turned up. Jeffreys spoke to the sergeant in charge of the party and told him to fire a volley into the air. This was done but again to little avail and the crowd became even more aggressive. 'The crowd charged the British party, they then lowered their rifles and put a volley into them and that finished the business,' he remembered.[50] When the dust had settled, the crowd had scattered, leaving several bodies lying on the ground.

 co

The violence at Delhi may have been overshadowed by the later events at Amritsar, but it could have resulted in widespread bloodshed if it had got out of hand. The police and military response was not disproportionate and at least one volley was fired into the air above the heads of the protestors (with little effect) before the authorities resorted to controlled firing. Given the small number of police and military on the scene and the evident hostility of the crowd, it is little wonder that lethal force had to be employed. Mr Jeffreys, who was hit several times by stones and bricks, recalled that the situation appeared 'desperate. The crowd was very close.' Although it would later be questioned whether more police and soldiers could have been used to overawe the crowd, this would not have been very wise. It is true that a group of 250 Nepali soldiers (Manipuris) were present at Delhi railway station during the disturbances – they were passing through the capital – but they were not armed and could not speak Hindi. Perhaps wisely, British officers on the scene chose to keep the Manipuris in the background. When asked why the Manipuris had not been used on 30 March, Jeffreys replied that 'It would have been a hideous massacre. Nobody could understand and give orders to the Manipuris. They would have killed the first man who provoked them.'[51]

The fracas at the railway station showed how quickly violence could happen when tempers became frayed and misunderstandings occurred. What really happened remains a little confused, but it seems that a group of around 20 men attacked a contractor, Ganga Singh, who refused to close his shop and join the *hartal* because he did not own the business.[52] Two men were arrested by the police, but they were released soon afterwards. It was alleged that the police beat the suspects and then started on those who tried to intervene. Although this is impossible to verify, there is no doubt that the police had a poor reputation in the city and were commonly seen as corrupt, aggressive and arrogant.[53] When news spread that people had been arrested at the railway station and were being beaten, it did not take long for angry crowds to make their way there and shout for their release. So despised were the police in Delhi that repeated entreaties to the crowd to leave and statements that the men had been released had no effect.

The nationalist movement in the city was somewhat taken aback by the events of 30 March. The local branch of the *Satyagraha Sabha* had been inaugurated on 7 March, and had been prominent in speaking out against the Rowlatt Bills, but owing to the mob violence, its leaders closed it down in May; burning the list of pledges that they had all signed, in such fervour, only two months before.[54] Indeed, it seems that most of those who took the *satyagraha* vow were dedicated to the Mahatma's goal of non-violent protest and earnestly believed that his vision was both realisable and effective. Nevertheless, *satyagraha* was not the rapier that Gandhi imagined it to be, but a crude instrument that had the potential to raise a storm of violence across the country. It was a vague movement, riven by contradiction, and unclear about which laws should be disobeyed and what form this would take.[55]

This confusion ultimately stemmed from Gandhi himself. Gandhi's *satyagraha* pledge committed its signatories to refuse to obey the Rowlatt Bills, but this was impossible *unless one actually became a terrorist*. Although this basic inconsistency was explained to Gandhi, he does not seem to have been too concerned about it, withdrawing into his religious and moral justification for *satyagraha*. For Gandhi at least, the form of the protest was not really important, only that his followers show sufficient moral purpose and self-suffering in order to impress upon the authorities that 'soul-force' and 'truth-force' were strong and could not be defeated. Nevertheless, the loose organisation for *satyagraha* and the lack of specific tactics for its employment did sap the morale of some of those who were supposed to be putting it into practice, including Swami Shraddhanand, who admitted that the doctrine of *satyagraha* was both too subtle for 'ordinary people' to understand and likely to lead to violence.[56]

On 18 April Gandhi called off his movement, still convinced that 'satyagraha had nothing to do with the violence of the mob'.[57] It would be incorrect to say, as some British did at the time, that Gandhi directly *caused* the violence of 1919, but it would also not be right to divorce him and his movement from the violence that did occur, as Gandhi tried to do. There is no easy answer to what caused the violence of 1919, but Gandhi must take his share of responsibility for devising and leading a movement that called for mass civil disobedience of authority without stating how this disobedience was to take place. Because it was unclear, apart from the closing of shops, what form the disobedience could take, and given the heightened feelings within Delhi, it only took a small incident – such as that at the railway station – for violent clashes to occur. Violence was all the more likely given the unpopularity of the police force and the widespread grievances within India at this time, from high prices and the Rowlatt Bills, to Muslim alarm at the fate of the holy places of Islam.

CHAPTER 4

Hartals, Processions and Arrests

The lower orders had got out of hand. The leaders were no longer able to control the crowd.

Hon. C.A. Barron[1]

Sunday 6 April 1919 was known as 'Black Sunday', a day of *hartals* across India when it was hoped that the true strength of feeling against the Rowlatt Bills would be revealed. In Bombay, Gandhi had invited people to come to the Chowpatty Beach, where flat sands broke upon the Arabian Sea. It was a popular meeting place that would allow his followers enough room to gather. After people had bathed in the water, they would then form a procession towards the Madhav Baug Temple. Further meetings would be held throughout the day and the *Bombay Chronicle* implored its readers, 'If you value your freedom, you will join.'[2] For Mahatma Gandhi, 6 April was to be a day of humiliation and prayer, not a triumphalist or violent expression of will, but a fitting gesture of respect for those killed at Delhi on 30 March. 'It is therefore absolutely necessary,' he exhorted his followers, 'that when the demonstrators go out to bathe and form the procession there will be no noise, no talking, amongst themselves, but that they will march in absolute silence and disperse likewise.' He wanted the behaviour of his followers to be 'worthy of the occasion'.[3]

One of the first to arrive at Chowpatty Beach was the Mahatma himself, accompanied by a small group of volunteers. At eight o'clock he walked the short distance to the Chowpatty sands, helped as ever by his volunteers. He was still suffering from poor health and was in no condition to give his speech so it was read instead by one of his followers.[4] Gandhi's speech began by stating that he was anxious not to say a great deal on such an occasion, what he called 'the most solemn of our lives', but that it was impossible 'to ignore the tragedy that was enacted at the capital of India last Sunday'. Gandhi then spoke at some length on the shootings at Delhi, particular the differences between the official accounts and those collected by his followers, and the unjust and vindictive way that the crowds had been dispersed. The authorities, Gandhi claimed, 'simply followed out the traditional policy of ignoring leaders and of overawing the people'.

The second part of Gandhi's speech concentrated on how they were to build up strength through self-sacrifice and self-discipline and how this was essential if India was to be free. And then, concluding, he asked the crowd to pass two resolutions: the first to show deep sympathy for those killed in the riots in Delhi, the second a 'simple prayer' to Edwin Montagu, asking him to advise the King-Emperor to withdraw the Rowlatt Bill. With his speech over, Gandhi and his followers made their way, in a vast procession, to the Madhav Baug Temple to offer prayers. An enthusiastic reporter from the *Bombay Chronicle* wrote that 'without the least exaggeration it could be stated that from the seashore to the Madhav Baug it was a solid mass of humanity, gathering its strength on the way. The houses on both sides were crowded with women and men and children.'

೧

The march to Chowpatty beach on the morning of 6 April 1919 has gone down in Gandhian legend as a moment of unique significance; the first time the Mahatma conducted a grand, India-wide movement against repressive laws. The meeting undoubtedly showed Gandhi's appetite for political theatre and his ability to gather a great deal of support, particularly in those areas like Bombay where he was blessed with much local influence. Indeed, the gathering on 6 April and the *hartal* that occurred throughout many parts of India was undoubtedly a great personal success for Gandhi.[5] He would later enthuse to Lord Hunter that, 'no violence, no real violence was offered by the people because people were being told the true nature of Satyagraha.' 'It was an amazing sight for me,' he added, 'to see thousands of people behaving in a perfectly peaceful manner.'[6] Nationalist historiography has echoed this, enthusing that Gandhi's call for action against the Rowlatt Bills was a 'wake-up call' to India's masses. According to this legend, Gandhi's fervent opposition to this legislation stirred the sleeping people, galvanised their sense of patriotism and urged them to action. As Louis Fischer explained, 'Gandhi's *hartal* idea spread throughout India. It united vast multitudes in common action; it gave the people a sense of power.'[7] Such is the stubbornness of this argument – that *satyagraha* received enthusiastic support from all of India's people – that on the seventy-fifth anniversary of the Jallianwala Bagh massacre, an Indian historian, Satya M. Rai, could still claim that Gandhi's call for *satyagraha* received 'nationwide support'.[8]

In truth, the support that Gandhi received against the Rowlatt Bills was patchy. Although it was undoubtedly strong in certain parts of India, particularly Bombay, Ahmedabad, Lahore, Delhi and Amritsar, many other areas of India remained unmoved in 1919.[9] Bengal, traditionally the home of Indian revolutionaries, was surprisingly quiet. Apart from Calcutta, where a large meeting of about 10,000 people was held, the rest of the province was uninterested in the Rowlatt agitation. The Bengali press was divided over the merits of Gandhi's call for action and several public bodies, including the Bengal National Chamber of Commerce, issued manifestos against *satyagraha*. In Central and Southern India there were few protests against the Rowlatt Bills, perhaps reflecting a combination of little political interest, internal dissention within the nationalist movement, and a lack of grievances. In the Central Provinces, there were attempts to make shopkeepers close their businesses, but these met, as a British intelligence report noted, with 'very limited support'.[10] A meeting of 5,000 people was held in Puri in the province of Bihar and Orissa, but little else occurred. No meetings were held in Assam. Burma was largely immune.[11]

The extent of Muslim support for Gandhi's *satyagraha* remains unclear. In certain parts of India, particularly in Delhi and the Punjab, some Muslims were enthusiastic participants in *satyagraha* and there were notable scenes of Hindu-Muslim unity, for example when Hindus were admitted to a prayer meeting in the Fatehpuri Masjid in Delhi.[12] At the same time as the Rowlatt Bills came into force, the Muslims of India were particularly sensitive over the fate of the Ottoman Empire, which had collapsed at the end of the war. At Madras on 19 March a large meeting was held in Bombay to consider the question of what would happen to the Caliphate and to discuss the protection of the holy places of Islam.[13] Gandhi was fortunate in being able to sweep up some of this Muslim concern into his own campaign, and because he was remarkably vague in discussing what exactly the Rowlatt Bills did, Muslims and Hindus were able to protest together against the tyranny of the British Government without too many problems. But as would be a recurring feature of Gandhi's campaigns over the next 20 years, wider Muslim opinion remained stubbornly resistant to the Mahatma's charms and there were some concerns expressed at his *satyagraha* campaign. Muslim newspapers in both Bengal and the United Provinces were more interested in discussing the future of Turkey and expressing sympathy for Egyptian nationalists than they were in the Rowlatt agitation. One Muslim newspaper even denounced the Muslims of Delhi for allowing Hindus into mosques.[14]

As was perhaps to be expected, the princely states of India, those ruled by princes loyal to the British Crown, did not witness any anti-Rowlatt Bill disturbances. As the situation worsened in the Punjab and as violence flared up across the province, the Government of India contacted these rulers and asked for their support in putting down the disorder.[15] Keen to display their loyalty and fidelity to the King-Emperor, the rulers of the princely states quickly mobilised their troops and by guarding railway lines, patrolling roads and securing telegraph infrastructure played a key role in preventing *satyagraha* and other political movements from spreading out of British India. This was done with efficiency and strength; the Maharaja of Bundi voiced a common opinion when he wrote to Lord Chelmsford on 24 April condemning those 'insensate people of anarchical ideas which are very condemnable and unaryan [*sic*] in their nature' and offering his full support to the Viceroy.

✑

Gandhi may have rejoiced about the 'perfectly peaceful manner' of the *hartal* (or at least what he saw of it in Bombay), but it was accompanied in certain areas by coercion and intimidation. British reports from Calcutta indicate that 'some attempt' was made to force shops to close and there were scuffles when groups of demonstrators tried to stop trams and force their passengers out onto the streets. In Bombay groups of mill workers tried to coerce other mills to close, but were dispersed by police.[16] Wherever it took place, the *hartal* was a boisterous affair, something akin to a holiday or a local fair where crowds would gather in large numbers and, perhaps inevitably, some would become aggressive and intimidating, particularly when tensions were high.

A greater level of coercion seems to have been employed in the Punjab, where the disturbances would reach their peak, and which attracted a greater level of official concern. For Sir Michael O'Dwyer, the events of 6 April in Lahore were deeply unwelcome. A large procession took place, and although there were no clashes with the police, there is some evidence that shopkeepers were afraid to re-open their shops.[17] O'Dwyer recorded that:

> The orders regarding public meetings were openly defied, menacing crowds with black flags paraded the streets, and only the presence of a large body of British and Indian troops, including cavalry, with machine-guns prevented them from forcing their way into the European quarter.[18]

Indeed, the crowds that gathered in Lahore did at times show a menacing hostility to police officers and other official representatives. When a police officer, Mr I.W. Bowring, attended a large protest meeting at the Bradlaugh

Hall, he recalled that, 'As soon as we entered the room the whole audience proceeded to howl and hoot and yell. It displayed every sign of animosity towards us.' Sayad Muhammad Shah, an extra assistant commissioner, came across a large crowd near Lohari Gate. He was stopped and told to remove his turban or else 'there would be trouble'. In his opinion it was not safe for any European to walk the streets on 6 April. Indian *sowars* (cavalry soldiers) who were on duty found themselves the victims of 'shouting, hissing, and hooting' and many in the crowd constantly clapped their hands to frighten the horses. People were also recorded as shouting '*Hai, hai King George mar gaya*' ('King George is dead').[19]

It was during the *hartal* that it became readily apparent to the British authorities that rumours about the Rowlatt Acts were becoming increasingly inaccurate and misleading. A British intelligence report complained that during an address at a labour rally in Madras, a speaker claimed that 'if a policeman coveted a handsome woman he would get the husband out of the way by means of the Rowlatt Act'. It was also stated that the government would double the amount of income tax everyone paid.[20] Such lies were becoming commonplace and having a destabilising effect. In the Punjab, ignorance about the Rowlatt Bills was widespread. The Deputy Commissioner of Amritsar, Miles Irving, complained about the 'wildest rumours' that were circulating in the city about the acts. These included for example:

> that more than four people would not be allowed to assemble together; that there would be a tax levied on every marriage; that Government would collect its revenue in kind by taking half the produce, and other very wild rumours of that kind ...[21]

He also noted that during a number of meetings (28 February and 1 March) in Amritsar, 'it was never said what the Rowlatt Bill actually was'. Irving recalled one occasion when 'some one asked what the Rowlatt Bill was and was told from the platform that it was not opportune to give the information. There was complete ignorance on the part of the people as regards the actual provisions of the act.' Whether such rumours were spread deliberately by *satyagrahis* is unclear. Gandhi had ordered them to explain the Rowlatt Bills faithfully, but its complexity meant that misunderstandings were quick to occur in the largely illiterate Indian population. Although the authorities did make some attempts to stem the flood of rumours and misleading information that they encountered, it was, perhaps inevitably, a forlorn hope. For example, by the time the Government of Madras had prepared vernacular leaflets and issued a statement to the *Gazette of India* explaining the need to remove misunderstanding over the new legislation, it was 14 April, a day *after* the Jallianwala Bagh massacre.[22]

The situation at Amritsar was of particular concern.[23] At a meeting on 5 April, the 'leading citizens' of the city informed the Deputy Commissioner, Miles Irving, that in their opinion a *hartal* would not be held the following day. Much to his consternation, large crowds did come together on 6 April and most of the shops were closed. Although there was no violence, Irving was so surprised and concerned that he warned Captain J.W. Massey (OC Amritsar) to be ready to carry out a plan to safeguard the European settlement if trouble broke out. The *hartal* of 6 April at Amritsar may have been peaceful, but for many British observers, including Irving, it was just the beginning of an uncomfortable rise in the political temperature. 'They were working up for some kind of mischief for some future time which I could not foresee,' he would later tell Lord Hunter.[24] One of the main points that emerges from British eyewitness accounts of the *hartal* was the spectacle, which some found extremely worrying, of Hindus and Muslims acting together in a spirit of co-operation. For Ian Colvin, Dyer's biographer, the spectacle of Hindus and Muslims drinking out of the same water vessels at Amritsar was a 'breach of caste ... strange, ominous, unprecedented'; a symbol that something was wrong, perhaps a portent of conspiracies whispered in dark alleyways.[25]

On 8 April Irving penned a letter to the Commissioner of the Lahore Division, A.J.W. Kitchin, which he also forwarded to O'Dwyer. It was an alarming letter, full of concern and suspicion, in which Irving explained what had happened during the *hartal* and admitted that he felt matters were slipping out of control. He regarded the situation with 'very grave concern'. Irving could not put his finger on who was responsible for the increasing unrest in the city. He did not believe that the leading local nationalist and president of the *Satyagraha Sabha*, Dr Kitchlew, was at the centre of the conspiracy, regarding him as 'the local agent of very much bigger men'. In order to restore the situation Irving pressed urgently for reinforcements. 'It is absurd,' he wrote, 'to attempt to hold Amritsar City with a company of British Infantry and half a company of Garrison Artillery. Any resolute action in the city would leave the civil lines almost undefended.' As well as pressing for more troops, particularly motor machine-gun units, Irving felt it might be necessary to do something more.

> Secondly, we cannot go on indefinitely with the policy of keeping out of the way, and congratulating ourselves that the mob has not forced us to interfere. Every time we do this the confidence of the mob increases: yet with our present force we have no alternative. I think that we shall have to stand up for our

authority sooner or later by prohibiting some strike or procession which endangers the public peace. But for this a really strong force will have to be brought in and we shall have to be ready to try conclusions to the end to see who governs Amritsar.[26]

Given what would happen in Amritsar, it is tempting to place more emphasis on Irving's letter than it perhaps merits and see it as evidence that the British were either readying themselves for a harsh reaction or (as some have claimed) even planning the Jallianwala Bagh massacre in advance.[27] The letter was certainly candid and perhaps said more than was either wise or diplomatic, but it was not necessarily evidence of the hysteria that critics, like E.M. Forster, have often assigned to the British community in India. In Forster's most famous novel, *A Passage to India*, he portrays them as hysterical, haunted by the Mutiny and prone to overreaction. Elements of Forster's novel are clearly inspired by the events at Amritsar, such as the assault on Miss Quested in the Marabar Caves, which is redolent of the assault on the English missionary, Miss Marcia Sherwood. After this incident, the European community huddles in its club and wants to 'clear the bazaars' and 'flog every native' in sight.[28] But this is a gross caricature. Rather than lashing out blindly, Irving was confused and increasingly frustrated at the growth of popular feeling, and feared that unless more troops arrived, the European population could become targeted. By all accounts Irving was a gentle and quiet man, but like many of his contemporaries, he was struggling to understand how to respond to recent political developments; how to deal with the new political landscape that was rapidly being redrawn across the subcontinent. Irving had spent most of his working life in the Punjab, living and breathing its ideals of paternalism and tradition. He was a man devoted to his career, who had no interest in seeing his work undermined, not someone who would panic in a crisis or advocate harsh repression. In April 1919 Irving felt (with some justification) that forces were gathering around them that he did not understand and which he was powerless to challenge.

Things were coming to a head. After the *hartal*, the Hindu festival of *Ram Naumi* on 9 April helped to maintain the momentum of the protest movement. Twenty thousand people gathered in Lahore and large crowds again gathered in Amritsar.[29] For his part, O'Dwyer had had enough. On the afternoon of 9 April, he decided to act, issuing orders for the removal of the leaders of the 'virulent agitation' at Amritsar, Drs Kitchlew and Satyapal, and calling for the reinforcement of the garrison.[30] Upon receipt of O'Dwyer's orders, Irving immediately summoned his closest colleagues and discussed with them how they were to be carried out. Present were Captain Massey, the police

officers (Rehill and Plomer), and Henry Smith, the Civil Surgeon.[31] Arthur
Swinson wrote,

> The feeling at this meeting takes little imagining. Here they were, just five
> Englishmen, with some 250 troops and seventy-five police at their disposal,
> to face a possible explosion from 160,000 Sikhs and Muslims. They had to
> carry out the orders; there was no question of that. But they also had to do
> everything possible to safeguard the lives of the European civilians, the women
> and children, and all law-abiding citizens.[32]

It was decided that no crowds would be allowed to cross the railway line.
Preliminary dispositions of troops were made and Massey was warned to enact
an Internal Defence Scheme if things got out of hand, defending the civil
lines along the railway bridges. Smith was to remove Europeans from the city
with his motor ambulance. Although the situation seemed tense, there was
no evidence to suspect that the arrests would provoke anything other than a
'disorderly demonstration' in front of the district court house. Indeed, Irving
was more worried about a possible rescue attempt. It was decided that Mr
Rehill, the only officer who knew the route, would accompany the prisoners
to Dharamsala.

At the same time that Irving was trying to maintain order in Amritsar, another meeting was taking place at Government House in Lahore. In *The Jallianwala Bagh Massacre* (1963), Raja Ram alleges that a 'premeditated plan'
was hatched during this meeting for 'shooting well' the population of Amritsar on 13 April.[33] According to this theory, Sir Michael O'Dwyer had calculated that the coming Sunday would most likely be the next date at which
another *hartal* would take place. Being (apparently) beside himself with rage
at the affront at which the Indian people had given him with their *hartal* and
their displays of Hindu-Muslim unity, O'Dwyer arranged with his civilian
and military advisers to provoke the people of Amritsar into violence, which
could then be suppressed. Ram argues that the massacre at the Jallianwala
Bagh was, therefore, a premeditated act of imperial mass murder intended to
strike terror into the Indian population. While this remains a popular theory
in India, there is no evidence to support it. The historian, V.N. Datta, demol-
ishes Ram's theory, complaining that this plan 'is a figment of the author's
imagination'.[34] In any case, as Datta complains, the contention that on 9
April – a day *before* the riot at Amritsar – the British authorities arranged to
fire in four days' time is ridiculous, totally lacking in supporting evidence.

The claim that the British authorities were planning the massacre in advance may be incorrect, but it is indicative of the confusion and misunderstanding that have surrounded our understanding of the official response to Gandhi's *satyagraha* campaign. The British were undoubtedly worried at the spread of disaffection across India, but never contemplated a vicious response. On 8 April the Viceroy, Lord Chelmsford, instructed the Home Department to begin to plan for future developments in the resistance campaign and ordered local governments to issue leaflets explaining the Rowlatt Bills, expressing sympathy for constitutional and legal protest, but at the same time stressing that any violence or terrorism would be met with ruthless force.[35] The British response was one of patience and surveillance, what Peter Robb has called 'tactical non-interference', with district officers regularly taking the political temperature and sending reports to the government, but not getting involved. It was a tense period, and the issue that had arisen before with Annie Besant and the Home Rule movement, once again reared its head; whether it was possible or correct to take action against statements and actions that were seditious, but which the Government of India may have been sympathetic to or which were in line with future official direction. As was now becoming the norm, the government was treading a thin tightrope.

What should happen to Gandhi? It was known that he intended to travel north to Delhi in the days after the *hartal* and this finally forced the government's hand. Given that violence had already taken place in Delhi, the Government of India was concerned about the possibility that it could explode into another outbreak of disorder and was anxious to seal off the capital from the unrest that was simmering elsewhere in India. O'Dwyer typically wanted Gandhi deported to Burma, that Malaria-ridden backwater of the Raj, but the government was wary of such a strong step and remembered the storm of protest and agitation that had greeted the internment of Annie Besant only two years before. They knew only too well that outright repression was neither desirable nor possible, but something had to be done. In the end the decision was a kind of halfway point; something in between doing nothing or imprisoning the Mahatma. Chelmsford was away for a few days, holidaying in Dehru Dun, where (as he cheerfully boasted to Montagu) he had caught a 40-pound (18 kilogram) *mahseer* (carp). He wrote to the Secretary of State on 9 April and although not making reference to Gandhi's imminent arrest, made it clear that he was steeling himself for action. He wrote,

> We must, as you will acknowledge, be perfectly firm over this matter, but there are many pitfalls in the way and we have to walk warily, especially as Gandhi is acting with the assistance of lawyers, and he and his crowd will be careful

as to their legal ground. You must not worry. It is my affair and I must see it through.[36]

In the absence of the Viceroy, the decision to exclude Gandhi from Delhi and the Punjab was taken by Sir William Vincent, the Home Member of the Government of India, in consultation with Sir J.S. Meston (Finance) and Sir G.R. Lowndes (Legal).[37]

It has become fixed in nationalist memory that Gandhi's arrest on 9 April was yet another rash act of repression by the Government of India. Pearay Mohan, a journalist from Lahore, complained that it was an act of 'astounding folly' that was 'unjustified and humiliating'. Gandhi was 'eminently a man of peace', he would declare, 'incapable of doing violence to man or beast'.[38] But this is to misunderstand the motives of the Government's decision, which was based on maintaining as light as hand on events as possible, but cautiously attempting to manoeuvre them in their favour, in line with tried and tested techniques. Guidelines were issued that Gandhi was to be treated with 'every possible consideration' and that no force was to be used unless he disobeyed the order.[39] The decision to arrest Gandhi, or at least keep him out of the Punjab, would mark a turning point in the Rowlatt *Satyagraha*, a moment that would have a great influence on what subsequently occurred and provoked outrage and anger across India. Events were now moving beyond anyone's control. Nothing would ever be the same again.

CHAPTER 5

Violence in Ahmedabad

I hope there will be no resentment about my arrest.

Mohandas Gandhi[1]

L ate on the evening of 9 April 1919, a small group of Indians were standing on one of the platforms at the Old Delhi railway station, anxiously waiting for the arrival of the Mahatma. Gandhi had wanted to travel north for some time, but had been too busy to make the journey, promising to come after he had seen the *hartal* in Bombay on 6 April.[2] The group were led by Swami Shraddhanand, president of the *Satyagraha Sabha* in Delhi. Shraddhanand was under orders to keep the arrival of the Mahatma as secret as possible, but word had somehow leaked out and around 30 or 40 people had turned up, standing alongside them, eagerly awaiting the arrival of their leader. When the train did arrive, there was some confusion. As the train came to a halt, some passengers put their heads out of the window and shouted to the waiting crowd, 'Arrested!' Members of Swami's group ran along the platform, trying to find where Gandhi was, but it was of no use and he was not to be found. Eventually, they were greeted by Mahadev Desai, his secretary, who told them what had happened.[3]

Gandhi's part in the Rowlatt *Satyagraha* ended at the small dusty station of Palwal, on the Punjab border, about 37 miles (60 kilometres) from Delhi. The train that had been carrying the Mahatma pulled up alongside the platform and a small party of police officers boarded. They soon found Gandhi in a second-class carriage, surrounded by adoring acolytes. One of the officers approached him and showed him an order from the Punjab Government, which prevented him from entering the province. Gandhi politely refused to agree to these terms and told the officer that he fully intended to continue his journey to Delhi. The officer then placed a hand on Gandhi's shoulder and said, 'Mr Gandhi, I arrest you.' Gandhi's luggage was removed from the train and then, under a police guard, he was escorted back to Bombay. These were, he later recalled, 'all the simple ingredients of a proper arrest'.[4] But as Gandhi

returned to Bombay, quietly chatting to his companions and the police officers who sat alongside him, news was spreading across India and anger was
flaring up. The Government of India was about to learn that taking action
against the Mahatma, even action as gentle as this, could provoke his fellow
countrymen to acts of extraordinary violence. It was a lesson they would never
forget.

✌

The first province to feel the bonfire of violence and disorder that news of
Gandhi's arrest created was the Bombay Presidency. The unrest was worst in
Ahmedabad in Gujarat, the second largest city in the province and an im-
portant industrial centre. What happened in Ahmedabad between 10 and 12
April rarely appears in accounts of 1919, but it should not be overlooked. The
Indian National Congress made no investigation into the events in the city,
preferring instead to concentrate on 'revealing' the 'repressive regime' of Sir
Michael O'Dwyer in the Punjab, and it was certainly convenient to bypass
what happened there. But the actions of dangerous and co-ordinated mobs
and their attack upon the authorities in Ahmedabad are worth recalling because they undermine the commonly held perception that the unrest in India
was not as serious as the British claimed or that the authorities responded in
a heavy-handed manner.

By 1919 Ahmedabad had a population of over 300,000 people and was
a centre for the textile industry; known as the 'Manchester of India' with
51 mills, employing over 40,000 workers.[5] Perhaps because of this it had been
a politically aware city for many years with a long history of protest and support for the Home Rule movement. Although the city was prosperous with
a vibrant economy, the war years had inevitably introduced hardships and
strains, with rising prices and shortages of rolling stock interfering with the
supply of coal to the mills.[6] And it was here that Gandhi's power base lay.
He had been born in Gujarat and on returning to India he had become interested in the growing industrial tension in the city, conducting a *satyagraha*
campaign in 1918 on behalf of the mill workers for higher wages and better
conditions.

The news that Gandhi had been arrested on his way to Delhi arrived in
Ahmedabad sometime on the morning of 10 April and spread through the
city with alarming speed. Many mills immediately closed and crowds began to
gather in the city, shouting the Mahatma's name and denouncing the Rowlatt
Bills. Mr Chatfield, the District Magistrate, heard that there was 'excitement
in the town' at about 9 a.m. He spoke with the District Superintendent of

Police about what could be done to calm the situation and sent down groups of armed police to reinforce those who were already in the city. Matters remained tense for the next few hours, with large crowds gathering near the railway station and forcibly closing all the shops. A cinema was burnt, police were stoned, and two British men, both employees of a mill, were attacked as they drove through the city.[7] Although these men, both weaving masters, managed to escape, a police officer who helped them was beaten to death by the mob.[8]

At 3.30 p.m. Chatfield was sitting in his office in the cantonment when he received a phone call from Mr Smith, the Assistant Commissioner. Smith told him that a police station was being attacked by a 'riotous mob' and that a crowd was also 'besieging' a group of Europeans and police officers somewhere in the city. Chatfield decided to go and find out what was happening, asking the District Superintendent of Police, Mr R.R. Boyd, to order his reserve of 24 armed police into the city, and sending his car to pick him up.[9] Chatfield and Boyd drove to the city and reached Delhi Gate at about 5 p.m. The group of armed police had marched ahead and could not be seen. Chatfield edged forward until they saw a large crowd, apparently surrounding the police officers. He knew that once they had moved closer it would be extremely difficult to communicate, so he scribbled down a note for the OC Ahmedabad updating him on what had happened and telling him to send a military force to restore order. The people were hostile, but offered no violence, pulling back as Chatfield and his men approached. They eventually found the group of armed police guarding the five prisoners and attending to four wounded *sepoys* (Indian soldiers), one of whom was seriously injured. The situation at this point was extremely tense. Every so often someone in the crowd would push forward and give a cheer for Mahatma Gandhi. When they did this the crowd would reply 'Gandhi Mahatma *ki jai*!' Chatfield and the police officers, assisted by two *satyagrahis*, did their best to keep the crowd back by marching up and down and talking to them.[10] They remained where they were for one and a half hours, anxiously awaiting the arrival of soldiers. At 6 p.m. 200 men of 1/97th Infantry, led by Colonel G.S. Frazer, arrived. They formed a line of troops across the road, advanced and cleared the area. Chatfield and the armed police were then evacuated and a platoon was left to garrison the streets.

The leading nationalists of Ahmedabad, those who were members of the *Satyagraha Sabha* (many of whom were barristers or pleaders), did their best to prevent violence, but with limited success. The secretary, V.J. Patel, was engaged with the jostling crowds on 10 April, trying to control them, when he heard that there had been a shooting at Prem Gate and some people had been wounded. With some of his colleagues, he decided that it would be better if the crowds could be removed from the centre of the city as soon as possible, so it was arranged that a meeting would be held on the river bank, alongside the Sabarmati River, where the people could be calmed down and told what had happened.[11] Once the crowd had settled down, they read out a note explaining that Gandhi had been turned back from entering Delhi and had returned to Bombay. Furthermore, the Mahatma had penned a message to his countrymen, expressing his satisfaction at his arrest and hoping that there would be no resentment towards the authorities. He urged people to continue to uphold the values of truth, non-violence and Hindu-Muslim unity.[12]

That evening Patel and his fellow *satyagrahis* seem to have been reasonably confident that the violence was over. They were, however, to be grievously mistaken. By 8.30 a.m. more rumours were circulating in the city. This time they concerned not Gandhi, but one of his co-workers, Miss Anasuya Sarabhai, who it was believed had been arrested. Although this was not the case, Anasuya was well known in the city and fears for her safety sparked more frustration among angry mill workers.[13] Soon menacing crowds were moving up through the side streets, brandishing long sticks, shouting 'Anasuya *mata ki jai!*' Mobs then began to burn down buildings that had any association with government and attack any Europeans they could find.[14] The eleventh of April would be a day of unprecedented danger.

The first troops to arrive in the city reached Prem Gate at eleven o'clock and immediately saw that the situation had passed out of control. Thick clouds of black smoke hung over the city. Many buildings were on fire, which was an unwelcome addition to the fierce heat of the morning sun. Loud, abusive crowds were gathered in the streets, many of whom were carrying burning torches.[15] Major W.C. Kirkwood, who commanded 150 men of 1/97th Infantry, had been given orders that if rioters approached to within 25 yards of his men in a threatening manner, he was to issue a warning. If the situation continued to deteriorate he was ordered to open controlled bursts of fire to disperse the crowds. Determined to regain control of the city, troops began to move in and by noon had control over most of the northwestern area. Unfortunately, Kirkwood did not have enough men to gain control of the rest of Ahmedabad and had to be content with securing the most important areas. During the afternoon troops were despatched to various other locations, including residential areas, the waterworks, the Sabarmati railway bridge and the police headquarters.[16]

Because what happened in Ahmedabad remains relatively unknown, one could be forgiven for thinking that it was little more than an uncontrolled outburst of anger at the arrest of Gandhi (and later Anasuya Sarabhai) that subsided almost as soon as it had occurred, and that it was not as sinister or as brutal as that which would take place in the Punjab. The violence was certainly short in duration – largely being spent by 12 April – but one should not downplay the seriousness of the situation. Far from being peaceful crowds, many of the rioters were armed with *lathis*, sticks, bill hooks and various other weapons including swords and kerosene oil, which was used to burn government buildings. These clashes at times resembled bitter urban street fighting, with mobs gathering in large numbers at key points in the city, throwing stones, and then scattering into the side streets when the authorities attempted to push them back. The old town was a maze of narrow alleyways and side streets that could easily have swallowed entire platoons, so the layout of the city worked to the advantage of the mobs and allowed them to outflank the soldiers. Groups of armed police and soldiers would then march down the main streets issuing regular warnings to the crowds to disperse, inevitably without success, before resorting to controlled bursts of firing. It is easy to see why many nationalists chose to forget such ugly scenes.

A typical example of what happened in Ahmedabad was recorded by R.R. Shirgaonkar, the Deputy Superintendent of Police. On the morning of 11 April, Shirgaonkar led a small group of armed police to reinforce the beleaguered garrison at the Khas Bazaar *chowky* (police station), which had been surrounded by abusive, stone-throwing mobs. Organising his men into two lines, Shirgaonkar began to march towards those who had gathered outside the *chowky*; a crowd that he estimated to number somewhere between 500 and 1,000 people. He shouted at them to fall back and disperse, but was answered by jeers and showered with stones. He ordered his men to fix bayonets and they continued edging forward, the crowds gradually retreating before them. Shirgaonkar's party had gone as far as the *Tin Darwaza* (a famous monument known as 'the triple gateway') when the crowd began to increase in size and the stoning became heavier. Shirgaonkar again asked them to disperse, but without success. He warned them that if they did not do so he would fire, but again, this had little effect and stones continued to fall on them. Shirgaonkar then ordered a volley to be fired, with each man discharging one round of buckshot. Unfortunately, this had no effect on the crowd, possibly because the rounds did not reach them. Hurriedly reloading their rifles, this time with ball ammunition, they discharged another round. The crowd fell back, throwing stones as it did so.[17]

It would later be accepted that there was no conspiracy behind the violence on 10 and 11 April, but the mobs did not act without direction or organisation. Indeed, by the second day the rioters in Ahmedabad were operating with a remarkable degree of sophistication, certainly when compared with those that gathered at Delhi and elsewhere, which were far more spontaneous. Lieutenant J. Fitzpatrick, a cantonment magistrate, saw mobs being given food by 'very respectably dressed Hindus' and also noted that there were dedicated stretcher-bearers who, as well as looking after the wounded, acted as runners carrying messages between different groups. They would 'slip down the streets and get in amongst the crowd, and they would raise their hands and then went the "*chalo*", "*maro*", and all these sort of things'. More seriously, Fitzpatrick found piles of stones and bricks that had been collected in the shops of fruit-sellers and deliberately concealed beneath white cloths; evidently used as ammunition by the mobs.[18] A number of other witnesses also found baskets of stones that seemed to have been positioned around the city, and this helps to explain the level of resistance that greeted the authorities when they tried to restore order to Ahmedabad.

As well as showing cohesion and organisation when facing the authorities, the mobs in Ahmedabad also exhibited this when they decided to burn and loot buildings. The buildings were carefully chosen and the destruction was conducted with deliberation and care. All buildings with any connection to government were systematically burnt to the ground, including the collector's office, the city magistrate's office, the sub-registrar's office, a court house, and the telegraph and post offices.[19] When fire engines attempted to move through the crowds and extinguish the flames, they were stoned and abused and had to abandon their efforts. Indeed, such deliberate arson was particularly noticeable when considering the attacks upon 18 *chowks* on 10 and 11 April, which effectively paralysed the police force in the city. Those which bordered private houses were first of all, wrecked, and then most of the furniture was burnt out in the road, in order that there would be no damage to private homes. The way in which the police were attacked also proved how fragile government authority in the city had become. The police in Ahmedabad were completely disarmed within a few hours. Those who were in the streets were seized, had their uniforms torn off and burnt, and told to go home.[20]

Major Kirkwood described the rioters he saw in Ahmedabad as 'hostile, extremely hostile', who were throwing stones, flourishing sticks and making obscene gestures at his men.[21] Particularly threatening was that many of the rioters were carrying weapons. Two temples had been raided on 11 April by mobs looking for swords. Lieutenant A. St. J. Macdonald (2/10th Jats) saw a large crowd near the station that day. 'They were all armed,' he claimed. 'The crowd of two thousand people had sticks and *lathis* in their hands, bill hooks and things of that sort.' Another British officer, Lieutenant H.S. Larkin, was commanding a group of 50 soldiers when they were attacked by a group of *lathi-* and sword-wielding rioters. Larkin ordered three of his men to fire, but this had little effect; the mob running past them and disappearing into the side streets. Another attack was launched shortly afterwards. Larkin ordered all his men to fire, but this could not prevent one of the attackers, carrying a sword, from breaking into their lines and reaching Larkin. Steeling himself, the Lieutenant drew his revolver, pointed it at the man and fired. Unfortunately his weapon jammed and his opponent was able to assault him, slicing his arm with the sword. Larkin was wounded, but survived. His assailant was quickly overpowered.[22]

The violence in Ahmedabad was from the start an anti-European and anti-government movement. Because all Europeans were regarded as being representatives of the government, they were targeted, as well as those who either worked for British officials or in some way could be seen as buttressing the regime. A British police officer, Sergeant Fraser, was trying to hide in a shop on Richey Road, when he was found by the mob. He was dragged into the streets and killed.[23] The manager of the Electric Power House, Mr Duncan Brown, was attacked by a mob, who forced their way inside and beat him with *lathis*.[24] Similarly, Lieutenant H.S. Macdonald was threatened by a mob outside Prem Gate and would have been killed had troops not rescued him. But it was not just British officials who were targeted. A student from Gujarat College was stoned because he was wearing his khaki student uniform and Bulakhidas Bapuji Trivedi, the personal assistant to the collector (Mr Chatfield), was threatened with murder and had his house looted and ransacked. Everyone who wore European clothes was stoned and the Parsees of the city took to removing their hats and replacing them with skull caps to avoid the attentions of the mob. Mobs even went to the Grand Hotel on 11 April, broke into the reception and demanded to know if there were any Europeans staying there because they wanted to murder them. In certain parts of the town graffiti was daubed on the walls in charcoal calling for the murder of all Europeans, and several officials also remembered seeing an Indian *sadhu* (holy man) stalking the streets carrying a curved stick, muttering that he wanted 'white flesh'.[25]

Who were responsible for these outbreaks of disorder? Most accounts record that the crowds were chiefly composed of mill hands and youths, which, given the great textile industry within Ahmedabad, is not particularly surprising. The fact that the crowds consisted mainly of mill workers, who presumably worked together, perhaps explains why there was a greater level of organisation and deliberation in the disorders in Ahmedabad than would be seen elsewhere in 1919. The mill workers had a history of agitation and strike action, particularly regarding their wages, and they had been successful in achieving their demands on a number of occasions. The District Magistrate, Chatfield, admitted that one of the results of the struggles in 1917 and 1918 for higher wages was that they 'became well-organised, used to meetings, to common counsels, to concerted action' and who were willing to obey orders 'for the most part [from] the Jobbers and mill foremen'. The crowds were led by a small number of people and various accounts mention five or six men dressed in black caps and coats.[26] The wearing of black, the colour of mourning, may have been worn to express sorrow at the treatment of Mahatma Gandhi.

By darkness on 11 April, government control was gradually being re-established in Ahmedabad. Between 600 and 800 soldiers had been rushed into the city and a proclamation had been issued, stating that any gathering of over ten people would be fired upon.[27] This proclamation seems to have had some effect and although nationalists would later complain bitterly about it, normality gradually returned to Ahmedabad. By 14 April most of the army had been removed from the city and the police had resumed full duties. In the course of the violence, 28 people had died and another 123 were wounded.[28] Although some have suggested that the British approach to controlling the violence was heavy handed, such criticism ignores the context of violence in Ahmedabad; the claustrophobic, narrow streets, the organisation and discipline of the rioters, and the vicious attacks on small groups of soldiers.[29] Those officers tasked with restoring order were in much closer contact with rioters than was usually the case, meaning that there was often no time to use other, less violent forms of crowd dispersal. This restraint seems to have been in evidence throughout 10 and 11 April, testimony both to the professionalism of the forces called into Ahmedabad to restore order and the dangerous situation that existed in the city.

෴

Like ripples on the surface of water, the effect of Gandhi's arrest continued to spread across the subcontinent, producing unrest wherever it went. A special edition of the *Bombay Chronicle* was printed on the evening of 10 April announcing the arrest and, in response, several cloth and bullion markets in the city began to close. As news spread, tempers began to rise. On the following day, Friday, large numbers of businesses were closed and groups of people, mainly Hindu shopkeepers, began to move out onto the streets, reading the announcement of Gandhi's arrest and discussing what should be done. They were joined later on by Muslims coming home from Friday prayers.[30] By mid-morning thousands of people were on the streets, shouting 'Hindu Mussalman *ki jai*' and 'Mahatma Gandhi *ki jai*', and trying to re-enact the *hartal* of 6 April. Mobs then stoned those businesses that had decided to continue trading and many tramcars were stopped, their windows smashed and their occupants forced to get out. Fortunately, the level of anti-European violence that had been seen in Ahmedabad was not repeated. Although the police had to deal with large number of stone-throwing crowds, they refrained from firing, instead making several *lathi* charges that afternoon, mainly around Abdul Rahman Street in the Pydhownie district of the city.[31]

At Viramgam, about 40 miles (64 kilometres) from Ahmedabad, violence broke out on 12 April when angry mobs went to the railway station to stop the morning train from Ahmedabad. As elsewhere during the unrest the mobs were mainly youths – labourers and mill hands – who were excited by news of Gandhi's arrest and were determined to have their revenge. The mobs seriously assaulted Mr MacIlvride, a traffic inspector, and then burnt the station to the ground. Various other buildings, including the police *chowky*, post office and several goods wagons and signal boxes were either looted or burnt, and the *kacheri*, a local court house, was attacked several times during the day. For Manilal Nagarlal, a terrified clerk in the *kacheri*, the situation was deeply frightening, being surrounded by angry crowds shouting 'beat' and 'Victory to Mahatma Gandhi' while throwing stones and trying to get into the compound. The mobs then set fire to parts of the building and were only dispersed after police, desperate to protect themselves, repeatedly fired at them.[32] A third-class magistrate, Mr Madhavlal, was murdered and a further attack on the *kacheri* occurred later on, with the rioters managing to loot the treasury, before being dispersed by the arrival of police reinforcements.[33]

Gandhi arrived back at Bombay at about 3 p.m. on 11 April, surrounded by his followers, and was briefly caught up in the unrest in the streets. Several days later he made his way to his *ashram* and spoke out against the violence, urging people to refrain from all violence and repent for their sins.[34] By now the government was watching him closely. On 15 April, a police officer, Mr J.A. Guider (Deputy Inspector-General of Police, CID, Bombay), arrived in Ahmedabad after being ordered to take charge of the investigation into what had happened. His inquiries did not, however, get very far. Although Gandhi admitted that he knew who had organised the disturbances on 10 and

11 April, he would not reveal their names. Guider was understandably frustrated and disappointed and tried to elicit information from the other members of the *ashram*, but they too would not speak; it was apparently 'against their principles'.[35]

Guider reported to his superiors at Poona on 17 April, explaining Gandhi's refusal to divulge the names of those whom he suspected of being responsible for the unrest. When he read Guider's report, his superior at the CID, Sir Charles Cleveland, thought the moment was right to take action against Gandhi, arguing that his refusal to name guilty parties was a criminal offence that should be punished. But typically, the Viceroy shied away from taking firmer action against the Mahatma and nothing was heard of the suggestion again.[36] By that point the moment had passed. Some even felt that Gandhi might be useful in controlling public opinion in the future and were anxious to mollify him as much as possible; a fundamental mistake that later viceroys would repeat.[37] But anyway, attention was now moving away from Bombay and Gujrat to what had happened in the north, in the Punjab, where great mobs had gathered, people had been killed and the unrest had been at its most fierce.

CHAPTER 6

O'Dwyer in the Punjab

When confronted with a serious situation, I have generally found that
prompt action is the best way of dealing with it.

Sir Michael O'Dwyer[1]

Watered by five great rivers and bordered by the Himalayas to the north and the Rajasthan Desert to the south, the Punjab was the great agricultural province of British India, which by the 1920s produced a tenth of its cotton crop and a third of its wheat.[2] The province was split between the three main religious groups in India, Hindus, Muslims and Sikhs, with the main Muslim districts (which made up over half of the population) being in the west of the province, areas like Jhelum, Shahpur and Multan. The eastern districts were dominated by the other two religious groups, the Hindus and Sikhs. The Hindus of the Punjab were particularly active in the economic life of the province and were deeply involved in trade and money-lending, while the Sikhs, although only a small proportion of the total population, were an important minority and a trusted source of recruits for the Indian Army. In the Punjab, power meant having control of land and in their search for loyal allies the British relied upon local landowners and tribal chiefs to a greater extent than elsewhere in India. In a subcontinent that was undergoing considerable change, it was felt that by ensuring the loyalty of such allies, this could provide a bulwark to the political advances then seeping into other parts of India and contain the spectre of communal violence that was always a possibility within the Punjab, which did not have an ethnic or religious minority able to dominate the rest.

Despite Gandhi's strong support in the western districts of India, it would be in the Punjab where the Rowlatt *Satyagraha* would make its biggest mark. It was here where the disorders would reach their peak and where the authorities would resort to the strongest action. According to the Indian National Congress, the reason why the Punjab saw such disorder was the way in which the province was run and the oppression of its Lieutenant-Governor,

Sir Michael O'Dwyer. It alleged that his rule was marked by the systematic abuse of the Defence of India Act, the emergency legislation that had been drafted in during the war to deal with revolutionary crime. His recruiting policies were also heavily censured. So zealous was O'Dwyer in his drive to fill the depleted ranks of the Indian Army that he (allegedly) employed a variety of illegal methods to fill his quota, including coercion, threats, bribes and extortion.[3] Indeed, O'Dwyer's allegedly 'strong government' was the source of some concern among a number of senior officials in both India and Britain. Edwin Montagu, Lord Willingdon (Governor of Madras) and Sir George Lloyd (Governor of Bombay) all believed, to varying degrees, that the way in which O'Dwyer had run the Punjab had been a major contributing factor in the disorders.[4]

Given these concerns (which most modern historians have repeated), it is little wonder that O'Dwyer is one of the most vilified figures in the history of the Raj with a sinister reputation for authoritarian rule, repression and terrorism who has been commonly blamed for what happened in 1919. Although he has at times been overshadowed by Reginald Dyer, the importance of O'Dwyer to events in India in this period is beyond doubt. It was he who governed one of the most important provinces in the British Empire during the Great War (providing over 60 per cent of total Indian Army manpower) and who had dealt strongly with several anti-British conspiracies, ranging from the 'silk letter' plot to the Ghadr movement.[5] Finally, it was O'Dwyer who was murdered by an enraged Sikh, Udham Singh, in March 1940, not Dyer, who had died quietly in his bed at Long Ashton in Somerset, England, in the summer of 1927.[6] But what is the truth behind this controversial figure?

అ

Born in 1864, the son of a landowner in County Tipperary, Ireland, O'Dwyer had received a first-class degree in Jurisprudence from Balliol College, Oxford, and joined the Indian Civil Service (ICS) in 1885.[7] On arrival in India that November, he was sent to Lahore, the capital of the Punjab, which as he recorded in his memoirs, had 'a pervading sense of dust and disorder, relics of the rough Sikh dominion' that had only recently fallen to the British.[8] This environment of 'dust and disorder' was to be O'Dwyer's home for the next 20 years, as he worked on land revenue settlement work, first in Shahpur, then in Gujranwala, Rajputana and finally in the newly established North-West Frontier Province (NWFP).[9] O'Dwyer rose rapidly owing to what one Indian historian has described as his 'satanically energetic' personality.[10] He was fiercely intelligent and physically able to cope with the considerable pressures that life in India presented, yet without being too morose or serious. In his memoirs he described himself as a man for whom 'public cares' never caused him the loss of even 'half an hour's sleep', and who 'never believed in taking one's work too seriously'. Although he shouldered an immense burden of 'work and responsibility', he had:

> rarely allowed those to encroach on my morning ride and afternoon game of golf or tennis; while in the cold weather at Lahore one had two mornings a week with the hounds. Then there were the occasional duck-shoots in Bahawalpur, pig-sticking in Patiala, and one glorious week after stag in Kashmir, where my files, however, followed me. Our hunting days at Lahore were Thursday and Sunday, and we met at 7 a.m.[11]

Combined with this air of confidence, was a man who was very aware of the importance of the Punjab to the Raj and of the special traditions that guided British rule there.

In 1889 Michael O'Dwyer was appointed Settlement Officer in Gujranwala in the flat districts of central Punjab, about 40 miles (64 kilometres) from Lahore on the road to Peshawar and the North West Frontier. He was just 25 years of age and had been put in sole charge of some 3,000 square miles (7,700 square kilometres) with a population of almost 750,000 people.[12] It was an experience that would remain with him for the rest of his life. O'Dwyer lived in the dilapidated former residence of a legendary Sikh general, Hari Singh Nalwa; a sprawling mansion with a garden, tennis court and enough stabling for 12 horses. He was totally committed to his work and imbued with that sense of purpose the ICS was famous for; spending hours in the saddle everyday, traversing the fertile plains, meeting villagers, dispensing justice, settling disputes. The peasants were mostly Jat Sikhs, who were, as O'Dwyer quipped, 'as handy with the sword and the bayonet as with the plough and the water-lift'. It was a life that he thoroughly enjoyed. The Settlement Officer, he would claim in his memoirs,

> offers the best life and the most fascinating work to be found in India. It is the basis of all real knowledge of the rural masses. For six to eight months a year he lives and works among them, almost exclusively. He learns their inner life, their trials and hardships, their joys and their sorrows. He deals with them in their fields and their villages, where they are at their best, rather than in the law courts, where they are at their worst.

O'Dwyer emerged from the Punjab with not just an ability to ride well and calculate the appropriate land revenue from a collection of fields, but also with a set of principles that would later bring him into conflict with members of the growing nationalist movement, as well as with a variety of reforming politicians in London and Delhi. He was asked to replace Sir Louis Dane as Lieutenant-Governor of the Punjab in December 1912 and took up his appointment in May the following year aged 51. He remained in Lahore for the next six years and although he thoroughly enjoyed his responsibilities, he became increasingly distressed by the political developments in British India, particularly the idealistic schemes of Montagu and Chelmsford for reform and consultation. Indeed, if Edwin Montagu epitomised British liberal attitudes towards India, with its instinctive sympathy for the educated classes and distrust of the administration, then Sir Michael O'Dwyer represented its opposite pole. Contrary to their beliefs, he maintained that British policy should not be directed at importing a 'sham' democracy to a handful of Western-educated, so-called 'advanced' Indians, but at improving the life and conditions of the rural masses. He was not afraid of voicing his opinions and when he made disparaging remarks about the reforms in a speech on 13 September 1917 – barely a month after Montagu's August declaration – Lord Chelmsford regarded this as a 'deliberate flouting' of government policy and ordered him to apologise.[13]

When O'Dwyer moved into Government House in Lahore in May 1913 he inherited a style of administration that was nearly 70 years old. The 'Punjab School of Administration', as it was known, had emerged out of the wars of annexation in the 1840s and was based upon what has been described as 'paternalistic despotism'.[14] The Punjab had traditionally been a highly militarised frontier region and in the aftermath of the Second Sikh War (1848–9), the presence of large numbers of demobilised, but still potentially restless, Sikh soldiers was a cause of concern to the newly installed British administration. As a result, it was decided, possibly out of expediency more than anything else, to retain a greater military presence in the region than in other areas of India.[15] Ever since its annexation in 1849, the Punjab had been regarded by the British as a distinctly different part of their Indian empire and one that required a special type of administration; what was technically referred to as a 'non-regulation province'.

Over time a unique system of administration evolved in the Punjab. At the highest levels, executive power was restricted in the hands of the Lieutenant-Governor. Until 1920 he was in sole control of the administration and did not have an Executive Council.[16] The province was split into five divisions, each controlled by a commissioner, which were subdivided into 29 districts. The main administrative position across British India was the District Officer, but in the Punjab, where there was no separation between the executive and the judiciary, this was known as the Deputy Commissioner.[17] The Deputy Commissioner of the Punjab was supposed to represent the very best of the ICS, able to set an example of duty and selflessness to the people and continue the tradition of the early British rulers of the Punjab – the legendary figures of Henry and John Lawrence, John Nicholson, James Abbott and others – who were able to dominate a warlike province through their will, determination and formidable ability.[18]

✌

Of all the provinces of India none would be more important to the British Empire during the First World War than the Punjab. At the outbreak of war 66 per cent of cavalry, 87 per cent of artillery and 45 per cent of infantry were Punjabis.[19] When war broke out in 1914, O'Dwyer was convinced that the Punjab should rally to the flag and, as in the past, contribute significantly to the British war effort. During four years of war, the Punjab contributed 446,976 soldiers to the Indian Army – approximately 13 per cent of all men of military age – almost twice as much as its nearest competitor, the United Provinces.[20] Yet the demand for more Indian manpower only intensified as the war went on. By 1916 recruiting arrangements in the Punjab were 'wholly inadequate' to meet the demands of the war. In order to keep existing units up to strength and to form new ones, it was essential to raise dramatically the numbers of soldiers who were recruited into the Indian Army. Only through the overhaul of existing recruiting arrangements, more systematic civil-military co-operation and the active collaboration of local elites, was India able to meet the demands of military service. Before the war recruitment in the Punjab had been confined to restricted military districts that dealt with a particular class of recruit. O'Dwyer restructured this so that the catchment areas for recruitment corresponded to the administrative divisions of the province and, therefore, had access to pools of manpower that had hitherto not been tapped.[21]

In February 1917 the civil administration in the Punjab assumed direct responsibility for recruitment in the province.[22] Various means were employed by the government to increase recruitment figures: it held recruiting fairs; published manpower totals (to stimulate rivalry between different districts); and relied heavily upon local non-official elites to use their influence. As well as this, rewards were given to those who joined up. Over 180,000 acres of valuable land were put aside for those who had served with distinction during the war and by 1917 the Government was offering a variety of monetary rewards to increase recruitment. Every new recruit would be given a bonus of 50 rupees as well as a further 15 on the completion of their training. From 1 June 1918 *sepoys* would also receive a war bonus after every six months of service.[23]

For all the efforts of the Punjab Government, the demand for recruits grew larger as the war went on. By the beginning of 1918 the increasing intensity of army recruitment in the Punjab was beginning to have a negative effect on the province and local officials were becoming aware of tension. At the end of February the Commissioner at Rawalpindi complained of the 'tiredness' that the recruitment campaign was creating.[24] In response O'Dwyer appealed to the Adjutant-General on 31 March to suspend recruiting for ten weeks. This was agreed. Unfortunately, O'Dwyer could do little when the war turned against the British Empire in the spring of 1918. The massive German offensive on the Western Front ushered in the final crisis of the war and the Government of India was forced to break its promise. On 13 April, barely two weeks after recruitment in the Punjab had been suspended, it was resumed. To make matters worse, the numbers of troops required was far more than been previously considered and between April and October 1918 the Punjab raised a further 77,000 men.[25]

It has become commonplace to suggest that the pressure of recruitment was one of the factors that led to the disorders of 1919; that the Punjab had been squeezed to its limits and could not give any more, and that the Rowlatt *Satyagraha* was the spark that set the tinder alight. This does, however, remain a simplistic and limited explanation. For his part, O'Dwyer denied that recruitment had been pursued in illegal or unscrupulous ways. He admitted that 'some over-zealous agents may have exceeded the limits and may have used pressure', but he stated that 'over and over again in various places I deprecated any coercion being resorted to and any improper methods being used. I deprecated the bullying of recruits.'[26] There is little doubt that recruiting methods were more intensive than elsewhere in India – the Punjab was, after all, the main manpower pool of the Indian Army – and it undoubtedly became more so as the war dragged on and traditional sources of recruits dried up. Yet despite intensive recruitment in the rural areas of the Punjab, it was the towns and cities that witnessed the worst outbreaks of violence and disorder in 1919. In a written statement to the Hunter Inquiry, Mr F.H. Burton, former Deputy Commissioner at Amritsar, provided information on the level of recruitment that the city had provided. Between April 1918 and April 1919 Amritsar city was excluded from the requirements for the province and that, in any case, 'Very few recruits came forward from the city proper.' Between

January and June 1918 only 51 men were recruited, 26 of which were non-combatants.[27] One of the factors that mitigated against this was the reliance of the Indian Army on rural recruits and a corresponding reluctance to take city-dwellers. Burton also stated that the district recruiting officer made sure that those people who came before him 'were willing to serve before they were sworn in'.

The net from which the British could draw recruits widened significantly during the Great War, but the percentage of the population that went into the Indian Army, even for a province such as the Punjab, was remarkably light when compared to European figures.[28] Though O'Dwyer was certainly a keen believer that India should send her sons to fight for the Empire, he was not unaware of the consequences of large-scale recruitment and his government employed a variety of means to address the concerns arising from the recruiting districts. His call for the suspension of recruitment in 1918 (which unfortunately could not be heeded) reflects well upon him; a call, incidentally, which is never mentioned in nationalist accounts, perhaps because it jars with the myth of him as a ruthless imperial governor who bled the Punjab white for his own ends.

Nevertheless, there is little doubt that daily life became increasingly hard. Although the outbreak of war had not resulted in a massive dislocation to everyday existence, a severe outbreak of plague in the Punjab in 1915 increased the death rate and prices were affected badly by the poor harvests of that and the following year.[29] By the end of 1918 high prices was a major cause of discontent. Although average prices had risen less than they had in Europe, they had a more significant effect on the population. The failure of the monsoon in 1918–19 only made things worse. The amount of rainfall in India was 19 per cent less than average, badly affecting farming and producing the worst crop failure for ten years. The total annual production of food in India should have been around 80 million tons (81 million tonnes), but it was estimated that around a quarter of this had been lost. This had a considerable effect over wide areas of India and during 1919 famine (or scarcity) was recorded in Bengal, Bihar and Orissa, the United Provinces, Rajputana, Central India, the Central Provinces, Bombay, Hyderabad and Madras.[30]

☙

The Great War had undoubtedly affected the Punjab in a variety of ways and by 1919 it was suffering from numerous complaints, ranging from war weariness and high prices, to an upsurge in political agitation and unrest. Much of this has been blamed on O'Dwyer, but such an explanation is too simplistic and does not pay adequate attention to the reality of recruitment in the Punjab during the Great War. The British were remarkably adept at drawing resources from their possessions without compromising the basic structure of their rule. O'Dwyer did what he could to support the war effort of the British Empire, but he was always aware of the delicate balance that had to be maintained in the Punjab and the importance of not pushing the people too hard; lessons that had been ingrained in his mind since his time in Gujranwala. He was no fool and did what he could do mitigate the effects of recruiting pressure in the Punjab, and, to a certain extent, his administration was successful at doing this.

So, if recruitment is an unsatisfactory explanation, then what else could have caused such violence? Some have claimed that the violence was a response to government brutality or some other kind of provocation, but this explanation misses a number of crucial points, including the nature of the nationalist movement in the Punjab and the role of the press. The Punjab may not have been as politically 'advanced' as other parts of India, but it had become home to a number of revolutionary movements during the war and it had struggled for some years with a critical press, much of which spread anti-government propaganda throughout the province.[31] Indeed, there is considerable evidence to show that feelings against the British were heightened in the Punjab, more than elsewhere, by the tone of the press. In Bombay there was admittedly a 'storm of protest' against the Rowlatt Bills by most newspapers, but at least five, including two Hindu and Muslim publications, supported the legislation and accepted the Viceroy's assurances on how the acts would be enforced.[32] In Bengal the press was divided over the *satyagraha* movement, with several newspapers, including the *Bengalee*, denouncing Gandhi's schemes as damaging to the forthcoming reforms. Similar divided views were contained within the United Provinces, with more moderate publications criticising the passive resistance movement, but praising the spectacle of Hindu-Muslim unity. The conduct of the rioters in Lahore and Amritsar was condemned by all newspapers in the United Provinces with the exception of the *Independent*.[33]

The nationalist press in the Punjab was, on the contrary, considerably more forceful in its criticisms of government and contributed to growing public anger. By the second half of March, the general topic of discussion was agitation against the Rowlatt Bills and the *Tribune* in Lahore declared its approval of the passive resistance campaign. In Amritsar, the *Waqt*, which was associated with the Home Rule movement, was especially violent in its condemnation of government, producing cartoons showing the Viceroy in the act of murdering Mother India and the goddess of Liberty with a black snake.[34]

Contributing to the general sense of unrest and unease was the appearance of threatening posters in the Punjab during April and May 1919. Some were poetic laments at the present state of India and her apparent betrayal by Britain, but many were more sinister. On 12 April, a poster was torn from one of the walls of Yakki Gate in Lahore, which referred to the British as 'monkeys' and urged Indians to 'Kill and be killed' and 'to turn these mean monkeys from your holy country'. Three days later a poster was found on Lohari Gate urging people to 'wake up' and rise against the 'tyrannical Faringee'.[35] It was these sinister manifestations of hatred and distrust that O'Dwyer was watching in March and April 1919, determined to resist it if he could; a battered breakwater standing firm against the onrushing tide.

Given the importance of the Punjab to the Raj and the worrying growth of seditious movements within its borders, it is little wonder that O'Dwyer was concerned. He had always maintained that tipping the political balance in such a province was bound to lead to disaster and that the British must remain firmly in charge. On 9 April he issued orders for the deportation of the two leaders of the agitation at Amritsar (Drs Kitchlew and Satyapal); men whom he regarded as being central to the spread of disloyalty throughout the Punjab. He was convinced that if these men could be prevented from continuing their campaign, it would be possible to keep a lid on the simmering discontent that had been raised during the Rowlatt *Satyagraha*. But it would be one of the most controversial decisions of his life; provoking the very situation that he had wanted to prevent. The Punjab was about to explode.

PART TWO
DISTURBANCES

CHAPTER 7

A 'Great Calamity' in Amritsar

I am a revolutionary and I will also be a violent non-co-operator,
if I see that non-violence does not succeed.

Dr Saifuddin Kitchlew[1]

S hortly before ten o'clock on the morning of 10 April 1919, four Indian men arrived at a large bungalow in the civil lines of Amritsar. The party consisted of Dr Kitchlew (a Muslim barrister), Dr Satyapal (a surgeon), and their two attendants, Hans Raj and Jairam Singh.[2] Kitchlew and Satyapal were the leading Indian National Congress representatives in Amritsar and during the preceding months they had played a major role in organising meetings within the city and making speeches on a variety of issues, particularly the tyranny of Sir Michael O'Dwyer, the evils of the Rowlatt Bills and the need for Hindu-Muslim unity. Both had taken Mahatma Gandhi's *satyagraha* vow and had been prominent in the *hartal* on 6 April when businesses had closed and processions had taken place. This had not gone unnoticed and like many leading political speakers they were being watched. By 30 March both men had been banned from speaking at political meetings or writing to the press under the Defence of India Act. Orders for their arrest had been issued on 9 April and the following morning they had been asked to visit the Deputy Commissioner at his home in the cantonment.

Dr Saifuddin Kitchlew – known within nationalist legend, somewhat bizarrely, as 'the hero of the Jallianwala Bagh' – was 31 years old and had been involved in local politics for many years; apparently stirred by the taunts he received as a student at Peterhouse College, Cambridge, where he studied from 1907 to 1909.[3] He had returned to India in 1912 (after a year studying in Germany) and started a prosperous legal business in Jullunder. Forced to leave because of his antagonism with the local Deputy Commissioner, Kitchlew moved to Amritsar and delved into local politics, helping to found local branches of Congress and the Muslim League. His colleague, Satyapal, was a lesser-known figure, originally hailing from Wazirabad in the Punjab.

A respected surgeon with a practice in Amritsar, he was deeply interested in politics and supported a variety of Hindu charitable organisations, as well as becoming involved in a campaign to reform the issue of railway platform tickets to Indians.[4]

As soon as they were invited into the bungalow, Kitchlew and Satyapal were handed arrest warrants and told that they would be leaving Amritsar at once. Protesting, they were placed under military guard, escorted out to two cars and then driven at high speed to Dharamsala where they were taken into custody. These arrests marked the beginning of the disturbances in the Punjab. Many writers have seen these actions as hasty, ill-considered and unnecessarily provocative. Louis Fischer, the biographer of Mahatma Gandhi, complained that the 'banishing of the leaders removed from Amritsar the two men who might have restrained the populace'.[5] Although some historians continue to view these arrests with indignation and scorn, they were not necessarily unjustified. Indeed, it is a little strange to defend Kitchlew and Satyapal on the grounds that they would have 'restrained' the population, given that they had been doing the exact opposite for years. Kitchlew, in particular, was someone who had skirted around the edges of what was acceptable in political discussion for a long time; a man who was fiercely committed to the Home Rule and civil disobedience movements and who sometimes went beyond what the government regarded as being constitutional.

Kitchlew had first met Gandhi in 1909 – hosting a dinner for him in his rooms at Cambridge – and became an enthusiastic *satyagrahi* after his call for a passive resistance movement against the Rowlatt Bills. Kitchlew was a good speaker; energetic, passionate and idealistic, and soon attracted a strong regional following. He had signed the *satyagraha* vow, but sat uneasily within the movement, and sometimes (as his biographer admitted), 'he was impatient and even asked the people to take direct action if the goal was not achieved by non-violent means'. Like many of those who took Gandhi's vow, Kitchlew did not speak at length on the exact provisions of the Rowlatt Act, but made passionate appeals against them, damning it as an extraordinary and unnecessary measure. In March 1919 he asked an audience 'to think calmly what horrors it would bring to them and their coming generations', but this was impossible given the widespread ignorance of the act. Kitchlew's speeches were usually 'simple and expressed ideas in a manner that his audience appreciated and easily understood', concentrating on 'resistance' to an autocratic government. He did not promote a violent armed revolt against British rule, but the content of his speeches and his great activity in trying to rouse peoples' opinions against the Rowlatt Bills came close to advocating open resistance.[6]

છ૭

It took less than an hour for word to spread through the city that Kitchlew and Satyapal had been arrested. By 11.30 a.m. crowds were beginning to gather in Hall Bazaar, the main thoroughfare in the city.[7] Great numbers of people then began to move towards the civil lines, apparently being intent on speaking with the Deputy Commissioner and pleading with him for the release of their leaders. In order to reach the civil lines, the crowds would have to cross the railway tracks by means of two bridges, a narrow footbridge and a wider road bridge. It was at the Hall Road Bridge where the first collision occurred. When the crowd tried to cross, they were stopped by a mounted picquet of 12 British and Indian soldiers. The situation was stable for an hour or so, but with the gradual swelling of the crowd, things began to deteriorate. Mr R.B. Beckett, the Assistant Commissioner, reached Hall Bridge at about 1 p.m. and was deeply alarmed by what he found. A handful of troops were keeping back what was by now a vast crowd that 'stretched as far as I could see'. Beckett tried to get them to disperse by shouting, but he could not be heard above the noise of the crowd. Gradually they were pushed back across the bridge. Protestors had started hitting the horses (they 'were absolutely frantic') and when the crowd reached the end of the bridge they came across a heap of bricks and stones that lay at the side of the road. Then they began stoning the British troops.[8]

Miles Irving arrived at Hall Bridge a little later, finding the picquet under a hail of brickbats. 'They were totally unable to hold back the crowd,' he remembered. 'They were being driven back. I endeavoured to rally them and get them to charge. But the horses would not face it.'[9] He decided to withdraw the picquet about 100 yards (91 metres). Irving told Beckett to return to the civil lines and call for reinforcements because the situation was slipping out of control. Shortly afterwards a small group of mounted soldiers, probably about six or seven strong, arrived at the bridge, led by a Lieutenant Dickie. By this time the stoning was becoming fiercer, with bricks and metalling from the road being ripped up and hurled at the soldiers. There was very little Dickie's men could do in such a situation so they began trotting back at some speed. It was at this point that an extra assistant commissioner, Mr F.A. Connor, arrived. He was alarmed to find that the picquet 'were practically bolting into the civil lines' so he told them to stand. Dickie was evidently in some distress, dramatically shouting to Connor, 'Oh, for God's sake send reinforcements.' Connor told him that the crowd must not be allowed into the civil lines. Several members of Dickie's party dismounted, levelled their rifles and fired three or four rounds. The firing seems to have had the desired effect; the shouting, stone-throwing crowds immediately stopped and retreated back a few steps.[10]

The firing at Hall Bridge prevented the British positions from being over-run and the authorities were bolstered with the arrival of a group of 24 police and seven *sowars* (Indian soldiers) under the command of Reginald Plomer, the Deputy Superintendent of Police. Plomer arrived at a critical moment. He could see hundreds of people streaming over the footbridge next to the railway station and knew that they could outflank him. His men managed to clear the building and – assisted by two Indian pleaders – push the crowd back towards the telegraph office on the other side of the railway lines. How-ever, by about 2 p.m., another large group of people began to approach the bridge, apparently being intent on pushing past the armed picquet and trying to enter the cantonment. After attempting to parley with the crowd, Plomer eventually gave an order to a non-commissioned officer (NCO) in charge of the picquet to fire. This time the firing was a more sustained and lethal volley than earlier in the day and caused more casualties, with bullets ripping into the front ranks of the jostling, pulling crowd and stopping them in their tracks. Official sources are vague on exact number of Indian casualties from the first and second firings. The Hunter Inquiry agreed that 'three or four individuals' were shot in the first firing and there were 'between 20 and 30 casualties' in the second, more prolonged, episode.[11]

The firings on the bridges may have secured the European settlements to the north of the city, but for those still inside the walls, it only made things worse. Elements of the crowd rapidly turned into enraged mobs and stormed back through the streets to commit various acts of murder, assault and ar-son. This seems to have occurred after 1 p.m., but the exact timing of events is difficult to finalise with any certainty. At the National Bank, Mr Stewart, the manager, and Mr Scott, the assistant manager, were murdered and the building was looted and burnt. At the Alliance Bank, Mr Thomson, the man-ager, was killed, although the building remained largely undamaged.[12] The Chartered Bank was also attacked, but the arrival of a small party of police under the Deputy Superintendent of Police, Khan Sahib Ahmed Jan, pre-vented much damage from being done. The banks remained the major target for the mob, but a number of other buildings were not spared. The town hall and the sub-post office were set on fire, the telegraph office was looted and its instruments smashed and the station goods yard was stormed and dam-aged. The Indian Christian Church and the Religious Book Society's depot and hall were burnt and an attempt to torch the Church Missionary Society's Girl's Normal School was prevented by the timely arrival of a police picquet.

Three other sub-post offices within the city were also looted.[13] It was during this period that an employee of the North Western Railway, Mr Robinson, was murdered and Sergeant Rowlands, an electrician, was also killed.[14] Serious assaults took place on Mr Bennet, the Station Superintendent, Mr Pinto, the Telegraph Master, and Miss Marcia Sherwood, a missionary.

∽

As soon as the firing on the bridges took place, Henry Smith, the Civil Surgeon, knew that he must act. With his motor ambulance he managed to evacuate between 30 and 40 Indian Christian women from the city and dropped them off at the cantonment. For him 'the whole violence went off practically at once in the different parts' of the city. 'I was doing a cataract on the operating table,' he explained, 'a thing that does not take more than a minute, and my assistant told me, "They are firing, Sir." These were the first shots, the hospital being quite close to the position.' 'My observation of the facts in regard to the attack on the Telegraph office, Banks, Church, Town Hall, school, a gang arriving to dispose of the ladies in the hospital, all acting simultaneously in different places,' he would tell Mr Justice Rankin, 'makes me say that did not occur without organisation.'[15] Smith also complained that all telephone wires were cut 'immediately after' the first picquet had fired.

Henry Smith's claim that the violence was all part of pre-planned conspiracy was discussed extensively by the Hunter Committee and remains perhaps the greatest mystery about the events of 10 April: was the violence a response to the firings, or were the mobs intent on murder and destruction from the beginning? It is difficult to be certain. As with much of the historical debate about the Punjab disturbances, opinions are polarised. Indian writers have argued that the crowds were peaceful and that the violence came from a fringe element that had 'lost its head' when fired upon unnecessarily. The Minority Report found that the crowds attempting to see Irving, 'had no intention of committing any excesses', but after the first firing, 'they lost their heads and [were] seized by a mad frenzy'.[16] According to Main Feroz Din, an honorary magistrate, 'The people were barefooted and bareheaded and unarmed, without even sticks in their hands.'[17] This was later repeated by the Congress Punjab Inquiry, which talked of a crowd of 'mourners – bareheaded, many unshod, and all without sticks'.[18]

British accounts of the crowd differ considerably from the bareheaded crowd of pure *satyagrahis* that has become part of Indian legend. On the contrary, soldiers and officials were unanimous in recording the hostility and size of the crowds they faced that day. According to Miles Irving, 'They were very noisy, a furious crowd, you could hear the roar of them up the long road [leading to Hall Gate], they were an absolutely mad crowd, spitting with rage and swearing.'[19] One of the protestors apparently shouted, 'Where is the Deputy Commissioner? We will butcher him to pieces.'[20] Irving also claimed that the crowd turned violent soon *after* the first shots were fired on Hall Bridge. Soon after the crowd had retreated, he claimed that 'smoke was coming up at this time from the National Bank there'. This evidence was accepted by the Hunter Report, which concluded that this happened between 1 and 1.30 p.m., although it has since been disputed.[21] Another British official who saw the crowds that day, Beckett, remembered that, 'The crowd were all shouting and behaving in a most fanatical manner, making faces, waving their hands.' Indeed, many British witnesses even recorded similar adjectives of the attitude and demeanour of the crowds that gathered at various points, particularly at Hall Bridge. At least three British witnesses all recorded that the crowds were 'howling'.[22]

Whatever the attitude of the crowds, they were of staggering proportions. According to F.A. Connor, the whole city was 'full of a mob' about 30,000 strong. Captain J.W. Massey (OC Amritsar) thought there were about 40,000 people.[23] Given that the population of Amritsar amounted to about 150,000 people, these crowds represented a significant proportion of those living in the city, even if a considerable proportion were in the city for the religious festivals scheduled for the weekend.[24] As well as recording their fears at the approach of such a large and apparently hostile crowd, several British observers also claimed that they were faced with openly criminal elements. According to Miles Irving,

> They were of the lower classes of the city, very largely organised gangs. There is a great tendency for what I may call the hooligan class to be organised under led captains, and they were very much to the fore. They were of all classes. A great number were Kashmiri Muhammadans, of whom there are numbers in Amritsar, and others were Hindus, such as *Khatris* and *Aroras* of the poorer classes.

Mr Plomer believed that the crowd was (in part) composed of 'riffs-raffs' and 'hooligans' under the control of two notorious locals, Bhugga and Ratto. Similarly Henry Smith claimed that local gangs of 'hooligans' were organised on the night of 9 April, with a butcher attached to each group.[25]

It may not be possible to make any final statements on the motives and demeanour of the crowds that gathered on 10 April, but there is no doubt that the authorities were faced with large numbers of angry and determined people. Given the threatening situation – the shouting, the jostling, the stone throwing – the authorities were justified in firing when they did. Indeed, it is not clear what else they could have done, other than let the crowds into the cantonment, which would have been extremely dangerous. It is unlikely that any statement or appearance by Irving would have calmed the situation – when he did go to the bridge he was stoned – and they could not engage in other, less violent methods of crowd control because of a lack of troops. They could also do very little when the temper of the mobs changed soon after the second firing at the bridges.[26]

✑

The murder of Europeans in Amritsar was, for the British at least, the most sinister episode of the entire disturbances; a frightening example of 'native' resentment that simmered under the surface and threatened to break out at any moment.[27] The first incident, a ghastly portent of what was to come, occurred just after the police had fired for the second time. A group of men made their way to the National Bank and smashed their way inside. According to Basant Singh, the head clerk, a mob broke into the bank at around 1.30 p.m. ('just after my Sahibs had returned from tiffin') and collected in the main hall, using their *lathis* to smash everything they could. Although it is difficult to confirm what happened next in any detail, the manager, Mr Stewart, and his assistant, Mr Scott, were both attacked and killed. The bank was then ransacked and burnt and the adjoining *godown* (warehouse), where large amounts of cloth and other valuables were stored, was looted.[28] A subsequent investigation concluded that the attack had been led by two locals, Rattan Chand ('Ratto') and Bhugga, assisted by about 20 others, including several butchers armed with hatchets.

One of the other major European banks in the city, the Alliance Bank, was also not spared. Sometime around 2 or 2.30 p.m., an angry crowd, armed with *lathis*, gathered outside. The Indian staff desperately tried to get the mob to move on and shouted that the manager, Mr G.M. Thomson, was not inside. Unfortunately, they were ignored and the mob broke in, searching for any Europeans. Thomson, who was armed with a revolver, ran up to the roof but was seen by the mob and pelted with bricks and stones. Not wishing to 'die a dog's death', he returned downstairs to confront the mob on the staircase. Some of those in the main hall then rushed at him, but Thomson defended himself with his revolver. In a scene eerily reminiscent of the famous death of General Gordon at Khartoum, Thomson stood there firing at his assailants and managed to kill one of them. This, however, only provoked the mob and amid a welter of *lathi* blows he retreated to a rear office. At this point several of Thomson's Indian colleagues tried to save his life, by dragging him away and saying that the *sahib* had died. Undeterred, the mob continued upstairs, broke into where Thomson was lying and murdered him. His body was thrown off the balcony and then set on fire with a canister of oil.[29]

At roughly the same time, the Chartered Bank was being attacked, although fortunately, the European manager, Mr J.W. Thomson, and his assistant, Mr Ross, managed to evade the mob by hiding in an upstairs room. A crowd of about 2,000 people set fire to the building, but they were scattered by the timely arrival of a picquet of 25 policemen led by Khan Sahib Ahmad Jan who had received word that 'the lives of two Sahibs were in great danger'. When he arrived at the bank, Ahmad Jan found it on fire ('I found a lot of papers burning outside the Bank') and rushed forward shouting '*pakaro, pakaro!*' ('seize them, seize them!').[30] Most of the crowd fled at their arrival and they were able to search the bank, find the Europeans and bring them to the *kotwali*. The two British managers of the Chartered Bank were not the only ones to have a narrow escape that afternoon. Shortly after 1 p.m. Miss Marcia Sherwood, the superintendent of the Amritsar Mission School, was cycling through the city when she encountered one of the mobs. They were evidently out of control and looking for trouble. Someone shouted, 'Kill her, she is English.' Desperately trying to escape, Miss Sherwood turned her bicycle around and pedalled off. Unfortunately, in the chaos of the old town, she became lost and had to retrace her steps. It was at this point when she met the mob again. A group of eight men attacked her, pushed her to the ground and hit her with *lathis*. When she staggered to her feet she was again chased and hit on the head. With that the cry went up that she was dead and the mob moved off shouting for victory. Miraculously Miss Sherwood had not been killed. Although grievously wounded, she was taken in by a group of Hindu shopkeepers who treated her injuries and tried to make her as comfortable as possible.[31]

Mrs Easdon, a doctor at the municipal Zenana Hospital, was the second British woman to be targeted by the mob that day. She was fortunate to remain hidden in the hospital when a mob broke in and searched for her, ransacking the hospital as they did so. Why they tried to kill her remains unclear; among nationalist accounts there is a persistent suspicion that she laughed at some of those who had been wounded at the bridges and shouted that they 'deserved it'.[32] Although it is impossible to verify whether Mrs Easdon did this, it is clear that those who broke into the hospital were acting in a more methodical manner than the mobs that attacked the banks and simply killed any

European they found. Mrs Nelly Benjamin, a sub-assistant surgeon, helped to hide Mrs Easdon and courageously faced the mob, telling them that she was not in the building. The hospital was repeatedly searched. Beds were overturned, cupboards were thrown open, but Mrs Easdon remained hidden and was finally escorted to safety by Muhammad Sharif, a sub-inspector of Police. Shocked at how close she had come to meeting a violent fate, Mrs Easdon left the city that evening, wearing Indian pyjamas and a *burka*, her feet dyed black with ink.[33]

ɛ⁄ɔ

The violence that day was the worst single outbreak of disorder to be seen anywhere in India during 1919 – what Miles Irving referred to as 'the greatest calamity since the Mutiny' – and it would burn itself in the memory of those officials who were tasked with restoring order in the city, haunting their imaginations for years to come. In retrospect the attempt to forestall violence by deporting Kitchlew and Satyapal had backfired badly and merely prompted the unrest that the authorities had been seeking to avoid. Some would claim that violence would have happened anyway, and that it was all part of a pre-planned revolutionary conspiracy, but this is unlikely to have been so. The arrests of the leaders at Amritsar and the violence that would follow were a reflection of the misunderstandings and confusions that were so potent in April 1919, between, on the one hand, those British officials who were tired of letting Kitchlew and his colleagues preach sedition unmolested and who decided to take action, and, on the other hand, those Indians who believed the worst about the Rowlatt Bills and felt that the actions of the authorities were all part of some sinister plan of repression.

CHAPTER 8

A 'Terrible Quietness'

The Club was fuller than usual, and several parents had brought their children into the rooms reserved for adults, which gave the air of the Residency at Lucknow.

E.M. Forster[1]

By the afternoon of 10 April the civilian authorities had lost control of Amritsar. That evening, as parts of Amritsar burned and baying crowds marched through the streets brandishing *lathis* and boasting about their exploits, the surviving Europeans, including the *burka*-clad Mrs Easdon, made their way into the fort on the other side of the city walls, where they could be protected. The condition that existed there was a constant source of complaint by the European community. The idea of terrified women and children huddled together in stuffy, unsanitary fortifications brought back vivid reminders of the Mutiny of 1857.[2] Frank McCallum, a young officer of 1/9th Gurkhas who had detrained at Amritsar that afternoon, went to the fort and saw for himself the lines of camp beds and cots that made up the accommodation. 'I was greatly shocked to see,' he recalled, 'by chance a barrack room of women and children who had been brought into the Fort from the Civil Lines for safety. There was a terrible quietness in that barrack room. The ladies seemed so bemused and sad.'[3]

For Miles Irving, the situation remained 'very critical' for the next two days. 'We were able to hold the outskirts of the city,' he recalled, but could make 'no impression on the city. The city was still impertinently hostile.' Furthermore, 'It was freely said that it might be the Raj of the Sarkar outside, but inside it was *Hindu–Musalmanon ki hakumat*.'[4] A senior ICS official, A.J.W. Kitchin, Commissioner of the Lahore Division, was ordered to Amritsar that afternoon. He drove to the city and met Captain Massey who was busy supervising the evacuation of women and children. Kitchin acted decisively. He established his headquarters in the railway station and discussed with Massey about whether they would be able to hold the railway line.[5] It was possible, he said but it would require more troops. The evening witnessed frantic activity as small numbers of reinforcements arrived from Lahore. At 3 p.m. a train carrying 270 Gurkhas (on its way to Peshawar) was detained and the troops were sent out to guard the fort, the station and the cantonment. Later at 11 p.m. Major Macdonald arrived from Lahore with 300 men from 1/124th Baluchis and 216/Royal Sussex Regiment.

As well as trying to secure the fort and cantonment, Kitchin had to find some way of restoring order, but how this was to be done was not immediately apparent. Furthermore, from the moment he arrived a question arose that required his attention and which would come to have enormous consequences: just who was in charge – the civilians or the military? This question is important because of the widely held belief that the civilian authorities at Amritsar abdicated their responsibilities to the military, particularly Dyer, who arrived on 11 April. Sir Valentine Chirol, a journalist well acquainted with India, condemned the civilian authorities for the 'wholesale surrender' of their authority to the military in what he called 'a disastrous departure from the best traditions of the Indian Civil Service'.[6] It was this, so the story goes, that allowed Dyer to take such drastic action in the Jallianwala Bagh on 13 April.

೧

So what had happened? At some point on the evening of 10 April, Macdonald, commander of the 300 men who had come from Lahore, was told that 'the situation was beyond our control and that he must take such immediate steps as the military situation demanded'. Although it has often been assumed by this act that Kitchin not only deprived the Deputy Commissioner (Miles Irving) of his authority but also completely handed over all power to the military, this was not the case. In his evidence to the Hunter Inquiry, Kitchin said he had not deprived Irving of command and stated that he had 'handed over charge to Major Macdonald of the military situation. He would take such steps as were required. I said nothing about civil administration.'[7] In hindsight it may be possible to draw such a clear separation and judge the civilian authorities in Amritsar to have been at fault. For his part, Kitchin was deeply concerned by what he found in Amritsar and felt that a strong military response was both desirable and necessary. There was simply no way that situation could be restored without military help, yet there was no suggestion that the civilian authorities would simply disappear.

Kitchin's defence may have fallen on deaf ears, but before Dyer's arrival there was no dramatic abdication of civilian responsibility. Certainly, as Nigel Collett has observed, 'the lines of civil authority were already growing confused', but the civilian officers remained deeply involved in what was going on.[8] Ironically perhaps, the loss of Amritsar city forced British civil and military personnel to work closely with each other, even if ultimate authority was unclear. After the firings on 10 April, the British authorities closed ranks and, consequent with the need to maintain communication and receive reinforcements, remained in the railway station. According to Kitchin:

> In those days we all lived together. I might make the point a little clearer. In those days not only in Amritsar but in other places too in the first two days everybody lived in his boots in the railway station, *the civil and the military lived, ate and slept together.* [9]

One of the main problems they encountered was the difficulty of communication. During the morning of 11 April, rumours were circulating about what else was going on in the Punjab – that troops were mutinying and how Lahore fort had fallen – leading to a state of considerable unrest for those British officers in Amritsar. Kitchin remembered how 'telegraph lines were cut at Gurdaspur and Dhariwal and other places, some stations were being burnt. The lines between Lahore and Amritsar were unsafe; no train could move without danger'. The cutting of telegraph and telephone wires around Amritsar was deeply chilling. According to Miles Irving, 'The attempt to cut communications was certainly organized. Directly after I got down I naturally tried to communicate with Lahore, but found communications down and I learnt that the wires had been cut with a hammer and a cold chisel.' Fortunately, Kitchin managed to send a garbled message to Lahore using a phonophore.[10]

For Miles Irving, the situation certainly seems to have got the better of him. He had only taken up his position at Amritsar in February 1919 and was conscious that he did not know the city as well as some of the more forceful Europeans present, particularly Kitchin and the Civil Surgeon, Smith. Irving found 10 and 11 April difficult days, having to come to terms with what had occurred under his watch and trying to remain in charge. Most of the writing on Amritsar is critical of the Deputy Commissioner. Alfred Draper found that he was 'well meaning' and 'well intentioned', but did not command a great deal of respect.[11] He was certainly shocked at what had occurred and may have panicked. When he was asked by the Hunter Committee to justify his actions, he became animated, comparing what had happened to the Mutiny of 1857. 'Frankly,' he snapped, 'I did not at the time get out my law books and look at the precedents of the High Court.'[12] Indeed, it is difficult to be too harsh on Irving. The arrival of Kitchin (and later Dyer) took much of the power out of his hands and there was very little he could have done in such a situation. Furthermore, there was a constant circulation of civilian and military superiors through Amritsar between 10 and 13 April, which only added to the confusion in the railway station. Kitchin, perhaps the most important person, arrived at the city on the evening of 10 April, returned to Lahore the following day, went back to Amritsar on the morning of 12 April, before leaving again that evening. Major Macdonald arrived on 10 April and then was replaced by Dyer the following day. It is little wonder that Irving felt bewildered.

Combined with the confusion over who was in charge was the inexperience of the key personnel in dealing with the type of situation they faced. Because both Kitchin and Dyer did not know Amritsar very well (and Miles Irving had only been Deputy Commissioner since February), there was a lack of detailed knowledge of the city, which perhaps explains why Henry Smith, the Civil Surgeon (who had many years' experience), was included in their discussions.[13] The police officers also lacked familiarity and expertise in dealing with the difficult situation that would enfold in the city on 10 April. The Chief Inspector of Police (Muhammad Ashraf Khan) admitted that in 27 years' service in the police he had never had to deal with a riot before. Likewise, the Deputy Superintendent of Police (Khan Sahib Ahmed Jan) made similar comments.[14]

Turning to the role of the police, according to most accounts one of the major factors that allowed such mob violence to occur was the relative inactivity of the police reserve, stationed in the *kotwali* in the centre of the city.[15] As well as allowing the Town Hall to burn down, little was done to prevent the attack on the National Bank and no attempt made to find out what was going on elsewhere in the city and restore order.[16] The Hunter Report was very critical of the two senior police officers on duty on 10 April. Both Khan Sahib Ahmed Jan and Muhammad Ashraf Khan 'failed either to grasp, or to attempt to cope with, their responsibility' and showed a 'lack of initiative'.[17] Indeed, one of the few points where the Hunter and Congress Reports were in agreement was on the inaction of the police.[18]

A Criminal Investigation Department investigation into the inactivity of the police reserve blamed four factors: the lack of co-operation between Ahmad Jan and Ashraf Khan; fear of the large crowds; want of definite orders; and poor detective work.[19] This was all well and good, but in many ways, the criticism of the handling of the police reserve at the *kotwali* is unfair. Although there were rumours of disagreements between Ahmed Jan and Ashraf Khan over who was in charge, they were placed in a difficult situation and did about as much as could reasonably be expected.[20] Both Ian Colvin and Arthur Swinson, who wrote extensively about the situation at Amritsar, did not blame the police. They pointed to the fact that there was no European officer present in the *kotwali* and, in any case, no definite orders had been issued.[21] Muhammad Ashraf Khan, the Inspector of Police, believed that they had done as much as they could – despatching a small party to the National Bank and helping to quench the burning Town Hall – but that they were simply too few in number to cope with the size and ferocity of the mobs in Amritsar and had very little information on what was happening. He had also only received one order from Mr Plomer and that was simply to remain in reserve until Plomer himself came to take command, so it is perhaps understandable that he did not act with more urgency.[22]

✧

The attitude of the British authorities during this period was, according to one participant, one of 'deep indignation'. Very few British went into Amritsar in the following days, and even then only with a sizeable military escort. When questioned about whether he had gone into the city after 10 April, Miles Irving shook his head. 'Neither cared, nor were allowed by the Military authorities. None of us were such fools as to put our heads into a hornet's nest.' When Kitchin discussed with Macdonald the possibility of organising a mission into the city (on the evening of 10 April) to make contact with the police reserve, it was anticipated that this would involve 'street fighting of a dangerous kind'. Fortunately, before plans could be finalised it was confirmed that all the surviving Europeans had been safely removed from the city and placed in the fort.[23] The railway station was soon turned into a veritable fortress. When Girdhari Lal, a local businessman, reached Amritsar on the morning of 11 April, he saw 'batches of policemen guarding the railway lines'. 'When the train steamed into the station here,' he recalled, 'the whole place looked like a regular military post, with soldiers and guns scattered all over ... At every step outside the city, one could see nothing but only military or police as [*sic*] short distances with rifles and bayonets. Not a single policeman was to be seen on duty anywhere in the city.'[24]

For those political activists who had been at the forefront of the *hartal*, the detention of Kitchlew and Satyapal left them without any recognised leaders. One of those present at this time was the secretary of the *Satyagraha Sabha*, Hans Raj, who had been with the leaders when they were arrested. He would later turn approver and become the key prosecution witness in the so-called Amritsar Conspiracy Case of 1919, when Kitchlew and Satyapal (with 13 others) were found guilty of sedition and sentenced to transportation for life.[25] Hans Raj's testimony has often been criticised as being unreliable, but it does offer important clues to what happened in the city between 10 and 13 April, which has remained something of a mystery. According to Raj, after the arrest of Kitchlew and Satyapal, the person 'to go to for orders' was a Dr Hafiz Mohammed Bashir. Little is known about him. He was a 33-year-old resident of Amritsar and was regarded by the authorities as being so dangerous that he was later sentenced to death. From Raj's testimony, he appears as a major figure, taking a leading role in the Ram Naumi celebrations of 9 April when he rode through the streets on horseback, covered in garlands. He gave a speech in the bazaar saying that if Hindu and Muslim unity was maintained, then 'it would not be difficult to take back Hindustan from Government'. It was also alleged that he led the mob that attacked the National Bank, urging the crowd to loot the premises and kill the *sahibs*.[26]

After the violence on 10 April, those who had signed the *satyagraha* vow looked to Bashir for guidance. Views on what to do were mixed. Some argued that the *hartal* should be stopped and an official application made to the Deputy Commissioner to release the leaders, but Bashir was unimpressed. When Hans Raj suggested that they should end the *hartal*, Bashir told him that he was 'a child' who did not understand 'such matters'. Furthermore, 'if we lose the present opportunity we shall never had [*sic*] a chance again'. On 12 April Bashir ordered Hans Raj to organise a meeting at the Hindu Sabha High School, where a telegram from Dr Kitchlew would be read out and speeches would be made. But Bashir never turned up. When Raj saw him the following day – 13 April – Bashir told him to arrange another meeting in the Jallianwala Bagh that afternoon. When he protested that martial law had been proclaimed and that no meeting should take place, Bashir did not agree. 'Government is not so foolish as to fire at such a meeting,' he is reported to have said.[27] And once again, Bashir never arrived at the Jallianwala Bagh.

Given the amount of claims and counter-claims about what was going on in the city during this period, it is difficult to be certain of anything, particularly the role of Dr Bashir. Nevertheless, Hans Raj's testimony highlights how uncertain and fluid the situation was and how quickly it could change. The *satyagrahis* may have not been planning an armed uprising against British rule, but they were certainly willing to defy the authorities, continue the *hartal* and keep the spirit of defiance alive. The situation in the city between 10 and 12 April was relatively calm, if tense. Sometime on the afternoon of 10 April the water supply was cut off. This has been seen in nationalist writing as yet further evidence of a determined British plan to terrorise and punish the civilian population, but this was not so. It was cut off because rioters had smashed many of the hydrants and there was a rumour that the water had been poisoned, which meant that the British could not use water from this source as well.[28] Groups of citizens from 'respectable' families patrolled the streets and kept order, but many others, perhaps afraid of British reprisals, stayed in their homes. Shops remained closed and a number of funeral processions were held, but very little else occurred.[29]

The funerals of those killed on 10 April did, however, present the British with an acute problem. If the authorities allowed these processions to take place, which were likely to attract considerable numbers of people, there was a danger that the crowds would get out of control. For the British, it was, therefore, essential to try and limit the number of people who were allowed to take part. After considerable wrangling between Irving and Maqbool Mahmood, a High Court pleader, it was finally agreed that the funerals could take place with processions of not more than 2,000 people and crowds could attend in any number. Everyone must return to the city by 2 p.m. or else they would be fired upon. The funeral processions took place that afternoon with 'great enthusiasm' and were finished by one o'clock.[30]

Considering the violence that had been exhibited against the small European community the previous day, the authorities were remarkably magnanimous on 11 April in allowing so many people to gather. Yet again this episode reveals a greater sense of responsibility than is usually given in nationalist accounts, which often present the scenes at the railway station as evidence of a hysterical overreaction. Nevertheless, Kitchin was dissatisfied with how things were going and wanted stronger, more decisive action, particularly from Major Macdonald who had not wanted to interfere with the funerals. It was only after the processions had returned that Macdonald took a small party of troops to the *kotwali* and posted men at various points along Hall Bazaar.[31] Kitchin was more forthright than either Irving or Macdonald and wanted a firmer response to the crisis, one that was not simply one of responding to developments. This was very much in line with Kitchin's training in the Indian Civil Service (ICS) and with his experience in the Punjab. He knew that British rule rested upon prestige and, to a certain extent, bluff, and was well aware that sometimes decisive action was required.[32]

Kitchin left Amritsar that afternoon, determined to see Michael O'Dwyer and consult with him about how best to restore order. After consulting the Lieutenant-Governor, Kitchin wrote a letter to the commander of the British troops in Lahore, Major-General Sir William Beynon, and informed him that Major Macdonald had 'done nothing to quell the rebellion'. Ominously Kitchin requested that Beynon 'send an officer who is not afraid to act'.[33] In response, Beynon summoned Macdonald's commanding officer in 1/124th Baluchis, Lieutenant-Colonel M.H.L. Morgan, and showed him Kitchin's letter. Beynon then told him to go to Amritsar as soon as possible and regain control of the city. Morgan clicked his heels, saluted and hurriedly made his way out. He travelled to Amritsar that evening, unsure of the situation that would confront him, but expecting the worst. When he arrived he found – to his complete surprise – that he was not the only senior officer present: Brigadier-General Dyer, the commander at Jullunder, was there too. Because he was no longer the senior officer present, Morgan suggested that he should return to Lahore, but Dyer disagreed and ordered Morgan to stay in the city for the time being.[34]

What on earth was going on? Dyer's arrival seems to have been a surprise for most of those present in the railway station (and in Lahore), but they quickly accepted his authority. Although Dyer would claim that he was ordered to Amritsar at two o'clock that afternoon by Beynon, this does not seem to have been the case and Beynon had, in fact, sent Morgan. Dyer went on his own violation; probably having heard news of serious unrest in the city and being anxious to take decisive action.[35] Dyer's sudden arrival at Amritsar and his decision to keep Morgan with him has been viewed with suspicion and there are rumours that it was all part of some sinister plan to terrorise the population and restore order in the most violent way possible. But this is to misread the situation. Communication was undoubtedly difficult at this time with rumours circulating through the Punjab about widespread looting, violence and murder and such a mix-up was an almost inevitable result of the situation. In any case, Dyer was not solely responsible for Jullunder and it would have been somewhat strange of him not to have taken an interest in a major incident at Amritsar, which was within his area of operations, particularly when Jullunder itself was reasonably quiet. Morgan was an experienced officer and a tough fighter, just the type of person that Dyer was drawn to and who he would want by his side in such a dangerous environment. They started making preparations for restoring order.

ↈ

Dyer's arrival had a dramatic impact in Amritsar and galvanised the British administration, and it seems that this was the point when civilian authority was superseded. He immediately transferred his headquarters from the railway station to the Ram Bagh gardens and began thinking about what he could do next. His decision to transfer his headquarters to the Ram Bagh was a symbolic statement that Dyer – in other words, the military – was now in sole command and would deal with the situation as he saw fit. The days of military and civilian authorities living and eating together were over and the change in atmosphere was not lost on those present, including the Deputy Commissioner, Miles Irving. At ten o'clock on the morning of 12 April Dyer led a strong party through the city: 120 British and 310 Indian troops supported by two armoured cars. He met a mob at Sultanwind Gate, which he managed to disperse peacefully, although he would later admit to have considered opening fire.[36]

Dyer's actions once he arrived in Amritsar have attracted considerable criticism. Nigel Collett has criticised him for not acting with sufficient vigour on 12 April, arguing that he should have continued Major Macdonald's policy of slowly gaining control of the city by gradually increasing the number of picquets. This strange lack of action, Collett suggests, prevented Dyer from being able 'to regain the upper hand in much of the city'. Apparently, Dyer did not do this because for him at least, much more punitive action was required. It was not simply a matter of returning the city to normalcy but of suppressing a revolt and punishing the people.[37] Yet this is again unconvincing. The claim that Dyer should have split his force and placed smaller detachments throughout the city would not necessarily have been a wise move. At Ahmedabad, which witnessed anti-European violence of similar intensity to Amritsar, the police were deployed in small groups throughout the city and by the evening of 10 April had been completely disarmed by the mobs. The District Magistrate, Mr G.E. Chatfield, was asked numerous times by the Hunter Committee as to why he had not employed the military in force in the city. Although standing by his decision, Chatfield did admit that the deployment of police in Ahmedabad showed 'the great danger of putting small bodies of men to guard points'.[38] Even if parties of police and military forces had been stationed in Amritsar between 11 and 13 April, this is unlikely to have been popular and – from what we know from Lahore and Delhi – may have been regarded by the population as a deeply unwanted and aggressive move. Indeed, a constant request from the *satyagrahis* of Delhi and Lahore was that troops should *not* be brought into the city but kept out of the way as far as possible. Simply posting more picquets through the city was not going to solve the problem. In any case, Dyer's responsibilities were not just to Amritsar, but to 45 Brigade's area of operations in the Punjab. He was, at this point, only too aware of the unrest around him being regularly informed of the cutting of wires and the derailing of trains. Revolt seemed to be engulfing the entire province.

CHAPTER 9

Protest and Response in Lahore

When you go and call on the Lieutenant-Governor, you take visiting cards, you do not take brickbats.

Lieutenant-Colonel Frank Johnson[1]

Thirty miles (38 kilometres) to the west of Amritsar lay Lahore, the capital of the Punjab. Its beating heart may have lain in the narrow streets and crowded bazaars of the old city, but the seat of political power (and indeed throughout the province) lay elsewhere.[2] Across Lahore, past the European quarter and the fashionable hotel, Faletti's, was Government House. Behind the two-storey portico and white walls, this sprawling mansion was the home of successive lieutenant-governors, the present occupant being the 'satanically energetic' Irishman, Sir Michael O'Dwyer. When Sir Michael returned to Lahore in 1913, after many years spent working in the NWFP and Central India, he found that much had changed. The atmosphere of 'dust and disorder' that he had enjoyed as a new recruit to the ICS in 1885 had developed into 'one of the finest stations in India'. British rule had resulted in a great expansion of the city to the south and east, with a new cantonment and a variety of public buildings being erected, including Government House, which had been built upon the tomb of a seventeenth-century Mughal ruler, Muhammad Kasim Khan. It was a building suitable to the British rulers of the Punjab, and where O'Dwyer would reside during some of the most testing times of his governorship, when it was feared that the forces of agitation and sedition would take their struggle to its very walls.

Lahore had not witnessed a *hartal* on 30 March, but it did so on 6 April when demonstrations were held and businesses were closed. The anti-Rowlatt campaign in Lahore was strong among the city's middle classes; its lawyers, businessmen and students, and was led by the secretary of the Indian Association, Duni Chand. Also prominent in the discussions over how to resist the new legislation was Lala Harkishen Lal, a barrister and financial entrepreneur; Ram Bhaj Dutt, a High Court *vakil* (lawyer); the barrister, Gokul Chand Narang; and Fazal-i-Husain, a leading representative of the Muslims of Lahore.[3] As at many places across India, there was no unified response to Gandhi's call for a passive resistance movement on the lines of *satyagraha*. Gandhi's influence was not as pervasive in Lahore as elsewhere in India, although there was strong feeling against the Rowlatt Acts. At a meeting on 4 February, it was decided that 'untold misery would be caused to the Punjab if the law was enacted, [so] we were determined to oppose their new proposals in all constitutional ways open to us'.[4] On 9 March another meeting was held, during which Dr Kitchlew of Amritsar gave a speech. A resolution was made that should the Rowlatt Bills become law, a passive resistance movement would begin.

The atmosphere in the city during this period, as across many parts of the Punjab, was unsettled and there was unrest over a number of issues, not just the Rowlatt legislation. There was resentment, in certain quarters at least, towards O'Dwyer, and there had also been much hardship after the Punjab banking crisis of 1913, which had destroyed the savings of hundreds of middle-class families. On 2 April, at a joint gathering of the Indian Association and the Provincial Committee of the Indian National Congress, it was finally decided to endorse Gandhi's call for a *hartal*. Things were now coming to a head. On 4 April a number of civilian officials had tried to persuade the chief organisers and 'agitators' to suspend civil disobedience. Alarmed at the growth of feeling in the city and aware of what had happened at Delhi, Mr F. Fyson, the Deputy Commissioner, met the leading members of the movement and told them that they must help to maintain peace on the *hartal* day and refrain from forcing people to close their shops. In return he would promise not to interfere with any demonstrations or gatherings.[5] 'We repeatedly pointed out,' Mr E.P. Broadway, the Senior Superintendent of Police, remembered, 'that they were stirring up forces they might not be able to control.'[6] It took news of Gandhi's arrest to bring these forces into the open.

⁋

If 6 April was a difficult and trying day for the military commander in Lahore, Major-General Sir William Beynon, 10 April was far worse. It was an uneasy day of watching and waiting, trying to stay cool in the suffocating heat and reading the telegrams and despatches that periodically came in from the different areas under his command. Beynon had been informed the previous evening that trouble was expected in the next few days, but it was not until the afternoon that things began to happen. The news that Mahatma Gandhi had been arrested and escorted back to Bombay, while on his way to the Punjab, reached Lahore at about 3.30 p.m. It was followed an hour later by rumours of unrest and disorder at Amritsar.[7] Beynon told Brigadier-General Clarke (GOC 43 Brigade) to get troops into the city as soon as possible. Unfortunately, because Thursday was a military holiday some delay was encountered in getting the men together, many of whom had been enjoying a brigade sports day in the cantonment.

On the other side of the city, in Government House, Sir Michael O'Dwyer held an emergency meeting with his civilian and police chiefs that afternoon. Among those present were Fyson, Broadway and Mr G.A. Cocks, the Deputy Inspector-General of the CID (Punjab). O'Dwyer inquired as to what arrangements had been made in case the news of Gandhi's arrest caused trouble in the city. Including the police there were 580 troops available in Lahore, although many of them were either on leave or playing sports because of the military holiday.[8] As they were discussing the disposition of police forces and how they could deploy their troops, news was received that large crowds were streaming out of the old city, through Lohari Gate and down Anarkali Bazaar. The Lieutenant-Governor quickly drew the meeting to an end. Mr Montgomery, the Chief Engineer, suggested that he would collect the European women and children and put them under guard in Government House. Fyson and Cocks headed to the mall, while Broadway drove to the civil lines to bring up his reserve of mounted police.

News of Gandhi's arrest and the violence at Amritsar spread through the city with alarming speed. By 5 p.m. groups of people were going through the bazaars shouting that Gandhi had been arrested. The people do not seem to have been led by pleaders or leading citizens and were just groups of locals, excited by the news and intent on making some kind of protest.[9] The crowd that formed late that afternoon numbered somewhere between 6 and 7,000 people; not as many as would gather in Amritsar, but still large enough to present the authorities with a major challenge to law and order.[10] The crowds soon reached the Government Telegraph Office, but this was defended by a detachment of 40 British soldiers with fixed bayonets. The protestors changed direction and moved off down the mall, evidently heading for Government House, but were blocked off by a small party of police officers. It was at this point that Fyson and Cocks drove up. As he left the car, Cocks watched several police officers trying to push the crowd back. 'They were quite unsuccessful,' he declared. For a next few minutes the police tried to hold back the crowd, shouting at them and trying to get them to move on, but the situation only got worse. Fearing that the small group of police were in danger of being overrun an order to fire was given.[11] In the quick volley that followed, one man was killed and seven wounded. The crowd broke off and disappeared around the O'Dwyer Soldiers' Club.[12]

Despite the firing the crowd did not dissipate, but gradually began to re-form again outside Lohari Gate at the edge of Anarkali Bazaar. Mr Broadway recalled that it had 'formed into a compact mass' and had also 'swelled to huge proportions'.[13] The situation in front of Lohari Gate remained extremely tense for some time; the police enduring volleys of stones and brickbats while trying to get the mobs to disperse. As at Amritsar, at the front were a number of Indian activists endeavouring to get people to go home, but again without success. One of these was Chaudhri Ram Bhaj Dutt, a senior local figure in the *Arya Samaj* (Hindu reform movement).[14] Mr Broadway spoke to Dutt several times and they both warned the crowd that they would be fired upon if they did not disperse. Dutt was then given a horse, but he could not control it and was thrown from the saddle. After picking himself up, he climbed onto an electric switch box on the pavement. From there Dutt waved a white cloth and shouted at the crowd, although his words were drowned out in the noise. Things were getting out of hand.

Mr W.G. Clarke, the Deputy Superintendent of Police, later described the noise as 'like an electric engine'. He later recalled,

> I waited there for a few minutes, thinking of course the mob would disperse; I saw it was getting larger. So I decided to push them back; I gave an order to load and warned them that if they did not disperse, I would fire; at the same time I blew the alarm whistle; I had a very rough time of it then.

Shortly afterwards, Mr Fyson arrived and gave the crowd two minutes to comply with these orders. After the time had elapsed, and with no improvement in the situation, he gave Broadway the order to fire. Five or six rounds were fired, with three people being killed and another 12 wounded. The crowd broke and streamed back towards the city and Broadway immediately ordered the ceasefire. Shaken but relieved, the police then moved up to Circular Road and began to clear the adjoining streets and gardens of rioters. A number of cavalry, under the command of Mr Clarke, then rode up to Delhi Gate, on the outskirts of the old city, and dispersed another mob in Landa Bazaar.[15]

Despite the usual claims that the actions of the police on 10 April were unjustified and aggressive, it seems that, once again, they were perfectly reasonable. The idea that the authorities should have allowed the crowds to either reach the civil lines or Government House is unconvincing. The crowds consisted mostly of youths – probably students[16] – who seem to have been unarmed, but they were clearly hostile and aggressive. Some evidence suggests that the crowds outside Lahori Gate also contained many Muslim workers and artisans; apparently tougher and more difficult to control than the Hindu middle classes.[17] The authorities showed a great deal of patience on 10 April and contrary to the opinion of the Congress Inquiry, took numerous 'intermediate stages' before firing. Aided by several local pleaders, including Ram Bhaj Dutt, the police tried to get the crowds to disperse before resorting to lethal force. Not only did some youths in the crowd try and steal rifles from the hands of police officers – an extremely serious offence – but (as at Delhi) they were also throwing barrages of stones and brickbats. Broadway, the Senior Superintendent of Police, complained that:

> For about three-quarters of an hour we remained there being stoned from in front and from the roofs to our left and right front, being occasionally pushed back a few yards and again pushing forward. We were all hit with brick bats, etc., including the Cavalry Officer. I was hit five or six times – once rather severely on my right shoulder blade, apparently by a brick from one of the house tops. My left hand and thigh were also cut – people on some low roofs to our left front in particular were so troublesome that two or three rounds of buck-shot were fired in their direction which eased the situation.

The problem was, as Mr Fyson would later write, 'It was difficult to distinguish what they were shouting or to ascertain their object.' It was also, he added, 'the third day on which illegal processions had taken place and there was no saying when the temper of the mob would change or what effect of their reaching Government House would be'.[18]

The thought that crowds of angry, violent protestors, several thousand strong, could gain access to the seat of provincial power was the stuff of nightmares, particularly given the grave news that was entering the city from Amritsar. For O'Dwyer, bloodshed had already occurred at Amritsar and he was under no illusion that it was going to happen again. It was, therefore, essential that British lives were protected and any mobs dispersed as soon as possible. Indeed, there was the whiff of panic about the Lieutenant-Governor on 10 April. He had called for the deployment of troops in Lahore since 2 p.m., but did not hear anything until 6.30 that evening and he went through 'some hours of the most terrible suspense', pacing up and down his office, snapping at his attendants. By this time he was feeling increasingly uneasy: 'From my verandah,' he wrote, 'I could hear the ominous cries, $1^1/_2$ miles off, and there was only a small body of armed police to block their way.'[19]

☙

The firings and the arrival of British cavalry that evening may have dispersed the mobs and secured the safety of Government House, but as the day drew to a close British authority had collapsed in many parts of the city. Owing to the disturbed situation all the police stations within the old city were abandoned and their officers withdrawn to safer locations. This may have helped to calm the situation, but, as at Amritsar, such a withdrawal meant that British forces were immediately without good intelligence on what was going on inside the city walls.[20] Ravinder Kumar argues that the firings 'dramatically transformed the political climate of Lahore' and 'undermined the control which the local administration exercised over the crowded bazaars and *mohallas*' and he seems to be correct.[21] In the old walled city, the shops remained closed the following day; the narrow streets brimming with 'intense resentment ... and a persistent clamour for the return of the dead bodies and the release of the wounded'.[22]

O'Dwyer held a meeting with representatives of the Punjabi 'martial classes' at Government House the following morning. He believed that this was a 'critical moment' that allowed him an opportunity of 'seeing how men are tested by a crisis'. Although one member suggested opening negotiations with the leaders of the mob, O'Dwyer recorded – perhaps with some pride – that the rest were 'of one opinion', namely that only 'prompt and drastic action by Government would avert a serious rising'. O'Dwyer told them that he would willingly accept any co-operation and help they could provide, but he would not negotiate with any mob leaders and government was, in any case, quite ready to restore the situation on its own if necessary.[23] Despite O'Dwyer's confident tone, the British authorities could do little on 11 April. Groups of people armed with *lathis* forced the closure of the booking office at the Golden Temple that morning and an extremely large and noisy crowd gathered outside the fort, home to a small and isolated British garrison. Lieutenant-Colonel W.F. North, the officer in charge, watched as the crowd – several thousand strong – tried to pull down the railings. Not only were the crowd armed with *lathis* and 'bamboos with iron axes fixed on top', they were also shouting abuse at the garrison: 'Let us kill the white pigs' was one expression he remembered. Fortunately the defences prevented the crowds from getting inside the fort.[24]

There were two areas of major concern for the authorities in Lahore. The first was the railway workshops at Moghalpura, a suburb on the northern out-skirts of the city, which employed over 12,000 people by 1918.[25] It was feared that the workers were either unsteady in their loyalty and could launch strike action or that they would become a target for the mobs. Although Moghalpura and its surrounding stations did not witness strike action during this period, there were persistent attempts to interfere with their work. Sikh students stood outside the station distributing passive-resistance leaflets and at times up to 30 per cent of the railway workers were absent without leave.[26] The second was the formation of a *danda fauj* (a 'rebel' or 'bludgeon army') on 11 April. That had been organised by a man called Chanan Din who recruited people, gave them *lathis* and marched them around the city declaring his loyalty to the Amir of Afghanistan and the Kaiser of Germany.[27] Despite its mock-military appearance (with their sticks slung over one shoulder), the *danda fauj* was not a trained, rebel army on the lines of the *sepoys* who had risen in 1857. Nevertheless, it should not be just dismissed. The *danda fauj* was perhaps the most open manifestation of rebellion to be seen in the entire Punjab disorders; a clear example of how unrest and ill feeling had turned into open resistance, and it does not take a great deal of imagination to see that in the narrow, claustrophobic streets of Lahore, large numbers of young men armed with *lathis* could have been a sizeable threat to any columns the British sent in.

That day a large meeting was held in Badshahi Mosque in the centre of the old town, a huge seventeenth-century Mughal building made of red sandstone. It was then one of the biggest in India and beneath three great white marble domes, it could hold over 50,000 worshippers. On 11 April there was an extremely large gathering in the mosque, perhaps numbering around 35,000 people, and it was remarkable for the unprecedented spectacle of huge crowds of both Hindus and Muslims entering the mosque and drinking water from the same glasses. Inside the doors a large banner had been draped across the walls with a Persian motto written upon it: 'The King who practices tyranny cuts his own root underneath.' At 1.30 p.m. the meeting began. According to a CID report, several people spoke during the afternoon, including a Muslim, Khalifa Shujjadin, who lectured on Hindu-Muslim unity and explained his discussions with the Deputy Commissioner, namely that he had been asked to restore peace to the city. He then read a message from Gandhi, imploring the people to observe his instructions and not to create disorder. Ram Bhaj Dutt spoke next, decrying the firings of the previous days as 'folly' and 'cruelty', and stating that whatever would happen was in the hands of God. Dutt then took questions from the audience, about whether passive resistance and the *hartal* should continue, whether the shops should open or if they should follow Gandhi's instructions. Because he could not come to a decision, Dutt suggested that a committee should be formed to decide upon these matters.[28]

This committee – the so-called People's Committee – was formed that afternoon. Ten representatives were put forward, including Lala Harkishen Lal, Duni Chand and Gokal Chand Narang. The committee met twice that day and after discussions with leading shopkeepers and others, it was decided that four conditions would have to be fulfilled before peace could be restored to the city and the *hartal* called off.

1. Withdrawal of the military from the city, including the Circular Road.
2. Dead and wounded to be made over to their relatives, except those who wanted to remain in the hospital.
3. All persons arrested to be released on their furnishing adequate bails, if necessary.
4. To prevent recurrence, there should be an advisory committee to advise Government and to maintain order.[29]

With that the meeting broke up and thousands of people streamed out of the mosque into the surrounding streets. Feelings were running high that afternoon and for those still brimming with anger, there was little else to do but form a procession and make as much noise as possible, shouting slogans for those killed at Delhi and Amritsar. The *danda fauj* were out in force, marching up and down the streets brandishing their *lathis* and taking out their frustration on any pictures of the British royal family that they could find. On their way to one of the bazaars, pictures of King George V were torn down from one house and the sign advertising the services of a contractor, Fakir Chand, on which the king and queen were portrayed, was pulled down and kicked to the cries of '*Hai hai George mar gaya.*'[30]

For the next three days the People's Committee was the 'sole repository of power in Lahore', meeting daily to review the situation, discussing the progress of *satyagraha* and negotiating with the local administration over the termination of the *hartal*.[31] Because Lahore contained a relatively large number of the politically aware classes, from barristers to students, and because none had (as yet) been arrested, it was not surprising that the leading citizens of the city came together and formed a committee to come up with a unified set of demands. As perhaps was to be expected, the response from the authorities, chiefly O'Dwyer, was not encouraging. For Sir Michael, the very existence of a 'People's Committee', let alone the four conditions that had been laid down, was arrogant, insulting and dangerous. 'I need hardly say,' he wrote in his memoirs, 'I refused to consider these terms. I was not prepared to abdicate to rebels.'[32] O'Dwyer was going to take the city back.

☙

On 12 April Lieutenant-Colonel Frank Johnson was given command of a body of 800 soldiers and police officers and, as he put it, 'told to go into the city and re-establish police and military control there'. Johnson entered at about 9.30 a.m. and left four hours later. He was clearly worried about what could happen when his troops entered the old city, which he regarded as the 'centre' of the disturbances. He would later tell Lord Hunter that 'I was very glad that I had over 800 [men] with me when I went.' He had made a number of rather novel and imaginative arrangements for aerial support. After halting at the entrance to the old city, Johnson told the leaders of a crowd that if a bomb was thrown at his men or if a shot was fired, then he would be forced to call for air support, which would 'clear the route' for the column. Before his troops went in, two aeroplanes would fly as low as they could and watch for a 'Very' flare that Johnson would fire. If Johnson fired *two* flares this would be the signal that something had gone wrong and that bombs should be dropped 200 yards ahead of his column. Although it is doubtful whether this scheme would have been very effective – given the difficulty of dropping bombs accurately from the aircraft then available – Johnson evidently felt that the situation was serious enough to warrant such extreme measures.[33]

Johnson's column managed to wind its way through the streets without trouble until it reached Hira Mandi, an open square next to Badshahi Mosque. It arrived just as a meeting was being held inside. The official version of events recorded by the Hunter Inquiry states that after a magistrate was sent into the mosque to warn the people that they must leave, crowds gradually began to pour outside. This crowd continued to increase in size, and fearing that it was not going to leave, Mr Fyson (who was alongside Johnson) gave a warning to the crowd to disperse. This was answered with jeers and a fusillade of stones. Fyson then told his police officers that they could engage the crowd. Eight rounds of buckshot were fired, one man was killed and another 28 were wounded.[34]

Indian accounts of what happened at Hira Mandi differ significantly from the official version. A number of those interviewed by the Congress Report stressed both the innocence of the crowds and that there was no need to fire. Sardar Diwan Singh, the Sub-Editor of the *Leader*, stated that people could not leave Hira Mandi because the crowds were so thick, that 'no opposition was offered by the people' and that there were no stones thrown. Similar accounts were recorded by Lala Madan Gopal (a resident); Sardar Sardul Singh Caveeshar (a Sikh journalist for the *New Herald*); and Lala Bankey Dyal (a press reporter for the *Jhang Sial*).[35] In reality, the clash at Hira Mandi was the result of confusion and panic and was not part of a determined attempt to terrorise the population (as some accounts allege). Johnson and Fyson had been ordered to show the people that the Government was still in control and to make sure that they left in good order. The people, coming out of the meeting after being told that it was unlikely any British troops would be in the city, were immediately faced with soldiers, including a group of cavalry, which naturally alarmed them. Several British biplanes, swooping low overhead, only added to the sense of panic and fear rippling through the crowd. Because the crowds were so large and leaderless, it seems that both sides, British and Indian, felt that they were being surrounded. Those British officers present recorded a constant movement of people around the sides of Hira Mandi, perhaps only trying to leave, but which increased their sense of danger.[36] In such a delicate situation it could only take a few stones or a strong movement forward by either side to spark off a violent response.

The brief firing at Hira Mandi dispersed the crowd, which fled in the nearby streets. Unfortunately, as the column made their way out of their city, Johnson's rearguard were ambushed by large numbers of people, brandishing *lathis* and hurling stones, while bricks were being thrown from the roofs of nearby houses. This was exactly what Johnson had feared. He galloped back and despite being hit by a brick thrown from a four-storey window, ordered the police to fire a few rounds, which they did, promptly restoring the situation. Johnson established picquets at three places in the city, garrisoned by groups of British and Indian troops and police, and issued orders that no parties were to move about in groups of less than 200.[37] The attempt to regain control of the city on 12 April may not have gone entirely to plan, but the height of the disorders in Lahore had now passed. The following day the Deputy Commissioner declared the city to be under the Seditious Meetings Act, where all gatherings of more than ten people would be deemed unlawful. On 14 April, the principal leaders of the *satyagraha* movement in Lahore, including Ram Bhaj Dutt, Lal Harkishen Lal and Duni Chand, were arrested. After these orders had been served, the unrest in the city rapidly collapsed.[38] The days of the 'People's Committee' were over.

CHAPTER 10

A 'Serious Rising' at Kasur

They were shouting saying that the English Raj had come to an end as 'Gandhi ki jai, Kitchlew ki jai' *and* 'Satyapal ki jai'.

Bawa Kharak Singh[1]

On 12 April, Lieutenant H. Munro of 2/17th Infantry was reading a newspaper when the train in which he was travelling – the nine o'clock from Ferozepore – stopped unexpectedly about 500 yards (457 metres) from the station at Kasur, a town 34 miles (55 kilometres) southeast of Lahore.[2] Several moments later one of Munro's fellow passengers, a captain in the Royal Engineers called Limby, drew his attention to the flight of Indian passengers from the train, many of whom were running up and down the bank on the right side of the track, apparently in a state of some excitement.[3] They then noticed that another passenger, Mr Sherbourn, had also got off. Aware of the disturbances that had occurred across the Punjab in recent days, Munro and Limby disembarked to see what was going on. Once he had jumped out, Munro looked towards the station and saw a large crowd of Indians carrying 'flags of different descriptions', 'pieces of cloth' and *lathis*. Ominously, parts of the station were also on fire. It did not take long before Munro was spotted. As soon as members of the crowd saw him, they began shouting '*Afsar Sahib hai, mar do, mar do*' ('Here is an officer, kill him, kill him'). Although Munro was not too alarmed at first, he re-entered the carriage and consulted with the remaining Europeans about what they should do.

It was agreed that they must get out of the train until it could be restarted. With the help of their fellow passengers, including a travelling inspector of accounts (Mr Khair-ud-Din), the Sherbourns left the train and took shelter in a small gateman's hut on the side of the track next to a level crossing.[4] Both Munro and Limby then tried to restart the train. They ran along the tracks up to the engine and clambered into the driver's carriage. Unfortunately, the guard and driver either could not or would not help them and by this time they had been overtaken by the mob. After fighting, being pelted with brickbats and hit with *lathis*, Limby and Munro managed to run off and escape from the crowd, finding shelter in a nearby Sikh village. Meanwhile, the rest of the mob closed around the gatekeeper's hut and tried to get in. The door and windows were smashed and two corporals of 1/4th Queens (Battson and Gringham), who had been guarding the door, were dragged off and beaten.[5] Mr Khair-ud-Din protested with the crowd, appealing to them 'that I had my purdahwalla family inside and not to disturb us', and he was assisted by a local pleader, Mr Ghulam Mohi-ud-Din. Sherbourn recalled that as soon as this pleader arrived and spoke to the mob 'they quietened down immediately' and began to disperse. The Sherbourns finally emerged out of the gatekeeper's hut several hours later, when they were escorted to a nearby village and then onto the bungalow of the District Superintendent of Police.

The Sherbourns were evidently fortunate to survive the attack on the Ferozepore train, but the two other British warrant officers, Conductor Selby and Sergeant Mallett, who had remained in the carriage, were not so fortunate. It is not clear why they stayed with the train when the rest of their passengers had deserted it, but it seems that both were armed with revolvers and had some inkling that something would happen.[6] A short while after the mob had attacked the gatekeeper's hut, the train finally moved off and arrived at the station. At this point Selby and Mallett got out onto the platform, where they were confronted by elements of the mob that were still milling around. They were jeered at and had stones thrown at them. Evidently fearing for their lives, Selby and Mallett fired several rounds from their revolvers, at which point the mob rushed towards them and attacked them.[7] Selby was killed soon after and Mallet, severely injured, died later in hospital. Although it has been suggested that by firing the two officers had provoked the crowd into attacking them, the Hunter Report concluded, probably correctly, that they were justified in doing so because anti-European violence had already taken place.[8]

Following the attack on the two warrant officers, elements of the mob made their way across the town, looted and set fire to the main Kasur Post Office. The mob then launched a full-scale assault on the two main government buildings in the town, the *tahsil* (revenue office) and the Munsif's Court, the latter of which was set on fire. According to a municipal commissioner who was present that morning, the crowd shouted: 'Let us loot the treasury and release the prisoners.'[9] A police garrison was stationed at the *tahsil* and fearing that the mob was trying to break down the doors and get inside, they fired several shots into the air. This did not have any noticeable effect upon the crowd, which it was later estimated was approximately 1,500 to 2,000 strong. At this point Mr Mitter, the Sub-Divisional Officer, and the Deputy Superintendent of Police arrived. Upon realising the seriousness of the situation, fire was ordered against the crowd. Fifty-seven rounds were fired, killing four men and causing an unknown number of wounded. After this firing the mob gradually dispersed. The disorder at Kasur was over.

೪

What had caused the violence on 12 April? Reports were inconsistent. According to Sir Michael O'Dwyer, Kasur witnessed a 'serious rising' that 'followed the example' of the mobs in Lahore and Amritsar.[10] Mr Marsden, the Sub-Divisional Officer, was certain that the rioting and murders were caused by four factors: the rumours that were circulating, many of them false, about the provisions of the Rowlatt Act; the role played by local leaders in 'stimulating the excitement of the people'; fears of a trade boycott if Kasur did not 'fall into line' over the *hartal*; and the *hartals* of 11 and 12 April in the town.[11] Furthermore, he maintained that the nature of army recruitment and any alleged provocation by the Punjab Government had no effect on the outbreak of the disorders. On the contrary, Lala Mohan Lal Seth, a municipal commissioner in the town, blamed high prices, the overzealous collection of war loans, friction over recruitment, the 'unsympathetic attitude' of Sir Michael O'Dwyer, the provisions of the Rowlatt Act and the 'forced return' of Mahatma Gandhi to Bombay. In his testimony before the Hunter Inquiry, he also stated that the civil authorities were 'really mistaken in thinking there was a general rising of the town'. He noted that by 2 p.m. on 12 April 'it was just nothing', with people sitting in their homes or shops.[12]

As with many of the crowds that gathered in the Punjab during April 1919, descriptions of them often vary greatly and seem to depend, to a significant degree, on the nationality and ideological standpoint of the witness. Nevertheless, some consensus did emerge from personal accounts. According to one witness, 'The rioters were of all castes, led by discontented persons, pleaders and school boys', and were composed of 'butchers, leather and cotton and factory hands and menials', or as he scornfully put it, 'the very scum of the City'.[13] Although the British would later insist that the small number of pleaders and other educated men in Kasur played a key role in leading the mob, this does not seem to have been very likely. Most of those who saw the mobs claimed that no 'respectable' people were present.[14] Unlike Amritsar and Lahore, Kasur had almost no political life or activity before April 1919, and it was considerably smaller (with a population of just over only 31,000).[15] It had not taken part in the *hartal* on 6 April and feelings about this within the educated community were not encouraging. Few of the local pleaders were in favour of it. There seems to have been fears about possible punitive action from the Punjab Government, and it was only when they began to receive taunts from neighbouring towns about their lack of activity, and when some traders were given their *hundis* (promissory notes) back, that interest in the *hartal* revived.[16] News of the outbreak of violence at Amritsar reached Kasur on the evening of 10 April, apparently from traders who worked there, and caused a great deal of excitement.[17] The news of the return of Mahatma Gandhi to Bombay also created much anger. On the morning of 11 April a procession led by a local shopkeeper, Nadir Shah, went through the streets insisting upon the closure of all shops and businesses.

The *hartal* continued on the following day (12 April) when a crowd of up to 700 people gathered and marched through the streets.[18] The crowds were boosted by the arrival of a considerable number of people from nearby villages, apparently eager for loot. That morning most of the local pleaders were assembled in their houses, deliberating how they could stop the *hartal*, when they heard news that 'boys are committing mischief at the railway station'. At the forefront of this crowd were a group of students led by Kamal Din who were carrying a *charpoy* (bedstead) on which a black flag had been laid, supposedly representing the death of liberty. The crowds went through the streets, closing any businesses as they went, before arriving at the railway station at 9.45 a.m. They had apparently chosen the railway station because they wanted the passengers to see them.[19] The crowd at this point seem to have been peaceful, but after a number of speeches had been delivered, one by Nadir Shah and the other by Kamal Din, the crowd became violent. Barely 15 minutes later, the station was a scene of chaos. Around 2,000 people had rushed into the building, totally overwhelming the railway staff. The ticket office and waiting rooms were vandalised, the telegraph equipment was destroyed and the lamproom had been looted and set on fire. A wagon of some kind had been placed on the middle platform, laced with oil and set alight, sending thick acrid black smoke into the sky.[20] It was at this point when three trains reached the signals at the outer edges of the junction, from Lahore, Patti and Ferozepore, the latter containing a small group of British passengers, including Munro and the Sherbourns.

From British accounts of this incident, there is constant suspicion that the railway officials were in league with the mob; a number of witnesses criticising the attitude of the railway officials and the failure to reverse the Ferozepore train out of danger.[21] Mr Kehar Singh, the Assistant Stationmaster, denied that the railway officials – about 30 in all – were in league with the mob. When he arrived at the station at about 10 a.m., he found that his staff were desperately trying to disperse the mob and extinguish the fires. Nevertheless, some of them do seem to have become involved in the riot. Mr Raynor complained that the staff at Kasur were 'most inactive' and did not send a wire to Ferozepore alerting the authorities to the disorder until it was too late and the wires had been cut. He also complained that they showed 'a very sullen attitude towards identifying people' in the subsequent search for the offenders. Because the permanent stationmaster was on leave, the person in charge that morning was an assistant called Chuni Lal. According to Mr Khair-ud-Din (who was endeavouring to save the Sherbourns from the attentions of the mob), the leader of one of the groups who tried to enter the gatekeeper's hut was Chuni Lal. Before the Hunter Committee, Khair-ud-Din said that:

> I had some talk with him. I told him that this was no good. I gave him a small lecture and advised that he should not do so and so on, and he accepted it at once. After that he pleaded on my behalf and assisted me.[22]

Although it seems that Chuni Lal quickly forgot his allegiance to the mob and made efforts to protect them, he was curiously aggressive towards Mr Sherbourn, telling Khair-ud-Din to 'Damn Sherbourn and damn the English Government.' Shortly afterwards, Mr Ghulam Mohi-ud-Din arrived and helped to disperse the last of those still milling around the gatekeeper's hut.

It will probably never be known for certain whether any railway officials were in direct collusion with the mob that attacked Kasur station, but one is left with the suspicion that in the heat of the moment, a number of them either joined the mob or simply melted away. Four railway staff were later arrested, including Chuni Lal, and one (Bhagat Ram) was flogged. The mob that stormed through Kasur station on 12 April seems to have been of a slightly different consistency to others that formed in the Punjab during this period. The lack of political activity within the town and the apparent reluctance of many of the pleader class to wholeheartedly support a *hartal* perhaps explains why students were so prominent in the disturbances. Given the large number of traders resident in Kasur, the threat of a trading boycott from the rest of the Punjab was a serious concern, especially given the high prices and economic dislocation that India was currently undergoing. A large gathering on 12 April was, therefore, seen as an opportunity to make up for what a municipal commissioner called 'their past omission' in missing the *hartal* on 6 April.[23] Exactly when and how, and under what stimulus, the crowd turned violent at the station is unclear; it may have been then that determined looters took matters into their own hands.

After the events at Amritsar on 10 April, the attack on the Ferozepore train at Kasur was the worst incident of anti-European violence that was seen during the Punjab disorders of 1919. When news filtered to Ferozepore and Lahore, the civil authorities were deeply alarmed and sent a battalion of Sikh troops, commanded by Lieutenant-Colonel H. McRae, to restore the situation. McRae's troops loaded onto a special train and left Ferozepore just after 2 p.m., unsure of what they would find when they arrived. They proceeded carefully and were met by a small delegation of local civilians and police who told them what had happened. Kasur was relatively quiet by this time, the fury that had inspired the morning's violence quickly subsiding after the firing at the *tahsil*. McRae decided to drive through the town to see for himself. He found the situation to be tense although not violent. 'All the shops were closed,' he remembered, 'and the inhabitants were standing in silent groups at every corner and crowded the roof tops and windows ... They appeared sullen and as if they were afraid of reprisals.'[24]

ల∕ు

Back in Lahore, Sir Michael O'Dwyer was becoming increasingly concerned at the spread of disorder across the province. During the evening of 12 April, another stifling evening of worry and anxiety, news arrived in Lahore that indicated that violence was now spreading along the railway lines, first at Amritsar and then onto Kasur and elsewhere. The station at Bhagtanwala, south of the Golden Temple, was burnt, at Taran Taran a Government Treasury was attacked, and a goods train was derailed between the nearby villages of Chheharta and Khasa. As well as targeting the stations, no less threatening for the authorities was the damage that was being caused to telegraph wires. Wires were being cut at regular intervals all over the province, particularly around Amritsar, which played havoc with British communications.[25] By the following morning, 13 April, O'Dwyer had decided that further action must now be taken to restore law and order. He consulted with Major-General Beynon and with Chief Justice, Sir Henry Rattigan, about what could be done and together they came to the conclusion that the Government of India must act. At three o'clock that afternoon he sent a despatch off to Delhi listing the attacks on the communication and transport infrastructure and stating that 'open rebellion' now existed in parts of the province, particularly Lahore and Amritsar. Owing to the damage to the telegraphic service it was not received until the following day and it took another 24 hours for a decision to be made. On 15 April the Government of India agreed with O'Dwyer's findings and authorised the necessary measures.[26]

At three o'clock on the morning of 14 April, while Lahore was still waiting for the Government to declare martial law, two British officials woke
Sir Michael and handed him a despatch from Amritsar. It was written by
the Deputy Commissioner, Miles Irving, and told him that Dyer had fired
upon the crowd in the city with heavy casualties. This was the firing at the
Jallianwala Bagh, which had happened about ten hours earlier. Without offering an opinion on what had happened and before receiving the military
report, O'Dwyer summarised the situation as then known and sent off another despatch.

> At Amritsar yesterday Brigadier-General Dyer and Deputy-Commissioner read
> proclamation in city forbidding all public meetings. Prohibition proclaimed
> by beat of drum and read and explained at several places in city. In spite of
> this, meeting attended by six thousand was held at 4.30 contrary to Deputy
> Commissioner's expectation. Troops present under command of General Dyer
> fired, killing about two hundred. Deputy-Commissioner not present. Military
> report not yet received.

Later that day Dyer's superior, Beynon, spoke with the Lieutenant-Governor
and gave him more details on what had occurred. He told O'Dwyer that he
believed Dyer's actions had ended the rebellion and that he was conveying
his approval. Furthermore, he asked whether he could add the Lieutenant-
Governor's support. O'Dwyer hesitated at this point because the actions concerned were military ones, but he did eventually agree to endorse Beynon's
approval.[27]

Indian nationalists would always remember O'Dwyer's support for Dyer
in 1919 and it would later emerge as one of the reasons behind the assassination of the former Lieutenant-Governor 21 years later.[28] But given the
situation at the time, his approval of the shooting at the Jallianwala Bagh
was reasonable. From the information that Beynon had provided, Dyer had
fired because he realised that his force 'was small and to hesitate might induce attack'. This was an acceptable legal justification and was in line with
the established British tradition of the use of 'minimum force' during such
disturbances. In any case, it was widely accepted that the firing had put down
the rebellion in the Punjab. For Miles Irving, the effect of the firing at the
Jallianwala Bagh on 13 April was 'electric'. He reported,

> The news ended all danger of further disturbance in the district. It was taken
> far and wide as an assurance that the hand of Government was not, as it was
> thought, paralysed and all who were waiting on events hasted to declare for
> constitutional authority.

Irving was far from alone in regarding the controversial actions at the Jallianwala Bagh as bringing to an end the most serious uprising in India since 1857. When Mr A.J.W. Kitchin, Commissioner of the Lahore Division, was told about the shooting on the morning of the following day, he was satisfied that 'the trouble was over' and for William Beynon, the Jallianwala Bagh incident 'crushed the rebellion at its heart'.[29]

The news of the shooting at Amritsar took some time to spread across the province, during which time the violence and vandalism continued. Contrary to the commonly held perception, the day that violence broke out (10 April) was not the peak of the disorders. Arguably the worst day was 14 April, what Sir Michael O'Dwyer called the 'high-water mark of the rebellion'.[30] By this point attacks on British communications had reached alarming proportions, with 12 attacks on the telegraph grid being recorded, three times more than the previous day.[31] Serious riots and disorders took place at a variety of other locations, including Gujranwala, Lyallpur, Sheikhupura and Gujrat. In Delhi, scene of a violent clash with police on 30 March, a CID officer was assaulted at a protest meeting in one of the city's parks and police began to notice more and more *lathis* spreading through the city; an alarming portent of hostility towards the authorities. It has been argued that General Dyer's action at the Jallianwala Bagh was one of the major *causes* of the violence that subsequently occurred in the Punjab, particularly its rural areas. Nigel Collett writes that from a record of events, including the attacks on communications after 13 April, 'it is quite clear that the violence was a reaction to events in Amritsar, and that far from being "the Saviour of the Punjab", Dyer's action at the Jallianwala Bagh was a major cause of the danger it was in'.[32]

For critics of Dyer the uncomfortable truth that his actions may have restored a semblance of order to the Punjab has always been resisted, yet there are good grounds for believing that this was actually the case. Collett's argument is based on simple chronology: that because the events in question occurred *after* 13 April, then they must have been *caused* by the shooting at the Jallianwala Bagh. But it was not so straightforward. In the days after 13 April a potent mix of half-truths and rumours were in circulation across the Punjab, which did much to unsettle previously quiet districts: that Gandhi had been arrested; that police had fired on crowds in Delhi and Lahore; that there had been riots in Amritsar; that the Golden Temple had been bombed; that Sikh girls had been outraged; that a regiment of the Indian Army had mutinied; that a railway strike was spreading, and so on.[33] The instances of violence and disorder in a number of outlying regions, such as Gujranwala and Lyallpur, were caused by a complex mix of factors and were not necessarily a reaction to Dyer's shooting at the Jallianwala Bagh. In any case, news of this event did not reach many outlying areas of the Punjab until several days later; the extensive damage to the communication and transport infrastructure hampering the spread of word across the province. Sir Michael O'Dwyer noted that after 18 April, 'by which time the news had penetrated over the Province, it was not necessary to fire another shot'.[34] Once news of Dyer's actions became widely known, the disturbances in the Punjab were effectively over, but until then the situation would remain unsettled. Indeed, for those officers in the more outlying districts their problems were only just beginning.

CHAPTER 11

The 'High-Water Mark'

We knew there were Europeans there and we did not know what had happened to them. We were very anxious about all the outlying Europeans at that time.

Major-General Sir William Beynon[1]

At 12.15 p.m. on 14 April, Captain A. Harwood of 1/Durham Light Infantry was ushered into the office of the commander of 2nd (Rawalpindi) Division, Major-General Sir Charles Dobell. He was told that situation in Gujranwala, a town of around 30,000 inhabitants 140 miles (225 kilometres) to the south, was dangerous and that the European community there was in danger. He was to go there at once and restore order. Harwood marched with a detachment of 25 men to the railway station and caught the *Bombay Mail* south. They stopped at Wazirabad to pick up an extra 50 men of the South Lancashire Regiment and then continued onto Gujranwala. At the small station at Rahwali they were told that they could go no further for the moment because the line had been cut. Proceeding later on with some railway engineers, they continued on their journey, which as Harwood complained, was 'dead slow' and took all afternoon. Harwood's party finally arrived at Gujranwala at 8.30 that evening. He was stunned by what he found. He recorded that

> everything was blazing, the station, the goods yard, post office and church. That was as far as I could see at that time. They were absolutely gutted; it was quite impossible to save them as they had been burning for a number of hours.

Violent unrest had now spread out of the main cities of the Punjab.

The disorders in the more outlying districts of the Punjab, particularly in and around the town of Gujranwala, may not have been the most violent or the most destructive of those that occurred in April 1919, but they did cause acute anxiety to the British authorities in Lahore. The appearance of angry crowds outside the railway station on the morning of 14 April and the widespread damage that was caused to the town, where a number of buildings, including the post office, railway station and *tahsil* were set on fire, showed that the disturbances were spreading and had the potential to pull British resources even thinner than they already were. When Sir Michael O'Dwyer was informed of the destruction, he immediately contacted the military commander at Rawalpindi and asked what they could do. Unfortunately, little help could be sent at that moment because there was no one available; testimony to the crippling shortage of British troops in this part of India. O'Dwyer wrote,

> He informed me that the Pindi Division, which was about 200 miles to the north, had received information about the situation at Gujranwala that morning; he also told me he had no troops to send, and even if he had them to send, there was no means of sending them owing to the communications being cut.[2]

The first British reinforcements to arrive at Gujranwala were Harwood's party of 75 men just after eight o'clock that evening.

Harwood would have been forgiven for thinking, as he gazed at the blazing wreckage of the station and church, that the entire town had been razed and the small European community (barely 15 people plus a small group of American missionaries) massacred, but this had not occurred. The overstretched police forces had fired on large crowds several times during the day and Royal Air Force biplanes had flown overhead, bombing and machine-gunning gatherings from the air, but there were no serious European casualties. The most unfortunate aspect of the disorders in Gujranwala was, as Harwood had found, the attack on British communications. Walking back along the railway line from the station he found that 'Practically all the wires along the railway right in front of the native city were cut, the wires were flat on the ground and absolutely destroyed.' In his report to the Hunter Committee, Mr J.M. Coode (Director of Telegraph Engineering, Northern Circle) stated that on 14 April 20 wires were cut in Gujranwala and that telegraphic instruments were destroyed at the station and the telegraph office. The line was damaged for two and a half miles (four kilometres) and 450 insulators were smashed.[3]

ꙮ

What had caused the violence at Gujranwala? When asked about the origins of the disturbances by the Hunter Committee, a number of witnesses stated that there were three main factors: anger at the Rowlatt Bills (although much of this seems to have been based on fabrications and rumours); the arrest of

1. Conference of Governors and Heads of Provinces, Delhi, 21-26 January 1918. Lord Chelmsford (with walking stick) and Edwin Montagu (with pith helmet) are seated next to each other on the front row. Sir Michael O'Dwyer is seated second from left

2. Sir Michael O'Dwyer, photographed by Walter Stoneman, 1920

3. Gandhi in the late-1920s

4. Brigadier-General Dyer

5. Anarkali and Lohari Gate, Lahore

6. Narrow street inside the city walls, Ahmedabad

7. National Bank, Amritsar

8. Alliance Bank, the room where
Mr Thompson was murdered

9. Graves of Europeans murdered on
10 April 1919 in Amritsar Cantonment
Cemetery, Putligarh

10. Musafi, Kasur

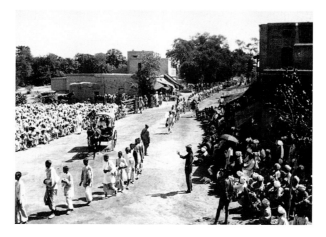

11. View of detainees, Kasur

12. Railway station, Gujranwala

13. Courts, Gujranwala

14. Narrow entrance to Jallianwala Bagh (today)   **15.** Entrance to Jallianwala Bagh, 1919

16. Location of firing, Jallianwala Bagh

17. Panorama of Jallianwala Bagh

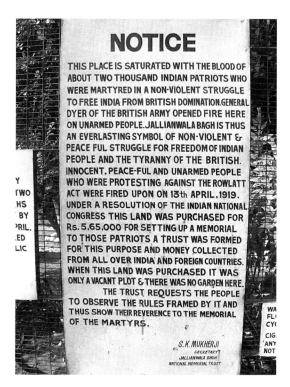

18. Notice at entrance to Jallianwala Bagh

19. Framed bullet hole, Jallianwala Bagh

20. Memorial, Jallianwala Bagh

Mahatma Gandhi at Palwal on 9 April; and the news of unrest at Amritsar and Lahore.[4] Lieutenant-Colonel A.J. O'Brien, the Deputy Commissioner, believed that many of the causes lay elsewhere because the people of Gujranwala had 'no economic causes' for unrest and few recruiting concerns because the vast majority of wartime recruits came from the rural areas.[5] Contrary to the findings of Nigel Collett, news of the firing at the Jallianwala Bagh was *not* a contributing factor in the disturbances on 14 April. There had been a *hartal* in Gujranwala on 6 April, but the following six days were quiet and there was no local desire to hold another.[6] It was only when news arrived on 12 April of the riots at Amritsar and Lahore that a meeting of the District Congress Committee took place, during which there was a 'long discussion' over the advisability of taking action. Opinion was divided on whether to stage another *hartal*.[7] Local traders complained that they would lose profits if their businesses were to close on 13 and 14 April, the days of the *Baisakhi* festival.[8] However, at another meeting the following day it was finally decided that it would go ahead, now on 14 April.

The confusion within the District Congress Committee about whether to stage a *hartal* or not on 14 or 15 April was not appreciated by Mr J.B. Nevill, the Assistant Superintendent of Police. He complained that this last-minute change was a deliberate attempt to foil their arrangements. He told Lord Hunter,

> It was well known that we have very few police. It was also on that day that lots of local people had gone to attend a durbar held by the Lieutenant-Governor at Lahore. We were all told that this was deliberately done by the leaders.[9]

Nevill and his men were certainly placed in a difficult situation, but the change of date was less about undermining the response of the authorities to civil disobedience, and more to do with disagreements at the local level, with different leaders wanting different things, and being influenced by a variety of rumours that were moving through the Punjab. Manohar Lal, a local pleader and member of the District Congress Committee, argued that there was no conspiracy to wage war against the King-Emperor and even as late as the evening of 13 April, the likelihood of a *hartal* on the following day was 'doubtful', with 'no definite programme' and no place for a proposed meeting of the committee.[10]

Crowds began to form at Gujranwala much earlier in the day than previously seen in the Punjab. By 8 a.m. large numbers of people were moving through the city, many of whom were going around making sure shops were shut and shouting against the Rowlatt Bills. As at Delhi and Kasur, the railway station was to be the scene of confrontation between crowds and the authorities. Many people had gone to the station to catch the train to Wazirabad, a traditional destination for those going to celebrate the *Baisakhi* festival. The train arrived at 9.30 a.m. and was extremely crowded. It was at this moment that sinister rumours passed through the crowds, both around the station and in the train, that a calf had been found dead on one of the railway bridges. This seems to have been the spark that set Gujranwala alight. As soon as the Deputy Superintendent of Police found out about this (shortly after 7.30 a.m.) he buried it, evidently fearing what effect news of this could have within the Hindu community with its well-known antipathy to cow killing. Although there was no evidence to suggest this, it was rumoured that the calf was killed by either the police or the CID to instigate communal violence.[11] Ironically, news of the calf did not produce a Hindu-Muslim riot, but a great swelling of anti-government feeling. An angry crowd got off the train and 'a few rotten sleepers lying by were piled up on the culvert and set on fire probably by means of a live coal taken from the Railway engine'. Another group then made their way to a further bridge, the Katchi, and also damaged it severely.

The police force at Gujranwala fired at crowds in two places that day.[12] The first clash occurred at 11 a.m. when Mr Heron, the Superintendent of Police, led a small detachment along the railway line after hearing news that a mob was trying to destroy a signal on the track going towards Lahore. When they met the crowd, Heron repeatedly asked them to disperse, but without success. The Assistant Commissioner, Ferdinand Wace, recorded his admiration at the composure of Heron who 'had to deal for several hours with a shouting and threatening crowd' and the 'foul abuse' that was directed at him. He noted that the 'front ranks of the crowd were composed almost entirely of small boys in order to deter him from employing firearms in dispersing it'.[13] Despite being threatened with murder and coming under a barrage of stones and bricks, Mr Heron refused to order his officers to fire.[14] It was only when someone rushed towards him that he acted. The police responded with gunfire, wounding two or three people.

The mob fled to the other side of the railway fencing, but did not disperse, while the police wisely retraced their steps back to the station. The situation in Gujranwala gradually deteriorated during the afternoon. The post office, next to the station, was set on fire and a mob prevented the fire engine from putting out the blaze. Other groups then made their way into the town and, as at Amritsar and Ahmedabad, attacked all those buildings with any connection to government authority. The *tahsil,* the *dak* bungalow, the church and the district court were all set on fire, the police lines were attacked and finally, the railway goods shed and an industrial school were burnt. By 2 p.m. small groups of police officers, often working independently and trying to disperse the mobs as best they could, fired at crowds whenever they were sighted. Mr Nevill, the Assistant Superintendent, was horrified at what he saw when he reached the civil lines. 'There the mob had scattered all over the place. They were burning down any building they came across ... They practically burnt everything.'[15]

Contrary to the great disagreements over which crowds gathered in Lahore and Amritsar, there is consensus about the nature of those in Gujranwala. Lala Ralya Ram Chopra, a retired inspector and governor, saw the crowds at the railway station at 11 a.m. He remembered how they were 'shouting and howling and throwing stones at the doors of the station building'.[16] A secretary of the municipal committee, Mr Iqbal Narain, went to the railway station that morning and found a crowd of about 500 people, some of whom were armed with crowbars, hammers and *lathis*. Many of these implements were used on two bridges, the Katchi and the Gurukul, which were both set on fire during the day. The damage that was caused to the two bridges was not just small-scale vandalism, but a determined attempt to interfere with British communications. At the Gurukul bridge a pile of wooden logs were heaped on the track, doused in petrol and set alight, and the Katchi bridge was so badly damaged by fire that it was unsafe to allow trains to cross.[17]

As at many places throughout the Punjab during April 1919, many of the educated men of the town, pleaders or doctors, tried to prevent violence, but without much success. A local pleader, Manohar Lal, was involved, from very early in the day, in drawing crowds away from the centre of town to large meeting grounds where they could be kept occupied with speeches and discussions. It was only when several wounded men arrived – apparently caused by the first firing ordered by Mr Heron – that, as he put it, 'utter confusion followed'. Many people, apparently worked up into an 'uncontrollable rage', left the meeting and went to the post office and railway station where they clashed with the police.[18] Several members of the District Congress Committee, including its president, Din Mahomed, and its secretary, Labh Singh, were also involved in the efforts to avert violence at the railway station. An onlooker recalled that these men 'rendered incessant and conspicuous service to the police' on 14 April, helping them to put out fires and trying the best they could to get crowds to disperse by pleading with them and, as Manohar Lal had tried, to lead groups of people away from the station.[19]

The action of the authorities at Gujranwala was reasonably restrained, particularly given the critical lack of police officers in the town. Owing to a shortage of recruits, each station was two or three men short and on 14 April the total strength of the police was only about two-thirds of full strength.[20] One of the other problems at Gujranwala was the dislocation of command at such a critical time. The Deputy Commissioner, Lieutenant-Colonel A.J. O'Brien, had been transferred to Ambala on 12 April, but was hastily sent back to Gujranwala two days later when violence broke out. His replacement, Khan Bahadur Mirza Sultan Ahmad, was not as decisive as O'Brien and he was criticised by the Hunter Committee for 'committing an error' for failing to fire upon the mobs that burnt down the post office. 'If effective measures had then been taken to disperse the mob and restore order,' the report concluded, 'the later incidents of the day might have been avoided.'[21]

℘

The most controversial aspect of the manner in which the disorders in Gujranwala were dealt with concerns the use of aircraft.[22] That afternoon three aircraft of the Royal Air Force flew to Gujranwala, dropped eight bombs on the town and machine-gunned a number of crowds in the vicinity. Nationalist accounts of this incident pray heavily upon the indiscriminate and unjustified bombing and machine-gunning of the people of Gujranwala. According to one eyewitness, 'The noise that the bombs made was like rapid firing. These aeroplanes came very close to the housetops and, it appears, threw bombs on all sides of the city.' Ilahi Bux, a carpenter, claimed that he was bombed while walking with two companions near the village of Dhulli. Bombs also fell on the Gulab Singh Khalsa Hotel. Bhai Inder Singh, the Superintendent, recalled how

> I felt a shock (like earthquake) and the yard of the hostel was enveloped in smoke. We all ran towards the *deori* (porch) and stopped there. When the smoke vanished, we came to know that a big bomb had fallen, and had made a big hole, about 5 or 6 feet in circumference and about a foot in depth, in the paved platform in front of the kitchens, where our students used to take meals, and meet for congregational prayers.[23]

The Congress Report made much capital out of this, writing that the use of aeroplanes was 'unjustified', 'thoughtless' and conducted 'in order to terrorize the people'. Furthermore, aircraft should not have been used in this manner because there was 'no danger threatening life or property'.[24] More recently, one historian has complained that 'unarmed market crowds and schoolhouses were strafed with hundreds of rounds of ammunition and then carpet bombed' by aircraft sent from Lahore.[25]

A different version of what happened was recorded by one of the pilots, Captain D.H.M. Carberry, a Flight Commander in No. 31 Squadron, who arrived above Gujranwala about 3 p.m. that day. Glancing down at the situation beneath him, Carberry noticed that the railway station was full of people and seemed to be on fire. He also noticed that a train was burning on one of the tracks. He then saw that flames were coming from the church and several houses in the civil lines. He had been given three instructions from his commanding officer. The first was that the 'native city' was not to be bombed. Second, that he was to bomb crowds only if they were in the open, and finally that he must try and disperse gatherings in the surrounding villages if they were going to or coming from Gujranwala.[26] Contrary to nationalist hyperbole, Carberry's orders reflected the British wish to avoid unnecessary civilian casualties and the concern that looters and other bands of men would come into Gujranwala from the surrounding districts. If these groups could be prevented from doing so, then there was a much greater chance that the disorders could be contained. Carberry (he was followed shortly after by two other aeroplanes) dropped eight 20-pound bombs in total on 14 April, although it seems up to half of them did not explode: three on a large crowd moving towards the town; two on a crowd near the village of Gharjakh, and finally three more in Gujranwala itself, one on Khalsa High School and Boarding House and another two near the railway goods shed.[27] The Deputy Commissioner, O'Brien, calculated that 11 people were killed and 27 wounded, although whether by police action or the aircraft is unclear.

Carberry's mission and his efforts to prevent crowds from gathering in Gujranwala were certainly not an ideal way of crowd control. As one historian has recently written, this was 'highly questionable' and undoubtedly resulted in some innocent lives being lost.[28] Nevertheless, the use of aircraft was indicative of the desperation and fear that gripped the British authorities that day and arguing over whether these actions violate the principle of 'minimum force' is perhaps to miss the point. Employing aircraft in such a manner was not something that the authorities had ever planned or wanted to do.[29] News of the disturbances at Gujranwala was received at Lahore 'rather as a shock' and the decision to send aeroplanes was not motivated by punishment or revenge. On the contrary, the Chief Secretary to the Punjab Government argued that sending aircraft to Gujranwala was the 'only possible way' of restoring the situation. It was the result of, as Sir Michael O'Dwyer put it, 'a very dangerous situation ... there were no troops there and very few police'.[30] According to O'Dwyer, on hearing of renewed disorders,

> The military authorities at once dispatched a few aeroplanes which arrived in the nick of time – about 3 p.m. – to save the Treasury building (in which the few European women and children had taken refuge) and the jail, which the rebels – having destroyed all other public buildings – were threatening.

He believed that the use of aircraft had been very effective, dispersing 'the rebellious mobs' and 'restoring the situation' until troops could arrive in strength later that night.

The use of aircraft at Gujranwala was possibly the first use of such machines during a period of civil disorder in history and it raised profound issues about the employment of aircraft in such circumstances. The Hunter Report stated that the use of aircraft had been justified, but noted the 'special problems' that arose when bombs and machine guns were used to disperse crowds and called for a careful inquiry by the Royal Air Force into this matter.[31] Nevertheless, its impact on what happened in Gujranwala is impossible to discount. Almost all of those who were asked by the Hunter Committee about the effect of the arrival of aircraft over Gujranwala replied in positive terms; Mr E.K. Shaw, a district engineer, even going so far as to say that without it, 'the whole of the civil lines would have been destroyed'.[32] Ferdinand Wace also believed that the mobs were only 'finally dispersed by the arrival of an aeroplane from Lahore'.[33] And even though it may be suggested that these testimonies were just official bias, Carberry's aircraft did arrive at Gujranwala at an acute moment – 3 p.m. – when it seemed, at least to the hard-pressed police forces, that they were not going to be able to restore the situation. The appearance of aircraft, flying low over the town, was enough to make most of those on the streets, including the mobs, scatter and disperse, and give the authorities a much-needed breathing space before troops could arrive from Rawalpindi.

જ

The events at Gujranwala had the potential to be the worst outbreak of violence seen during the whole period of the disturbances. The determined nature of the crowds, many of whom were carrying *lathis* and hammers, combined with the shortage of police officers, meant that British control over the town disintegrated during the afternoon. It is likely that had there been a larger European community in Gujranwala or had it been more exposed, there would have been many more casualties. Fortunately, the small European contingent had been notified of trouble at noon and made their way into the Treasury, a square walled enclosure, where they could be protected.[34]

There was also extensive unrest in the surrounding districts during this period, particularly against the transport and communication infrastructure. Indeed, travelling through the Punjab by rail in mid-April 1919 was not for the faint-hearted. On the same day that violence broke out in Gujranwala, Lieutenant Tatem of 2nd (Rawalpindi) Division was travelling on the 8.16 from Lyallpur when he encountered the same hatred. Just before he arrived at Hafizabad, things began to go wrong.[35] A large crowd was milling around the station, brandishing sticks and shouting slogans. When they saw Tatem they screamed at him and tried to get into the carriage, battering the doors in with their *lathis*. Deciding to take his chance on the platform, Tatem got out and tried to reason with the crowd, asking them what he had to do with the trouble, but they would not listen. He was struck in the stomach with a *lathi* blow, so he ran off down the platform and back inside the carriage. Eventually the train moved off from the station and continued on its journey, with Tatem shocked and bruised, but alive. 'The carriage was smashed a bit,' he would later recall, 'the three windows, glass, venetians and wire, were all smashed.'

Hafizabad was not the only place to witness unrest and violence on 14 April. In Gujrat, an agricultural town 75 miles (120 kilometres) north of Lahore, a *hartal* was held that morning. Upon hearing that trouble was brewing, Mr H.S. Williamson, the Deputy Commissioner, led a party of 20 police officers down to the bazaar and spoke with a crowd of shopkeepers. He told them that he would protect them from intimidation and advised them not to be bullied into closing their shops. His words had little effect, however. At three o'clock that afternoon a large procession was formed, waving black flags and shouting anti-government slogans. Williamson again made his way into town with a small police guard and met the crowd, but thanks to a thunderstorm and a sudden downpour of heavy rain, by the time he had arrived 'the ardour of the crowd was cooling'. Presently the procession broke up and people returned indoors, but the situation remained far from normal and as a precaution Williamson sent for reinforcements.

At 10 a.m. on the following morning (15 April) a crowd, mostly consisting of young men, gathered in the streets with black flags, proudly displaying a large portrait of Gandhi. The authorities, bolstered by the arrival of 70 troops of 37/Dogras, decided that it was necessary to disperse the crowds and force shopkeepers to end the *hartal*, but were anxious not to be too provocative. By 4 p.m. the situation had deteriorated considerably. Three schools had been attacked by elements of the crowds, with windows and doors broken, and several masters being assaulted, but the most serious incident was (as in Kasur, Delhi and Gujranwala) at the railway station. Once the crowd reached the station, it began to smash the telegraph and telephone instruments, break up furniture and destroy any official records that could be found. The police, monitoring the situation carefully all day, now decided that they must act. They made their way into the station, but because the crowd was too scattered, it was not possible to fire a volley into them. The most senior sub-judge present then ordered independent firing and after a few rounds the crowds ran off. On the following morning, notices were issued throughout the town under the Police Act explaining that all meetings and processions without a licence were banned. That day the police were out on the streets in force. With that the situation rapidly improved.[36]

∾

Although the railway infrastructure continued to attract violent mobs in the next few days, by 16 April the disturbances had reached and passed their high-water mark. By now the authorities were moving swiftly to restore normal conditions. Whenever they were available, armoured trains travelled up and down the railway tracks mending the lines and firing upon those who were suspected of damaging them.[37] Somewhat belatedly, stringent efforts were now being taken to curb the tide of misleading and inaccurate information that was circulating about the provisions of the Rowlatt Act. Across India vernacular leaflets were being issued to explain what it meant, and various printing presses that had published *satyagraha* material were also being suppressed. Acting under the Defence of India Rules of 1915, newspapers in the Punjab were banned from making reference to the disorders, three editors were prosecuted and formal warnings were given to 20 publications.[38]

Elsewhere, mobile columns were fanning out across the province in a show of strength, visiting villages that had been suspected of damaging infrastructure, arresting suspects and levying fines.[39] A civil officer was also attached to each column and specially directed to give lectures explaining to people the exact provisions of the Rowlatt Acts and correcting the rumours that had swept over the country. Mobile columns had been employed by the British to quiet troubled districts for many years, most noticeably in the Punjab during the Mutiny of 1857, and they were relied upon to do the same in 1919.[40] According to the Joint Deputy Commissioner of Sheikhupura, they were extremely effective, showing 'the value of armoured cars along railway communications, and of Mobile Machine Gun Sections for other parts of the district'. 'Such an armed force,' he concluded, 'should always be ready for emergencies in the Punjab, where everything depends on quickness.'[41] The presence of mobile columns and armoured cars across the province and the spread of news of the firing at the Jallianwala Bagh may have helped to calm the situation and intimidate lawless elements, but there was much work to be done. Now the authorities would have to try and find those who were responsible for what had happened and punish them. On 14 April Lord Chelmsford made a decision of far reaching implications. Martial law was about to begin.

CHAPTER 12

Causes and Conspiracies

We really did not know what was happening.

Lieutenant-General Sir Havelock Hudson[1]

March and April were punishing months in India, when the heat and dust of the plains would become unbearable and exhaust even those who were accustomed to the Indian climate. For those who were fortunate enough, the worst of the hot season could be avoided by retreating to one of the many hill stations that the British manned, where it was cooler, greener and reminded one of home. In time honoured tradition, the Viceroy, Lord Chelmsford, retreated to Simla during the hot season of 1919, the genteel Himalayan town that had become the summer capital of the Raj in 1864. Like many who served in India, Chelmsford recognised the importance of the hill stations and found it easier to work in the fresher climate of Simla, with its grand vistas of the snow-clad Himalayas, than in the stifling offices of New Delhi.

Perhaps reflecting the unease that he had always felt about the British administration in India, such enthusiasm was not shared by his superior in London, Edwin Montagu. During his visit in the winter of 1917–18, Montagu had taken the long, winding train journey up to Simla. 'The scenery is, of course, gorgeous,' he would write, 'but four hours round hairpin curves is very tiring, and I had quite enough of it when we arrived on a perfect, though cold, day at Simla, with the glorious hills stretching all round it.' Montagu disliked the summer capital and found the method of conveyance up to Government House – by native rickshaw – distasteful and remarked that it 'seems to me quite horrible. Hill stations ought not to exist.'[2] Indeed, Montagu had stumbled upon a moot point. The problem with moving to Simla was that it left Chelmsford and the administration open to criticisms that they were out of touch, enjoying the spectacular views and cool breezes of the foothills, while the rest of the British officials in India, those who maintained British rule every day, sweated and toiled down in the plains below, particularly when grave disorders were taking place. Lieutenant-Colonel H. Morgan, the command-ing officer of one of the Indian Army battalions that would help to restore order in 1919, was not alone in complaining about the lack of guidance that was received from the administration during the unrest in the Punjab. 'They let those sweltering down in the plains do the dirty work and then censure them for doing it.'[3]

The response of Lord Chelmsford to news of the seriousness of the vio-lence was one of disbelief and confusion, and did little to banish his reputa-tion for being out of touch. The Viceroy had always been unimpressed with Gandhi and his doctrine of *satyagraha* and had not taken it as seriously as per-haps he should have done, even being away on holiday (camping in the hills near Dehra Dun) when Gandhi was arrested. Chelmsford had met Gandhi in Delhi on 4 March but the meeting was unproductive. Gandhi recalled that it was 'extremely cordial and friendly'. 'I got the impression,' he recalled, 'that both of us understand each other but neither succeeded in convincing the other.'[4] He again telegraphed Chelmsford on 12 March. 'Even at this eleventh hour,' Gandhi pleaded, 'I respectfully ask his Excellency and his Government to pause and consider before passing Rowlatt Bills.'[5] Chelmsford remained unmoved. He explained to Montagu,

> I think he is trying to frighten us, and I propose to call his 'bluff'. In any case no other course in open to us. The fact is he had got passive resistance on the brain and cannot suppress it any longer. We can congratulate ourselves that he has not chosen his ground better. I am quite happy in defending my present position.[6]

The Viceroy wrote to Montagu on 9 April, a day before the storm broke.

> Dear me, what a d—d nuisance these saintly fanatics are! Gandhi is incapable of hurting a fly and is as honest as the day, but he enters quite light-heartedly on a course of action which is the negation of all government and may lead to much hardship to people who are ignorant and easily led astray.[7]

Barely a week later, Chelmsford's confidence that Gandhi's movement was bound to fail and leave the Government of India stronger than before had been brutally shattered. Chelmsford was certainly guilty of not realising the serious-ness of purpose held by Gandhi and clearly underestimated the power of the 'saintly fanatic' to garner support throughout the subcontinent. Chelmsford maintained that the war was really to blame. 'Strong Mussalman feeling; a population in many parts inclined to lawlessness; a large number of disbanded soldiery, some puffed up by victory, other discontented at being demobilized,' he would write. As well as the high price of food, he believed that the violence was 'a reaction from all the strain which the war was put upon them. We have kindled them with excitement for our own purposes during the war. Is it to be wondered at they should now be in a state of nervous strain?'[8]

One of those certainly under 'nervous strain' was Edwin Montagu. He had been questioned on the disorders in the House of Commons and had, somewhat uncomfortably, replied that 'no one cause could be alleged'. After speaking in the House, Montagu returned the short distance to the India Office, the elegant Italianate building designed by Sir Gilbert Scott in 1858, overlooking St James's Park. Anxiously, he penned a letter to the Viceroy.

> I am anxiously awaiting your next letter which will give me in the form of which telegrams are no substitute your innermost reflections. For myself I have warm admiration for the promptness and firmness with which you tackled what must at one moment have seemed a truly alarming position.

Montagu then turned his thoughts to the origins of the violence. 'How suddenly the embers burst into flame,' he wrote, 'and how extraordinarily widespread were the points at which the troubles broke out.' He suspected that there were a number of factors that had contributed to the outbreak of the disorders, but could make no firm conclusions. He believed that 'High prices, the Rowlatt Bills, the unrest which is now so universal throughout the world, and, as regards the Mahomedans, alarm as to the fate of Turkey, all enter into the picture,' but he also wondered 'whether it is possible to single out any particular factor as more responsible than others'.[9]

☙

Had Sir Michael O'Dwyer been privy to the correspondence between Montagu and Chelmsford, he would undoubtedly have scoffed at their confusion and told them, directly and bluntly, that the cause of the violence was quite simple. It was a nationalist rebellion, which sprang from a pre-planned conspiracy to overthrow British rule. In his evidence before the Hunter Inquiry, he explained that about six months before the outbreak of the disorders, he had become aware of an increasing amount of agitation and propaganda that had taken place in the Punjab. This had occurred mainly in Lahore and Amritsar by what he called 'extreme politicians'.[10] He believed that various 'revolutionary forces' were at work in Punjab and were beginning to make common cause. He pointed to the violence that had occurred since 1907, including agrarian unrest, the attempted assassination of the Viceroy, Lord Hardinge, in December 1912, the emergence of the Ghadr movement and the 'silk letter' conspiracy. O'Dwyer believed that opposition to the Rowlatt

Bills 'cemented' a loose alliance of these disparate groups, which all shared the same anti-government agenda. He would later repeat this in his memoirs, chapter 17 of which was entitled 'The Punjab Rebellion of 1919'.[11]

Were the Punjab disturbances a 'rebellion'? O'Dwyer was not alone in claiming that they were. Asked if he believed there was a rebellion in the Punjab, Mr J.P. Thompson, the Chief Secretary to the Punjab Government, replied, 'I do not think anybody entertained any doubt on that subject, Sir.' Numerous other civilian and military officers quizzed by the Hunter Inquiry responded similarly.[12] Indeed, it soon became an article of faith within the Punjab Government that it had defeated a rebellion in 1919. The timing of the disorders seemed to be ominously familiar; taking place at roughly the same point in the year as the Indian Mutiny had done in 1857. It was widely believed in 1919 that the disturbances had also been timed to coincide with the arrival of the hot weather, which would erode the fighting capabilities of British troops and make it more difficult for them to restore order.

One of the major props in the belief of a rebellion was the disruption caused to the railway and communication network throughout April and May. This was of major concern to the British authorities, particularly when considering the threat from the Afghan invasion, which began in May.[13] The seemingly systematic attack upon communications gave important support to the idea that the disturbances were dangerous and did come from a revolutionary conspiracy.[14] In his evidence before the Hunter Committee, Lieutenant-General Sir Havelock Hudson (Adjutant-General in India) concurred. He argued that the destruction of railway lines in the Punjab 'had every appearance of a systematic attempt to isolate the province'. Because all telegraph lines seemed to have been 'systematically cut', Hudson maintained that 'there were good grounds for believing that the disturbances or possible elements of disorder were by no means local', but 'the work of some central and guiding organisation'.[15]

The outbreak of the Third Afghan War in May 1919 added extra weight to those who argued that the events of March and April had been pre-organised, probably in concert with Afghanistan. O'Dwyer argued that Afghan troops and frontier tribesmen began a 'concerted attack' on the frontier at the end of April; 'encouraged by the belief that the Punjab was seething with rebellion and ready to receive them with open arms'. Although the Hunter Report found no direct connection between the disorders in the Punjab and conspirators from Afghanistan, O'Dwyer was unimpressed. 'No impartial critic,' he wrote, 'will *now* accept the conclusion of these authorities that there was no evidence of an organised conspiracy.'[16] Indeed, although it was certainly tempting to agree with O'Dwyer and make firm connections between the two events, the origins of the Afghan invasion lay firmly within the internal dynamics and strains of that country. The pro-British amir, Habibullah, had been murdered on the night of 19/20 February and after a coup, his nephew, Amanullah, had assumed control. Having come to power with the support of various anti-British elements within Afghanistan and on a wave of nationalism, Amanullah began to make preparations for a war that would free Afghanistan from British interference. It is clear that he knew that there was serious unrest in the Punjab in April and May, and hoped to capitalise upon this, but it is highly unlikely that there was any direct contact with disgruntled elements in India, and certainly not with Gandhi.[17]

Despite overwhelming circumstantial evidence, conclusive proof of a conspiracy remained elusive and the authorities struggled in vain to establish a clear connection between the outbreaks in the Punjab and any organised revolutionary cells. The problem was a lack of evidence. When Malcolm Hailey, a gifted member of the ICS, was sent to Lahore to investigate, he was not able to find 'any definite evidence that there had been a carefully prepared plot by the Congress for creating an uprising in the Punjab'.[18] Although O'Dwyer disagreed strongly with Hailey, he was forced to admit that he had no proof of a 'central organization' for the rebellion.[19] Similarly, when asked by the Hunter Inquiry whether there was any organisation, 'secret or otherwise, the object of which is to overthrow the British Government', G.A. Cocks, the Deputy Inspector-General of the CID in the Punjab, replied that his answer was 'probably in the negative' and that he could find no such evidence.[20]

༒

The Government of India always remained somewhat confused about what had happened in 1919, but for others the answer was simple. The British could not find any evidence of a conspiracy because there was nothing to find. It did not exist. Nationalist accounts, both at the time and ever since, have tended to follow the arguments first aired in the Minority and Congress Reports, both of which were published in 1920. According to the Minority Report, the problem with official explanations was their failure to appreciate 'The Real Nature of the Disorders'.[21] It presented the disturbances as 'the natural consequence of economic hardships and political unrest'. It noted that the Great War had 'strained' the resources of India 'to the utmost', which had made a major contribution to the war effort with over 400,000 men being recruited from the Punjab alone. When this sacrifice was combined with price rises, the failure of the monsoon in 1918 (which led to famine), disappointment over the lack of political reform in India and the introduction of the Rowlatt Acts, unrest was inevitable. There was no organised conspiracy, no rebellion and no anti-British feeling, but rather 'mobs seized by the frenzy of the moment'.[22] These sentiments were echoed by the investigation conducted by the Indian National Congress. It blamed the unrest on Sir Michael O'Dwyer's policies in the Punjab, which ranged from the forcible levy of war loans to the gagging of the press, the abuse of emergency legislation and the illegal compulsion of large numbers of men into the Indian Army.[23] In addition, the authors of the Congress Report made the accusation that 'he subjected the Punjabis to the gravest provocation, under which they momentarily lost self-control'. The dissatisfaction that the Rowlatt Bills created – 'a storm of opposition unknown before in India' – was also mentioned.[24]

Of all the issues that Lord Hunter and his committee had to grapple with, the question of what had caused such violence was, in many ways, the most vexatious problem they faced. In the end, as Montagu suspected, no clear answer emerged. According to the report, the disorders stemmed from a number of interrelated issues, particularly the 'general state of unrest and discontent among the people' following the end of the Great War. Among other factors it cited the increase in 'political agitation' brought about by those advocating Home Rule; anger towards the introduction of the Rowlatt Bills, which had been heightened by the 'bitter and determined' criticism of them in nationalist newspapers (as well as the many false rumours as to their particulars); the popularity of Mohandas Gandhi and his *satyagraha* movement; and unease over the possible fate of the Ottoman Empire. Economic factors were also considered, including the high prices throughout India after the war, which had not been helped by the poor harvest of 1919. Lord Hunter did, however, state that his committee could find 'no evidence in the material before us of antecedent conspiracy as the mainspring of the disorders'.[25]

Writing about the origins of the mutiny, Judith Brown has argued that single explanations do not work. Instead we should see a 'confused patchwork' with the degree of disorder (and the causes of that disorder) varying greatly between regions.[26] The year 1919 was similar in this respect and the causes of discontent still remain difficult to measure with any precision. The disturbances were mainly urban in origin, yet the towns and cities of the Punjab had suffered relatively lightly from the pressures of recruitment. There were certainly high prices and food shortages, but prices in India had risen slower than they had in Europe and it was mainly government servants, with fixed wages, that had suffered most. Famine had been recorded in many parts of India in 1919, but not in the Punjab, which was always well supplied with food. The Rowlatt Bills undoubtedly aroused a great deal of opposition, but little was known of their exact provisions and they were not widely read. Extensive damage had been caused to the communication and transport network of the Punjab, but no evidence emerged of revolutionary cells dedicated to violent upheaval. Given these contradictions, it is little wonder that Montagu and Chelmsford, as well as numerous later writers, were confused about what happened.

Whatever British officials might have felt at the time, the disturbances that shook northern India during 1919 had little in common with the Indian Mutiny of 1857. The mutiny was primarily a *sepoy* rebellion, concerned not with independence, but with other demands that centred on terms of service and the interference with caste and religion. Although there seems to have been a number of isolated attempts to tamper with the loyalty of Indian battalions, these episodes remained the exception rather than the rule.[27] Whereas the events of 1857 had been preceded by the appearance of mysterious *chapattis* (small cakes of unleavened bread which were spread from village to village, a presage of rebellion) across central and northern India, which apparently signalled the oncoming uprising, there were no similar signals in 1919.[28] As a consequence, the failure of Lord Hunter (and others like Malcolm Hailey) to find proof of an 'antecedent conspiracy' behind the disorders has been taken by many writers as conclusive verification that the unrest in 1919 was not as serious as was claimed by O'Dwyer and others. Because there was no revolutionary conspiracy and no hardened terrorist cells behind the violence, then, therefore, the unrest was not serious and that the measures taken to restore order were unjustified and disproportionate.

These conclusions are a dangerous misunderstanding. Though Hunter and others failed to find evidence of a conspiracy to overthrow the British Government on the lines of earlier revolts, perhaps like Bengal in 1905 or the Bolsheviks in Russia in 1917, he did admit that 'open rebellion' was an 'apt and accurate' description of what had happened in the Punjab in April 1919.[29] It is, of course, possible to be revolutionary without advocating violence, and this is perhaps what confused many British officials who were used to looking for small, dedicated cells of violent extremists – like those behind the 'silk letter' or Ghadr plots – and insisted they were to blame. While the degree of disorder certainly differed across India, and the reasons why certain crowds gathered and others became violent undoubtedly owed much to local factors, at the heart of what happened was Gandhi's *satyagraha* campaign. It was this that caused crowds to gather and protest against the Rowlatt Bills, although knowing very little about what they actually did.

There is no evidence that the Mahatma directly organised or called for violent resistance to the Raj, but his objectives were revolutionary in that they openly disobeyed the authorities and tried to overthrow government legislation. His methods may have nominally been non-violent, but this should not blind us to the seriousness of the challenge that Gandhi issued to the government in March 1919, and his important role in stoking the tension and frustration within India. The call to non-co-operation and the constant repetition of the 'horrors' of the Rowlatt Acts was bound to result in clashes with the police and military, particularly after the events in Delhi on 30 March. As O'Dwyer and many other British officials had warned, when crowds gathered, they could often get out of hand and quickly gain a violent momentum. Lord Hunter, as so many others would do, insisted in believing what Gandhi said about his movement and taking the Mahatma's word for his actions; that *satyagraha* was not a threatening conspiracy, but a display of purpose that would helpfully guide the authorities back to the path of righteousness. Gandhi was no friend to the Government of India, but one of its most dedicated enemies, albeit clothed in the *dhoti* of a humble man and armed with only the power of his words. Such a misunderstanding says more about Hunter's naivety than it does about the man from Porbandar.

PART THREE
AFTERMATH

CHAPTER 13

The Introduction of Martial Law

Government have taken off the gloves.

A.J.W. Kitchin[1]

The Punjab was isolated, cut off from the rest of India; a thick veil seemed to cover it and hide it from outside eyes. There was hardly any news, and people could not go there or come out from there... Odd individuals, who managed to escape from that inferno, were so terror struck that they could give no account. Helplessly and impotently, we, who were outside, waited for scraps of news and bitterness filled our hearts.[2]

This description of martial law in the Punjab was written by Jawaharlal Nehru, the future prime minister of India, and it has come to define the events that followed the shooting at the Jallianwala Bagh. Mahatma Gandhi felt that the abuses that occurred under the cloak of martial law were, in many ways, even *worse* than the shooting at Amritsar. In *Young India* he complained that

the fury that has been spent upon General Dyer is, I am sure, largely misdirected. No doubt the shooting was 'frightful', the loss of innocent life deplorable. But the slow torture, degradation and emasculation that followed was much worse, more calculated, malicious and soul killing, and the actors who perform the deeds deserve greater condemnation than General Dyer for the Jallianwala Bagh massacre. The latter only destroyed a few bodies but the others tried to kill the soul of a nation.[3]

Writing on the disorders in the Punjab has been dominated by the shooting at the Jallianwala Bagh. The important period of martial law that followed has receded into the background. Although some aspects of it – particularly General Dyer's notorious 'crawling order' – are well known, how martial law was imposed and conducted remains only as an afterthought in most discussions of the Amritsar Massacre.[4] But this period left an impression of brutality and coercion that – in Gandhi's case at least – was never forgotten. Perhaps the earliest writer to draw attention to the abuses that occurred under the cloak of martial law was journalist Guy Horniman, whose scathing account was published in 1920.[5] The report compiled by the Indian National Congress was also dominated by discussions of the brutal and seemingly arbitrary punishments inflicted upon innocent civilians. It concluded that as well as there being 'no necessity whatsoever for the promulgation of martial law', it was 'unduly prolonged', 'unnecessary, cruel, oppressive' and 'an abortion of justice'.[6] These criticisms have been repeated ever since.[7]

The Lieutenant-Governor of the Punjab, Sir Michael O'Dwyer, would not have agreed. In his memoirs he wrote a staunch defence of his administration and complained bitterly about the 'unscrupulous propaganda', which had been 'pursued by the extremists to discredit the weapon which had foiled their designs and to vilify those who had made use of it'. He noted with anger the 'widespread impression both in England and in India that the authorities, military and civil, went out of their way to inflict racial humiliation on Indians'. This, he believed, was 'grossly unjust'.[8] O'Dwyer did, however, distance himself from the more unsavoury elements of martial law, noting that it was not 'his business' to justify orders for which he had not been responsible, particularly the 'crawling' and 'salaaming' orders, the 'fancy punishments' and the floggings. But the question remains as to how the British administered martial law and whether it was an attempt – in Gandhi's stinging phrase – to 'kill the soul of a nation'.

ço

In response to a request from O'Dwyer on 13 April, Lord Chelmsford issued Ordinance No. 1 the following day.[9] He was 'satisfied that a state of open rebellion against the authority of the Government exists in certain parts of the Province of the Punjab' and thus suspended the functioning of 'ordinary Criminal Courts' and authorised the introduction of martial law within selected districts across the Punjab.[10] Martial law was proclaimed in Amritsar, Lahore and Gujranwala on 15 April, Gujrat followed on 18 April and Lyallpur two days later. It remained in force until the night of 9/10 June in Amritsar, Gujranwala and Lyallpur, and until midnight on 11 June in Lahore. Because of the critical dependence of the NWFP on the railway network that ran from Lahore to Peshawar and Quetta, selected railway lines remained under martial law for some time to come.[11] During this period, 852 people were arrested and 581 were convicted, the majority being charged with 'waging war against the King Emperor' and sentenced accordingly.[12]

The introduction of martial law in the Punjab was not a step that was taken lightly. O'Dwyer was reluctant to admit that the situation had passed out of his control, but felt that he had no other choice. Although much would be made of this decision by those critical of O'Dwyer, his actions had the backing of the Government of India.[13] On 16 April, Chelmsford informed Montagu that 'bands' were roaming the districts of Amritsar, Lahore and Gujranwala 'looting and destroying' and that 'summary justice' was 'the only thing for wandering bands of freebooters'. He also believed that the firing at Amritsar had given the city 'a very severe lesson'.[14] Although Chelmsford would later try and distance himself from the measures taken under martial law, he wrote to O'Dwyer on 30 April explaining that he would support him in all 'actions necessary to put down these troubles sternly'.[15] From the outset O'Dwyer was keen to retain some level of civilian authority, but this was problematic because during martial law the normal relationship between the civil and military authorities was reversed and the military would become responsible for law and order and the restoration of normality.[16] However, there was considerable confusion about what this actually meant in practice and how it was to be administered. Indeed, the confusion over this matter was the cause of a bitter dispute between Lahore and Simla, from which many of the subsequent problems experienced during this period can be traced.

According to O'Dwyer, he had worked out a scheme for the administration of martial law with his Chief Secretary (Mr J.P. Thompson) that was similar to that which had existed during the Mutiny of 1857. According to this scheme, the civil government would remain in command and would only use the military to *enforce* this authority. He believed that this would be the best way of dealing promptly with the disorders without abdicating all civilian control. Unfortunately, the Government of India disagreed and informed him that there could be 'no half measures' and that the civilian power was 'entirely to cease', being replaced by military rule. Thompson explained to the Hunter Inquiry at length the confusion that existed in the Government of the Punjab about the legal position of martial law:

> I do not know whether it has yet been brought out that there was considerable confusion at first to know which the correct source of authority was when we first got sanction of the Government of India to the proclamation of Martial Law. We had a meeting at Government House at which we went into the question and we came to the conclusion that while Martial Law was on the General Officer Commanding was the law. Then we got hold of some papers which I should like to put in. I have obtained sanction from the Army Department to put them in. Instructions were issued by the Adjutant-General when Martial Law was proclaimed and it was then pointed out that there were two kinds of

> Martial Law – statutory and non-statutory – and the general idea given was that
> the civil power was supreme when statutory Martial Law was declared and that
> military power was supreme when non-statutory Martial Law was declared.

In this, Thompson was correct. Official guidelines stated that statutory martial law allowed the military to take exceptional measures, but without civilian control being entirely relinquished.[17] On 16 April Lahore was convinced that 'the civil authority was still supreme', but on the following day a message from the Government of India ruled that this was not the case. The military would remain in charge.[18]

Historian Peter Robb is unimpressed with O'Dwyer's arguments that the Government of India effectively sidelined Lahore and handed all control over to the military. He writes that 'there was no suggestion that the civil authority should be abrogated' and quotes a communication between Chelmsford and O'Dwyer, written on 26 April 1919, to argue that the Viceroy had counselled for moderation in the administration of martial law and, therefore, that any breach of this was (partly at least) O'Dwyer's fault.[19] Chelmsford's two 'cardinal principles' were that no greater force should be used than was necessary to maintain law and order and that actions should leave as little bitterness behind as possible.[20] This was all well and good, but, as shown above, this was *ten days too late* and it was in the days after 15 April, when martial law was first declared, that the Punjab Government was trying to maintain some level of control over the military. It was in these first, crucial days of martial law that they were denied the support from the Government of India that they needed and when the majority of the abuses occurred. A simple glance at the chronology of the correspondence between the Punjab and the Government of India shows that it was made very clear to O'Dwyer that he was *not* in charge of the administration of martial law.[21] Given O'Dwyer's experience and administrative ability, it was a serious mistake to sideline him.

એ૭

O'Dwyer was in regular contact with the Viceroy and from the end of April with Sir Edward Maclagan, who was to be his successor at Lahore.[22] He had been scheduled to leave the Punjab on 30 April, but because 'it was considered desirable that I should see the disturbances through and that my successor should not be associated with the measures necessary to suppress them' he stayed on until 26 May. During O'Dwyer's final days in Lahore, he was his usual 'satanically energetic' self. Every day he would ride to the city gates (without an escort) and then make his way through some of the main bazaars, trying to assess the temper of the people. It was a typical act of courage and determination from the Lieutenant-Governor who had been brought up in the traditions of British rule in the Punjab and knew that it was essential to present a bold front and show the people that he was not afraid.[23] 'We are getting our martial law machinery into work,' O'Dwyer explained on 16 April.[24] Lieutenant-Colonel E.D. Money was appointed Administrator of Martial Law and various proclamations and orders were distributed by 16th Division throughout the Punjab.[25] Of particular importance was *Instructions for Guidance of Officers Administering Martial Law*, which was issued on 19 April. Although martial law had often been associated with undisciplined violence against the civilian population, this order made it clear that officers had to 'exercise restraint over their feelings' and that there 'should never be any suspicion of resentful retaliation'.[26]

It soon became evident that there was a great deal of confusion over what exactly martial law was. Almost daily meetings – what O'Dwyer called 'pow-wows' – were held in Government House at which military officers reported on the day's events and then discussed what else could be done.[27] According to Thompson, 'there was a great deal more done orally than in normal times' during the disturbances and this was perhaps understandable given the gravity of the situation and the novelty of what they were doing.[28] There were sometimes sharp disagreements. Four days before Chelmsford would iterate his two 'cardinal principles', O'Dwyer had admitted that 'I keep on impressing on the military authorities at our daily Conference, that nothing revengeful should be done which would leave any justifiable resentment behind'.[29] Chelmsford does not seem to have been aware of this and on 30 April complained to Montagu that O'Dwyer's methods were not suitable to any other province in India (except the Punjab) and that 'If only people would realise that the day has passed when you can keep India down by the sword!'[30] The same day news reached Simla of a highly unusual and deeply offensive order at Amritsar where Indians, who wished to pass along a certain street, would have to do so on all fours. Chelmsford was incensed. 'Now I have no wish to make your task harder,' he lambasted O'Dwyer, 'but I would ask you, does not this particular form of punishment offend against the canons of wise punishment?'[31] Chelmsford wanted the order cancelled immediately.

What Chelmsford was referring to was Dyer's so-called 'crawling' order, which was perhaps the most notorious single episode in the history of martial law. The 'crawling order' was in force at Amritsar between 19 and 24 April and required Indians, who wished to pass along the street that the English missionary, Miss Sherwood, had been assaulted, to pass along on all fours.[32] The lane, known as the Kucha Kurrichhan, was about 150 yards (137 metres) in length and was picqueted on both sides by British soldiers. This order, which soon attracted a notoriety that almost equalled that of the Jallianwala Bagh massacre, was criticised in the Hunter Report for causing 'unnecessary inconvenience' and for being an 'act of humiliation', which 'has continued to be a cause of bitterness and racial ill-feeling long after it was recalled'.[33] The Congress Report made much out of this, complaining that 'The crawling order and other fancy punishments were unworthy of a civilized administration, and were symptomatic of the moral degradation of their inventors.'[34] Even Ian Colvin, Dyer's biographer, passes over the incident without discussing it in any great detail, and Arthur Swinson calls it 'the stupidest act of his entire career'.[35]

How did this order come about? A number of sources suggest that Dyer may not have been the (sole) author of this punishment or that it simply came about by accident, but this remains unconvincing.[36] Dyer was clearly outraged by the assault on Miss Sherwood and 'searched' for some 'fitting punishment' that would impress upon the city that such acts could not be tolerated.[37] He also maintained that 'crawling order' had been 'much misrepresented', was a misnomer (because it only required Indians to pass along it on all fours, not to crawl) and was a 'trivial accident' and 'minor incident'.[38] In any case, Dyer believed that the attempted murder of Miss Sherwood to have been of such gravity – he called it a 'most dastardly outrage' – that the location of the assault should be seen as 'holy ground' and only by treating it with an almost religious significance could Indians understand how serious it was. The assault on Miss Sherwood seemed to strike at the heart of British prestige in India, asking the question of whether the British could protect their womenfolk and raising dark spectres of Cawnpore, of Lucknow and other places where British women and children had been mercilessly butchered by rebels in 1857. Given the character of Dyer, a man deeply imbued with the values and attitudes of the Raj, and who apparently always enjoyed the company of women, his fury at this assault is understandable, if overzealous.

The 'crawling order' would become a bitter symbol of British oppression that would never be forgiven, but what is striking about the incident is its insignificance. It was only in force *along one lane* for five days between the hours of 6 a.m. and 8 p.m. and only 50 people crawled along it.[39] It may have been an insensitive and misguided order, but it was hardly evidence of a brutal and widespread policy of British repression as most accounts allege. Sensitive to the criticisms that Chelmsford had made (or at least implied), O'Dwyer wrote a passionate defence of his position and his role in the administration of martial law on 1 May. Regarding the 'crawling order', O'Dwyer agreed that it was improper and admitted that it caused him 'as much of a shock as it did to Your Excellency'.[40] He also confirmed that as soon as news of this order reached him it had been stopped. Furthermore:

> I am now doing what I can in communication with the General Officer Commanding, Division, and his Brigadier to prevent any abuse of martial law orders. But where martial law has been proclaimed, the military authority supersedes the civil in the ground covered by martial law orders and all I and my officers can do is advise and suggest.

He was, of course, completely correct, although it could hardly have been satisfying pointing this out to Chelmsford, who had insisted that the military authorities superseded the civilian ones. O'Dwyer then stressed that although he had approved the martial law orders in Lahore before they were issued ('as a matter of courtesy'), it was impossible for him to do so for areas outside the city. He would, therefore, be unable to accept responsibility for orders to which he had not been informed.

☙

Dyer's 'crawling order' has often been seen as a reflection of its author's fractured personality, but it was not the only episode in the administration of martial law that has been heavily criticised. Perhaps the most vigorous proponent of martial law, even more so than Dyer, was Lieutenant-Colonel Frank Johnson. He was the man who had tried to restore order to Lahore on 12 April and soon attracted an infamy that almost rivalled that of Dyer.[41] Between 15 April and 29 May, Johnson was responsible for the Lahore Civil Area, in which around 240,000 people resided. Johnson commanded a combined force of 1,500 soldiers and police and acted with considerable energy. He put in place a curfew between 8 p.m. and 5 a.m., had 66 people flogged, curtailed railway travel (by banning third- and intermediate-class tickets), made sure that shops were opened, commandeered electric lights and fans, and also commandeered vehicles.[42] But his most controversial orders – what Helen Fein has described as 'the most outstanding case of collective punishments'[43] – concerned the students of Lahore. He restricted their movements and forced many to attend several roll calls each day. He even punished the staff and students of King Edward Medical College because a martial law notice had been pulled down from its walls. Staff and students were marched to the Lahore Fort and detained for 30 hours.[44]

The orders that Johnson was most proud of concerned the economy of Lahore. On 25 April he took steps to control the price of certain goods, and over the following month the price of milk, salt, vegetables, mutton and *atta*

(wheat) were reduced. Johnson took even more drastic action with milk sup-
plies. He issued strict orders about the adulteration of milk, which could in
no way be justified as keeping the peace or restoring order, but to 'improve the
low standard of business morality' in Lahore. He believed that these actions
did not go beyond his remit and that it was his responsibility to see that the
people could get the 'necessaries of life' at 'reasonable rates'; something that
he believed was absolutely essential to the 'preservation of peace and order'.[45]
Indeed, evidence suggests that given the high prices for food at this time
this was a popular measure that assuaged some of the grievances of the city.
Major J.C. Hunter of the North Western Railway told the Hunter Inquiry
that in January his workmen had 'complained bitterly' about the exorbitant
price of food, but that under martial law they had 'no trouble' getting any.
'The food was controlled and they got food at reasonable prices and if the
bania (shopkeeper) refused to sell he was dealt with immediately.'[46]

Understanding the nature of martial law in Lahore depends on appreciating Frank Johnson. A former adventurer and mercenary, Johnson was, in
many ways, a typical British *conquistador*, 'handsome, aggressive and self-
confident',[47] used to operating without close guidance from his superiors and
a passionate believer in British supremacy. He had made his name in South
Africa as an adventurer and pioneer and in 1890 played a leading role in the
operation to secure Matabeleland under the guidance of Cecil Rhodes. Indeed, J.P. Thompson found Johnson to be a good soldier, but 'a little too
"colonial"'.[48] He certainly controlled Lahore in an insensitive and often over-
bearing manner. His martial law orders were strict and in many cases unnecessary, such as the order banning more than two people from walking abreast,
his decision to ban cycles and his commandeering of lights and fans.[49] These
instructions may have been irritating and unhelpful, but they were not part
of process of terrorisation and had practical uses, such as the curfew, which
allowed him to rest his troops and save them from endless patrolling. Indeed,
martial law was not always enforced on a solely racial basis (as has often been
assumed) and he fined four Europeans for not allowing their vehicles to be
used by the martial law authorities.[50] In any case he believed that the people of Lahore had actually benefited from his administration, comparing it
with the previous rule that their 'forefathers' had been used to. It seems that
Johnson saw martial law as a tool that allowed him to improve life in Lahore,
by restarting the economic life of the city and reminding people of the need
for 'loyalty' and 'honour'. Johnson may not have been the most sympathetic
of British officers, but he was not the tyrant of legend and deserves some credit
for doing a thankless task in a highly difficult situation.

დ

Martial law in Amritsar and Lahore may not have been as punitive as subsequent writers have claimed, but it had not all gone to plan and there was some friction and misunderstanding that undermined the restoration of normality. Johnson clearly acted in a more decisive manner than other commanders in the Punjab and seems to have been given a free hand. A revealing comment can be found in the testimony of William Beynon, Johnson's superior, when he was asked about the orders that had been passed in Lahore: '*Colonel Johnson made a mistake*,' he said.

> He was Officer Commanding the Civil Area. When Martial Law is proclaimed the officer proclaiming Martial Law appoints administrators of Martial Law who carry out his orders, draw up rules, collate information as regards punishments, sentence and generally anything which has to do with Martial Law.[51]

The 'Supreme Military Authority' within the 16th Division was Colonel Money, *not* Johnson. Beynon issued orders under martial law, which were then administered by Money. If Money felt any orders were incorrect then he would advise Beynon accordingly. Although Johnson could issue orders in his own area, they had to be 'consistent' with these directions. So it seems that Money was really to blame, but because he was not called to speak before the Hunter Committee we know little about him. For O'Dwyer this confusion was unhelpful and underlined why he should have remained in charge. He kept a close eye on what was going on, but he was unable to shape martial law as much as he would have liked. Johnson consulted him about many issues, particularly those 'connected with the ordinary life of the citizens', but he did not discuss those issues that 'were more or less purely of a military nature'.[52] Although Johnson was present at Government House frequently in April, this close collaboration was allowed to lapse during May and June.

The lack of control over martial law was not unique to those areas under Frank Johnson's command and in the coming weeks similar situations would reoccur in other areas of the Punjab, particularly those that did not fall under Sir Michael's hawkish gaze, at Kasur, Gujranwala and Sheikhupura. But this was not something that the authorities wanted or would have approved of, but a reflection of the confused situation in the Punjab and the lack of understanding of how martial law was to be administered. Nationalist writers were not slow in accusing the authorities of masterminding a process of terrorisation and humiliation against the population, however, this was never in the minds of O'Dwyer and Beynon (and indeed they had issued guidelines that strictly forbade such things from happening). But they did clearly believe that martial law was of benefit and helped to restore a sense of 'business as usual' to those areas in which it had been declared. However, as the population settled down to life under martial law, in those long days of May and June, the authorities in Simla and London were feeling increasingly uneasy about what was going on. Rumours were now spreading that made the 'crawling order' look tame, of other 'fancy punishments', of mass floggings, of indignities on holy men, that they began to rethink their earlier enthusiasm for military control, retreat from the firm stance they had taken and betray the support they had freely offered to those officials tasked with restoring order to the Punjab.

CHAPTER 14

'Fancy Punishments' and 'Erratic Acts'

The tendency of the present day is to abolish respectfulness. An Indian father will tell you that sons are not respectful even to their parents.

Lieutenant-Colonel A.J. O'Brien[1]

Anxiously awaiting news in Simla, Lord Chelmsford became increasingly nervous about the continuation of martial law during May. His earlier desire for 'summary justice' for those involved in the violence now began to diminish. He wrote to O'Dwyer on 12 May,

> I cannot disguise from you that everyday's continuation of martial law makes the future situation more difficult, and I firmly believe that if you were to say we have crushed this rebellion I am now going to go back to normal conditions, this would do more to impress people with the success of your policy than any drawn-out continuance of martial law.[2]

But Chelmsford would find that trying to withdraw or control martial law, once the genie was out of the bottle, was not as simple as he had imagined and he did not seem to understand that it was not O'Dwyer whom he should have been petitioning. The ruling on 16 April that civilian control was entirely to cease in the areas where martial law was declared now came back to haunt the Government of India. His decision to ignore Lahore and place the administration of martial law entirely in the hands of the military prevented him from being able to shape it as fully as he would have liked. There was no use nagging O'Dwyer. The army was now in charge.

Chelmsford may have been the Viceroy, but peering down at the plains from his lodge in the hills of Simla – somewhat unkindly lampooned as 'Mount Olympus' – his influence was limited. On 14 May a meeting was held at Government House, Lahore, at which the arguments over whether martial law should be removed were aired. Although the military authorities were 'unanimously opposed to any immediate or early discontinuance of

Martial Law', it was agreed to relax it as far as possible by ending the curfew, returning commandeered items to their owners and stopping the roll calls.[3] On the evening of 26 May, O'Dwyer left Government House for the last time. He sent a final communication to the Viceroy that evening informing him that 'apart from a comparatively small disaffected section in the towns, the feeling throughout the province is generally healthy and in more places actively loyal'.[4] O'Dwyer's successor was a trusted friend and colleague, Sir Edward Maclagan, another distinguished member of the ICS. If Chelmsford had hoped that Maclagan would be more flexible and supportive of his position than O'Dwyer had been (or more willing to end martial law for that matter), he was to be disappointed. As early as 21 May, Maclagan had informed the Viceroy that although he was 'very anxious to get back the normal conditions as soon as possible,' he had no wish to 'endanger our progress in this direction by a premature relaxation of present arrangements before the more important trials are concluded and before we know how we stand as regards the new military and political problems which have arisen since martial law was imposed'.[5]

During May and June the authorities were desperately trying to find those responsible for the disorders, pressurising informants, searching houses and tracing scraps of intelligence across the province. Of the 532 people arrested, 386 were convicted. Of these 77 were sentenced to the maximum of two years' imprisonment, while eight people were imprisoned for one year.[6] Towards the end of May the main subject of discussion between Lahore and Simla was whether legal practitioners from outside the province should be allowed to act for those who had been tried by the martial law authorities. A ban was put in place 'from a military point of view', probably because, as O'Dwyer explained to Chelmsford, many of those who wanted to come into the Punjab were 'extremist politicians' who would have only whipped up anti-government feeling.[7] This was bitterly resented by many nationalists and seen as yet further evidence of the despotic and authoritarian instincts of the British. This step in curtailing travel was undoubtedly a serious point, but the criticism masks a deceptively simple explanation. Although O'Dwyer clearly felt that it would have made things more difficult for the authorities if large numbers of lawyers came into his province, the curtailment of travel across the Punjab was not specific to any class of person, but as Beynon explained to Lord Hunter, *to prevent all movements without specific permission*, a common part of martial law.[8]

The decision to continue martial law for so long remains a controversial one. The Hunter Report stated that the wisdom of continuing it until

August was 'more open to criticism' than the original decision to declare martial law and the Congress Report is full of vitriol about the continuation of
emergency measures.[9] Most British officials in the Punjab during April and
May were keen for it to remain in place for the time being, at least on the
railways where there was a grave danger of attacks on the vital transport and
communication infrastructure, and this was understandable. Although it is
likely that martial law could have been relaxed in some areas, it was felt that
'it was a risk not worth taking' and given the threat from Afghanistan this was
a reasonable conclusion.[10] In any case it should not be thought that it was kept
in place in order to terrorise the Punjabi population. O'Dwyer – hardly sympathetic to nationalist demands – believed that martial law should have been
relaxed earlier, and he was not the only one.[11] A sad irony was that for government bureaucracy martial law could have been withdrawn a fortnight earlier.
However, 'an unfortunate misunderstanding between the Home Department
and the Army Department' ('due to the present system of circulating files')
prevented this from taking place.[12]

✧

One of the worst outbreaks of violence in the Punjab during 1919 had been at
Kasur, just south of Lahore. On 12 April mobs had looted and burnt the *tahsil*
and the railway station, and attacked the Ferozepore train, which contained a
small party of Europeans. Four British soldiers had been beaten and two warrant officers had been murdered. Lieutenant-Colonel H. McRae, commanding 2/15th Sikhs, arrived at Kasur that afternoon with orders to 'take all measures to restore order'. As soon as martial law came into force, McRae acted
swiftly. He marched through the town on 16 April reading out the proclamation of martial law and, in co-operation with local police officers, made a
number of arrests.[13] Two days later he ordered the assembly of all local schoolboys and had six of them whipped. In order to identify those people who had
played a role in the violence on 12 April, McRae also ordered the entire male
population of Kasur to be assembled on two occasions. He was assisted by the
arrival of Mr P. Marsden as a sub-divisional officer, and the appointment of
Captain A.C. Doveton (1/30th Punjabis) as martial law officer.

A great deal of criticism has been levelled at those officers who administered martial law in Kasur. A statement given to the Hunter Inquiry by a municipal commissioner (Lala Mohan Lal Seth) claimed that there was 'no reason
or occasion' for martial law to be introduced and that it was administered in
a 'very strict' manner. He also mentioned, what he called, 'erratic acts' committed by military officers that included hundreds of arrests, house searches,

travel restrictions, looting and 'various indignities' on wandering holy men (*sadhus*).[14] According to the Hunter Report, Doveton invented a number of minor punishments such as forcing prisoners to work in the railway goods sheds; allowing a prisoner to undertake a 'skipping exercise' if he wanted to be excused from such work; another was asked to write a poem in praise of martial law; and a salaaming order whereby those who were convicted had to touch the ground with their forehead.[15] It was these so-called 'fancy punishments' that would become one of the most notorious episodes from this period; a propaganda disaster for the Government of India that would become forever etched in the memory of Indian nationalists. The report commissioned by the Indian National Congress made no attempt to hide its disgust at McRae and Doveton. 'In some respects,' the report read, 'these two officers excelled their brother officers in their inventiveness, irresponsibility and total disregard of the feelings and sentiments of those who were affected by their orders.'[16]

Despite the mythology surrounding martial law in Kasur, the effects of these so-called 'fancy punishments' should not be overstated. One of the incidents much repeated in nationalist accounts was that of a holy man who was apparently 'whitewashed' by Doveton. This incident of apparently shocking racial humiliation fitted perfectly with their dim view of British officials, but it can be explained in a perfectly reasonable way. Some men, perhaps including a *sadhu*, worked in the goods yards during martial law and had to take delivery of a consignment of lime. Because the siding was blocked, it was necessary to remove the lime by hand. Unfortunately, as it was the rainy season, the workers soon became covered in lime 'from head to foot'.[17] Someone must have seen these men and spread rumours that this had been done on purpose. Over time this story has gradually solidified into historical fact, when it was, in truth, nothing of the sort.

Orders similar to the so-called 'fancy punishments' invented by Doveton in Kasur also occurred in the more outlying areas of the Punjab. When people met European civil or military officers in Gujranwala they had to alight from any transport, close any umbrellas, and salute. This salaaming order was, according to the Minority Report, 'calculated to humiliate the whole Indian population'.[18] In Malawakal and Sheikhupura males were either given sanitary work or told to sweep the streets[19]; and schoolboys in Wazirabad were made to salute the union flag daily, a disciplinary measure employed because some of the boys had taken part in the unrest.[20] These punishments were widely criticised. The Hunter Report censured several officers involved in these orders including Marsden at Kasur, Lieutenant-Colonel A.J. O'Brien (Deputy Commissioner, Gujranwala) and B.N. Bosworth-Smith (Joint

Deputy Commissioner, Sheikhupura).[21] When several of these officers pe-titioned the Government of India for a hearing in 1920 they were all refused; eloquent testimony to how serious these offences were taken and how devas-tating the conclusions of the Hunter Committee were to a number of British officials, not just Dyer.[22] Therefore, to claim that the authorities attempted either to downplay or hide the mistakes of martial law is simply untrue.

What strikes one about these 'fancy punishments' is that although they may have been distasteful and irritating, they were, like the 'crawling order', on a very small scale and were in no way evidence of an attempt to terrorise the civilian population. Indeed, they were, in effect, *a way of reducing punishment*. Doveton argued that instead of flogging people or throwing them in jail, he would, for example, order them to serve in the railway sheds, something that would not burden his officers with more work (and which, in any case, would have been preferable for those who had been arrested). 'My idea,' he argued, 'was to reduce punishments, because, on the whole, order had been restored and people were inclined to behave themselves as a whole better, and I was try-ing to cut down punishments.'[23] Indeed, in the outlying areas of the Punjab martial law was remarkably 'light'. In Gujranwala, there was some resistance to it, but it seems to have been mainly concerned with the introduction of a curfew order, designed to clear the streets at night. When local people com-plained that it interfered with the movement of carts and animals to market, the order was swiftly repealed. There were 16 cases of flogging in Gujranwala, and only a single punishment took place in public. After this it was stopped. At Wazirabad, the administrator, Major C.W.J. Smith, was mainly concerned with the difficulty of getting a clerk for his office. Manpower was so stretched at this point that he was forced to do all the administrative paperwork himself. Only two people were imprisoned at Wazirabad; a telegraph clerk who dam-aged government property and a drunken European who was charged with 'indecent conduct'.[24]

℘

As well as the 'fancy punishments', one of the chief criticisms of martial law was the amount of flogging that took place. Guy Horniman regarded flog-ging as being 'a common feature of the administration of Martial Law'[25] and the Hunter Report admitted that 'too many' sentences of flogging were pronounced.[26] So concerned was Mahatma Gandhi about the rumours that were circulating about the apparently widespread use of flogging that he sent a telegram to the Viceroy's Private Secretary on 21 April warning him that if people were being whipped it would rouse the 'gravest indignation'.[27] Most of those officers on the ground believed that flogging was a suitable and swift punishment. For Frank Johnson in Lahore, flogging was 'kindest method of punishment' because of its supposed deterrent effect. He wrote that he 'would sooner have been deprived of the services of 1,000 rifles than the power of inflicting corporal punishment'.[28] Limited jail accommodation at Lahore was another factor. Because it would have been impossible to imprison everyone who contravened martial law orders, Johnson had to use other ways to administer punishment quickly and efficiently.

The experience of Mr J.E. Keough, an extra assistant commissioner, who was involved in trying 22 cases for breaches of martial law (mainly relating to the curfew order) is instructive. Of the 22 prisoners he tried, Keough had only 12 flogged. The highest number of 'stripes' given was 18 but the usual number was between six and eight. Public flogging took place on 17 April before it was cancelled the following day. Prisoners were marched from the *kotwali* a short distance (about 25 yards/23 metres) to the Market Square, fastened to a triangle that had been erected, stripped virtually naked and then flogged with a thin cane. Keough maintained that flogging was the 'most salutary punishment that could be awarded' given the circumstances and that it was, in many cases, the preferred option. Because many of those who were flogged were from the 'lower strata of society', it was preferable to the payment of fines.[29] Furthermore, if a prisoner was 'obviously not fitted' for flogging on age or health grounds, then they would be excused.

Another member of the ICS, James Penny, had a similar experience when he was sent to Sheikhupura to help administer martial law in May. The chief difficulty, he found, was what sentences to impose on those convicted of offences because of the lack of jail space and the difficulty of collecting fines. Most settled for caning, which was conducted, as he put it, 'lightly and quickly'.[30] Indeed, martial law may not have been ideal, but it was not administered with anything approaching 'Prussian frightfulness'. It was, on the contrary, conducted sensibly and with the best of intentions. The issue of public flogging also highlights another feature of the administration of martial law: when abuses or practices that were considered illegal or undesirable were reported to the central authorities, they were cancelled immediately. Although these sentences were painful and demeaning for those involved, flogging was not part of a process of terrorisation. As far as J.P. Thompson could remember, 'flogging in public did not come to our notice till practically after it ceased'.[31]

Flogging was not unique to Lahore and corporal punishment was also used at Kasur. Forty people were whipped, each suffering approximately 18 'stripes'. This included six schoolboys, ranging between 13 and 17 years of age who were given between three and six 'cuts' with a bamboo cane. Although the decision to cane schoolboys was attacked bitterly by several local pleaders, as well as by Congress, McRae argued – like Johnson had – that it was a just and appropriate punishment, particularly given the role that a number of students had played in the mobs at the railway station on 12 April.[32] And while this may seem at first glance to be yet another example of British brutality, the school was supportive of the punishments and had asked for military help. In any case, McRae's punishments were not far removed from the use of corporal punishment in British schools, which was widely accepted and understood at the time. Indeed, however distasteful the flogging and whipping was, however painful and demeaning, it should be seen in context. Flogging and whipping were not unknown in India, or indeed throughout the Punjab. Although those sentences inflicted by the military were conducted with a rope 'in military fashion', and were somewhat more severe than usually given by a *rattan* cane in jail, whipping was a common practice. During the hearings of the Hunter Committee, Mr Herbert, the government advocate, made the point 'that 600 to 700 floggings are meted out in a year in the Punjab', a statistic that helps to place the punishments of martial law in context and allows us to move beyond the hysterical, simplistic condemnation that can be found in most accounts of this period.[33]

ౚ

By 11 June Nehru's 'thick veil' of martial law had been withdrawn from large parts of the Punjab and only remained in place on selected railway lines. So concerned were the authorities about the threat to British civilians that between April and May, 311 women and 307 British children had been evacuated to hill stations.[34] British officials were uniform in their opinion that martial law was a necessary step in the restoration of order in the Punjab, particularly when considering the danger from Afghanistan in May. Indeed, they were probably right. Martial law was an important and necessary step in the restoration of order and gave the authorities the powers they needed to control troubled districts and search for those responsible. Unfortunately, this period has become synonymous with repression and brutality; laced with infamous tales about 'fancy punishments' and endless flogging and regularly compared to German violence against the Belgian civilian population in 1914. But such a narrow view does not provide a complete explanation for how the authorities attempted to restore order in the Punjab. Undoubtedly, there were instances of abuse, Dyer's 'crawling order' and Doveton's 'fancy punishments' being the most obvious examples, but these were limited in scope and execution and were not part of an organised plan. As soon as many of these orders came to the attention of higher authorities, either in Lahore or Simla, they were cancelled immediately; hardly the 'killing' of 'the soul of the nation' as claimed by Gandhi. Indeed, it is difficult to avoid the conclusion that at certain times, martial law orders were actually *popular* among the people, particularly those measures that reduced prices and prevented the adulteration of milk. For example, in Sangla, where schoolboys were made to salute the union flag, it was soon noticed that the boys enjoyed the novelty of being in regular contact with British soldiers.[35]

Does Sir Michael O'Dwyer deserve the vitriol that has been heaped upon him? A study of him during this period gives lie to many of the accusations that have been made against him. On the contrary, he acted with remarkable foresight and skill. He was acutely aware of the potential legacy of bitterness that martial law could leave among the people and continually stressed the importance of this to the military authorities. At various times he disagreed strongly not just with Beynon, but also with Dyer and Johnson, in his efforts to relax martial law. He intervened to prevent Amritsar from having a large fine levied on it; he thought the salaaming order in Amritsar was 'ridiculous' and suggested it should be cancelled; he was instrumental in getting Dyer to cancel the 'crawling order'; he suggested to Frank Johnson that the distances for students to march in Lahore should be shortened; and he also insisted that the population of Lahore was not totally disarmed (as Johnson wanted).[36] Given these efforts, it is difficult to see O'Dwyer as the cartoon villain of Congress imagination. Furthermore, his original wish to retain civilian control of martial law, which was vetoed by the Government of India, seems remarkably farsighted. Although O'Dwyer still had an important role to play in how martial law was administered, he could not *order* Beynon to do anything. He offered his opinion, but the military authorities sometimes 'did not act as promptly as I had hoped ... they always took notice of my suggestions and the suggestions of my officers and sooner or later, sometimes sooner, sometimes later, took action on them'. Therefore, his claim that any abuses 'were not those of my administration, they were the orders of the Martial Law authorities' was correct.[37]

It should not be thought, however, that the story of martial law was simply one of military brutality and repression. The Indian Army was in a highly unenviable position. The Adjutant-General in India, Havelock Hudson, complained that the introduction of martial law caused British troops 'very great loss and extra pain and suffering' because it prevented them from returning home, many of whom had not seen their families for five years.[38] Enforcing martial law was not particularly easy for those British officers and soldiers who were tasked with it. It was all the more difficult in the outlying regions, areas that could not rely on large numbers of troops to quell disorder and where only a light hand of government was pressed. In any case, none of the officers involved, both senior and junior, had any experience of martial law in India, something that had not been declared in over 60 years. Many of those in senior military and civilian positions during the disturbances confessed to their unfamiliarity with what they were being asked to do. Many had completely different ideas as to what martial law actually was.[39] This confusion was certainly understandable and the Adjutant-General also made the very relevant point that the *Manual of Military Law*, the soldiers' guide, contained 900 pages, but only one page was allotted to martial law and that the 'soldier has got very little to go upon'.[40]

Undoubtedly, martial law in the more outlying areas of the Punjab, from Kasur to Gujranwala, was not always administered as well as it should have been. Lacking the numbers of staff necessary, many British soldiers and officials struggled to deal with the vast administrative and judicial tasks that they had been given. They were aware of the murders of Europeans and the swiftness with which violence had broken out, and felt that unless order was restored quickly and efficiently, it could happen again. It is clear that O'Dwyer consulted with the military authorities 'every other day or so' in Lahore, however, the same could not be said of those officers who were operating further afield.[41] The declaration of martial law presented those officers in more rural parts of the Punjab with considerable challenges, particularly given their lack of experience in dealing with this kind of situation and a dearth of official instructions in how they were to proceed. Bosworth-Smith had never been to Gujranwala before he was sent there on 21 April and O'Brien was not issued with any instructions about martial law, apart from a brief telephone conversation with J.P. Thompson who told him that he might have to take certain actions hurriedly, but that they would be legalised afterwards if they were conducted 'in good faith'.[42]

Why then has this period been seen for so long as one of spiteful repression and torture? In truth, historians have been guilty of over-exaggerating certain incidents and of not paying sufficient attention to the documentary record. The incident of the 'whitewashed' *sadhu* is particularly instructive and shows how Indian nationalists were effective at taking numerous events out of context, often embellishing and exaggerating them, and always ascribing the worst possible motives to the British officers, men like Dyer and Doveton,

Johnson and McRae. Although there is no evidence that a Hindu holy man was abused in this fashion, it has gradually become part of the Amritsar legend and continues to be repeated to this day. An allegation by the American sociologist, Helen Fein, was that the British use of terror was a 'spontaneous invention' by those officers who were allowed great responsibility in districts where martial law was declared. She argued that 'The use of terror was consistent with the officers' conviction that they, the British, were in a state of war with the Indians, who could no longer be regarded indulgently, like children, but must be treated sternly as enemies.'[43] This may have been true on rare occasions when tempers flared, but the men who were given such responsibility in 1919 were not all ruthless zealots dripping with hatred for Indian civilians. They were professionals who knew the seriousness of the situation and feared that unless strong action was taken, British rule would weaken, if not collapse. They were all aware of the legacy of bitterness that martial law could produce and did their best to lessen it. Most had been educated and brought up in a world of so-called 'muscular Christianity', a world of benevolent imperialism and the 'white man's burden', where it was their duty to set an example of civilisation and rigid order before their subjects.[44] Indeed, if anything emerges from the testimonies compiled by the Hunter Committee, it is that many officers felt martial law was a process that allowed them to *educate* the Indian population, not terrorise them, something which was very much in line with this emphasis on benevolent imperial direction. However, distasteful this may now seem, these actions can only be understood within the context of 1919 and the settled, hierarchical world of the British Empire.

CHAPTER 15

Lord Hunter and the Disorders Inquiry Committee

I do not believe that the Government has anything to fear from a searching enquiry.

Edwin Montagu[1]

C restfallen at what had happened in the Punjab, Gandhi issued a statement to the Indian press on 18 April suspending his campaign of civil disobedience. 'It is not without sorrow,' he wrote, 'that I feel compelled to advise the temporary suspension of civil disobedience ... I am sorry, when I embarked upon a mass movement, I underrated the forces of evil and I must now pause and consider how best to meet the situation.'[2] Gandhi's decision to suspend his campaign, combined with the stringent efforts now being made to stamp out any dissent by the Government of India, meant that the Rowlatt *Satyagraha* gradually faded away during late April and May 1919, particularly in those areas where he did not have reservoirs of local support. Gandhi continued to preach non-violence and spread his views through his newspapers, *New India* and *Navajivan*, but his reputation had been battered by the events in the Punjab and he was assailed from both sides, by those who believed that he should not have stopped his campaign, but pressed on into the teeth of official resistance, and those who said that he had only himself to blame for the toll of dead and wounded that was being counted across the Bombay Presidency and the Punjab.[3]

The summer of 1919 was a turbulent one for India. At the beginning of May the Third Afghan War had broken out with columns of Afghan troops, joined by tribal militias, marching down from the hills into the Punjab via three invasion routes: the Khyber, Khost and Kandahar.[4] Although the war ended relatively quickly – an armistice had been signed on 3 June – the invasion was a further shock to those who had hoped the ending of the Great War in November 1918 would herald a new era of peace and security for the Raj. With the ending of the war with Afghanistan and the gradual lifting of martial law, news began circulating about what had happened in the Punjab, provoking nationalist outrage and fuelling a sustained anti-government campaign in the Indian press. The Nobel Prize-winning author, Rabindranath Tagore, wrote to the Viceroy on 31 May expressing his disgust with the measures taken by the authorities to restore order. These measures, he wrote, have 'with a rude shock, revealed to our minds the helplessness of our position as British subjects in India'. Accordingly, he asked Chelmsford to release him from his knighthood.[5]

On 8 June the All India Congress Committee met in Allahabad and appointed a sub-committee to begin its own investigation into the events in the Punjab, to be led by a member of Imperial Legislative Council, Madan Mohan Malaviya, and a well-respected barrister, Motilal Nehru. They travelled to the Punjab on 25 June and began to compile evidence on the disturbances and the reaction of the government to them.[6] Anger at the happenings in the Punjab was also combined with a growing fury emanating from sections of the Muslim community, angry at the fate of Turkey and anxious about the future of Islamic holy places in the Middle East. Over the next year this would turn into the Khalifat movement, which although never organised on national lines and unrepresentative of all of India's Muslims, posed yet more problems for Chelmsford's beleaguered administration. *Satyagraha* may have been suppressed, the danger from Afghanistan averted, but political unrest and agitation in India would only continue into the winter of 1919–20 and highlight the alarming spread of political discontent across the subcontinent.

❧

Lord Chelmsford gave the opening speech at a meeting of the Imperial Legislative Council on 3 September.[7]

> Since the close of the last session there have been events of a grave character disturbing the peace and tranquillity of this country, and I cannot pass them over without mention. For some time past my Government has been in correspondence with the Secretary of State upon the question of an enquiry into these disorders. We have both been anxious to settle this question as quickly as possible, but an announcement has been delayed largely by the difficulty of procuring the services of a suitable chairman.

But now, Chelmsford could reveal, this difficulty had been overcome and Lord William Hunter, an eminent Scottish judge, had been appointed. It would begin the following month. The proceedings of the committee would be held in public, but the chairman had the right to direct them *in camera* if the 'public interests so require'. 'I trust that people of all classes of opinion,' he added, 'will do nothing to add to their difficulties by the needless importation of irrelevant or intentionally inflammable material.'

Chelmsford was clearly uncomfortable at the meeting of the Legislative Council, unhappy over the decision to have an inquiry, fearful of what it would produce and whether it would result in further disorder. But Edwin Montagu was not to be dissuaded and it was from the Secretary of State that the pressure came. Far from attempting to downplay the disorders, he was convinced that an inquiry was exactly what India needed, a searching and impartial investigation that would restore faith in the British Government and its promises of reform. As early as 1 May, Montagu warned Chelmsford that he believed they should hold 'an enquiry into the causes of and the treatment of the riots that have occurred in India'. Although Montagu was at pains to point out that this did not necessarily imply that the Government of India was at fault, 'it always seems to me', he reassured the anxious Viceroy, 'that one ought to investigate allegations of needless brutality'.[8] Montagu saw the inquiry as an opportunity to re-engage with Indian nationalists, particularly Gandhi, and create a more favourable reception to his policies, but it would be deeply unwelcome to the authorities in India. Both Bengal and Bombay were opposed to it, and Sir William Vincent, the Home Member, argued that it would only 'renew old bitterness now wiped out' and provide an opportunity for extremists to indict government policies.[9]

Despite the almost unanimous opposition to an inquiry from the authorities in India, Montagu would not listen and showed his stubborn streak, pressing ahead with it anyway, although he did state that Indian members would only be chosen if they could command the respect and confidence of the 'moderates' in India. As was perhaps to be expected, deciding upon the composition of the committee was a delicate task and there were considerable difficulties in securing the acceptances of its members, particularly the chairman. Montagu would later complain of his angst at not being able to secure the services of a man of 'really outstanding merits', but by late August he had decided that it must be Lord William Hunter, a former solicitor general in the Asquith Government and a senator of the College of Justice in Scotland.[10] The Viceroy was not particularly enamoured with Montagu's suggestion. On 20 August he expressed his 'great surprise' and regret that they had not secured 'someone with a more high-sounding name than Lord Hunter'.[11] Montagu wrote back a week later, arguing that Hunter was 'level-headed', 'conscientious' and a 'wise man', but this could not dispel the profound lack of confidence that was reposed in him.[12]

Whether Lord Hunter was fit to lead the inquiry was an open question among the authorities that autumn. For his part, Montagu had faith that Hunter was the right man. On 29 August he wrote to him, urging him to avoid producing a 'whitewash'. 'The object that we have in instituting this enquiry,' he said, 'is in short to take with confidence and with courage all the steps necessary to restore public confidence.'[13] The same day he wrote to Chelmsford.

> We are in for this enquiry and we must make the best of it. I am satisfied that in order to make the best of it, we must have a fearless enquiry. Nothing would be worse than an enquiry which was held to be prejudiced and before which evidence was not produced.[14]

The Hunter Committee was finally appointed on 14 October to investigate the causes of, and measures taken to cope with, the 'recent disorders' in Delhi, the Punjab and Bombay Presidency. It consisted of seven members, not including its chairman: Mr Justice G.C. Rankin (Judge of the High Court, Calcutta); Mr W.F. Rice (Additional Secretary to the Government of India, Home Department); Major-General Sir George Barrow (GOC Peshawar Division); Pandit Jagat Narayan (Member of Legislative Council, United Provinces); Mr Thomas Smith (Member of Legislative Council, United Provinces); Sir Chimanlal Setalvad (Advocate of High Court, Bombay); and Sardar Sahibzada Sultan Ahmed Khan (Member for Appeals, Gwalior). Together they would take part in one of the most important and controversial investigations in the history of British rule in India.

ඐ

The Hunter Committee began its hearings in Lahore on 29 October. Although some of the interviews (such as those with Michael O'Dwyer and the Adjutant-General, Havelock Hudson) were held in private (in a tent in the garden of Faletti's Hotel), the majority were held in an open hall where members of the public were invited to attend. Given the wide interest in the case and the controversy of what had happened in the Punjab, it was perhaps inevitable that large crowds were drawn to the committee, many of whom were students and political activists. One of the constant criticisms of those that came before Lord Hunter and his colleagues was the atmosphere in the court, which was sometimes extremely hostile to British officials and soldiers, and Hunter constantly struggled to maintain order. At one point during the testimony of Reginald Plomer (one of the senior police officers at Amritsar), his voice was drowned out by laughing in the public gallery. Hunter was forced to intercede. 'There should be no demonstration of any description by any member of the audience. It is only on these conditions that this enquiry is to be conducted in public.'[15] It would not be the only occasion when the atmosphere in the courtroom was far from ideal.

Even though Indian writing has often presented the Hunter Committee (and its subsequent report) as little more than a one-sided official whitewash designed to bury the blame for the outbreak and suppression of the disorders, in reality this was not the case. Montagu tried desperately to make sure that the committee was as impartial and objective as possible, even writing to Chelmsford on 29 August imploring him not to defend every action that had been taken by the authorities during the disorders. If the inquiry was a whitewash, Montagu complained, 'we shall have achieved nothing and we shall have done more to embitter feeling than anything'.[16] Indeed, the approach taken by the committee was far more rigorous than is usually assumed. While the British members of the inquiry were restrained and respectful, the Indian members were able to conduct their cross-examination of witnesses almost unchecked and more than lived up to their reputations as sharp, critical barristers.

One of the constant features of the hearings was the atmosphere of distrust between the official and non-official members of the committee; something that may have been entirely predictable, but was nevertheless deeply damaging. Setalvad recorded in his memoirs a row between himself and Lord Hunter who accused him of wanting 'to drive the British out of the country'. Setalvad bristled at this comment and accused Hunter of being 'short-sighted' and 'intolerant'.[17] This spat, which took place at Agra when the reports were being drafted, was indicative of the discord that threatened to fracture the entire process. The Indian members of the committee were barely on speaking terms with Hunter afterwards. One of the problems was that Lord Hunter was either unable or unwilling to rein in members of his team. According to one writer, Hunter was 'not out of the top drawer', was 'completely ignorant of India' and could not speak 'one word of any Indian language'.[18] Sir George Barrow would recall that Hunter was 'a mild man somewhat dazed on his entry on a new stage, where diaphanous oriental draperies replaced the weightier tartans of his own land' and even Montagu would notice that Hunter was 'more than a little diffident' about India.[19]

As the hearings got underway, there were many tense standoffs between the Indian members of the committee, particularly Pandit Narayan, and those who were called to give evidence. Narayan was a fiercely intelligent man and a fervent nationalist, and his questions and assumptions often upset those whom he interviewed. He certainly made life very difficult for the British soldiers and officials who gave evidence, repeatedly probing their responses, trying to pinpoint weaknesses in their arguments and provoking them with criticisms of their actions. Even Gandhi felt that Narayan's questioning was 'extremely severe' and 'harsher than it need be'.[20] This was particularly the case with military officers who felt that Narayan was treating them in a disrespectful and, at times, insulting manner. Major-General Beynon was incensed when Narayan accused him of treating Lahore 'as the Germans treated Belgium', implying that the authorities had committed widespread abuse of the civilian population. He would also complain that Narayan was not putting 'plain questions' to him, a common criticism of so-called 'clever Indian lawyers'.[21] Fierce exchanges also occurred between the Indian members and Lieutenant-Colonel Frank Johnson, who had been commander of the Lahore Civil Area during martial law. Johnson was not a man to be easily intimidated and seemed to revel in the pressured atmosphere of the courtroom, confident in his actions and unwilling to back down before the committee. On one occasion when Johnson referred to Indians as 'natives', Setalvad reminded him that the term was offensive and to use the expression 'Indian' instead. With tension thick in the air, Johnson would later claim that the people of India would 'never be fit for self-government' until they had 'become a nation'.[22] This clash was indicative of the controversies and disagreements that ran through the committee's work.

The testimony for which the Hunter Report will always be known – the testimony that sparked fierce controversy and which continues to bedevil our understanding of the Amritsar Massacre – belonged to Brigadier-General Dyer. He appeared before the committee on 19 November and spent the day answering questions and talking about what had happened at Amritsar. The hearing took place in Lahore with the hall full of onlookers as usual, including many students, all eager for a glimpse of the general. Dyer was not in the best of condition. He had only returned from operations against Afghanistan in June and, aggravated by the intense heat and strain, his health was gradually failing. He was also worried about his Brigade Major, Tommy Briggs, who was then in hospital awaiting an operation for a suspected appendicitis. Briggs's absence meant that Dyer was without many of his personal notes and papers and also without the support of a trusted friend with a thorough knowledge of the events in question.[23] Although some of Dyer's colleagues had warned him about saying too much in front of the committee, he does not seem to have listened to them. His commanding officer in Lahore, William Beynon, apparently told Dyer, 'There are on this Inquiry several extremely clever Indian lawyers, who are out to get you. For God's sake, stick to the facts and keep your mouth shut.'[24] Unfortunately, Dyer did not heed these words. He was a man in great physical pain, shaken, unprepared for the fierce arena he was about to enter.

The committee asked Dyer about a range of subjects related to this time in Amritsar, such as the nature of the disorders, the actions of the civilian authorities (particularly how and when he was handed authority), and his decision to institute the so-called 'crawling order', but his actions in the Jallianwala Bagh took up most of the day. The committee was interested in trying to assess Dyer's motivations on 13 April and why he had fired into the crowd. Lord Hunter asked Dyer why he had continued to fire into the crowd at the Jallianwala Bagh even though they had tried to flee by moving to the exits. 'I thought it my duty to go on firing until it dispersed,' Dyer replied. 'If I fired a little, the effect would not be sufficient. If I had fired a little I should be wrong in firing at all.' Hunter went on, asking Dyer whether he believed the crowd would not have dispersed had he asked them to do so. Dyer shrugged, admitting that 'I think it quite possible that I could have dispersed them even without firing.' Somewhat alarmed at Dyer's response, Hunter gave him another opportunity to put his actions into context, asking him why he did not do this. 'I could not disperse them for some time; then they would all come back and laugh at me, and I considered I would be making myself a fool.' A short while later he added that he had not taken his decision to fire lightly; he looked upon it 'as my duty, a very horrible duty'.[25]

After Lord Hunter had completed his questions, he was followed by G.C. Rankin, who also was interested in Dyer's motivations, particularly when he had made his mind up to go and fire at the gathering. Dyer maintained that the situation was 'very, very serious' and that he had made up his mind to 'do all men to death if they were going to continue the meeting'.[26] 'Excuse my putting it in that way, General,' Rankin then asked, somewhat perturbed by his choice of words, 'but was it not a resort to what has been called "frightfulness" for the benefit of the Punjab Districts as a whole?' Dyer categorically denied this was the case.

> I think it was a horrible duty for me to perform. It was a merciful act that I had given them chance to disperse. The responsibility was very great. I had made up my mind that if I fired I must fire well and strong so that it would have a full effect. I had decided if I fired one round I must shoot a lot of rounds or I must not shoot at all.

It seemed clear from what Dyer was saying that his actions were premeditated and had been decided upon before he arrived at the Jallianwala Bagh.

Dyer was then asked about the 'crawling order' in Amritsar, when he had closed the street where Miss Sherwood had been assaulted, and the floggings that had been inflicted upon six men for this offence. Although Dyer did not have any proof that the six men had been guilty of striking down Miss Sherwood, 'the chances were', he said, that they had been involved in the assault and he would not run the risk of letting them go free, so he had them flogged. Dyer maintained that 30 lashes was the limit proscribed by the government and that 'In the old days it used to be many hundreds of lashes. Now-a-days I look upon it as not a very severe sentence.' This comment did nothing to endear Dyer to the committee and reinforced the growing sense that this was a man of brutality and severity, or at the very least, a monumental lack of tact.

The next to interview Dyer was Chimanlal Setalvad, the first of the Indian members of the committee. He talked Dyer through his proclamation and his arrival at the Jallianwala Bagh and the responses seemed to confirm that Dyer had decided upon his actions in the Bagh before he had arrived and that they had been premeditated. At one point he posed a question about the width of the entrance to the Jallianwala Bagh and supposing that it had been wider, whether Dyer would have employed the armoured cars (with their mounted machine guns) on the crowd. Setalvad was fond of asking such suppositions, which although may not have been strictly relevant to what had actually occurred, helped to keep up the pressure on Dyer. Setalvad could sense that more revelations would follow if he kept probing him, but he could not have been more surprised when his quarry took the bait, replying simply that, 'I think probably yes.' This was perhaps the most shocking of all Dyer's claims, a scandalising admission that he would have used machine guns upon an unarmed crowd and caused many more casualties, but had been unable to. The shock in the hall was palpable.

After pausing for a few moments, Setalvad then asked Dyer whether his decision to open fire in the Bagh was designed to 'strike terror' into the population. 'Call it what you like,' Dyer replied, with a touch of disdain. 'I was going to punish them. My idea from a military point of view was to make a wide impression.' Undaunted, Setalvad continued, querying whether it was designed to make an impact throughout the Punjab. Dyer agreed, replying that he wanted to reduce the 'moral' of the rebels. When he was asked, once again, whether this constituted 'frightfulness', Dyer thought not and maintained that 'it was my duty to do this' and that 'they ought to be thankful to me for doing it'. He went on to state that 'I thought I would be doing a jolly lot of good and they would realize that they were not to be wicked.'[27] Dyer finished his testimony that evening, exhausted after having been subject to detailed questioning for most of the day, but still proud of his performance. Although he remained robustly confident in what he had said, perhaps very glorifying in the stand he had made, Dyer should have known what kind of impact his statements would make. The backlash was about to begin.

❧

The Hunter Committee finished its hearings in January 1920 and retired to the Government Guest House in Agra to prepare their report. There, beneath the glorious white dome of the Taj Mahal, the tensions that had been seen throughout the hearings, between the official and non-official members, now widened still further. During this time the committee were constantly talking about the events they had investigated, arguing over different claims and trying to agree a satisfactory position to present to the Government of India. But it was to no avail and agreement was not reached. Setalvad noticed that there was 'a definite cleavage of opinion' between the European and Indian members on three main points: the justification of the application for martial law, its continuance and the level of condemnation that should be placed upon the firing at the Jallianwala Bagh and other allegedly 'oppressive measures'.[28] The European view (which would be confirmed in the Majority Report), considered that the unrest in the Punjab was open rebellion and justified most of the actions taken by the British authorities before and during martial law, except for the firing at the Jallianwala Bagh and a number of 'fancy punishments'.[29] The Indian members felt far more strongly on these issues, believing that 'the Government of India had taken an exaggerated and panicky view of the disturbances and had wrongly persuaded themselves to believe that the disturbances showed the existence of open rebellion'. Setalvad complained that the Europeans – Hunter, Rankin, Barrow, Rice and Smith – took a 'somewhat halting and apologetic' approach to these incidents.[30] Indeed, far from settling the matter once and for all, the Hunter Report only brought the issues into greater focus and prepared the ground for over 90 years of controversy.

Dyer's testimony remains at the heart of the matter and it would end his career. Indeed, it has been suggested that it was his unwise and often salacious admissions before the inquiry, rather than his actions in Amritsar *per se*, that fatally compromised his defence, and there is probably some truth in this. Aware of the brewing storm that his testimony had created, Dyer soon began to backtrack on some of the comments he had made. In June 1920 he drafted a statement with a team of solicitors in London. This was then sent to the War Office where it was hoped that it would lead to a reconsideration of his treatment. Although Dyer's request was not accepted, it gave him an opportunity to criticise the way that the inquiry had been conducted, including the way he had been cross-examined, the lack of notice of any charges against him, and being unable to review his transcript and correct verbal inaccuracies. Dyer concluded that 'this procedure was not in accordance with the course of justice normally observed at the hearing of complaints or charges against an individual' and that 'the procedure was wholly irregular according to military law and custom'. Therefore, he requested that the Army Council not consider the findings of the Hunter Committee as in any way final but to draw their own conclusions 'of my conduct as a soldier'.[31]

There was certainly some truth in Dyer's criticisms of the Hunter Inquiry, and indeed he may have received better treatment at a formal court-martial. At the very least he would have been able to check the transcripts of his interview, which he always maintained were inaccurate.[32] Although it is not possible to state with any certainty whether the text that was recorded was a completely accurate version of what was said – there would undoubtedly have been a number of errors – the main problem was the nature of the inquiry itself. The testimonies before the committee were not taken on oath and witnesses did not have access to any legal representation. It was not in any way meant to be a trial of those responsible for the disorders or those who suppressed them, but at times it came close to becoming one. Dyer would not be the only British officer who went before the committee unsure of what would happen. Lieutenant-Colonel A.J. O'Brien, the Deputy Commissioner of Gujranwala, would make a familiar complaint when he told Chimanlal Setalvad that 'I did not expect to be cross-examined.'[33] Dyer seems to have become convinced that he had saved the Raj and deserved praise not criticism. He was a strong-willed man, prone to vanity, and – like many who came before the committee – he bristled at being questioned in a searching and, at times, critical manner, particularly by Indian lawyers.

With the 'Dyer affair' now reverberating throughout the empire, perhaps Montagu was beginning to realise the magnitude of the mistake he had made in ordering an inquiry into the disorders in the Punjab. His pious hope that Lord Hunter would be able to author a report that would simultaneously heal the wounds from the Punjab, undermine nationalist accusations of partiality and official bias, and bring about a renewed sense of trust between the government and the nationalists was in tatters, shown to be the naive illusion it always was. The decision to include members such as Pandit Narayan and Chimanlal Setalvad, to ensure it would be acceptable in some form to nationalist opinion, was revealed as a fallacy, because before Lord Hunter had even been appointed, the All India Congress Committee had begun their own investigation and had a natural interest in criticising Hunter's work. Yet the inclusion of the Indian members meant that it was highly unlikely that they would come to an agreed position with Lord Hunter and the other official members, and merely highlight the discord within India. Furthermore, because the inquiry was not independent, no matter how much Montagu nagged Hunter to conduct a 'fearless' investigation, his conclusions were likely to be viewed as nothing more than official 'whitewash'.

In some respects, the Hunter Inquiry gave Montagu the worst of both worlds. It was never likely to be acceptable to Gandhi and the more extreme wing of the Indian National Congress, yet at the same time, it alienated many British officials and soldiers who came under searching cross-examination without protection or representation. The apparent 'revelations' that leaked out of their testimonies did enough to hint that a great deal of brutality and 'imperial terrorism' had occurred in the Punjab, but been suppressed by Lord Hunter and his committee. Had Montagu listened to those in the Government of India who had cautioned him against taking such a dangerous step, he would not have been in such a parlous position. There undoubtedly would have been an outcry against the Jallianwala Bagh, but it would have been manageable and easier to survive. Now with Dyer's testimony sprawled across the front pages of the press in Fleet Street, and renewed clamouring from the nationalists in India, Montagu was faced with a propaganda disaster and a major crisis of confidence in his leadership. His failure either to understand or appreciate the implications of Hunter's inquiry, meant that he was responsible for undermining support for the Raj in a period of acute difficulty. This was not the way to run an empire; it was, on the contrary, a recipe for complete and utter disaster.

CHAPTER 16

Debates and Disagreements

There could be no reasonable doubt in my mind that any villagers in the meeting were there as sympathizers and adherents of the insurrection.

Brigadier-General Reginald Dyer[1]

In March 1920 Dyer was summoned to Delhi and informed, much to his surprise, that owing to the conclusions of the Hunter Committee, he was to be immediately relieved of command. He could expect no further employment in India. Shocked and disgusted at how he was being treated, Dyer protested, but to no avail. He left India two months later, buoyed by a torchlight procession from his men, but wracked with physical as well as mental pain. Once back in London he tried to have his case reviewed, petitioning the Army Council for a court martial, but his efforts were unsuccessful and, by the summer of 1920 there was nothing else to do but pick over the ruins of his career and brood on ambitions unfulfilled.[2]

On 8 July the House of Commons debated the affair. A motion had been put forward by critics of Montagu to have the salary of the Secretary of State for India reduced by £100 in order to express their disapproval of his actions over the Punjab. In a noisy, bitter exchange, the supporters and critics of Dyer's actions clashed on what had happened, how he had been treated and what issues were at stake. Dyer was in the gallery sitting next to Sir Michael O'Dwyer and watched the proceedings in silence.[3] The debate that Montagu had hoped to silence with the Hunter Inquiry, and with his assiduous cultivation of Fleet Street, was now out of control. He opened the debate, arguing that Dyer's actions were totally unjustified and brought up fundamental choices about the way in which India was to be ruled. Montagu was speaking from the heart. As the author of a set of reforms that he believed would result in a new way of governing India, a new way based, to a certain degree, on Indian opinion and a greater regard for Indian feeling, he could in no way justify the Jallianwala Bagh.

In his speech Montagu did not go into the details of the Dyer case, but concentrated on what he believed were the broader issues at stake. He believed that it was a simple choice between terrorism and democracy. If you were going to fire upon a gathering and keep shooting 'to teach somebody else a lesson', if you were going to have the 'crawling order' or other 'fancy punishments', then you were 'enforcing racial humiliation' and 'indulging in frightfulness'. He would have none of this. Furthermore:

> Are you going to keep your hold upon India by terrorism, racial humiliation and subordination, and frightfulness, or are you going to rest it upon the goodwill, and the growing goodwill, of the people of your Indian Empire.[4]

Montagu believed that this was 'the whole question at issue', but his comments and the way in which he had defined the debate – that it was a choice between terrorism and goodwill – would infuriate a vocal minority across the floor, who had never been impressed with the Secretary of State and whose sympathies lay firmly with Dyer. His opponents were in the mood for a fight that afternoon; one of them even shouting out, 'What a terrible speech!'

The debate raged for seven hours and covered all aspects of the Amritsar incident: the origins of the disturbances and whether there had been a revolutionary conspiracy; the nature of the violence and the size and composition of the crowds; the Jallianwala Bagh incident; the role of Sir Michael O'Dwyer; the administration of martial law; the effect of censuring Dyer on the future of the Empire, and so on. Eventually, at 11 p.m. a halt was called to the proceedings and a vote was held over whether the Secretary of State should have his salary reduced. Only 37 members voted yes, the remaining (247) members of Parliament voted no. Montagu had survived. The House may have approved the decision to deprive Dyer of his command with a large majority, chiefly Labour and Liberal votes, but the victory was won at a great personal cost to Montagu, who never recovered from the verbal battering he received from the floor – what Sir Michael O'Dwyer called his 'pitiful exhibition' – having alienated large swathes of conservative opinion by his emotional and passionate appeal against racism and terrorism.[5]

By now the case had begun to attract a powerful group of supporters who sympathised with the position of Dyer and believed that it was essential for the future confidence of the Raj that he was supported. Bloodied but unbowed the pro-Dyer lobby retreated to consider their tactics. The day after the commons debate, H.A. Gwynne, Editor of the arch-conservative *Morning Post*, opened a public subscription for him that eventually collected over £28,000. Dyer was initially opposed to it, but O'Dwyer persuaded him that it was the only way in which the public 'could show their sympathy for him and their disgust at his treatment'. On 19 July the House of Lords debated the affair. The supporters of Dyer were out in strength. A motion was put forward: 'That this House deplores the conduct of the case of General Dyer as unjust to that officer, and as establishing a precedent dangerous to the preservation of order in face of rebellion.' A sizeable majority voted for the motion, which was another embarrassment to Montagu and the Government of India, and highlighted how the Amritsar affair had polarised British political opinion.[6]

∾

During the debate in the House of Commons, one of the issues that continually cropped up was the gathering at the Jallianwala Bagh, whether it was a peaceful, unarmed crowd or a violent, revolutionary mob. In some respects this was the key question. In his classic statement on the crowd in the French Revolution, George Rudé has complained that historians who have looked at the composition of such gatherings have tended to do so 'according to their own social ideas, political sympathies, or ideological preoccupations'.[7] A similar tendency has occurred with the crowd in the Jallianwala Bagh. For those who sought to defend Dyer, the key to their argument was ascertaining the guilt and criminal intent of those who gathered. If it could be shown that the crowd had done so in *direct defiance* of the orders prohibiting large gatherings, then Dyer's actions could, more easily, be justified.[8] On the other side of the debate, however, were those who claimed that the people in the Jallianwala Bagh were innocent and had not heard of any proclamation. If this was the case then Dyer's actions would be totally unjustifiable.[9]

It may not be possible to settle these arguments conclusively, but some limited deductions can be made. Although it is true that Dyer did not visit every area of the city (including some important locations), it is clear that considerable numbers of people saw his proclamation. Several officials estimated that up to 500 people gathered in each location, and given that they stopped 19 times, this would have meant that between 7,000 and 9,000 people heard the proclamation.[10] According to the 1921 census of India, Amritsar had a population of just over 160,000 people; therefore, approximately five to six percent of the population would have witnessed Dyer's proclamation at first hand.[11] In any case, this figure is likely to have been higher, assuming that at least some of those who were present either mentioned it to their friends or gave them a copy of the written orders. It was certainly assumed at the time that word would spread rapidly through the city, and this was not unlikely given that Amritsar was one of the most congested urban areas in the Punjab, with a higher population density than either Delhi or Lahore.[12] Furthermore, knowledge would have spread indirectly because soon after Dyer's column had left the city, a counter-proclamation was made by a boy with a tin can shouting that a meeting would be held at 4 p.m. in the Jallianwala Bagh.[13]

Despite the efforts that had been made to dissuade people from gathering in large numbers, by the early afternoon of 13 April a crowd had begun to form in the Jallianwala Bagh. Given its importance to the history of India's independence movement, our knowledge of this meeting is remarkably thin. It had been organised by the secretary of the *Satyagraha Sabha*, Hans Raj, ostensibly on the orders of their leader, Dr Bashir. At 4 p.m. on 12 April Raj had spoken at Hindu Sabha High School and explained that he was organising a great meeting for the following afternoon. Two resolutions would be made: the first condemning the firing on 10 April and the second calling for the release of the leaders.[14] A letter from Dr Kitchlew would also be read out by his wife. It was for this meeting that the boy went around the city with a tin can after Dyer's column had left. One of the important facts about the gathering in the Jallianwala Bagh was that it was organised, to a certain extent, on *false pretences*. During various public meetings on 12 April, Hans Raj had repeatedly stressed that it would be presided over by Lala Kanhyalal Bhatia, an elderly High Court pleader who was widely respected in the city. Yet when questioned about his role on 13 April, Bhatia emphatically denied any participation. 'No one consulted me,' he complained. Furthermore, 'I never had any intention to speak at or preside over any meeting on that day, nor did I express any such intention to anybody.'[15] It is, therefore, unclear what Bhatia's role in the meeting at the Jallianwala Bagh was and that has led to a suggestion that all was not as it seemed on 13 April.

The role of Hans Raj has been a source of constant speculation. It has been alleged that he was a police informant guilty of luring Indians into the Bagh with the blessing of the British authorities. This accusation seems to have emerged soon after the massacre and can be found in Pearay Mohan's *The Punjab 'Rebellion' of 1919 and How It Was Suppressed* (1920). Mohan claimed that Hans Raj, 'a rudderless youth of an extremely dubious character', had been unable to find a stable career in Amritsar, being dismissed from several jobs because he stole money from his employers. He had apparently tried to join the police but was turned down. Mohan then claims that despite these setbacks, Raj was allowed to become a secret agent of the CID, the infamous Indian intelligence organisation. At this point (and despite having no political interest or inclinations) Raj began to attend political meetings in Amritsar, gradually 'worming' his way into the confidences of the leading public men in the city, before finally being appointed secretary of the *Satyagraha Sabha* on 8 April. During the disturbances Raj watched and reported on the movements of the nationalists within the city and was then ordered to arrange the meeting at the Jallianwala Bagh.[16] Alfred Draper has also suggested that he was seen talking to two CID officers that afternoon and then mysteriously disappearing just before Dyer's troops arrived.[17]

How valid is the argument that Hans Raj was at the centre of a British conspiracy to organise (and then suppress) a meeting at the Jallianwala Bagh? Although it has remained a constant suspicion in nationalist discourse it should be dismissed.[18] Like many conspiracy theories it focuses on minor anomalies and distorts them out of context and is highly unlikely. First, the idea that Dyer would have *wanted* huge numbers of people to gather in the centre of the city is nothing less than absurd. This was, from his perspective, the worst thing that could have happened and what he had been trying to prevent for two days. Second, Pearay Mohan could not point to any evidence that Raj ever met Dyer or any other senior British official, apart from circumstantial suspicions. In any case, the argument that Hans Raj disappeared before Dyer's troops arrived at the Bagh is also doubtful. Several eyewitness accounts agree that Raj was *still present* when the troops arrived and some even recall him speaking to the crowd. For example, one witness remembered that as soon as Dyer's men began arriving, Raj had told the people not to be afraid. When the first volley had been fired he again shouted 'these are blank shots'.[19] If Raj was at the centre of some conspiracy, then he was surely putting his own life at risk by remaining in the Bagh.

The activities of Hans Raj on 12 and 13 April point not so much to a sinister conspiracy with the British authorities, but more to the lack of nationalist leadership in Amritsar in the absence of Kitchlew and Satyapal, both of whom were widely known and respected. It seems that Raj, lacking both the wide following that the two leaders enjoyed and the charisma that would have allowed him to give a sparkling oration, simply used Bhatia's name – one of the few pleaders who had a strong following – to increase the turnout at the Jallianwala Bagh. The reputation of Hans Raj as an ardent and honest nationalist may have been undermined by his betrayal of his colleagues during the Amritsar Conspiracy Case, but before 13 April there is no reason to believe that he was not a committed *satyagrahi*, having found a purpose and direction that had so far been denied him in life; certainly not the only dissolute youth who would find his destiny in a nationalist struggle. He would later tell a British magistrate that a speech by Dr Satyapal had made such a 'great impression' on him that he had signed the *satyagraha* vow the following day.[20] Prominence in the nationalist movement gave Raj a platform that he otherwise would not have had. It was only when he was arrested by the police in late April that his new found zeal crumbled and he told them what they wanted to hear; that Kitchlew and Satyapal had been the prime movers in a province-wide conspiracy to overthrow the government with force.

જ

Hans Raj had been busy in the garden from about 2 p.m. A stage had been erected about 100 yards (91 metres) from the main entrance with a portrait of Kitchlew propped up against it. Eight speakers delivered orations on 13 April: Dar Singh, Abdul Majid, Brij Gopi Nath, Gurbax Rai, Abdul Aziz, Rai Ram Singh, Hans Raj and Durga Das. All were local nationalists who had been involved in the *hartal* movement and were colleagues of Kitchlew and Satyapal. It is unclear in which order they came, but it is often said that either Hans Raj or Durga Das came last, standing on the platform and speaking to the crowd when Dyer's troops entered.[21] The content of their speeches will probably never be known and, as discussed earlier, this remains a subject of some speculation, often mirroring the writer's ideological perspective. Contrary to some claims, the speakers in the Jallianwala Bagh do not seem to have been inciting the crowd to armed revolt or urging them to rush towards the railway station and cantonment and finish off the British. It is likely that had this been the case, the meeting would have been much shorter and the decisive clash with the authorities would have occurred earlier. As it was the speeches went on for about three hours and would have gone on for longer had Dyer not dispersed the crowd. The crowd was mostly unarmed. Some may have carried *lathis*, but no firearms were present.[22]

Nevertheless, the danger posed by the meeting should not be underestimated. The speeches were not aimed at pacifying or calming the crowd, or helping the authorities to restore normality, but at keeping the spirit of defiance and nationalism alive within the city. Those who gave speeches were not 'moderates' who wished for gradual constitutional advances to self-government, but men who wanted it much quicker. The speakers laboured on familiar topics: the cruelty and oppression of the British; the terror of the Rowlatt Bills; the importance of Gandhi's *satyagraha* campaign; and so on, and would have done little to lower tensions in the city. One of them, Gurbax Rai, mocked martial law, telling the crowd that no more than five people were allowed to gather in one place and urging them to 'look at the thousands here'. What could martial law do?[23] Another speaker was Brij Gopi Nath, a 23-year-old clerk at the National Bank. He was a budding poet and

had read what the authorities regarded as 'inflammatory and seditious' poems at a variety of meetings in Amritsar, including at the Jallianwala Bagh on
13 April.[24] Another speaker, Durga Das, was a 26-year-old employee at the
offices of *Waqt*, a notoriously anti-British newspaper. He had been involved
in the railway platform agitation and made a number of speeches critical of
the government.[25] At the meeting he called for two resolutions, the first asking for the repeal of the Rowlatt Act and the second to release Kitchlew and
Satyapal.[26] It is not clear what would have happened if the meeting had finished, but it would not have contributed towards the restoration of law and
order within Amritsar and may have provoked further unrest.

Given the confusion over the speakers in the Jallianwala Bagh, it is understandable that there has been little attempt to analyse either the size or the
composition of those who were listening to them. Most histories have noted
that two major events were taking place in Amritsar at this time and had resulted in a large number of outside villagers entering the city, most of whom (it
is assumed) had no knowledge of what was going on. On 10 April a cattle fair
had been held near the Govindgarh Fort and 13 April was *Baisakhi* day, the
beginning of the Hindu solar new year.[27] That day was also the day that Sikhs
commemorate the founding of the *Khalsa* by Guru Gobind Singh in 1689.
Professor Datta notes that 'as usual there was a large influx into the town
of people from adjacent areas who had come for a dip in the holy tank surrounding the Golden Temple' and 'quite a large number of villagers had found
their way to the Bagh'.[28] According to the Minority Report, at least 87 people who had been killed in the Jallianwala Bagh came from outside villages
and that the 'proportion of the outside people in the meeting must have been
appreciable'.[29] This has been reinforced by the Indian historian, Surjit Hans,
who claims that the number of victims that came from outside Amritsar was
about 23 per cent, or about one in five. Their presence, he concludes, cannot
be coincidental and they must have gathered for the *Baisakhi* and cattle fairs.[30]

Yet, the idea that large numbers of people had made their way into
Amritsar between 10 and 13 April (and were unaware of what was happening) is unconvincing for a number of reasons. Indeed, it is unlikely that by
13 April there were many people in Amritsar for the cattle fair at all. The
festival had begun on 10 April but owing to the violence and looting, many
of the cattle holders 'scattered with a considerable loss ... of cattle' in the following days. The importance of the *Baisakhi* festival in drawing people into
the city also seems to have been overstated. Fewer people made their way into
Amritsar for the festival than was usual that year. All third-class railway travel
to and from the city had been banned on 11 April. This was done by Kitchin

with the knowledge of the festival very much in his mind because 'we did not want to fill Amritsar with innocent people when the situation was grave'. Civil picquets were also out in force around Amritsar, stopping villagers and advising them not to attend the festival. Perhaps because of this one police officer recorded that the number of festival-goers was 'much less . . . than usual', consisting mainly of Jats, most of whom were townspeople.[31]

Furthermore, even if few of those in the Bagh were villagers, then it should not automatically be assumed that they were innocent or had no knowledge of what was going on in the city. Dyer believed that the presence of villagers was indicative of the desperate situation he was in and he may have been right. When he heard of the gathering in the Jallianwala Bagh, he knew there was a real danger that they would be overwhelmed by 'a combination of the city gangs and the still more formidable multitude from the villages'. For him, the presence of villagers in Amritsar 'only made the matter more sinister' because he claimed to have received news of extensive efforts to spread disorder into the rural areas by the 'rebels'.[32] The British knew that this was a common danger and had already occurred at Kasur and Gujranwala, when villagers headed into the towns for loot and plunder when they heard of the disorders. In any case, cattle fairs were notorious in northern India for being testing, and possibly dangerous, events, when people from all over the subcontinent, including hill men from the frontier and Afghanistan, would make their way into the city to do business.[33]

In terms of the composition of the crowd, some further points can be made. First, there seems to have been relatively few Muslims. Surjit Hans claims that only 59 Muslims were killed in the firing on 13 April, considerably fewer than either Hindus or Sikhs. He attributes this to the fact that there was a major Sikh festival underway (which Muslims would generally avoid), and also to the effect of Dyer's proclamation.[34] Muslims made up roughly 40 per cent of the population of Amritsar, mainly immigrants hailing from Kashmir who came into the city because of the cloth trade. They lived in the outer areas of the city, places like the Katras Khazana, Hakiman, Karam Singh and Garba Singh, which lay at the southern end of the city, close to the city walls.[35] Looking at the map of where Dyer made his proclamation, it seems that he spent a considerable amount of time in these southern portions of the city, meaning that knowledge of it would have been far greater in these areas than perhaps elsewhere. Furthermore, shortly after 4 p.m., a funeral procession for a Muslim killed on 10 April filed past the Jallianwala Bagh and many people left to join it. According to one resident, about 5,000 people went to follow this procession.[36]

Second, it is commonly assumed that the crowd that assembled in the Bagh contained a mix of men, women and children.[37] Scenes of women and children being slaughtered in the Jallianwala Bagh are shown in Richard Attenborough's Academy Award winning movie, *Gandhi* (1982), and although this is an emotive subject, it should be considered critically. According to Dyer's Brigade Major, when they entered the Bagh, 'we could see an immense crowd of men packed in a square'. He also remembered that 'The crowd was composed of men; no women or children were seen during the whole time we were there.'[38] Dyer also argued that he 'did not see a single woman or child in the assembly'.[39] Although it is understandable why the military authorities would maintain that the gathering in the Jallianwala Bagh contained no women and children, there is a surprising lack of evidence to suggest otherwise. The Congress Report made no mention of large numbers of women and children in the Bagh and Surjit Hans found evidence of only two female 'martyrs'.[40] More recently, the historian Purnima Bose has admitted that because Indian women 'did not begin to take an active role in the non-violent movement till the emergence of Gandhi as a national leader sometime after the massacre, it is unlikely that many were present in the Jallianwala Bagh'.[41] In any case, Amritsar had a noticeably lower proportion of females in its population than men. By 1921 there were only 646 Hindu women per 1,000 Hindu men and only 729 Muslim women for every 1,000 Muslim men.[42] Therefore, the vast majority of those in the Jallianwala Bagh seem to have been adult males.

It remains impossible to be precise on the exact numbers of people who made their way into the Bagh that afternoon. Although there may only have been a small contingent of outsiders present, a large number of city dwellers went to the Bagh. The vast majority did so, it would seem, to attend the meeting that Hans Raj had arranged and listen to the well-respected local pleader, Lala Kanhyalal Bhatia (who, of course, never turned up). The Hunter Report estimated that the crowd contained between 10,000 and 20,000 people and the Indian National Congress put this figure at around 20,000.[43] Most accounts have echoed these figures, with historians regularly converging on around 15,000. Yet, when reviewing many Indian accounts of the massacre, including those compiled by the Congress Inquiry and the recollections of Hans Raj, these figures seem underestimations, with eyewitnesses often recording anything between 20,000 and 30,000 people. If this is correct then the crowd could have been substantially bigger than is usually assumed; something that would have undoubtedly influenced Dyer's appreciation of the situation.

പ

Contrary to what most historians have assumed, there is a considerable amount of information available on the gathering in the Jallianwala Bagh. This can be used to analyse the composition of the crowd in greater detail that has previously been made and begin to test the assumptions and claims that were first aired in the House of Commons in July 1920 and which have been repeated ever since. Much of the statistical and anecdotal evidence points to conclusions that are contrary to accepted historical opinion. First, it seems that knowledge of the order banning meetings was more widely known than many have believed. Dyer's proclamation had spread through most of the Muslim districts and Hans Raj's role in publicising the meeting to his followers meant that it was well known that the authorities had banned large gatherings, but one would be held anyway in defiance of these instructions.

The other conclusions to be drawn are that the crowd was bigger than the Hunter Report suggested, swelling to upwards of 25,000 people, and that it mainly consisted of male Hindus. There were some women and children present, but they were not in any great numbers. Therefore, it seems that the gathering in the Bagh was, in reality, considerably different to the usual picture, the scenes that can be found in Attenborough's *Gandhi*, that the gathering was totally peaceful, contained women and children with no knowledge of any orders from Dyer. Although a number of writers have grasped, albeit tentatively, that the gathering in the garden may have been somewhat different to that enshrined in Indian national myth, there has been a reluctance to take these points to their logical conclusion and discuss what effect this may have had on Dyer, when he entered the Bagh shortly after 5 p.m.

CHAPTER 17

Dyer and the Jallianwala Bagh

Jalianwalabagh is shut in by buildings and is the perfect death trap.

Edward Thompson[1]

Weakened by a stroke in November 1921, Reginald Dyer retired to the small village of Long Ashton, near Bristol, where he was nursed by his devoted wife, Annie. He would live for a further six years, becoming less and less active as the years went by, gradually sinking into tiredness and lethargy, spending his days inspecting the flowers in his garden and reading to his grandchildren. He died on the evening of 23 July 1927.[2] It is evident from those that knew him in these twilight years that he still thought a lot about Amritsar and the actions that had taken place on 13 April 1919. But no matter how many times he recalled what he had done and wrestled with what else he could have done, no matter how many times he revisited in his mind the baking hot streets of Amritsar, or the dusty ground of the Jallianwala Bagh, he always seemed to come to the same conclusion: 'I would do the same again' he would frequently tell his wife. But the questions remain to be answered: why had Dyer fired upon the crowd in the Jallianwala Bagh and was he right to do so?

After 90 years the Amritsar Massacre maintains its sinister reputation and a degree of confusion and mystery about what exactly went on in that fatal walled garden. A variety of explanations and justifications have been offered for Dyer's actions, many of which concentrate on his psychological state prior to the massacre.[3] In trying to understand the events in the Jallianwala Bagh, Dyer's own words are of vital importance. However, these have become clouded because he made various pronouncements and explanations – which differed in some important respects – on at least four occasions between 1919 and 1920. In Dyer's initial report he justified firing without warning by stressing that 'my force was small and to hesitate might induce attack'.[4] However, in subsequent statements, Dyer expanded on this. By 25 August he was talking about creating a 'moral, and widespread effect'. 'It was no longer a question of merely dispersing the crowd,' he stated, 'but one of producing a sufficient moral effect, from a military point of view, not only on those who were present but more specially throughout the Punjab.'[5] He would repeat these claims before the Hunter Inquiry and write a more sophisticated version of them in his letter of July 1920. The difference between these two explanations was of vital importance because if Dyer's actions were premeditated and conducted out of a desire to spread terror and fear, then they could not be justified according to British military law.

၄၅

In order to understand what happened on 13 April it is necessary to draw away from the psychological explanations of Dyer's actions and look again at what information was available to him at the time. The key is to find out *when he was informed that the meeting at the Jallianwala Bagh was taking place*. His report of August 1919 stated that he was informed at 12.40 p.m. (while he was still in the city) that a 'big meeting' would be held at the Jallianwala Bagh later that afternoon. This was scheduled to take place sometime around half past four. He returned to his headquarters at the Ram Bagh (1.30 p.m.), where he was later given definite information by John Rehill (Deputy Superintendent of Police) that this meeting was taking place and that a number of people had already gathered.[6] Dyer's men started out at 4.15 p.m. and arrived about an hour later. Given these timings, it has generally been accepted that Dyer had between three and four hours to think about what action needed to be taken if a meeting was being held at the Bagh (i.e. between 12.40 and 4.30 p.m.). There has been a strong consensus that Dyer used this time to devise a sinister plan for the massacre. Related to this is the assumption that because Dyer took personal command of the mission to the Jallianwala Bagh, he was aware that his actions were going to break the law.[7] Accordingly, he arranged that senior company commanders were not present. Nigel Collett believes that this was 'neither necessary nor usual' and suggests that the size of the party could have been delegated to a major.[8] Similarly, Professor Datta claims this 'indicates that he was bent from the outset on the drastic step he took'.[9] By taking personal charge, however, 'Dyer ensured that there would be no officers present who might baulk at his plans.'[10]

This interpretation, which has found general agreement, is questionable, however, because Dyer was *not* the only British officer present in the Bagh. He was accompanied (in his motorcar) by Captain Briggs (his Brigade Major), Lieutenant-Colonel H. Morgan of 124/Baluchis and two bodyguards. Rehill and Plomer followed in another car and Captain Gerry Crampton of

9/Gurkhas jogged alongside on foot. At no stage during his time at Amritsar had Dyer delegated authority to a senior company commander and he was unlikely to do it now, particularly given the gravity of the situation as he saw it. He was first and foremost a 'soldier's general' and had spent over three hours going through the city during the morning with his troops reading out the proclamation banning all gatherings. As he would time and again throughout his career, Dyer willingly shared the deprivations of the private soldier and if there was any work to be done then he would do it. He undoubtedly felt that he would have been abdicating his duty if he had delegated this important task to a subordinate officer.

The afternoon of 13 April was long, slow and excruciatingly hot, and many of those British officials in Amritsar assumed that no meeting would take place. Dyer, in particular, believed that no crowd would gather and defy his authority; hence there was no need to make any plan. He was a man prone to arrogance, used to having his orders obeyed. Before the Hunter Committee he complained, 'I thought I had done enough to make the crowd not meet,' and 'I had warned them all day, this is, up to the time I went to Rambagh.' Dyer was not alone in thinking this. Several civilian officials at Amritsar also believed that it was unlikely that any crowd would gather in the Jallianwala Bagh. Miles Irving had heard 'certain rumours' of a gathering but 'did not attach any great importance' to them. Indeed, Irving seems to have been so convinced that nothing much would happen that he spent the afternoon at the fort.[11] Although in hindsight it seems that the meeting at the Jallianwala Bagh was always going to take place, it may not have appeared so to Dyer and his fellow officers.

The criticism that Dyer took no steps to prevent people from gathering in the Jallianwala Bagh is unfair and unrealistic. There was very little he could have done in the situation. It would have taken another hour to march to the Bagh, if not even longer because of the fierce heat of the early afternoon, which would have been a considerable strain on his already tired troops. Considering the reception that Dyer and his men had received during the morning, when they had been spat at and verbally abused, it is unlikely to have been a very popular decision. In any case, Dyer told the Hunter Inquiry that there was no way he could have prevented a meeting on 13 April because he did not have enough men.[12] There was no proof that a meeting would gather, *only that one had been organised*, and given the rumours that were circulating throughout the Punjab at this time, it is perhaps unsurprising that Dyer did not take immediate notice of it. Dyer's knowledge of Amritsar was patchy and he was not very familiar with the location and size of the Jallianwala Bagh. The

composition of the column that he took to the Bagh is also worth investigation. He had with him 25 Baluchis and 25 Gurkhas armed with rifles, and
40 Gurkhas armed only with *kukris*. Not including his immediate staff, Dyer's
party comprised just 90 soldiers, surprisingly small given the oft-repeated assumption that his actions were premeditated.

The three-hour time gap has confused the main issue. In truth, Dyer did
not have much time to do anything other than sketch out a route to the Bagh
and the locations where picquets would be stationed. He was only told at
4 p.m. by Rehill that a meeting was *definitely* taking place and barely 15 minutes later his men were on the move. Dyer's initial statement is worth recalling for the light it can shed on this point. This statement, which was written
immediately after he returned from the Bagh and then transmitted to his superiors the following day, states that

> On my way back from the city I was informed that the disaffected characters
> in the city had ordered a meeting in the Jallianwala Bagh at 16–30 hours. I did
> not think this meeting would take place in the face of what I had done.

After arriving, 'I realised that my force was small and to hesitate might induce
attack. I immediately opened fire and dispersed the crowd.'[13] Therefore, it
seems that at no point before entering the Bagh had Dyer decided what he
would do. He had undoubtedly entertained various scenarios should a crowd
begin to gather, but he had not resolved on anything specific.

Those who have analysed the reasons why Dyer fired in the Jallianwala
Bagh have failed to provide a convincing answer because they have confused
two separate issues. Historians have confused his actions *before* the massacre
and his actions *after* he reached the Bagh. They have assumed that because
he fired within seconds of entering and without giving a warning, then he
must have planned it in advance. This is unlikely. It should be remembered
that Dyer had never been to the Jallianwala Bagh before and the sight that
confronted him, of a large crowd in an open space, would have been shocking
and highly unnerving. Although Dyer had been told by Rehill (at 4 p.m.) that
a crowd of 1,000 people had already gathered, *he had no idea of the size of the
crowd before he arrived.*[14] What actions Dyer would take, therefore, depended
upon what he found in the Jallianwala Bagh and were not the result of some
premeditated plan. The narrow entrance to the Bagh was barely seven feet
(two metres) wide and did not offer a good view of what lay beyond. Indeed,
Dyer's first action once he was inside was to ask his Brigade Major, Briggs,
about the possible size of the crowd, clearly indicating that this was not what
he was expecting.[15] The size and density of the mass that lay in front of the

two officers made a deep impression upon them. It is likely that had Dyer found a much smaller crowd in the Bagh, or one that contained more women and children, he would *not* have fired. However, because he was faced with a vast crowd (upwards of 25,000 people) and because there were so few women and children, it seems likely that he decided to fire without waiting any longer, being convinced that he was facing the *danda fauj*.

The massacre at the Jallianwala Bagh was, in many ways, the logical outcome of a failure of intelligence. The withdrawal of the police and the abandonment of the city by the authorities on 10 April meant that very few officers had much information on what was happening inside the walls. An aeroplane did circle the city on 12 April, but it was not under Dyer's command and had come from Lahore. This meant that Dyer's intelligence was based on unreliable reports from detectives (who could not operate in the city for fear of their lives) or from the few spies he had (because there was no money to fund such activities in the city).[16] The episode of the armoured car amply illustrates this lack of intelligence. Dyer was heavily criticised for the remarks he made to the Hunter Inquiry about the possible use of machine guns mounted on the two armoured cars that accompanied him to the Bagh.[17] Dyer stated that if he had been able to get them through the entrance, he would have opened fire with them. This has become part of the Amritsar legend, apparently being yet further evidence that Dyer had hatched a plan, as well as testament to his brutality. Despite being repeated in all accounts of the massacre, Dyer's comments simply do not make sense and offer a warning about taking his testimony before the Hunter Committee too seriously.

First of all, if he was so keen to do this, then he could have quite easily detached the Vickers machine gun from one of the armoured cars (which were designed for dismounted use) and ordered a squad to carry it into the Jallianwala Bagh, which would have taken only a few seconds, but he did not do this.[18] In any case, if Dyer went to the Bagh with a plan already formed in his mind then it was a remarkably poor one given that the cars could not fit through the entrance, which would surely have been pointed out to him. Although he stated that the machine guns were there if 'the necessity arose, and I was attacked', it is still puzzling as to why he brought them along. It was probably a reflection of his rush in moving to the Bagh and his ignorance of the geography of the area.[19] Therefore, far from showing Dyer's prior intent or latent brutality, this episode reinforces the idea that he did not have a plan, or indeed, any hint of what lay before him in the Jallianwala Bagh. The longstanding assumption that Dyer was bent on machine-gunning the crowd is a myth. He had not devised a robust plan of action; he was making things up as he went along.

ଏ

The legality (or not) or Dyer's actions in the Jallianwala Bagh has aroused a great deal of controversy. Nigel Collett's *The Butcher of Amritsar* (2005) devotes considerable attention to this question, concluding that from an examination of British Law, the Code of Criminal Procedure, Army Regulations (India) and the *Manual of Military Law*, Dyer's actions were illegal on three counts: that he opened fire without warning; that he did so upon a crowd that was not violent and which had not threatened him; and that he fired for longer than was strictly necessary to achieve the aim of dispersing the crowd. Legal justification for Dyer's actions, as Collett notes, depended upon proving that the crowd that gathered in the Jallianwala Bagh was revolutionary and intent on violence.[20] Chapter 13 of the *Manual of Military Law* ('Summary of the Law of Riot and Insurrection') defined three types of gatherings: unlawful assemblies, riots and insurrections.[21] Dyer and his lawyers, drafting his defence in London in the spring of 1920, maintained that the crowd in the Bagh was 'a defiant, organized, and rebellious mob', in other words, the most serious type of gathering (an insurrection), and that any amount of force could be used to deal with it.

Dyer's lengthy explanation for his actions has often been disputed. Collett argues that his defence was fatally flawed because of the Hunter Report's conclusion that there was no insurrection in the Punjab in 1919 and that, in any case, he did not employ minimum force in dispersing the crowd.[22] There are two objections that can be raised to this interpretation. First, the Hunter Committee may have decided that there was no conspiracy behind the unrest, but it also admitted that there was 'open rebellion' in the Punjab in April 1919.[23] Like many at Amritsar, Dyer was convinced – with some justification – that he was faced with a dangerous rebellion and the size and composition of the crowd in the Jallianwala Bagh would have done nothing to lessen his fears. Second, the criticism that Dyer did not employ minimum force and that he fired for longer than was required (in order to disperse the crowd) is also problematic and rests entirely upon his various testimonies.[24] Because he had talked about creating a 'moral' and 'widespread effect' and justified his actions on the grounds of sending a message throughout the Punjab, then this clearly violated the 'minimum force' philosophy and could not be justified.[25]

That Dyer's actions were premeditated has also been given additional support by the length of time that firing was kept up. Most accounts agree that the shooting at the Jallianwala Bagh lasted between six and ten minutes. *But why?* On returning from the Bagh, Dyer apparently told Gerard Wathen, the principal of a local Sikh college, that 'he had to decide quickly or his men would have been overpowered' and that he continued to fire to teach the crowd a lesson. Wathen also recorded Dyer's suggestion that he could not order the troops to stop firing because of the impossibility of giving orders over the sound of gunfire.[26] Dyer continued to fire for one very simple reason: *there were still people in the Jallianwala Bagh and it was his duty to disperse them.* Although he would later suggest that he continued to fire to punish them, the key factor was that the Jallianwala Bagh still contained large numbers of people. The difficulty with trying to assess what level of force was sufficiently 'minimum' in this case concerns the reliability of Dyer's testimonies. Indeed, even Collett admits that 'Dyer condemned himself out of his own mouth' and had he stuck to his first and most simple explanation – that he fired because he feared imminent attack by the crowd – then he would have been absolved of any blame.[27]

The argument that Dyer should have fired only until the crowd dispersed again misses the point that *this is exactly what he did.* According to Lieutenant-Colonel Morgan, the decision to ceasefire was only taken after the Bagh was 'absolutely empty' and this seems to have been the case.[28] Dyer's report of August 1919 states that 'I fired and continued to fire until the crowd dispersed' and he would later maintain that 'When 1,650 rounds or thereabouts had been fired, and roughly ten minutes from the time of opening fire, the whole crowd had dispersed.'[29] Admittedly, it took a considerable amount of time for the thousands of people to disperse because there were only several small exits out of the Bagh, but Dyer would not have known this. Therefore, from a purely legal perspective, Dyer *did* fire until the crowd dispersed. Unfortunately, it took ten minutes for this to occur. Had there been more exits, Dyer's men would not have had to fire for so long.

The Amritsar Massacre is undoubtedly one of the most emotive and contentious events in modern Indian history, which has been reflected in the lively debates that have surrounded it. To some, Dyer's actions were deliberate, planned and methodical: when he received notification about the gathering, he decided (for a variety of reasons) that he must fire and that he did so once he reached the Bagh. Others have suggested that Dyer suffered some form of mental collapse and accidentally gave the order to fire. All are incorrect or at least flawed. A reconstruction of Dyer's actions during 13 April highlights the very limited time in which any decision to fire could have been made. Because Dyer had ignored the possibility of any large-scale gatherings

actually taking place, it was only when Rehill brought him definite information that crowds were forming in the Jallianwala Bagh at 4 p.m. that he realised
he had to return to the city. As has been shown, within minutes he was on the
move, having had precious little time to do anything other than organise his
dispositions. In summary, he had not resolved to do anything specific until
he actually got to the Bagh. It was once he was inside and confronted with a
crowd of unexpected proportions (and with a seemingly sinister composition)
that he made his decision to fire, either fearing that there would not be time
to issue another warning, or that it would have been too dangerous to have
done so.

℘

How many people were killed or wounded in the Jallianwala Bagh? Estimates
have ranged between 200 and 2,000 dead.[30] Upon returning to the Ram Bagh,
Dyer discovered that his troops had fired 1,650 rounds. Each man carried 100
rounds and they had fired roughly 33 each, meaning that Dyer could have
continued to fire for a considerable time had he chosen to do so.[31] He divided
1,650 between five and six ('I am in doubt whether by 5 or 6') and calculated
the number of dead to be 300, with many more casualties. Official estimates
put it a little higher, ranging somewhere between 400 and 500 killed,[32] and
the Hunter Report later settled upon the figure of 379 dead with probably
three times as many wounded.[33] Lord Hunter's figure has, however, often
been regarded as too low and there was a clear political interest in pushing the
figures as low as possible. The Congress Punjab Inquiry concluded that 1,000
deaths 'is by no means an exaggerated calculation' and the visitor's notice at
the Jallianwala Bagh memorial makes reference to 'the blood of about two
thousand Indian patriots'.[34]

The exact number of casualties that Dyer's men caused in the Jallianwala
Bagh will never be known and unless dramatic new evidence comes to light,
it is likely to remain a point of contention. Because Dyer did not tend to the
wounded or compile precise statistics in the Bagh it was necessarily much later
when the authorities attempted to do this, by which time much valuable information had been lost. A local government inquiry would have examined
this question much earlier, but because of the formation of the Hunter Report, this did not take place; in order to avoid any 'embarrassment' if the
two reports disagreed.[35] The Government of India issued a proclamation on
7 August asking for information on people who had been killed, but this was
not notably successful. Pandit Jagat Narayan gloomily pointed out one of the
main problems with this when he complained, 'Don't you think that anybody

and everybody who was wounded or the relatives or killed persons in that fair would be funky [*sic*] to come forward and say that he was one of the rioters?'[36]

A subsequent investigation by F.H. Burton, an Indian civil servant, concluded that approximately 415 people had been killed; somewhat higher than the 379 dead that the committee would publish.[37] He estimated that the crowd was 60 per cent Hindu and 33 per cent Muslim (the rest presumably being Sikh). Of this total, Burton argued that between 20 and 25 per cent came from villages outside the city. Trying to get a full and accurate statistical breakdown of the casualties in the Jallianwala Bagh was a near-impossible task that would rumble on into the 1920s as the Government of India tried to draw a line under the affair. It would ultimately pay out over 18 *lakhs* of rupees as compensation for those killed or wounded on 13 April. After much consideration the government eventually compiled its own list of dead and wounded and this document – which has remained neglected by historians – can add to the figures given by Burton in 1919. The government concluded that the vast majority of the dead in the Jallianwala Bagh were from Amritsar city (142), closely followed by those from Amritsar *tahsil* (30). The rest (72) came from further afield including Tarn Taran, Lahore and Gujranwala. Of the wounded, again most of them came from Amritsar city (89), then from Amritsar *tahsil* (43), with the rest being from outside districts (56).[38]

The figures that have been presented here cannot be regarded as final or necessarily complete, but they add to our understanding of the nature of the crowd in the Bagh and how many became victims of Dyer's fire. Taken together they undermine the commonly held perception that the Jallianwala Bagh was full of villagers who had come into the city for a religious festival or a cattle fair. On the contrary, Dyer's proclamation may have been more successful than many historians have argued. Because the majority of those killed and wounded were from Amritsar city and because most of them were Hindus, it seems reasonable to assume that the vast majority of those who gathered in the Jallianwala Bagh on the afternoon of 13 April had done so in defiance of Dyer and that only a small proportion were there because of the *Baisakhi* and cattle fairs. And it was this that unnerved Dyer when he first saw the crowd, which seemingly confirmed his worst suspicions; that a crowd had gathered in defiance of his orders and to challenge his authority.

ↂ

Those who saw Dyer after he returned from the Jallianwala Bagh all tell the same story: that he was unnerved and deeply upset about what had happened. One witness recorded that Dyer was 'distraught' and apparently Miles Irving found him 'all dazed and shaken up'.[39] The sight of the previously imperturbable general now visibly traumatised made a deep impression upon those who were at the Ram Bagh; his shaking hands struggling to light the cigarettes that he always seemed to be smoking. Although Dyer's condition upon returning from the city has often been discounted or ignored, it provides further evidence that casts doubt upon the traditionally accepted version of his actions. *This was hardly the response of a man who had steeled himself to commit a premeditated act of mass murder.* His actions in the Jallianwala Bagh were not part of some sinister master plan, but were, on the contrary, a response to a number of unexpected things: the nature and composition of the crowd and the geography of the Bagh, particularly its lack of exits.

The nature of the Jallianwala Bagh is of crucial importance. Dyer did not know Amritsar well and he was clearly unaware that there was no easy way out. When Dyer entered the Bagh, he did not have time to survey it and his attention was focused upon the huge swell of the crowd in front of him. In any case, after he had given the order to fire, the storm of dust that was kicked up as thousands of people tried to flee, rendered visibility very difficult. When Dyer met Sir Michael O'Dwyer several days later he told him that on entering the Bagh he saw an 'enormous crowd'. Knowing that he only had a handful of troops and fearing that he would be cut off, he opened fire. After the first volley, the crowd began to move to the sides and he momentarily thought they were going to rush him, so he kept on firing. Dyer later admitted that this was probably a mistake.[40] Someone who noticed this was the writer and member of the ICS, Edward Thompson. In *A Letter From India* (1932), Thompson claimed that during a dinner party with Miles Irving many years later, he had asked the Deputy Commissioner what Dyer had said to him on returning from the Bagh. Irving replied, 'Dyer came to me all dazed and shaken up, and said, "I never knew that there was no way out."' One of the others present, Mr F.G. Puckle (Financial Secretary to the Punjab Government), also said that Dyer had told him, about six months after the massacre, 'I haven't had a night's sleep since that happened. I keep on seeing it all over again.' Writing in the bitter year of 1932, when the British Raj was visibly crumbling, Thompson wrote, somewhat sadly, that 'The story of the last dozen years would have been immeasurably happier had we realized that Jalianwalabagh was the scene of a mistake and not of calculated brutality.'[41]

If this was indeed the case, that the Jallianwala Bagh massacre was to a certain extent *a mistake* on Dyer's behalf, then why did he later maintain that he knew exactly what he was doing? Why did he say that he fired to produce a 'moral' effect throughout the Punjab and that his actions were premeditated?

In short, Dyer had no other option. *He could never admit that he panicked or that he was shocked by what he found in the Jallianwala Bagh.* Thompson claimed that 'pressure of outside congratulation helped him to build up the conviction that he saved the Empire', and there is probably much in this. Sir Charles Gwynn, author of a widely respected work, *Imperial Policing* (1934), believed the same, arguing that Dyer was emboldened by the vocal support he had been given by Sir Michael O'Dwyer and others, and being somewhat vain, he started to enjoy his new role as the 'saviour of India' and expanded on his initial motivations and 'exaggerated the ruthlessness of his attitude and the deliberateness of his action'.[42] By August 1919 Dyer may indeed have convinced himself that his actions were justified. For those who knew him well, this boastful pride was not terribly surprising because the general was a vain man, convinced of his own worth and who by 1918 had become increasingly frustrated at the slow progress of his career. He was bitter that he had not made major-general and was eager to see his actions in the Jallianwala Bagh as proof that he had the energy and strength of character to move further up the chain of command. As shall be seen, it was not the first time that Dyer reinterpreted his actions in such a glowing manner.

Three years before the Jallianwala Bagh, in February 1916, Dyer had become the commander of British forces in Eastern Persia (the Seistan Field Force), charged with countering German influence in the region, which was intended to destabilise the Raj at a crucial moment in the war effort. Dyer subsequently wrote a positive account of this campaign entitled *Raiders of the Sarhadd* (1921); a dramatic tale of high adventure and daring on the frontier, redolent of Henry Rider Haggard at his best. In *Raiders* Dyer portrays himself as a dashing hero, who uses bluff and bravery to make up for his lack of resources in a difficult and hostile area, and who only left the Sarhadd because of exhaustion. However Dyer saw himself, the truth was somewhat different. Dyer's conduct of this campaign, despite the positive account he subsequently wrote, was questionable. Not only did he make a rather clumsy attempt to annex parts of the Sarhadd into the British Empire, but he also ignored his primary mission (to prevent German infiltration) and became bogged down in punitive operations that tied down troops and caused much unnecessary devastation in the region. It is clear that by the time he came back to India the authorities were very concerned with his activities and his disobedience to their orders and made sure that he did not return.[43]

It is evident that a similar tendency to embellish the truth and to claim a far greater significance for his conduct than was perhaps merited would later emerge in Dyer's report of 25 August 1919 and in his testimony before the

Hunter Committee. Believing himself to be the 'saviour of the Raj' and affronted by the tone of Indian lawyers, he unwittingly made a series of unwise admissions that did not tell the entire story, but which have been taken by generations of writers as providing the truth to what really happened in the Jallianwala Bagh. But we must draw away from these theories and look instead to the information Dyer had at his disposal during the afternoon, which was extremely limited and unreliable. He simply did not know what was happening and was surprised at the size and composition of the crowd that faced him. He may have later maintained that he knew exactly what he was doing in the Jallianwala Bagh, but he was unlikely to have made any other admission. He was not the type of man to admit mistakes easily and it was in his first report, written hours after returning from the Bagh, that Dyer got closest to his real motivations. 'I realised that my force was small and to hesitate might induce attack. I immediately opened fire and dispersed the crowd.'[44] There is no better explanation of what happened that afternoon. Edward Thompson, whose brief account tells us much about this incident, wrote that the Jallianwala Bagh was the 'perfect death-trap'.[45] By a series of curious, unforeseen and tragic events it would indeed become one.

CHAPTER 18

Shadows of Amritsar

The shadow of Amritsar has lengthened over the fair face of India.

The Duke of Connaught[1]

As 1919 drew to a close and as Lord Hunter and his colleagues endeavoured to get to the bottom of what had happened in the Punjab and elsewhere earlier that year, the British desperately tried to stabilise the Raj, to return once more to 'business as usual' and to get back to administering their empire. On 23 December His Majesty the King-Emperor, King George V, issued a royal proclamation. Echoing Queen Victoria's Proclamation of 1858 (which had itself come at the end of a period of great violence and bitter recrimination), the proclamation was designed to draw a line under the disturbances, soothe feelings in the subcontinent, and help retain an atmosphere favourable to the introduction of the new reforms. 'A new era is opening,' it read. 'Let it begin with a common determination among my people and my officers to work together for a common purpose.' The proclamation discussed the forthcoming reforms – 'there now lies before us a definite step on the road to responsible Government' – and issued a clemency for those who had been arrested or imprisoned during the disorders. It was also announced that the king's son, the Prince of Wales, would come to the subcontinent over the following winter to inaugurate the constitutional changes in British India.[2]

King George V's proclamation was a remarkable act of clemency and forgiveness, perhaps even appeasement; testimony to how vulnerable the Raj had become in the last months of 1919 and how desperate it was to ensure that the forthcoming reforms would be given a chance to work. Much to the chagrin of those who still believed that the Raj had to keep its nerve and crush political dissent with the ruthlessness that the British had once shown in India, many of those who had been arrested in April and May were released under the terms of the proclamation, including Kitchlew and Satyapal. By the end of 1919, out of around 1,800 people who had been convicted by the courts for their involvement in violent disturbances only 86 remained in jail to serve their sentences; a fitting riposte to those who believe the worst of the British in India and maintain that their only weapon to deal with nationalist agitation was repression.[3] A British report at the end of 1919 proudly noted that the effect of the King-Emperor's proclamation was 'profound', helping to rally the 'moderate' wing of the Indian National Congress and prompting a great warmth of feeling towards King George V.[4] This may have been true initially, but it soon wore off. At the annual session of the Congress that month, held in of all places, Amritsar, the delegates expressed dissatisfaction over the events in the Punjab, but agreed to work with the forthcoming Montagu-Chelmsford reforms.[5] Unfortunately, this lukewarm support would soon disappear.

⁊

What move would the Mahatma make next? The suspension of *satyagraha* on 18 April could not have come a day sooner for the embattled authorities in India. Montagu wrote to Chelmsford,

> I will have no doubt that he [Gandhi] now sincerely regrets having acted as he did. He will have learnt that the masses who surround him are only too ready to outstrip the limits which he may set to the cause he champions, and that with a little encouragement the ignorant peasantry and townspeople may be led to actions which he would be the first to deplore.[6]

But, while Gandhi would always distance himself from the more unsavoury episodes of his various civil disobedience campaigns, Montagu clearly underestimated him and failed to realise the extent to which concessions and goodwill would satisfy Gandhi and the Indian National Congress. Montagu had pinned his hopes on the reforms and had shown a willingness to deal with the disorders in the Punjab in what he believed was an open, transparent and honest way. But this would not be enough. Indeed there were no lengths to which Montagu could go that would strengthen the 'moderates' sufficiently so that disorder and unrest would melt away. Montagu failed to understand the psychology of resistance and learn the lesson of the repartition of Bengal, which had only resulted in yet more terrorism and violence. He could not lead by a series of concessions.

Whatever had happened in 1919, it had not dented the Mahatma's determination to challenge the Raj. Spurred on by the Khalifat campaign and drawing support from the anger over the failure (as many nationalists believed) of the Government to deal adequately with what had happened in the Punjab and to punish those involved, Gandhi embarked upon a new campaign of non-co-operation the following year. On 1 August 1920 he wrote to the Viceroy to return the medals that he had been awarded for his work in the South African War and to express his dissatisfaction over the Khalifat question and the way in which the disorders in the Punjab had been investigated. Gandhi told the Viceroy that the sympathetic treatment of Sir Michael O'Dwyer had broken his faith in the Government of India. 'In my humble opinion,' he added, 'the ordinary method of agitating by way of petitions, deputation and the like, is no remedy for moving to repentence a Government, so hopelessly indifferent to the welfare of its charge as the Government of India has proved to be.' Gandhi was, therefore, beginning a movement whereby all those who agreed would withdraw their co-operation from government.[7]

The initial impact of Gandhi's call for a *hartal* was mixed. Although certain areas of India were immediately behind him (such as Gujarat and the urban centres of the Punjab), the *hartal* was not followed universally and many politicians across India were not keen. Gandhi had stressed that non-co-operation with the government required not just occasional displays of purpose, but a permanent state of mind, the most important element of which was the boycott of the new councils, scheduled for election in November 1920. Gandhi was convinced that if only those 'educated people' who were tempted to take up council seats could resist it, the government 'cannot run its administration for a moment'.[8] Worried about the effect that boycotting the new reforms would have on their local position, either by allowing their rivals to have a greater say in the corridors of power or by alienating the Government of India still further, many politicians hesitated to commit themselves to a movement that promised much, but was deeply antithetical to the long-standing Congress desire to have a greater amount of responsibility in the running of the administration. In the end Gandhi won them over. At a special session of Congress in September 1920, it was agreed – not without much dissent and criticism – that Gandhi's programme would be undertaken until such time as the Government of India paid sufficient attention to the 'wrongs' of the Khalifat and the Punjab. Titles would be surrendered, foreign goods would be boycotted and there would be a 'gradual' withdrawal from government schools and law courts.[9]

Gandhi's campaign began in 1921 with a wave of resignations from schools and law courts and between August and November the Government of India recorded disturbances and riots all over the subcontinent.[10] Although Gandhi repeated his desire for a non-violent movement, as had happened in March and April 1919, by spreading rousing tales of British oppression and 'wrongs', it was only a matter of time before the campaign turned violent. There were 89 assaults on police during 1921 and throughout India police officers were boycotted, ostracised and prevented from buying food. By November, the visit of the Prince of Wales to India was the cause of acute anxiety to the administration, eager to present it as a success, but worried that it could turn into a publicity disaster. Gandhi called for a *hartal* to coincide with his arrival, and fierce rioting broke out in Bombay, leaving 55 dead and over 400 wounded. The 'non-co-operation' movement was slipping out of control.[11]

The official response to Gandhi's campaign of non-co-operation was one of patience and surveillance, watching and waiting, aiming to give Gandhi and his followers enough room to manoeuvre in the hope that something would happen to cause the collapse of their campaign without official interference. Outright repression was considered to be dangerous and ran the risk of further alienating those 'moderates' who were deemed essential to the working of the Montagu-Chelmsford reforms.[12] Chelmsford explained his policy towards non-co-operation in a letter to Montagu on 4 August 1920. He was determined to avoid what he saw as the mistakes of the past, claiming that 'It is not worth while making martyrs if you can possibly avoid it. When once you have made a martyr you do not know where his martyrdom may land you.' The arrests of Annie Besant and Gandhi still cast a long shadow over him. Chelmsford was convinced that this was the only way to proceed; indeed it would be followed by his successor, Lord Reading, who was appointed Viceroy in 1921. But this was not an easy strategy and it would stretch the loyalties of many provincial governors who were anxious about the spread of discontent in their areas and concerned about the loss of prestige that Gandhi's campaign was causing to the administration. The campaign would only end after more and more violence broke out, leaving scores of dead and wounded, including 23 policemen killed at Chauri Chaura in the United Provinces; an event that came to symbolise the difficulty, perhaps impossibility, of conducting large-scale *satyagraha* that was in harmony with its ideals.

The King-Emperor's hope that his proclamation would usher in a 'new era' of trust and teamwork between the administration and the nationalists was consumed in the flames of Chauri Chaura. On the morning of 4 February 1922, a huge crowd of about 2,000 villagers from the Gorakhpur District (in the United Provinces) marched to the police station at Chauri Chaura. It was rumoured that police officers from this station had prevented Congress activists from protesting outside a bazaar several days earlier. The crowd were out for revenge. Led by several determined volunteers, waving *swaraj* (self-rule) flags and shouting anti-government slogans, the crowd attacked the *chowky*, set fire to the building, and then murdered those officers who tried to flee.[13] The freedom struggle was now no longer confined to genteel, elite debating societies that would meet every Christmas and make resolutions, but an open movement that cut across all races and religions in India, a war of riots and street fighting, of mass imprisonments, of cotton *khadi* struggling against British khaki.

As had happened in 1919 once the violence had reached such alarming proportions, Gandhi had no option but to throw up his hands in despair. Six days after the murders at Chauri Chaura, he gave a speech to Congress volunteers at Bardoli and announced that, once again, he was suspending civil disobedience. 'What I have heard now confirms me in the belief that most of those who are present here have failed to understand the message of non-violence,' he said. 'I must, therefore, immediately stop the movement for civil disobedience.'[14] Gandhi was finally jailed for six years in March 1922, convicted of 'bringing into hatred and contempt ... the Government established by law in British India'.[15] At a stroke the non-co-operation movement faltered and India returned to something approaching normality. Support for non-co-operation had died in the aftermath of Chauri Chaura and gradually the always uneasy alliance between Congress and the Khalifat movement dissolved. The Government of India congratulated itself on how it had dealt with the non-co-operation campaign and Gandhi got used to incarceration under the British; a remarkably mild imprisonment that perfectly summed up the almost schizophrenic British attitude towards repression and coercion. Gandhi was allowed considerable freedoms and kept up a voluminous correspondence with his friends and followers. He served barely a third of his sentence and when he was taken ill with appendicitis in 1924 the Government of India panicked and released him, paranoid lest the Mahatma die in British captivity.

Despite Gandhi's growing reputation, the British remained blissfully unconvinced that he was acting against the interests of the Raj and the question that had first arisen with Annie Besant would be asked again and again. In July 1917 the then Secretary of State for India, Austen Chamberlain, had asked Chelmsford about what to do with Mrs Besant. 'It is obviously undesirable,' he noted, 'to complicate the political issue by a question of religious liberty or conscience, and I shall be glad if you are able to distinguish between her two spheres of activity, even though that may involve a censorship of what she writes.'[16] Chamberlain, Montagu and a myriad of successive British viceroys and secretaries of state failed to realise that, for Gandhi, the struggle for Indian freedom was not simply a question of politics, but of profound *religious* significance. For him there were not two spheres of activity, but only one. True freedom for India would not come when the British had left, but when the

Indian people embraced moral and personal purity, 'truth' and non-violence. Once they did this, the presence of the British would become anachronistic and irrelevant. The failure of the British administration to understand the nature of Gandhi's vision, and to take strong measures against him, would gradually sap the legitimacy and energy of the Raj.

☙

Despite the hopes of Montagu and Chelmsford, the reforms of 1919 did not immediately produce a new sense of cohesion and solidarity between 'moderate' Indian politicians and the administration. Even though official British publications would applaud the 'large body of very useful legislation' that had been passed by the new provincial councils, the implementation of diarchy was confusing in theory and fraught with difficulty in practice, with a lack of trust, misunderstanding and confusion marring the effectiveness of the reforms. The rules were not implemented equally in each province and depended on those Indians who were being considered for office and the willingness of the ICS to work with them. For example, in Assam an Indian was given the highly sensitive portfolio of police, judiciary and prisons, but in Bombay the Governor, Sir George Lloyd, kept law and order under a British official, citing Indian inexperience.[17] Even more disastrous was the British appeasement of some urban nationalists, such as Lala Harkishen Lal, a dubious financier who had taken an enthusiastic role in the 'People's Committee' of Lahore. Lal was appointed Finance Minister of Agriculture for the Punjab and immediately depressed the price of wheat. This caused great hardship among cultivators, but was of considerable benefit to himself because he was the owner of four flour mills.[18] Sadly, such abuse of power was not an isolated phenomenon.

By the time the new councils had been formed, any goodwill towards the Government of India had been burnt off in the bitter aftermath of the Punjab disorders and over the continual conflicts with non-co-operation, leaving the legislature weakened and vulnerable. In many cases, those Indians who were given portfolios were only too aware of the spread of non-co-operation and did not want to appear too supportive of Government; they, therefore, tended 'to assume an attitude, not of hearty co-operation, but of suspicious criticism.'[19] Unfortunately, given the extreme financial stringency of the Government of India in the post-war years, sufficient funds were not available for spectacular investment in those 'transferred' departments, such as education, sanitation or industrial development, which might have helped to convince wider Indian opinion that the reforms were serious and should be given wholehearted support. It was little surprise that no one was happy. By as early as September 1921, 'moderates' were formally requesting that the constitution needed further amendment before the scheduled review of 1929.

Britain's grip on her Indian Empire was now beginning to relax, with devastating consequences for public order. The Rowlatt Act, alongside a host of other apparently 'repressive' legislation (including the Press Act), was repealed in March 1922, three years after Gandhi's call for its abolition. Despite the dangers posed by the spread of the non-co-operation movement, this legislation was thought undesirable and 'inconsistent with the spirit of the new era'. Because Indians were being brought into the administration and their views were being given greater weight, the old autocratic structure of the Raj would have to change. The sea change ushered in by the August declaration was now obvious to all.[20] Further change would come with the Government of India Act of 1935 that took one of the final steps in winding up British rule. Provinces were given increased powers, diarchy was ended and the act introduced direct elections for the first time for a greatly expanded electorate, with provincial legislatures being amended so that there could be non-official Indian majorities. In all branches of provincial governments, Indians were now in charge.[21] In a world that was tragically being seduced by the antidemocratic movements of fascism and communism, Britain, alone amongst the great powers, was endeavouring, thanklessly, to lay the foundations of freedom and democracy in India.

Ominously, it was also gradually becoming apparent that the episodes of Hindu-Muslim fraternity and unity that had been witnessed at some places in March and April 1919 did not point to a wider reconciliation and unification between these two religious communities. The Lucknow Pact of 1916, where the Congress and Muslim League had joined forces and presented a unified position on the reforms, did not last and despite Gandhi's best efforts to champion the cause of the Khalifat and the imprisoned Muslim journalists, the Ali brothers, the religious communities increasingly looked at each other with distrust. Sir Percival Griffiths, author of a history of the Indian police, grumbled that 'For the next fifteen years or so, the annual Administration Reports recorded, with almost monotonous regularity, communal outbreaks, or occasions when police vigilance had been able to avert such troubles.'[22] Communal violence increased in the 1920s and 1930s, beginning in Malabar in 1921, and soon spreading to other areas of the subcontinent, testimony to the tensions that lay beneath the surface of British rule and how the Raj was losing control. The 'communal problem' only worsened as the British retreated from the provinces of India to the central government. The more they enlarged the franchise the more acute it became, exposing Montagu's belief that decreased British control would bring order and stability as the naive liberal fallacy it had always been.

℃♄

There could, of course, be no way that those civil administrators of 1919 could have foreseen the long years of non-co-operation and civil disobedience of the 1920s and 1930s, but there were some who believed that something must be done if a repetition of 1919 was to be avoided. Shocked at the level of opposition that the Rowlatt Bills had raised and bitter towards those nationalists who seemed to be spurning the British in an era of unprecedented reform, various suggestions were made about how to move on from such unhappy events. It was J.P. Thompson, the Chief Secretary to the Government of the Punjab and close ally of Sir Michael O'Dwyer, who suggested that a government party should be formed in order to prevent such nationalist opposition from emerging again. Writing to Sir William Vincent (Member, Home Department) on 13 June 1919, Thompson believed that given the larger and more consultative assemblies that had been created, it was undesirable for government to remain above party politics. Thompson suggested that a government party could be formed, which would bring pro-Raj, so-called 'moderate', Indians into the confidence of the administration and ensure that the Government of India was never again left to face 'the united opposition over the Rowlatt Bill' and could count on the support of between 10 and 12 non-official members. Unfortunately, for Thompson, his idea was never very popular; the official response called it a 'wild' proposal and it was shelved.[23]

The idea of a government party was not the only idea floating around the corridors of New Delhi in this period; how to make sure that future agitation on the scale of the anti-Rowlatt protests could never happen again. One of the ways in which it was felt that a better view of British policy in India could be spread was through the use of cinematic propaganda. The Commissioner of the Rawalpindi Division, Sir Frank Popham Young, was very keen on the idea and believed that the successful employment of propaganda was essential to the future of the Raj. In July 1920, he sent a proposal to his superiors stating that:

> It is absolutely incumbent upon the British Empire to go into the Moving Pictures business, and that forthwith. The field is immense. The soil is virgin. I think I have said enough to present the British Empire Travel Moving Picture idea. I can understand that it may not be a pleasing idea to many. But we must

all recognise the evils spring from misunderstanding the world over, we must all recognise the existence of a new and great force. Surely we must use that force to combat those evils...And to sit with hands folded whilst facts are being distorted and great issues are being made more and more complex by misrepresentation and misunderstanding is surely something to which a stronger word than 'mistaken' should be applied.[24]

A number of bids were made from film producers, most notably by a Captain E.J. Solano, but they all fell through. Solano was accused of wanting to secure a film monopoly for the forthcoming visit of the Prince of Wales to India, but what seemed to really go against the whole project was the very idea of propaganda itself, which – to the British at least – was fundamentally distasteful. C.W. Gwynne's response to the idea was illustrative of the difficulty that the British found in engaging in the kind of dirty propaganda war that would be required if Gandhi and his fellow nationalists were to be disarmed. 'There was a very great suspicion of Captain Solano's motives,' he wrote, 'and it was thought that any examination of the question of the utilization of cinema propaganda *should be free from all taint of motives of self interest.*'[25] In the grand bureaucratic tradition of avoiding a decision, it was agreed that no action could be taken at present, but that an 'expert adviser' was to be consulted on this matter in future. Thus if some had thought that the great misunderstandings and unnecessary anger that had greeted the Rowlatt Bills would have sparked a great British fight back, they were to be disappointed.

What to do? Responding to Thompson's idea of a government party, Sir William Marris (Secretary, Home Department) wrote a short but insightful note that summed up the British dilemma in India as it had become by 1919. The problem was essentially, Marris wrote, 'the same one which presented itself when Mrs Besant was interned; and again when Gandhi started preaching Satyagraha'.

> Is agitation conducted in the name of constitutional liberty which is likely to lead to disorder to be permitted up to the point at which disorder actually occurs; and if not, can we do anything to stop it beyond what we do now? We have the Press Act, the Seditious Meetings Act, and so forth: but the trouble is that they are all rather a denial of our own principles; we use them intermittently and reluctantly, and they are weapons too big and clumsy to deal with nine-tenths of the actual mischief.[26]

Marris thought that the problem went 'far beyond Delhi', but 'strikes right at the continuance of our administration'. He lamented the problem of agitation during a period of reform; 'inasmuch as reforms are themselves a halfway measure, such agitation there is bound to be: and yet under reforms repression will be harder than ever'. Marris's note ended in a depressed state.

> I certainly do not advocate repression but I think we must get the Secretary of State and Parliament to face facts ... tell him that the unrestrained freedom of misrepresentation is a menace to our administration, because it is largely conducted by irresponsible mischief mongers and addressed not to intelligent independent men, but to the ignorance and prejudice of those who differ from us in every possible way... Is Parliament prepared to give us more weapons of defence or if not is it prepared to see the administration weakened and brought to a standstill?

Whether he liked it or not, Marris was right: the Rowlatt *Satyagraha* had raised profound questions about whether the British had the necessary willingness to hold onto their Indian Empire.

Conclusion

Amritsar and the British in India

It would be pleasant to blot out the memories of the years that followed.

Sir Stanley Reed[1]

Go stay a night with a certain kind of English family and a portrait or a book will come out from the lumber-room, a sword or a writing-desk or a bundle of letters; he served in India, they will tell you, and gazing at the faded sepia of the photograph or the long-sloping characters of his hand, you try to picture the man and what he did, what he felt about his part in life and his fantastic exile in an empire seven thousand miles across the sea.

So wrote Philip Mason in 1954, seven years after India had gained her freedom, in his widely read two-volume work, *The Men Who Ruled India*.[2] His words were wistful, full of nostalgia for the empire 'seven thousand miles across the sea' and amazement that it had ever existed at all. Mason's view that the British had had a positive impact on India and deserved to be remembered with pride and sympathy has been echoed by those who had been part of the Raj and fervently believed that they had, in the words of one *memsahib*, loved India: 'Did we British bleed India for what we could carry away?' she wrote, 'Or did our men give their heath – their lives for her? . . . Well, whatever else we did, we loved her.'[3]

Some British in India may have loved the subcontinent, and many certainly trumpeted the values and achievements of the Raj, but there was always the shadow of repression and autocracy behind the British in India that even they could not deny. The incident that summed this up more than any other was the Jallianwala Bagh; an event that seemed to fly in the face of any attempt to justify or praise the British achievement in India, the ultimate riposte to any suggestion that the British 'loved India', an act that called into question all that had been done by the British in the subcontinent for 150 years. The Raj endured for another 28 years after Amritsar, but it is commonly seen as a turning point, becoming enshrined in national myth as a brutal act that turned India's people finally and irrevocably against their colonial masters, pushing them onto the road of non-co-operation and, eventually, independence. A popular account of the British Empire records how it was a 'terrible event . . . providing one of those markers in time . . . by which imperial patterns can best be traced' and 'the worst of all stains upon the imperial record'.[4]

There is no doubt that Amritsar was an important event, but it did not 'end the Raj' as some have claimed. The decline and fall of British imperial rule over the subcontinent was a complex and lengthy process with uneven periods of reform frequently followed by years of backsliding and stubborn resistance. The outcry that followed the massacre undoubtedly affected British morale and willpower across India, but the main processes that would shape the devolution of power and influence had been framed by Montagu's August declaration and by the Government of India Act of 1919, both of which had been devised before the bloody events in the Punjab. That the massacre has attracted such hyperbole and hysteria is perhaps understandable, but this should not cloud our understanding of the events of 1919, and allow a whole series of myths to continue that are unhelpful and, to the British authorities in particular, deeply unfair. Because historians have concentrated on the Jallianwala Bagh and the apparently demonic figure of 'Rex' Dyer, they have missed the larger processes at work and written lopsided, biased and frequently inaccurate accounts of these events. I wrote *The Amritsar Massacre: The Untold Story of One Fateful Day* to highlight these layers of myth and to show the massacre within a broader context, not only by discussing the full scale of the violence, but also by explaining the attempts to reform the Indian Empire and bring in more representative institutions. Only by understanding the role of reform can we evaluate the level of coercion that the British employed. I hope that this will redefine the debate on the massacre and end the lazy repetition of the myths of 1919 that were first peddled by the Indian National Congress 90 years ago and which have gone unchallenged ever since.

ᖇᖇ

What really happened in 1919? Previously accepted explanations for the disorders have remained heavily, even obsessively, biased against British rule in the Punjab, particularly the allegedly 'iron rule' of Sir Michael

O'Dwyer, but this is a shallow and unsatisfactory conclusion. Although the British may not have been able to uncover the golden clue that would link the Mahatma to an organisation dedicated to overthrowing the Raj with violence, it is clear that *satyagraha* was central to what happened. Gandhi's movement may not have been violent in origin or intention, and those *satyagrahis* who took the vows and directed the *hartals* do seem to have been genuine believers, but they disobeyed authority and urged others to do so with commitment and dedication. When *satyagrahi*, including Gandhi, discussed the Rowlatt Bills, they made no attempt to present an objective summary of its provisions, but simply used it as a tool to damn 'government oppression' with recklessness and mendacity. Grievances were common in India in 1919 and where tensions were already high, it took only small incidents – the scuffle at Delhi railway station or the arrest of the leaders in Amritsar – to turn a peaceful *hartal* into an enraged torrent of shouting, abusive mobs that moved against anything that seemed to be from the *sarkar* (government). Whether he liked it or not, Gandhi – the apostle of non-violence – was primarily responsible for these gatherings.

Furthermore, the reaction of the British authorities to the crowds and mobs that gathered in April 1919 was, contrary to Congress propaganda, not marked by any great overreaction or indiscriminate violence. At Delhi, Lahore, Amritsar and Gujranwala, the police fired because it was felt (with strong justification) that nothing short of lethal force would be effective. Indeed, in many cases, the reaction was remarkably moderate, such as at Gujranwala and Delhi, where the police and military were under intense stoning and on the cusp of being overwhelmed before they took action. Though some accounts have often tried to minimise or ignore the level of violence and intimidation that was shown against the British community in March and April 1919, it should be remembered how terrifying it must have been for those scattered Europeans, either in Kasur, Amritsar, Gujranwala or elsewhere, who narrowly escaped with their lives when faced with angry mobs brandishing *lathis*. To categorise the British attempts to restore order as acts of terror and retribution is to distort their motivations and pervert what was, in many cases, an earnest desire to protect life and property.

The account of the most notorious British response of this period, the Jallianwala Bagh massacre, contained within these pages is different to previous explanations. The fantasy, beloved of so many Indian nationalists, that the Jallianwala Bagh was the result of some shady conspiracy between Dyer and Hans Raj is simply not true and should be given up for the fiction it always was. On the contrary, Dyer was no premeditated murderer. His decision to fire in the Jallianwala Bagh was a sudden reaction to the size and composition of the crowd that he faced, something that was deeply surprising and which was considerably larger than previous estimates – upwards of 25,000 people – and was mainly composed of male Hindus who had entered the Bagh primarily for political purposes. Because Dyer had so few troops he had no option but to keep firing. And he kept going because it took so long for the crowd to disperse itself due to the lack of exits, something that he was unaware of. As a result, it is likely that the total number of casualties for the massacre are slightly higher than the official figures and could lie somewhere in the region of 400 dead.

It may be argued that this account is controversial, somehow justifying or excusing Dyer's actions. I have suggested that any discussion of Dyer in the Jallianwala Bagh must examine what his reaction was to what he found there. By explaining the massacre solely in terms of Dyer's psychology or his personal character, previous accounts have failed to appreciate both the sequence of events that brought Dyer to the Bagh and his reaction to what he found. *To suggest that the size and composition of the crowd in the Bagh had no effect on Dyer is highly unlikely.* In any case, trying to justify or demonise Dyer's actions is, in many ways, to miss the point. Whether he would commit a massacre (or otherwise) was not a choice that Dyer ever made, it was simply a product of unfortunate circumstances. And while he would later claim that he knew exactly what he was doing in the Jallianwala Bagh, Dyer had said the same thing about his rather sordid role in the Sarhadd campaign and this new bravado simply reflected his stubborn self-belief as well as lingering frustration with a career that had promised so much but failed to deliver.

For so long synonymous with so-called 'imperial terrorism', martial law was far less repressive than has often been assumed. Although there were undoubted incidents of abuse (such as Dyer's 'crawling order'), they have been greatly exaggerated. Often they only lasted a matter of days because as soon as the provincial government became aware of them, they were cancelled. Much of this can be blamed on the widespread lack of understanding about martial law, what it was, how it was administered, and most importantly, whether the civilian or the military authorities were in command. Because everyone seemed to have a different definition of martial law, and because the Government of India was slow off the mark in defining exactly how it would work, abuses were allowed to occur. During this period, the allegedly 'reactionary' and 'repressive' Sir Michael O'Dwyer – who was not in a position of authority – continually advised the military commanders to be more cautious and was also instrumental in toning down some of the more offensive orders that had been passed by the military, including the 'crawling order' and various 'fancy punishments' elsewhere.

The way in which the British dealt with the disorders of 1919 was, therefore, on closer inspection, much more restrained and responsible than has always been assumed. Unfortunately, history has recorded a different verdict and the 'horrors' of the Punjab 'atrocities' have become ingrained in popular myth. Indeed it is testament to the success of the Indian National Congress that it was able to shape the history of this period so fundamentally that its arguments still dominate the field today. In the bitter aftermath of the unrest the Government of India began to lose its nerve and believe what has been written about it in the nationalist press; that it was all about oppression, racism and 'imperial terrorism'. The nationalist outcry from 1919 had a devastating effect on British resolve in India. Although the Hunter Report supported every decision to open fire on crowds in the Punjab and the Bombay Presidency during the disorders (apart from the Jallianwala Bagh), the Dyer case was the critical one. The censure of Dyer and his forced retirement sent a clear message that in future the support of one's superiors could not be taken for granted. The failure to support Dyer, whatever the merits of his case, dealt a blow to British authority and morale across India.[5] Sir Charles Gwynn's book on imperial policing, published in 1934, complained that it is perhaps still 'widely felt that an officer who takes strong action which he genuinely considers is necessitated by the circumstances cannot rely on the support of the Government'.[6]

Whenever government officials or soldiers attempted to quell disorder, the shadow of Amritsar influenced their actions. By April 1920 the Government of India issued new guidelines for the conduct of martial law, which strongly reflected the experiences of 1919.[7] The military were instructed to co-operate with the civil authorities to restore civilian control as soon as possible. They were to act with care and sensitivity at all times. Stress was laid upon not doing anything that would offend racial or religious sensitivities. Whipping was not to be conducted except when it would have been otherwise permitted in ordinary law and all force was to be governed by the principle of minimum force. The 1921 *Manual of Indian Military Law* reinforced these developments, re-emphasising caution in riot control situations and making it explicit that officers must only disperse illegal assemblies or mobs using 'no more force than is absolutely necessary'. They were, under no circumstances, to punish rioters.[8] In a complete reversal of the position that Lord Chelmsford had taken in April

1919, when he had deprived Sir Michael O'Dwyer of authority for the administration of martial law (and handed it over completely to the military), secret instructions were issued in November 1921 that made it clear that in the event of martial law being declared, the civilian authorities would remain partly responsible for its administration and they were in no way to abdicate all control.[9] *O'Dwyer had been right after all.*

Even though these developments certainly help to codify and standardise the way that the British would respond to future unrest, the British willingness to clamp down upon disorder and suppress discontent was visibly weakening, an understandable reaction to the outcry from the Jallianwala Bagh. When violence broke out in Malabar in August 1921, a troublesome district within the Madras Presidency with a long history of revolt, the British were anxious to avoid a repetition of what had occurred in the Punjab and proceeded carefully. The unrest in the Punjab had been suppressed within weeks, but because of the severe restrictions that had been placed on the prosecution of martial law, British officers were unable to restore order to Malabar for many months. Communal strife led to 2,000 deaths and over 20,000 arrests.[10] The military commander, Major-General Sir John Burnett-Stuart, complained bitterly about the restrictions on his operations. 'One of greatest handicaps imposed on us so far,' he wrote, 'had been the inadequacy of the Martial Law Ordinance to meet the situation.'[11] He was in no doubt that the outcry from the 'Dyer affair' was to blame. Indeed, the cry of 'Dyerism' would be raised whenever the British attempted to retain control by military force to plague them during their remaining years on the subcontinent. So nervous were British officers about firing in Peshawar in April 1930 (being convinced that they would not be supported should there be an inquiry), that soldiers were ordered to stand passively in front of rioting crowds for over an hour. On at least two occasions, British troops were on the point of being overwhelmed before they were forced to break into uncontrolled firing.[12]

British control over India gradually retreated during the next 30 years. There were times when British resolve held firm such as between 1924 and 1929 when Lord Birkenhead was Secretary of State for India; a man who was not convinced of the viability of parliamentary democracy in India and chose to rebuff nationalist agitation in the way that Montagu never had. Again, at the height of the Second World War, with the British Empire mortally wounded by the Axis powers, Gandhi's 'Quit India' movement was dealt with firmly. But these events were exceptions to the rule. The outcry from 1919 and the weak response of the Government of India to it suddenly revealed that the edifice of the Raj was crumbling, weakened by promises of reform and lacking the will to restore British prestige. There could be no greater contrast between the decisive – if somewhat panicked – British response to the Rowlatt *Satyagraha*, and the miserable failure to halt the murderous communal slaughter of partition in the spring and summer of 1947; a failure tinged by the desire to avoid 'another Amritsar'.

ↄ

Sixty-four years ago, at the stroke of midnight, the British Empire in India died; its flags lowered and its few remaining garrisons evacuated, with due pomp and ceremony, through the Gate of India onto the last troop ship bound for home. The earnest hopes of Edwin Montagu in 1917 to bring about a new era of co-operation and trust between Britain and India appeared hollow in 1947 as the British left in undue haste; abandoning the subcontinent in the throes of a violent upheaval as the bitter red lines of partition drew themselves across the Raj and gave birth to two new troubled neighbours, India and Pakistan. It is not difficult to imagine what the two main British protagonists in this story, General Dyer and Sir Michael O'Dwyer, would have thought of this spectacle. Both were fervent believers in the British Raj, although perhaps for different reasons. For Dyer, always an insecure man, the Raj gave him a home and a mission, which he had not found elsewhere. For Sir Michael, British power in India was a vast and successful experiment in paternalism; a great example of good government that protected and furthered the interests of India's 'real' people, and not necessarily those of its western-educated elites. Both men could not imagine any replacement for British power in India and the actions that they had taken in 1919 had been defined by their understanding that the empire was in danger and that certain measures were justified.[13] It was perhaps just as well that both had not lived to see independence. General Dyer had died in 1927, still protesting his innocence, and Sir Michael had fallen to an assassin's bullet at Caxton Hall, London, in 1940.

For the Secretary of State for India, Edwin Montagu, the future was equally bleak; having never recovered from the torrent of abuse that had been directed at him in the House of Commons during what he would call that 'dreadful debate' on Dyer in July 1920. Montagu left the India Office in March 1922 a broken man; shattered by the failure of Indian 'moderates' to support his reforms with sufficient zeal. He joined the boards of a number of firms, but never found the enthusiasm and zest for his work that he had found in India and became increasingly sickly and depressed. He complained frequently of pain and stress-related illnesses and on his return from a financial mission to

Brazil he became seriously ill. He died on 15 November 1924 in a nursing home in London. He was just 45 years old.[14]

Given Montagu's good intentions and his earnest efforts to bring about a 'new era' in the subcontinent, it is hard not to feel sympathetic to his fate. He had once told Chelmsford of his hopes that whatever happened to his reforms 'that it will not be said – "He instituted this great work, but failed in its execution."'[15] His desire to 'do something big' that would be 'epoch-making', that would satisfy all sides and be a 'keystone' for future British control, was to be unfulfilled and the remaining British years on the subcontinent were marked by increasing friction and disorder. Whether he liked it or not, the O'Dwyers and the Pentlands were right. If the British were to stay in India, then they must stay as rulers and accept everything that came with it. But Montagu could never accept this. By failing to support those officials and soldiers who restored order in 1919, by ordering an inquiry and by denouncing what he believed was 'frightfulness' and 'racial humiliation', Montagu did immense damage to the British cause in India, but without strengthening his hand among Indian politicians. He may have believed that his strategy would work with the dwindling band of 'moderate' politicians, but in reality it won him few favours. As he told Chelmsford in May 1919, he was aware of how unpopular he was among the British community in India. 'In fact the only confidence that I have achieved,' he grumbled, 'is the wavering, flickering, fluctuating support of some Indians.'[16] As would become painfully clear in the coming years, this would not be enough to save the Raj.

For that other key figure in the events of 1919, Mahatma Gandhi, independence was not something to be celebrated because it came with the bitter price of partition. Gandhi spent 15 August 1947, the day India redeemed Nehru's 'tryst with destiny', in Calcutta, deep in mourning. Although huge crowds gathered in Delhi and Karachi to celebrate the birth of two new nations, Gandhi spent the day fasting and spinning to mark his identification with the poor. He would not take part in the rejoicing, which he called a 'sorry affair', but he did pray for the reunification of his beloved motherland.[17] By now Gandhi cut a lonely figure, ignored by those younger men in Congress, and seen by many as an incorrigible idealist; mistrusted by many Hindus, hated by many Muslims. He would finally meet his end before the smoking revolver of an ardent Hindu nationalist, Nathuram Godse, in the grounds of Birla House, New Delhi, in January 1948. Gandhi's death turned him into the father of the nation, acclaimed throughout India as an everlasting symbol of the triumph of non-violent non-co-operation, of reason and love, over the forces of imperialism and repression, which were symbolised more than anything else by the Jallianwala Bagh massacre, 29 years before.

The memorial to the 'two thousand' Indian 'martyrs' in the Jallianwala Bagh stands today as a symbol of the price India paid to be free of imperial domination. Every day hundreds of schoolchildren make their way up the lonely, narrow entrance to the Bagh and wander around the garden inside, regaled by the tales of British repression and 'imperial terrorism' that have become established as historical fact and which continue to be repeated to this day. An introductory text on Gandhi written by the historian David Arnold and published in 2001 states

> If a single event was to be chosen as the critical turning point in the entire history of India's nationalist movement, the Jallianwala Bagh massacre would surely be it, for it revealed the intrinsic violence of British rule, a savage indifference to Indian life, and an utter contempt for nationalist feeling and peaceful protest.[18]

This is, of course, terribly wrong. In struggling to unite a divided nation and deal with the difficult legacy of colonialism, India may have needed the myths of the Jallianwala Bagh and the so-called 'imperial terrorism' of Sir Michael O'Dwyer and others, but it is time to let them go.

At the dawn of the twenty-first century, with India on the verge of superpower status, it must find the courage to face its past with honesty and fairness, not cling on to the old nationalist myths. The massacre was a deeply sad and tragic event, ending the lives of hundreds of Indians, but it was also unique; not an example of premeditated imperial murder, but rather the result of a series of unfortunate and unexpected events that came together one afternoon with devastating results. Dyer did not enter the Jallianwala Bagh with a plan already hatched in his mind, but walked up that narrow entrance, alone and alert, unsure of what would confront him. It was only when he saw that vast space and the huge crowd that had gathered inside did he understand what had happened; it was only then, in those few precious seconds, that he allowed fear to grip him. There were thousands of them. There was no time for anything else. He had to open fire.

Epilogue

Operation Blue Star

The floors of the shrine were carpeted with spent cartridges. The white marble of the pavement outside was stained with blood.

Mark Tully[1]

Amritsar's unfortunate association with violence did not end in 1919, or indeed with the savage communal slaughter of 1947. During the 1980s the eastern half of the partitioned Punjab, now in India, was the scene of growing unrest between groups of extremist Sikhs and the Government of India. The British had known only too well that ruling the Punjab was impossible without the consent of the Sikhs, and had made numerous concessions to them, including handing over control of *gurdwaras* (places of worship) in the 1920s in response to what was known as the Akali movement; an agitation that threatened to undermine the flow of recruits to the Indian Army. But in post-partition India, the Sikhs wanted more than just control over their temples, and continually tried to improve their position in the Punjab, railing against the dominance of the Hindus in Delhi, and campaigning for greater independence and autonomy. But now the Government of India was far less interested in securing Sikh support, only weakening it. After 1977 the Punjab was ruled by an anti-Congress coalition that included the Sikh party, the Akali Dal, and this became an increasing annoyance to the Indian Prime Minister, Indira Gandhi, who had suffered a disastrous electoral defeat that year.

The struggle between the Sikhs in the Punjab and the Government of India gradually increased during the 1980s, with a darkening mood of militancy taking hold amid the growing calls for a Sikh homeland of Khalistan.

The unrest was centred on Jarnail Singh Bhindranwale, a charismatic preacher who led a growing insurgency in the Punjab. The unrest would culminate in the storming of Bhindranwale's headquarters in the Golden Temple in June 1984, and with the assassination of Indira Gandhi, by her Sikh bodyguards on 31 October, plunging India into its most dangerous and unstable period since independence. The assault on the Sikh stronghold – codenamed Operation Blue Star – began on the night of 5 June and fighting raged in and around the Golden Temple for two days. Bhindranwale and his followers were well armed and held a perimeter of buildings around the complex, as well as occupying a strong defensive position in the temple itself. Indian Army units tried to storm the stronghold at night, but the resistance was too formidable and the white marble pavements of the temple, usually criss-crossed by pilgrims and visitors, became a murderous no-man's-land, covered by machine guns and snipers, and blocked with dead and wounded. Artillery fire was directed in and around the temple, resulting in damage to the surrounding bazaars, before as many as six tanks and armoured personnel carriers were sent in against the Sikh stronghold.[2] The *Akal Takht* ('Eternal Throne'), the symbol of the temporal power of the Sikhs, where the last of the terrorists were holding out, was almost demolished by tank fire, before resistance ended. According to official figures, 576 people died in the operation, including 83 Indian soldiers, although unofficial sources claimed that the number of dead was far higher, perhaps as many as 1,000.[3]

Operation Blue Star has, on first glance, little to do with the firing at the Jallianwala Bagh, but there are a number of startling parallels. The commander of the assault, Lieutenant-General Krishnaswami Sunderji, believed, with some justification, that unless he acted swiftly and decisively against the Sikh militants in the Golden Temple, then he would soon find his troops under attack from a hostile, revolutionary population that was interfering with communications, cutting railway lines and urging their men to mutiny. Furthermore, if they did not take action and allowed the insurgency to continue unmolested, then it was felt the prestige of the government would be fatally wounded.[4] These were the same fears that had haunted Dyer and his officers in 1919; a need to act decisively in a difficult urban area before the situation worsened even further. Although the Indian Army was in much greater strength in Amritsar in 1984 when compared with the shortage of troops in 1919, their nervousness was testimony to the volatility of the Punjab and the fragility of order. Evidently, the Indian Army officers who were tasked with restoring order to Amritsar in 1984 acted in a manner that would have been entirely familiar to Dyer 65 years before.

Comparing the Jallianwala Bagh with Operation Blue Star (and subsequent events in the Punjab) provides a useful corrective to much of the conventional historical wisdom on 1919. Although the Indian National Congress (and later the Muslim League) would continually – almost obsessively – decry the nature of British rule in the Punjab, for its alleged brutality and violence, events in the Punjab since independence have undermined the validity of these accusations. The situation in and around the Golden Temple was undoubtedly serious, but the Government of India employed force on an extensive and indiscriminate scale, including the use of artillery and armour in a congested urban area. Furthermore, the period of so-called 'President's Rule', when the Punjab was sealed off and put under a form of martial law that was far more draconian than 1919, should not be forgotten. Under an amendment to the National Security Act, police in the Punjab were permitted to enter and search houses without a warrant, to arrest and detain suspects for up to six months without having to give a reason, and arrest anyone without trial for as long as two years; provisions that make the Rowlatt Bills of 1919 look weak in comparison.[5] In the immediate aftermath of the firing, large numbers of civilians in and around Amritsar – perhaps as many as 5,000 people – were rounded up by the army and interrogated. Soon rumours leaked out of beatings, torture and extortion. Houses were ransacked, property was looted, and it was even alleged that students and staff at Punjabi University, Patiala, were ordered to get on their knees and *crawl* before Indian soldiers; a sort of modern day 'crawling order', but this time perpetrated by Indians against their fellow citizens.[6]

The violence and unrest in the Punjab, and the difficulty of maintaining order and stability that was experienced by Indira Gandhi in 1984, would have been familiar to O'Dwyer and other British administrators of the Punjab. They always maintained that control of such a potentially violent and explosive mix of people was dependent upon a non-communal unionist government that sought the support of the rural population and took clear action against any threat.[7] The decision by Montagu and his successors to seek an accommodation, not with the landowners and 'natural rulers' of India, but with the new urban, educated elite of the Indian National Congress, undermined British rule and was detrimental to stability and order. Indira Gandhi made the same mistake in the 1980s. She destabilised the fragile communal balance in the Punjab and then proved unwilling to take decisive action against the Sikh extremist movement, leaving it to grow bolder and bolder. Bhindranwale masterminded a growing terrorist campaign that targeted Hindus and government officials, while gradually fortifying the

Golden Temple. Twice suspected of being involved in the deaths of political opponents, he was released and allowed to grow stronger. Soon Bhindranwale was seen, like Gandhi had been in the 1930s, as the only one able and willing to openly defy the government with impunity.[8] A dangerous opponent had been allowed to get out of control.

Then finally, the patience of the government snapped. Operation Blue Star was ordered, but rather than undertaking a lengthy siege of the Golden Temple and negotiating with the defenders, the Indian Army conducted a night-time raid that rapidly morphed into a full-blown daylight assault, with grave results for all concerned. It was an event, like the Jallianwala Bagh, that left a legacy of bitterness and anger that would end in assassination; Sir Michael O'Dwyer in 1940 and Indira Gandhi 44 years later. But looking at the violence in the Punjab in 1984, and at the scale of action taken by the Indian Army, gives the lie to the accusation that the British ruled the Punjab with anything approaching the 'iron fist' of legend. It was not just the events of 1984 in and around the Golden Temple that showed the level of brutality that the Indian state was capable of. The struggle against the Sikhs did not end in 1984, but rumbled on throughout the decade, with the Government of India taking increasingly draconian action in the Punjab, passing ordinance after ordinance aimed at stamping out the terrorist threat.[9] The use of torture was widespread and made the much-criticised 'fancy punishments' of 1919 pale into insignificance. An Amnesty International report of 1992 criticised the Government of India for failing to acknowledge the scale of abuse that occurred in the Punjab. Common methods of torture included hanging people from ceilings and beating them, forcing their legs apart so as to cause pelvic injury, crushing the thighs with wooden bars, rubbing chilli powder into sensitive areas of the body, electric shocks and fingernails being torn out. Thousands of people were also detained – including women, children and the elderly – often because they were the relative of a suspect, and held for months, even years, in secret detention facilities.[10]

The Indian Army's deployment peaked in February 1992 with 120,000 army personnel, 53,000 police officers, 28,000 Home Guards, 10,000 special police and over 70,000 paramilitary police, a huge number of troops in one relatively small province, which, needless to say, dwarfed the numbers employed by the British to maintain order in the much bigger un-partitioned Punjab.[11] Sikh extremists were dealt with ruthlessly and between 1981 and the mid-nineties approximately 25,000 people were killed in the violence, both civilians and militants, and somewhere between 20,000 and 45,000 people were illegally detained. The number of those who disappeared during the unrest is unknown. It is little wonder that conditions in the Punjab resembled that of a civil war, with brutal terrorist violence being met by a vigorous and highly aggressive official response, including orders to 'shoot on sight' suspected offenders and extensive use of shady paramilitary groups.

When looking at the history of the Punjab and the violence that has periodically shaken it, the remarkable thing about British rule is that it managed to maintain law and order, stability and prosperity for a hundred years without resorting to such levels of violence and repression; certainly much lower than that employed by the champions of the 'freedom movement', the Indian National Congress. The structure of British rule was that of a bureaucratic dictatorship that maintained order through landed elites and, in many instances, through prestige alone. In order for British rule to work, any dissent had to be nipped in the bud as quickly as possible, as happened in the Punjab in 1919. And even if one considers the British response to have been disproportionate or overly brutal, the number of dead and wounded from the disorders remains tiny when compared with the vast numbers who became victims of the struggles in the 1980s. The Indian National Congress began the decade on a crusade to win the Hindu vote and in the Punjab it could only do so by increasing communal tensions.[12] This was the reality of democracy in India, a far more volatile and unstable type of rule than the British imposed, and which showed its dark side in dealing with the Khalistan problem. But Congress won the battle of history and still distorts our view of the Punjab under British rule. It was they who fought against the British Raj and delivered India from her imperial oppressors, 'into life and freedom' as Jawaharlal Nehru had said, thus entering history as victors of the colonial struggle. It was somewhat ironic, therefore, that it would be Indira Gandhi, the daughter of Nehru, who would usher in such a disastrous set of policies, but this time it would not be done by an alien imperial regime, but by a democratic government of the people.

Notes

Preface

1. *The Congress Punjab Inquiry 1919–1920: Evidence* (Delhi, 1996; first published 1920), p. 53.
2. TNA: CAB 27/92 & 27/93, *Evidence Taken Before the Disorders Inquiry Committee* (7 vols, Calcutta, 1920) [Hereafter *Disorders Inquiry Committee*], III, p. 17.
3. *Disorders Inquiry Committee*, III, p. 24.
4. Dyer, Reginald Edward Harry (1864–1927): Second-Lieutenant, Queen's Royal West Surrey Regiment (1885–7); 39/Bengal Native Infantry (1887–8); Wing Officer, 29/Punjab Infantry (1888–1901); DAAG, Garrison School, Chakrata (1901–9); Major, 25/Punjab Infantry (1908–10); Lieutenant-Colonel, 25/Punjab Infantry (1910–14); Chief of Staff to Sir Gerald Kitson (1914–16); OC Seistan Field Force (1916–17); GOC Jullundur Brigade (1918–19); retired (1920).
5. LHCMA: Edmonds Papers, 'Memoirs', III/2/17, p. 21.
6. Reginald Dyer to Anne Dyer (his wife), 19 April 1917, cited in I. Colvin, *The Life of General Dyer* (Edinburgh & London, 1929), p. 117.
7. Colvin, *The Life of General Dyer*, pp. 29–30.
8. *Disorders Inquiry Committee*, III, p. 114.
9. IWM: 83/31/1, Account of Brigadier F. McCallum, p. 3.
10. *Disorders Inquiry Committee*, III, p. 115.
11. *Disorders Inquiry Committee*, III, p. 202.
12. A. Gauba, *Amritsar. A Study in Urban History (1840–1947)* (Jalandhar, 1988), pp. 19–22, 53–4.
13. V.N. Datta, *Jallianwala Bagh* (Ludhiana, 1969), p. 94. It was dictated to Dyer's Brigade Major, Captain Briggs. Printed copies were also distributed in Urdu. Reginald Plomer and Muhammed Ashraf Khan decided on the route. *Disorders Inquiry Committee*, III, p. 67. Command 681, *Report of the Committee Appointed by the Government of India to Investigate the Disturbances in the Punjab, etc.* (London, 1920) [Hereafter *Hunter Report*], p. 28.
14. *Disorders Inquiry Committee*, III, pp. 40, 67, 116.
15. Dyer to General Staff, 16th (Indian) Division, 25 August 1919, contained in *Disorders Inquiry Committee*, III, p. 202.

16. A. Swinson, *Six Minutes to Sunset. The Story of General Dyer and the Amritsar Affair* (London, 1964), p. 48; Datta, *Jallianwala Bagh*, p. 99.
17. A. Draper, *The Amritsar Massacre. Twilight of the Raj* (London, 1985; first published 1981), p. 89; Swinson, *Six Minutes to Sunset*, p. 47.
18. R. Perkins, *The Amritsar Legacy. Golden Temple to Caxton Hall, the Story of a Killing* (Chippenham, 1989), p. 185.
19. *The Congress Punjab Inquiry 1919–1920: Evidence*, pp. 69, 78.
20. See for example Draper, *The Amritsar Massacre*, p. 88; Swinson, *Six Minutes to Sunset*, p. 50.
21. *The Congress Punjab Inquiry 1919–1920: Evidence*, p. 8.
22. *The Congress Punjab Inquiry 1919–1920: Evidence*, p. 52.
23. *The Congress Punjab Inquiry 1919–1920: Evidence*, p. 77.
24. Notice at 'Martyrs' Well', Jallianwala Bagh, Amritsar.

Introduction

1. Command 681, *Report of the Committee Appointed by the Government of India to Investigate the Disturbances in the Punjab, etc.* (London, 1920) [Hereafter *Hunter Report*], p. 29.
2. *Report of the Commissioners Appointed by the Punjab Sub-Committee of the Indian National Congress* [hereafter *Congress Punjab Inquiry*] in *The Collected Works of Mahatma Gandhi* (Electronic Book), New Delhi, Publications Division Government of India, 1999, 98 volumes *http://www.gandhiserve.org/cwmg/cwmg.html* [hereafter *CWMG*], XX, p. 180.
3. D. Sayer, 'British Reaction to the Amritsar Massacre 1919–1920', *Past and Present*, 131 (May 1991), pp. 131–2.
4. V.N. Datta, 'Perceptions of the Jallianwala Bagh Massacre', in V.N. Datta & S. Settar (eds), *Jallianwala Bagh Massacre* (Delhi, 2000), p. 1.
5. Gandhi to Chelmsford (Viceroy of India), 1 August 1920, in *CWMG*, XXI, p. 106.
6. 'Jallianwala Bagh Massacre Stirs Britain', *The Times of India*, 27 December 2006, *http://timesofindia.indiatimes.com/articleshow/954296.cms* [accessed 7 June 2008]. The events in the Jallianwala Bagh had also caused controversy during an earlier Royal visit to Amritsar. See 'Colonial History Rebounds on Queen' in *The Times*, 18 August 1997, and 'Queen Heals Open Wounds of Amritsar' in *The Times*, 15 October 1997.
7. Criticism of O'Dwyer can be found in most accounts. A typical recent example comes from P. Brendon, *The Decline and Fall of the British Empire 1781–1997* (London, 2008; first published 2007), p. 260.
8. See N.L. Paxton, *Writing Under the Raj. Gender, Race, and Rape in the British Colonial Imagination, 1830–1947* (London & New Jersey, 1999), p. 233; S. Das, 'Calcutta in Turmoil: April 1919', in Datta & Settar (eds), *Jallianwala Bagh Massacre*, p. 165.
9. See for example, G. Singh, 'The Imperial Terrorism in Punjab: Its Nature and Implications (1919–25)', in Datta & Settar (eds), *Jallianwala Bagh Massacre*, pp. 38–51.

10. For a concise introduction to the historiography see S. Narain, *The Historiography of the Jallianwala Bagh Massacre, 1919* (South Godstone, Surrey, 1998).
11. Writing about (and by) some of the key actors: Sir G. de S. Barrow, *The Fire of Life* (London, 1941); J.M. Brown, *Gandhi's Rise to Power. Indian Politics 1915–1922* (Cambridge, 1972); I. Colvin, *The Life of General Dyer* (Edinburgh & London, 1929); Sir M. O'Dwyer, *India as I Knew it 1885–1925* (London, 1925); Sir C. Setalvad, *Recollections and Reflections* (Bombay, 1946).
12. A. Swinson, *Six Minutes to Sunset. The Story of General Dyer and the Amritsar Affair* (London, 1964); Colvin, *The Life of General Dyer*.
13. S.R. Bakshi, *Jallianwala Bagh Tragedy* (New Delhi, 1982); V.N. Datta, *Jallianwala Bagh* (Ludhiana, 1969); Datta & Settar (eds), *Jallianwala Bagh Massacre*; A. Draper, *The Amritsar Massacre. Twilight of the Raj* (London, 1985; first published 1981); H. Fein, *Imperial Crime and Punishment. The Massacre at Jallianwala Bagh and British Judgment, 1919–1920* (Honolulu, 1977); R. Furneaux, *Massacre at Amritsar* (London, 1963); B.G. Horniman, *Amritsar and Our Duty to India* (Delhi, 1997; first published 1920); P. Mohan, *The Punjab "Rebellion" of 1919 and How It Was Suppressed*, R.M. Bakaya, ed. (New Delhi, 1999; first published 1920); R. Perkins, *The Amritsar Legacy. Golden Temple to Caxton Hall, the Story of a Killing* (Chippenham, 1989); R. Ram, *The Jallianwala Bagh Massacre. A Premeditated Plan* (Chandigarh, 1978; first published 1969). Stanley Wolpert, author of numerous books on Indian history, has also written about the Amritsar Massacre in a novel entitled *An Error of Judgment* (Boston & Toronto, 1970).
14. N. Collett, *The Butcher of Amritsar. General Reginald Dyer* (London, 2005), p. 423.
15. See R. Kumar (ed.), *Essays on Gandhian Politics. The Rowlatt Satyagraha of 1919* (Oxford, 1971).
16. For example, Arthur Swinson's final chapter of *Six Minutes to Sunset* begins with the questions 'Dyer: Was he right? Was he justified? Was he guilty?' (p. 185). See pp. 185–205. Chapter 7 of Datta's *Jallianwala Bagh* is entitled 'Why Did Dyer Shoot?' The final chapter of Furneaux's *Massacre at Amritsar* also concentrates on Dyer's motives in the Jallianwala Bagh (pp. 171–9). Nigel Collett's *The Butcher of Amritsar* is an attempt to 'discover the real Dyer' and explain 'what it was that persuaded Dyer to act as he did' (p. x). Brian Bond, 'Amritsar 1919', *History Today*, 13/10 (1963), pp. 666–76, asks the question of 'Why did a high-ranking and extremely competent British officer act in this apparently callous way?', p. 667.
17. For two recent works that argue some of these points, see S. Wolpert, *Shameful Flight. The Last Years of the British Empire in India* (Oxford, 2006), p. 4 and M. Misra, *Vishnu's Crowded Temple. India Since the Great Rebellion* (London, 2008; first published 2007), pp. 149–52.
18. *Hunter Report*, p. iii.
19. *Hunter Report*, p. 63.
20. *Hunter Report*, pp. 29–31, 83.

21. See *Hunter Report* [Minority], pp. 91–7.
22. See NAI: *Report on Native Newspaper*, Punjab, Jan–Dec 1920 (*Bande Mataram*, 29 May 1920; *Partrap*, 30 May 1920).
23. 'The Amritsar Report. Sir M.F. O'Dwyer's Criticisms', *The Times*, 9 June 1920, p. 15; Swinson, *Six Minutes to Sunset*, pp. 95–6.
24. The team consisted of Motilal Nehru, Fazlul Haq (replaced by M.R. Jayakar), C.R. Das, Abbas Tyabji, Gandhi and K. Santanam. See Brown, *Gandhi's Rise to Power*, pp. 236–7.
25. *Congress Punjab Inquiry*, pp. 179–80.
26. *The Congress Punjab Inquiry 1919–1920: Evidence* (Delhi, 1996; first published 1920).
27. Jayakar cited in Brown, *Gandhi's Rise to Power*, p. 236.
28. M.K. Gandhi, *An Autobiography or the Story of my Experiments with Truth*, M. Desai (trans) (London, 2001; first published, 1927 & 1929), p. 429.
29. The introduction makes particularly sentimental reading. 'It was here [the Punjab] that the Aryas of Vedic times first made their home. It was here that the hymns of the Rig Veda were first chanted ... It was here that Osiris, King of Egypt, first touched Indian soil and Semiramis, Queen of Assyria, who at the head of her vast armies tried her fortune for the dominion of India, suffered a crushing defeat ...' *Congress Punjab Inquiry*, p. 1.

Chapter 1: The Raj in an Age of Change

1. E.S. Montagu, *An Indian Diary*, V. Montagu (ed.) (London, 1930), pp. 70–1.
2. Montagu, *An Indian Diary*, V. Montagu (ed.), pp. 1–2.
3. Montagu, Edwin Samuel (1879–1924): Liberal MP for West Cambridgeshire (1906–18); Liberal MP for the combined country of Cambridgeshire (1918–22); Parliamentary Private Secretary for H.H. Asquith (1906–10); Under-Secretary of State for India (1910–14); Financial Secretary to the Treasury (1914–15); Chancellor of the Duchy of Lancaster (1915); Financial Secretary to the Treasury (1915–16); Minister of Munitions (1916–17); Minister Without Portfolio (1917); Secretary of State for India (1917–22); Liberal MP for Cambridgeshire (1918–22).
4. A. Rumbold, *Watershed in India 1914–1922* (London, 1979), p. 102.
5. P.G. Robb, *The Government of India and Reform. Policies Towards Politics and the Constitution 1916–1921* (New Delhi, 1989), p. 86.
6. Montagu, *An Indian Diary*, V. Montagu (ed.), p. 8.
7. *A Handbook for Travellers in India Burma and Ceylon*, 13th edn (London, 1929), p. xlix.
8. Three Members of the Viceroy's Executive Council must have served the Crown in India for at least ten years and one had to be a barrister. There was no ban on Indian membership and by 1919 Indians had held the portfolios dealing with Legislation and Education.
9. See E.M. Forster, *A Passage to India* (London, 1988; first published 1924) and P. Scott, *The Jewel in the Crown* (London, 2005; first published 1966).

10. E. Buettner, *Empire Families. Britons and Late Imperial India* (Oxford, 2004), p. 15. See also D. Gilmour, *The Ruling Caste. Imperial Lives in the Victorian Raj* (London, 2005).

11. H. Dodwell (ed.), *The Cambridge History of India, Vol. 6, The Indian Empire 1858–1918* (Cambridge, 1932), pp. 111, 348.

12. G. Krishna, 'The Development of the Indian National Congress as a Mass Organization, 1918–1923', *Journal of Asian Studies*, 25/3 (May 1966), p. 413.

13. A.M. Zaidi, *INC. The Glorious Tradition. Volume One: 1885–1920* (New Delhi, 1987), pp. 17–19.

14. Curzon cited in J.M. Brown, *Modern India. The Origins of an Asian Democracy*, 2nd edn (Oxford, 1994; first published 1985), p. 146. See M.N. Das, *India Under Morley and Minto. Politics Behind Revolution, Repression and Reforms* (London, 1964), p. 14.

15. Rumbold, *Watershed in India 1914–1922*, p. 6.

16. J. Masselos, 'Tilak, Bal Gangadhar (1856–1920)', *Oxford Dictionary of National Biography*, Oxford University Press, Sept 2004; online edn, May 2007 [http://www.oxforddnb.com/view/article/41085, accessed 30 April 2008].

17. Curzon, 'Dinner Given by United Service Club, Simla', cited in *Lord Curzon in India. Being a Selection from his Speeches as Viceroy and Governor-General of India 1898–1905* (London, 1906), p. 364.

18. R.J. Popplewell, *Intelligence and Imperial Defence. British Intelligence and the Defence of the Indian Empire 1904–1924* (London, 1995), p. 101; Gilmour, *The Ruling Caste*, p. 110. More than 10,000 people were killed by snakebites in Bengal in 1878 alone (p. 95).

19. G. Johnson, 'Partition, Agitation and Congress: Bengal 1904 to 1908', *Modern Asian Studies*, 7/3 (1973), p. 543.

20. Curzon to Broderick, 2 February 1905, cited in Johnson, 'Partition, Agitation and Congress: Bengal 1904 to 1908', pp. 549–50.

21. This is taken from Johnson, 'Partition, Agitation and Congress: Bengal 1904 to 1908', pp. 533–88.

22. S. Gopal, *British Policy in India 1858–1905* (Cambridge, 1965), p. 274.

23. S.R. Wasti, *Lord Minto and the Indian Nationalist Movement 1905 to 1910* (Oxford, 1964), pp. 123–4.

24. Minto to Morley, 21 May 1907, cited in Wasti, *Lord Minto and the Indian Nationalist Movement 1905 to 1910*, p. 98.

25. Wasti, *Lord Minto and the Indian Nationalist Movement 1905 to 1910*, p. 128.

26. A.B. Keith, *A Constitutional History of India 1600–1935* (London, 1936), p. 229.

27. H.F. Owen, 'Negotiating the Lucknow Pact', *Journal of Asian Studies*, 31/3 (May 1972), pp. 561–2.

28. See Popplewell, *Intelligence and Imperial Defence*, pp. 80–92, 103.

Chapter 2: The Great War and Reform in India

1. IOC: MSS EUR E264/5, Chelmsford to Montagu, 27 August 1919.

2. Thesiger, Frederic John Napier, first Viscount Chelmsford (1868–1933): Fellow of All Souls College, Oxford (1892–9); Governor of Queensland,

Australia (1905–9); Governor of New South Wales (1910–3); Governor-General of Australia (1909–10); Viceroy of India (1916–20); Viscount (1921).

3. E.S. Montagu, *An Indian Diary*, V. Montagu (ed.) (London, 1930), pp. 16, 40.

4. P.G. Robb, *The Government of India and Reform. Policies Towards Politics and the Constitution 1916–1921* (New Delhi, 1989), p. 20. The 'creaky and lumbering machine' quote comes from a letter to Montagu, 28 April 1918.

5. See *India's Contribution to the Great War* (Calcutta, 1923), pp. 61–5.

6. See T.G. Fraser, 'Germany and Indian Revolution, 1914–18', *Journal of Contemporary History*, 12/2 (April 1977), pp. 255–72; R.J. Popplewell, *Intelligence and Imperial Defence. British Intelligence and the Defence of the Indian Empire 1904–1924* (London, 1995).

7. For the 'silk letter' conspiracy see Sir M. O'Dwyer, *India as I Knew it 1885–1925* (London, 1925), pp. 178–82.

8. For the Ghadr movement see T. Tai Yong, 'An Imperial Home-Front: Punjab and the First World War', *Journal of Military History*, 64/2 (April 2000), pp. 386–8.

9. O'Dwyer, *India as I Knew it*, p. 197.

10. G. Krishna, 'The Development of the Indian National Congress as a Mass Organization, 1918–1923', *Journal of Asian Studies*, 25/3 (May 1966), p. 413.

11. *Report on the Administration of the Punjab and its Dependencies for 1919–20* (Lahore, 1921), p. 144.

12. *Report of the Special Session of the Indian National Congress Held at Bombay on 29th, 30th, 31st August and 1st September 1918* (Bombay, 1918), p. 4. The Buddha achieved enlightenment under the Bodhi tree.

13. See H.F. Owen, 'Negotiating the Lucknow Pact', *Journal of Asian Studies*, 31/3 (May 1972), pp. 561–87.

14. H.F. Owen, 'Towards Nation-Wide Agitation and Organisation: The Home Rule Leagues, 1915–18', in D.A. Low (ed.), *Soundings in Modern South Asian History* (London, 1968), pp. 171–2.

15. P. Robb, 'The Government of India and Annie Besant', *Modern Asian Studies*, 10/1 (1976), pp. 107–30.

16. IOC: MSS EUR E264/3, Chelmsford to Austen Chamberlain (Secretary of State for India), 28 June 1917.

17. Montagu, *An Indian Diary*, V. Montagu (ed.), pp. 71, 135.

18. Montagu cited in C. Kaul, *Reporting the Raj. The British Press and India, c. 1880–1922* (Manchester, 2003), p. 137.

19. R.J. Moore, 'The Problem of Freedom with Unity: London's India Policy, 1917–47' in D.A. Low (ed.), *Congress and the Raj. Facets of the Indian Struggle 1917–47* (London, 1977), p. 375.

20. IOC: MSS EUR E264/4, Montagu to Chelmsford, 10 April 1918.

21. A. Rumbold, *Watershed in India 1914–1922* (London, 1979), p. 85.

22. *The Parliamentary Debates, Fifth Series, Volume XCVII, House of Commons* (London, 1917), cols. 1695–6.

23. J.M. Brown, *Modern India. The Origins of an Asian Democracy*, 2nd edn (Oxford: Oxford University Press, 1994; first published 1985), p. 204. See R. Danzig, 'The Announcement of August 20th, 1917', *Journal of Asian Studies*, 28/1

(November 1968), pp. 19–37; Rumbold, *Watershed in India 1914–1922*, Chapter 6.

24. Montagu, *An Indian Diary*, V. Montagu, (ed.), pp. 135–6.
25. See IOC: MSS EUR E264/3, Montagu to Chelmsford, 3 August 1917.
26. *Manchester Guardian*, 22 August 1917, cited in C. Kaul, *Reporting the Raj. The British Press and India, c. 1880–1922* (Manchester, 2003), p. 168.
27. Montagu, *An Indian Diary*, V. Montagu (ed.), pp. 125–6.
28. T.W. Holderness to Austen Chamberlain, 3 November 1917, cited in Robb, 'The Government of India and Annie Besant', p. 126. The Ilbert Bill was bitterly opposed by the Anglo-Indian community and provoked the infamous 'White Mutiny'. A compromise was eventually reached whereby Europeans would be tried by a jury at least half of which would be composed of fellow Europeans. Brown, *Modern India*, p. 136.
29. Robb, 'The Government of India and Annie Besant', p. 127.
30. Robb, *The Government of India and Reform*, pp. 87–88.
31. *Statement Exhibiting the Moral and Material Progress and Condition of India During the Year 1919* (London, 1920), pp. 180, 185–6. A Functions Committee later proposed a list of 'transferred' subjects within the provinces. These included medical administration, public health and sanitation, education, public works, agriculture, civil veterinary departments, cooperative societies, fisheries, forests, excise, registration of deeds and documents, registration of births and deaths, religious and charitable endowments, industrial development, weights and measures, and museums.
32. *Report of the Special Session of the Indian National Congress Held at Bombay on 29th, 30th, 31st August and 1st September 1918*, pp. i–vii.
33. See Kaul, *Reporting the Raj*, Chapter 7.

Chapter 3: Gandhi and the Rowlatt *Satyagraha*

1. TNA: CAB 27/92 & 27/93, *Evidence Taken Before the Disorders Inquiry Committee* (7 vols, Calcutta, 1920) [Hereafter *Disorders Inquiry Committee*], II, p. 108.
2. Gandhi to Magnanlal Gandhi, 11 January 1915, in *The Collected Works of Mahatma Gandhi* (Electronic Book), New Delhi, Publications Division Government of India, 1999, 98 vols *http://www.gandhiserve.org/cwmg/cwmg.html* [hereafter *CWMG*], XIV, p. 337.
3. Gandhi, 'Interview to "The Bombay Chronicle"', 9 January 1915, in *CWMG*, XIV, p. 335.
4. Gandhi, 'Speech at Reception, Ghatkopar', 15 January 1915, in *CWMG*, XIV, p. 337. Emphasis added.
5. *Disorders Inquiry Committee*, VI, p. 14.
6. Gandhi, Mohandas Karamchand (1869–1948): religious and social campaigner; called to the Bar (1891); lived in South Africa (1893–1914); returned to India (1915); conducted *satyagraha* campaigns (1917, 1918, 1919, 1920–22, 1934, 1942); author of *Hind Swaraj* (1909), *An Autobiography or the Story of my Experiments with Truth,* M. Desai (trans.) (London, 2001; first published,

·1927 & 1929) and *Satyagraha in South Africa* (1928). There are numerous bi-ographies. See L. Fischer, *The Life of Mahatma Gandhi* (London, 1997; first pub-lished 1951); J.M. Brown, *Gandhi. Prisoner of Hope* (New Haven & London, 1998, first published 1989).

7. A. Ewing, 'The Indian Civil Service 1919–1924: Service Discontent and the Response in London and Delhi', *Modern Asian Studies*, 18/1 (1984), pp. 34–9.

8. See V.N. Datta, *Jallianwala Bagh* (Ludhiana, 1969), pp. 29–30.

9. *Statement Exhibiting the Moral and Material Progress and Condition of India During the Year 1919* (London, 1920), p. 21.

10. J. Nehru, *An Autobiography* (London, 2004; first published 1936), p. 44.

11. See P.G. Robb, *The Government of India and Reform. Policies Towards Politics and the Constitution 1916–1921* (New Delhi, 1989), Chapter 6.

12. These were the Honourable Sir Basil Scott (Chief Justice of Bombay), the Honourable Diwan Bahadur C.V. Kumaraswami Sastri (Judge of the High Court of Madras), the Honourable Sir Verney Lovett (Member of the Board of Rev-enue, United Provinces), the Honourable P.C. Mitter (Additional Member of the Bengal Legislative Council) and Mr J.D.V. Hodge (Secretary).

13. IOC: MSS EUR E264/43, *Sedition Committee, 1918 Report* (Calcutta, 1918), pp. 129, 148. R.J. Popplewell, *Intelligence and Imperial Defence. British Intelli-gence and the Defence of the Indian Empire 1904–1924* (London, 1995), pp. 174–5.

14. For the Rowlatt Bills see A. Rumbold, *Watershed in India 1914–1922* (London, 1979), pp. 135–8.

15. See P. Mohan, *The Punjab "Rebellion" of 1919 and How It Was Suppressed*, R.M. Bakaya (ed.) (New Delhi, 1999; first published 1920), pp. 32–3.

16. Robb, *The Government of India and Reform*, pp. 153–4, 157, 158.

17. J.M. Brown, *Modern India. The Origins of an Asian Democracy*, 2nd edn (Oxford, 1994; first published 1985), p. 203.

18. Gandhi to V.S. Srinivasa Sastri, 9 February 1919, in *CWMG*, XVII, p. 280. See Brown, *Gandhi. Prisoner of Hope*, pp. 128–9.

19. Gandhi to Madan Mohan Malaviya, 8 February 1919, in *CWMG*, XVII, pp. 279–80.

20. Gandhi to Pragji Desai, 9 February 1919, in *CWMG*, XVII, p. 281.

21. Gandhi, *An Autobiography*, p. 413.

22. Gandhi 'Letter to the Press on Satyagraha Movement', 23 March 1919, in *CWMG*, XVII, pp. 343–4.

23. Gandhi, 'The Satyagraha Pledge', 24 February 1919, in *CWMG*, XVII, p. 297. It read as follows: 'Being conscientiously of opinion that the Bills known as the Indian Criminal Law (Amendment) Bill No. I of 1919 and the Criminal Law (Emergency Powers) Bill No. II of 1919 are unjust, subversive of the principle of liberty and justice, and destructive of the elementary rights of individuals on which the safety of the community as a whole and the State itself is based, we solemnly affirm that, in the event of these Bills becoming law and until they are withdrawn, we shall refuse civilly to obey these laws and such other laws as a Committee to be hereafter appointed may think fit and we further affirm that

in this struggle we will faithfully follow truth and refrain from violence to life, person or property.' It was signed by M.K Gandhi, V.J. Patel, C.M. Desai, K.M. Thakoor and B.A. Sarabhai.

24. Gandhi to W.S. Massey (Private Secretary of the Viceroy), 24 February 1919, in *CWMG*, XVII, p. 298.

25. *Report of the Commissioners Appointed by the Punjab Sub-Committee of the Indian National Congress* [hereafter *Congress Punjab Inquiry*] in *CWMG*, XX, p. 39.

26. Gandhi, 'Instructions to Volunteers', 26 February 1919, in *CWMG*, XVII, p. 316.

27. H.F. Owen, 'Organizing for the Rowlatt Satyagraha of 1919', in Kumar (ed.), *Essays on Gandhian Politics*, p. 74.

28. NAI: Home Political (Deposit) Proceedings, March 1919, no. 16, 'Fortnightly Reports on the Internal Political Situation in India for the First Half of February 1919'.

29. J.M. Brown, *Gandhi's Rise to Power. Indian Politics 1915–1922* (Cambridge, 1972), pp. 168–9.

30. Gandhi, 'Message to Madras Meeting', 30 March 1919, in *CWMG*, XVII, p. 364. See also Gandhi, 'Statement on Laws For Civil Disobedience', 7 April 1919, in *CWMG*, XVII, p. 391.

31. Owen, 'Organizing for the Rowlatt Satyagraha of 1919', p. 88.

32. Gandhi, *An Autobiography*, pp. 405–8, 412.

33. Sir M. O'Dwyer, *India as I Knew it 1885–1925* (London, 1925), p. 266.

34. *Disorders Inquiry Committee*, I, p. 124.

35. Gandhi, 'Speech on Satyagraha, Allahabad', 11 March 1919, in *CWMG*, XVII, p. 328.

36. Gandhi, 'Speech on Rowlatt Bills, Bombay', 14 March 1919, in *CWMG*, XVII, pp. 333–4. At Trichinpoly on 25 March Gandhi said that he 'need not' explain the Rowlatt Bills. Gandhi, 'Speech on Satyagraha Movement, Trichinopoly', 25 March 1919, in *CWMG*, XVII, p. 350.

37. Gandhi, 'Speech on Satyagraha Movement, Madura', 26 March 1919, in *CWMG*, XVII, p. 354.

38. Gandhi, 'Speech on Satyagraha Movement, Tuticorin', 28 March 1919, in *CWMG*, XVII, p. 358. At Nagapatam on 29 March, Gandhi studiously made no reference to what the legislation actually was, only that it should be removed. Gandhi, 'Speech on Capital and Labour and Rowlatt Bills, Nagapatam', 29 March 1919, in *CWMG*, XVII, pp. 360–4.

39. Gandhi, 'Message to Madras Meeting', 30 March 1919, in *CWMG*, XVII, p. 366.

40. Gandhi to V.S. Srinivasa Sastri, 9 February 1919 in *CWMG*, XVII, p. 280.

41. See D.W. Ferrell, 'The Rowlatt Satyagraha in Delhi', in Kumar (ed.), *Essays on Gandhian Politics*, pp. 189–235.

42. The reason why Delhi held a *hartal* on 30 April seems to have been down to a simple misunderstanding combined with the difficulties of re-arranging things at such short notice. When asked why this had happened, Dr Abdur Rahman, one of the general secretaries of the Delhi *Satyagraha Sabha*, replied that 'In the beginning we mistook the message. We were to have it on the Sunday next after the passage of the Rowlatt Bill. We recommended for the 30th and as everything

was arranged in fact we could not change it for the 6th.' *Disorders Inquiry Committee*, I, p. 116.

43. Command 681, *Report of the Committee Appointed by the Government of India to Investigate the Disturbances in the Punjab, etc.* (London, 1920) [Hereafter *Hunter Report*], p. 3.

44. Gandhi to Madan Mohan Malaviya, 3 April 1919, in *CWMG*, XVII, p. 372.

45. *Disorders Inquiry Committee*, I, p. 125.

46. For estimates of the size of the crowd see *Disorders Inquiry Committee*, I, pp. 21, 25, 36, 61.

47. *Disorders Inquiry Committee*, I, pp. 26, 82, 173.

48. *Disorders Inquiry Committee*, I, pp. 12, 52–3.

49. *Disorders Inquiry Committee*, I, pp. 176, 178.

50. *Disorders Inquiry Committee*, I, pp. 54, 183.

51. *Disorders Inquiry Committee*, I, pp. 53, 55.

52. *Disorders Inquiry Committee*, I, pp. 30, 86, 195, 199.

53. For complaints about the police in Delhi see *Disorders Inquiry Committee*, I, pp. 68, 77, 81.

54. *Disorders Inquiry Committee*, I, pp. 68–9, 71, 105. See also Brown, *Gandhi's Rise to Power*, p. 184.

55. *Disorders Inquiry Committee*, I, pp. 60, 75.

56. *Disorders Inquiry Committee*, I, p. 71.

57. Gandhi, 'Press Statement on Suspension of Civil Disobedience', 18 April 1919, in *CWMG*, XVII, p. 443.

Chapter 4: *Hartals,* Processions and Arrests

1. TNA: CAB 27/92 & 27/93, *Evidence Taken Before the Disorders Inquiry Committee* (7 vols, Calcutta, 1920) [Hereafter *Disorders Inquiry Committee*], I, p. 9.

2. 'Black Sunday' taken from the *Bombay Chronicle*, 4 April 1919, in *The Collected Works of Mahatma Gandhi* (Electronic Book), New Delhi, Publications Division Government of India, 1999, 98 vols *http://www.gandhiserve.org/cwmg/cwmg.html* [hereafter *CWMG*], XVII, p. 375.

3. Gandhi, 'Directions to Demonstrators', 5 April 1919, in *CWMG*, XVII, p. 376.

4. Gandhi, 'Speech at Chowpatty, Bombay', 6 April 1919, in *CWMG*, XVII, pp. 382–7.

5. Indian intelligence estimated that 80 per cent of the shops in Bombay were closed and up to 150,000 people gathered at Chowpatty Beach. NAI: Home Political (B) Proceedings, April 1919, nos. 284–300, 'Reports in Connection with the Observances of Satyagraha Humiliation Day on 6th April 1919', p. 6. See J. Masselos, 'Some Aspects of Bombay City Politics in 1919', in Kumar (ed.), *Essays on Gandhian Politics*, p. 177.

6. *Disorders Inquiry Committee*, II, p. 110.

7. L. Fischer, *The Life of Mahatma Gandhi* (London, 1997; first published 1951), p. 226. Emphasis added. This has been echoed by other writers. See for example, B.G. Horniman, *Amritsar and Our Duty to India* (Delhi, 1997; first

published 1920), p. 76; R. Ram, *The Jallianwala Bagh Massacre. A Premeditated Plan* (Chandigarh, 1978; first published 1969), p. 42.

8. S.M. Rai, 'The Jallianwala Bagh Tragedy: Its Impact on the Political Awakening and Thinking in India' in V.N. Datta & S. Settar (eds), *Jallianwala Bagh Massacre* (Delhi, 2000), p. 26.

9. See R. Kumar, 'Introduction' in R. Kumar (ed.), *Essays on Gandhian Politics. The Rowlatt Satyagraha of 1919* (Oxford, 1971), pp. 6–7.

10. NAI: Home Political (Deposit) Proceedings, July 1919, no. 46, 'Fortnightly Reports on the Internal Political Situation for the First Half of April 1919', pp. 9, 23.

11. NAI: Home Political (B) Proceedings, April 1919, nos 284–300, 'Reports in Connection with the Observances of Satyagraha Humiliation Day on 6th April 1919'.

12. *Disorders Inquiry Committee*, I, p. 125.

13. NAI: Home Political (Deposit) Proceedings, April 1919, no. 49, 'Fortnightly Reports on the Internal Political Situation in India for the Second Half of March 1919'.

14. NAI: Home Political (Deposit) Proceedings, July 1919, no. 46, 'Fortnightly Reports on the Internal Political Situation for the First Half of April 1919', pp. 10–12, 14.

15. NAI: Foreign & Political (Deposit) Internal, Proceedings, June 1919, nos 39–54, 'Co-operation of Certain Ruling Princes and Chiefs in Connection with the Disturbances'.

16. NAI: Home Political (Deposit) Proceedings, July 1919, no. 46, 'Fortnightly Reports on the Internal Political Situation for the First Half of April 1919', p. 6.

17. *Disorders Inquiry Committee*, IV, p. 137.

18. Sir M. O'Dwyer, *India as I Knew it 1885–1925* (London, 1925), p. 269.

19. *Disorders Inquiry Committee*, IV, pp. 86, 98, 92, 132. Original emphasis.

20. NAI: Home Political (Deposit) Proceedings, July 1919, no. 46, 'Fortnightly Reports on the Internal Political Situation for the First Half of April 1919', p. 1.

21. *Disorders Inquiry Committee*, III, p. 2.

22. NAI: Home Political (Deposit) Proceedings, July 1919, no. 46, 'Fortnightly Reports on the Internal Political Situation for the First Half of April 1919', pp. 2–3.

23. For the Rowlatt *Satyagraha* in Amritsar see K. Mohan, *Militant Nationalism in the Punjab 1919–1935* (New Delhi, 1985), pp. 19–23.

24. *Disorders Inquiry Committee*, III, pp. 2, 3.

25. I. Colvin, *The Life of General Dyer* (Edinburgh & London, 1929), p. 140.

26. Irving to Kitchin, 8 April 1919, contained in *Disorders Inquiry Committee*, VI, p. 3.

27. This letter has been discussed extensively in the literature on Amritsar, often being taken as yet further evidence of an official overreaction. A. Draper, *The Amritsar Massacre. Twilight of the Raj* (London, 1985; first published 1981), pp. 49–51.

28. E.M. Forster, *A Passage to India* (London, 1988; first published 1924), p. 190.
29. *Disorders Inquiry Committee*, IV, p. 88.
30. O'Dwyer, *India as I Knew it*, p. 269.
31. *Disorders Inquiry Committee*, III, p. 180.
32. Swinson, *Six Minutes to Sunset*, p. 18.
33. Ram, *The Jallianwala Bagh Massacre*, Chapter 7.
34. V.N. Datta, 'Perceptions of the Jallianwala Bagh Massacre', in Datta & Settar (eds), *Jallianwala Bagh Massacre*, p. 4.
35. P.G. Robb, *The Government of India and Reform. Policies Towards Politics and the Constitution 1916–1921* (New Delhi, 1989), p. 130.
36. IOC: MSS EUR E 264/5, Chelmsford to Montagu, 9 April 1919.
37. Robb, *The Government of India and Reform*, p. 131.
38. P. Mohan, *The Punjab "Rebellion" of 1919 and How It Was Suppressed*, R.M. Bakaya (ed.) (New Delhi, 1999; first published 1920), pp. 60, 62.
39. The Government of India never referred to it as an arrest because Gandhi was 'escorted' or 'sent back' to the Bombay Presidency. Robb, *The Government of India and Reform*, p. 131.

Chapter 5: Violence in Ahmedabad

1. Gandhi, 'Message to Countrymen', 9 April 1919, in *The Collected Works of Mahatma Gandhi* (Electronic Book), New Delhi, Publications Division Government of India, 1999, 98 vols *http://www.gandhiserve.org/cwmg/cwmg.html* [hereafter *CWMG*], XVII, p. 408.
2. TNA: CAB 27/92 & 27/93, *Evidence Taken Before the Disorders Inquiry Committee* (7 vols, Calcutta, 1920) [Hereafter *Disorders Inquiry Committee*], II, pp. 113–4.
3. *Disorders Inquiry Committee*, I, p. 63.
4. *Disorders Inquiry Committee*, II, p. 110.
5. See K. Gillion, 'Gujarat in 1919', in R. Kumar (ed.), *Essays on Gandhian Politics. The Rowlatt Satyagraha of 1919* (Oxford, 1971), pp. 129–33.
6. See J.M. Brown, *Gandhi's Rise to Power. Indian Politics 1915–1922* (Cambridge, 1972), pp. 111–22.
7. The news came from a telegram written by Mahadev Desai (Gandhi's secretary) to the Ahmedabad *Satyagraha Sabha* that morning, informing them that Gandhi had been arrested. See Gillion, 'Gujarat in 1919', p. 136.
8. Command 681, *Report of the Committee Appointed by the Government of India to Investigate the Disturbances in the Punjab, etc.* (London, 1920) [Hereafter *Hunter Report*], pp. 10–11.
9. *Disorders Inquiry Committee*, II, pp. 2–3.
10. *Disorders Inquiry Committee*, II, pp. 220–1, 227.
11. *Disorders Inquiry Committee*, II, p. 150.
12. Gandhi, 'Message to Countrymen', 9 April 1919, in *CWMG*, XVII, pp. 407–9.
13. On 7 April Anasuya had gone to Bombay to take part in the distribution of prohibited literature, which was a key element of Gandhi's *satyagraha* campaign. When she did not come back, rumours spread that she had been arrested by

the authorities. She had, in fact, refrained from returning home because of the uncertain situation. *Disorders Inquiry Committee*, II, pp. 49, 255.

14. *Disorders Inquiry Committee*, II, pp. 47, 231.
15. *Disorders Inquiry Committee*, II, pp. 26, 228–9.
16. *Hunter Report*, p. 12.
17. *Disorders Inquiry Committee*, II, pp. 51–2.
18. *Disorders Inquiry Committee*, II, pp. 27, 58–9. Original emphasis. 'Chalo' means 'let's go' and 'maro' means to kill or to hit.
19. *Hunter Report*, p. 12.
20. *Disorders Inquiry Committee*, II, pp. 34, 46, 48–9.
21. *Disorders Inquiry Committee*, II, p. 27.
22. *Disorders Inquiry Committee*, II, pp. 45, 57.
23. *Disorders Inquiry Committee*, II, p. 33.
24. *Disorders Inquiry Committee*, II, pp. 75–6.
25. *Disorders Inquiry Committee*, II, pp. 27, 41, 55, 68, 70–2, 77, 82.
26. *Disorders Inquiry Committee*, II, pp. 13, 53, 54, 219.
27. *Disorders Inquiry Committee*, II, p. 228.
28. *Hunter Report*, p. 14. The reaction of the police was hampered by their out-of-date equipment. The police used Martini-Henry smoothbore muskets and could either fire buckshot (which was often ineffective) or ball ammunition (which sometimes jammed). See *Disorders Inquiry Committee*, II, pp. 33, 52, 53.
29. For criticisms of the British in Ahmedabad see S. Shoul, 'Soldiers, Riot Control and Aid to the Civil Power in India, Egypt and Palestine, 1919–39', *Journal of the Society for Army Historical Research*, 86/346 (Summer 2008), p. 123.
30. The cloth and bullion markets in Bombay were mainly Gujarati and had been strong supporters of Gandhi for several years. J. Masselos, 'Some Aspects of Bombay City Politics in 1919', in Kumar (ed.), *Essays on Gandhian Politics*, p. 184.
31. Four policemen received 'grievous wounds' and 30 to 40 other officers were also hit by stones during the day. *Disorders Inquiry Committee*, II, pp. 180, 181.
32. *Disorders Inquiry Committee*, II, pp. 157, 164.
33. *Hunter Report*, pp. 15–6.
34. Gandhi, 'Speech at Mass Meeting, Ahmedabad', 14 April 1919, in *CWMG*, XVII, pp. 420–4.
35. *Disorders Inquiry Committee*, II, pp. 64–6.
36. P.G. Robb, *The Government of India and Reform. Policies Towards Politics and the Constitution 1916–1921* (New Delhi, 1989), p. 133.
37. Brown, *Gandhi's Rise to Power*, p. 179.

Chapter 6: O'Dwyer in the Punjab

1. TNA: CAB 27/92 & 27/93, *Evidence Taken Before the Disorders Inquiry Committee* (7 vols, Calcutta, 1920) [Hereafter *Disorders Inquiry Committee*], VI, p. 65.
2. I. Talbot, *Punjab and the Raj 1849–1947* (New Delhi, 1988), p. 39. Over 500,000 tons of wheat were exported from the province every year.
3. See *Report of the Commissioners Appointed by the Punjab Sub-Committee of the Indian National Congress* [hereafter *Congress Punjab Inquiry*] in *The Collected*

Works of Mahatma Gandhi (Electronic Book), New Delhi, Publications Division Government of India, 1999, 98 vols *http://www.gandhiserve.org/cwmg/cwmg.html* [hereafter *CWMG*], XX, Chapter 2 and B.G. Horniman, *Amritsar and Our Duty to India* (Delhi, 1997; first published 1920), p. 23.

4. P.G. Robb, *The Government of India and Reform. Policies Towards Politics and the Constitution 1916–1921* (New Delhi, 1989), p. 173. For O'Dwyer's 'provocation' of the Punjab see *Congress Punjab Inquiry*, pp. 24–5; R. Ram, *The Jallianwala Bagh Massacre. A Premeditated Plan* (Chandigarh, 1978; first published 1969), Chapter 5. This can be found in G. Singh, 'The Imperial Terrorism in Punjab: Its Nature and Implications (1919–25)' in V.N. Datta & S. Settar (eds), *Jallianwala Bagh Massacre* (Delhi, 2000), pp. 38–51.

5. T. Tai Yong, *The Garrison State. The Military, Government and Society in Colonial Punjab, 1849–1947* (New Delhi & London, 2005), p. 98.

6. *The Times*, 14 March 1940. See R. Perkins, *The Amritsar Legacy. Golden Temple to Caxton Hall, the Story of a Killing* (Chippenham, 1989).

7. See my 'Sir Michael O'Dwyer and "Imperial Terrorism" in the Punjab, 1919', *South Asia*, 33/3 (2010), pp. 363–80.

8. Sir M. O'Dwyer, *India as I Knew it 1885–1925* (London, 1925), p. 27.

9. O'Dwyer, Sir Michael Francis (1864–1940): Shahpur (1887–9); Settlement Officer, Gujranwala (1889–95); Commissioner, Rajputana (1897–1901); Revenue Commissioner, NWFP (1901–8); Acting Resident in Hyderabad (1908–9); Acting-Agent to the Governor-General in Central India (1910–12); Lieutenant-Governor of the Punjab (1913–19).

10. V.N. Datta, 'Perceptions of the Jallianwala Bagh Massacre', in Datta & Settar (eds), *Jallianwala Bagh Massacre*, p. 3.

11. O'Dwyer, *India as I Knew it*, pp. 314–5.

12. Details of Gujranwala taken from O'Dwyer, *India as I Knew it*, pp. 51–4.

13. IOC: MSS EUR E264/3, Chelmsford to Montagu, 5 October 1917.

14. Tai Yong, *The Garrison State*, p. 17. For a fascinating study into the mentality of the ICS, particularly the 'Punjab Commission', see C. Dewey, *Anglo-Indian Attitudes. The Mind of the Indian Civil Service* (London, 1993).

15. Tai Yong, *The Garrison State*, pp. 36–7.

16. O'Dwyer, *India as I Knew it*, pp. 232–3.

17. D. Gilmour, *The Ruling Caste. Imperial Lives in the Victorian Raj* (London, 2005), p. 160.

18. The Deputy Commissioner was assisted by five Extra Assistant Commissioners, who would work with a host of rural notables and act as mediators between the Government of India and the people of the villages. Districts were split into *tahsils* (approximately 150 villages), which were subdivided into *zails* (10 to 30 villages). Talbot, *Punjab and the Raj 1849–1947*, p. 35.

19. At the outbreak of war 66 per cent of cavalry, 87 per cent of artillery and 45 per cent of infantry were Punjabis. Tai Yong, *The Garrison State*, pp. 18, 71.

20. *India's Contribution to the Great War* (Calcutta, 1923), p. 277. See also *Census of India, 1921, Volume XV, Punjab and Delhi* (2 parts, Lahore, 1923), Part I, Report, pp. 50–1.

21. T. Tai-Yong, 'An Imperial Home-Front: Punjab and the First World War', *Journal of Military History*, 64/2 (April 2000), pp. 383, 390.
22. This is taken from Appendix VII 'Note on recruiting methods employed in the Punjab', in V.N. Datta (ed.), *New Light on the Punjab Disturbances in 1919* (2 vols, Simla, 1975), I, pp. 484–7.
23. Tai Yong, *The Garrison State*, p. 122 and *India's Contribution to the Great War*, pp. 242–3.
24. Appendix VII 'Note on recruiting methods employed in the Punjab', in Datta (ed.), *New Light on the Punjab Disturbances in 1919*, I, p. 485.
25. Tai-Yong, 'An Imperial Home-Front: Punjab and the First World War', p. 407.
26. *Disorders Inquiry Committee*, VI, pp. 51, 75.
27. *Disorders Inquiry Committee*, III, p. 194.
28. India raised 1,440,437 soldiers during the Great War, which amounted to 0.3 per cent of her population. See C. Barnett, *The Collapse of British Power* (London, 2002; first published 1972), p. 79. India suffered 121,598 casualties during the war. *India's Contribution to the Great War*, p. 176.
29. *Census of India, 1921, Volume XV, Punjab and Delhi*, Part I, Report, p. 49.
30. Since August 1914, food had increased by about 93 per cent, about 60 per cent for Indian-made goods and over 190 per cent for imported goods. Statistics taken from *Statement Exhibiting the Moral and Material Progress and Condition of India During the Year 1919*, pp. 63–6.
31. O'Dwyer, *India as I Knew it*, pp. 268–71.
32. NAI: Home Political (Deposit) Proceedings, April 1919, no. 49, 'Fortnightly Reports on the Internal Political Situation in India for the Second Half of March 1919', p. 5.
33. NAI: Home Political (Deposit) Proceedings, July 1919, no. 46, 'Fortnightly Reports on the Internal Political Situation for the First Half of April 1919', pp. 11, 14.
34. NAI: Home Political (Deposit) Proceedings, April 1919, no. 49, 'Fortnightly Reports on the Internal Political Situation in India for the Second Half of March 1919', pp. 14–15.
35. 'Specimens of Posters published in the Punjab during the Disorders' in Datta (ed.), *New Light on the Punjab Disturbances in 1919*, II, pp. 1008–14.

Chapter 7: A 'Great Calamity' in Amritsar

1. T. Kitchlew, *Saifuddin Kitchlew. Hero of Jallianwala Bagh* (India, 1987), p. 33.
2. *The Congress Punjab Inquiry 1919–1920: Evidence* (Delhi, 1996; first published 1920), pp. 603–16. See NAI: Amritsar Conspiracy Case 1919 (Acc No. 1829), Dr S.D. Kitchlew, Dr Satyapal and 13 others, p. 76.
3. Details taken from Kitchlew, *Saifuddin Kitchlew*, pp. 1–25.
4. V.N. Datta, *Jallianwala Bagh* (Ludhiana, 1969), p. 63; N. Collett, *The Butcher of Amritsar. General Reginald Dyer* (London, 2005), p. 230.

5. L. Fischer, *The Life of Mahatma Gandhi* (London, 1997; first published 1951), p. 230.
6. Kitchlew, *Saifuddin Kitchlew*, pp. 17, 20, 23.
7. A basic narrative of the disturbances is provided in Command 681, *Report of the Committee Appointed by the Government of India to Investigate the Disturbances in the Punjab, etc.* (London, 1920) [Hereafter *Hunter Report*], Chapter 3, pp. 19–33.
8. TNA: CAB 27/92 & 27/93, *Evidence Taken Before the Disorders Inquiry Committee* (7 vols, Calcutta, 1920) [Hereafter *Disorders Inquiry Committee*], III, p. 42.
9. *Disorders Inquiry Committee*, III, p. 4.
10. *Disorders Inquiry Committee*, III, p. 43.
11. *Hunter Report*, p. 23.
12. The five Britons who were killed on 10 April were buried side by side in the Amritsar Cantonment Cemetery. Sadly it is now neglected, overgrown, and home to a number of illegal dwellings.
13. At the Golden Temple, Hajith Mandi and Dhal Basti Ram.
14. There are scant details about the murders of Robinson and Rowland, possibly because they occurred outside the old city. Robinson was attacked on the footbridge while Rowlands was chased by a mob near the Rego Bridge and killed. See *Hunter Report*, pp. 24–6.
15. *Disorders Inquiry Committee*, III, pp. 51, 52, 55.
16. *Hunter Report*, p. 88.
17. *The Congress Punjab Inquiry 1919–1920: Evidence*, p. 15.
18. *Report of the Commissioners Appointed by the Punjab Sub-Committee of the Indian National Congress* [hereafter *Congress Punjab Inquiry*] in *The Collected Works of Mahatma Gandhi* (Electronic Book), New Delhi, Publications Division Government of India, 1999, 98 vols *http://www.gandhiserve.org/cwmg/cwmg.html* [hereafter *CWMG*], XX, p. 51. Later Indian writers have echoed this interpretation.
19. *Disorders Inquiry Committee*, III, p. 17. This is quoted approvingly by I. Colvin, *The Life of General Dyer* (Edinburgh & London, 1929), p. 145.
20. *Hunter Report*, p. 22.
21. *Disorders Inquiry Committee*, III, p. 4. Irving also claims that British civilians were coming in from the city at around 1 p.m., before the second firing (p. 5). See Fein's correspondence with Datta. Note 8 in H. Fein, *Imperial Crime and Punishment. The Massacre at Jallianwala Bagh and British Judgment, 1919–1920* (Honolulu, 1977), pp. 223–4. It was recorded in the *Hunter Report*, p. 23.
22. *Disorders Inquiry Committee*, III, pp. 42, 43, 48; IWM: 83/31/1, Account of Brigadier F. McCallum, p. 1. See D. Sayer, 'British Reaction to the Amritsar Massacre 1919–1920', *Past & Present*, 131 (May 1991), pp. 138–9.
23. *Disorders Inquiry Committee*, III, pp. 44, 47. Muhammed Ashraf Khan, the Inspector of Police, thought the total could even have been as high as 75 or 80,000, but this seems unlikely (p. 81).
24. *Hunter Report*, p. 19.

25. *Disorders Inquiry Committee*, III, pp. 9, 34, 52. Smith also suggested that the gangs burnt the Town Hall and the banks to destroy incriminating records and documents (pp. 54–5).
26. *The Congress Punjab Inquiry 1919–1920: Evidence*, pp. 27, 51; *Hunter Report*, p. 23.
27. See A. Draper, *The Amritsar Massacre. Twilight of the Raj* (London, 1985; first published 1981), pp. 64–5.
28. PSA: Home Judicial (C) Proceedings, May 1920, nos 268–322, 'Petitions and Orders in Amritsar National Bank Murder Case'.
29. PSA: Home Judicial (B) Proceedings, July 1919, nos 86–106, 'Letters for Mercy in the Amritsar Alliance Bank Case and Communication of Certain Sentences Passed Therein'.
30. *Disorders Inquiry Committee*, III, p. 141.
31. Details taken from 'Amritsar Assault Case', contained in P. Mohan, *The Punjab "Rebellion" of 1919 and How It Was Suppressed*, R.M. Bakaya (ed.) (New Delhi, 1999; first published 1920), pp. 328–9.
32. See *The Congress Punjab Inquiry 1919–1920: Evidence*, p. 39. The wounded had been brought to a dispensary opposite to the hospital and Mrs Easdon was apparently seen on her balcony overlooking the street.
33. PSA: Home Judicial (B) Proceedings, July 1919, nos 72–65, 'Communication of the Sentences Passed in the Amritsar (Mrs Easdon) Case'.

Chapter 8: A 'Terrible Quietness'

1. E.M. Forster, *A Passage to India* (London, 1988; first published 1924) p. 188.
2. There were 130 women and children in the fort by the evening. A. Draper, *The Amritsar Massacre. Twilight of the Raj* (London, 1985; first published 1981), pp. 70–1. For a dramatic description of the European flight from Amritsar and the conditions ('of hot and horrid discomfort') in the fort see I. Colvin, *The Life of General Dyer* (Edinburgh & London, 1929), pp. 147–8.
3. IWM: 83/31/1, Account of Brigadier F. McCallum, p. 2.
4. TNA: CAB 27/92 & 27/93, *Evidence Taken Before the Disorders Inquiry Committee* (7 vols, Calcutta, 1920) [Hereafter *Disorders Inquiry Committee*], III, pp. 6–7. Original emphasis. The phrase means Hindi–Muslim unity.
5. *Disorders Inquiry Committee*, III, p. 221.
6. Sir V. Chirol, *India Old and New* (London, 1921), pp. 177, 184.
7. *Disorders Inquiry Committee*, III, pp. 157, 172.
8. N. Collett, *The Butcher of Amritsar. General Reginald Dyer* (London, 2005), p. 236.
9. *Disorders Inquiry Committee*, III, p. 170. Emphasis added.
10. *Disorders Inquiry Committee*, III, pp. 5, 158. A phonophore was a telephone that used telegraph wires. If any wires were uncut it could still be used. Unfortunately, if it was dependent on one or two wires it tended to be extremely difficult to hear anything at the other end.

11. Draper, *The Amritsar Massacre*, p. 45.
12. *Disorders Inquiry Committee*, III, p. 24.
13. *Disorders Inquiry Committee*, III, pp. 116, 162.
14. *Disorders Inquiry Committee*, III, pp. 87, 144.
15. Criticism of the Amritsar police can be found in V.N. Datta, *Jallianwala Bagh* (Ludhiana, 1969), pp. 83–4; R. Furneaux, *Massacre at Amritsar* (London, 1963), pp. 59–60.
16. The Honourable Khwaja Yusuf Shah, a Municipal Commissioner and Honorary Magistrate, believed that the police simply lost control over the mobs. *Disorders Inquiry Committee*, III, p. 92.
17. Command 681, *Report of the Committee Appointed by the Government of India to Investigate the Disturbances in the Punjab, etc.* (London, 1920) [Hereafter *Hunter Report*], p. 24.
18. *Report of the Commissioners Appointed by the Punjab Sub-Committee of the Indian National Congress* [hereafter *Congress Punjab Inquiry*] in *The Collected Works of Mahatma Gandhi* (Electronic Book), New Delhi, Publications Division Government of India, 1999, 98 vols *http://www.gandhiserve.org/cwmg/cwmg.html* [hereafter *CWMG*], XX, p. 55.
19. *Disorders Inquiry Committee*, III, p. 198. Ashraf Khan was reduced in rank, while Ahmed Jan was not only reduced in rank but also retired from the service on a reduced pension. NAI: Home Military, No. 126 (April 1921), 'Punishment Awarded to Police Officers who failed in their duty at Amritsar during the Disturbances'.
20. Furneaux, *Massacre at Amritsar*, p. 59.
21. A. Swinson, *Six Minutes to Sunset. The Story of General Dyer and the Amritsar Affair* (London, 1964), p. 24; Colvin, *The Life of General Dyer*, pp. 150–5.
22. *Disorders Inquiry Committee*, III, pp. 81, 83.
23. *Disorders Inquiry Committee*, III, pp. 23, 30, 157, 172.
24. Girdhari Lal cited in *Congress Punjab Inquiry*, pp. 56–7.
25. Dr Saif-ud-din Kitchlew (transportation for life); Dr Satyapal (transportation for life); Badar-ul-Islam Khan (acquitted); Dr Hafiz Mohammad Bashir (executed); Kotu Mal (three years' rigorous imprisonment); Lala Narain das Khanna (three years' rigorous imprisonment); Sirdar Gurdial Singu Salaria (acquitted); Swami Anabhawa Nand (transportation for life); Dina Nath (transportation for life); Dr Gurbakhsh Rai (transportation for life); Ghulam Nabi (acquitted); Ghulam Mohammed (transportation for life); Abdul Aziz (transportation for life); Mohammed Ismail (acquitted); Moti Ran (acquitted). Five other accused (Durga Das, Khrishen Diual, Brij Gopi Nath, Jai Ram Singh and Abdul Majid) absconded and were never caught. NAI: Amritsar Conspiracy Case 1919 (Acc No. 1829), Dr S.D. Kitchlew, Dr Satyapal and 13 others, pp. 18–23.
26. NAI: Amritsar Conspiracy Case 1919 (Acc No. 1829), Dr S.D. Kitchlew, Dr Satyapal and 13 others, pp. 34, 75, 77. On 10 April, he is reported to have told Kitchlew that now was not the time for *satyagraha*, but for 'active work' and if they did not have guns, they could do the work with *lathis*.

27. NAI: Amritsar Conspiracy Case 1919 (Acc No. 1829), Dr S.D. Kitchlew, Dr Satyapal and 13 others, pp. 80, 34, 36.

28. *Disorders Inquiry Committee*, III, p. 25.

29. Datta, *Jallianwala Bagh*, p. 87. *The Congress Punjab Inquiry 1919–1920: Evidence* (Delhi, 1996; first published 1920), pp. 29, 42.

30. *The Congress Punjab Inquiry 1919–1920: Evidence*, pp. 5, 24, 40.

31. Collett, *The Butcher of Amritsar*, p. 239.

32. A contemporary described Kitchin as 'a very able man, certainly no firebrand'. CSAS: Sir J. Penny Papers, 'Punjab Memories 1910–1945', p. 94.

33. IWM: 72/22/1, 'The Truth About Amritsar' by Lieutenant-Colonel H.M.L. Morgan, p. 3. Morgan states (incorrectly) that this meeting was on the evening of 12 April.

34. IWM: 72/22/1, 'The Truth About Amritsar' by Lieutenant-Colonel H.M.L. Morgan, p. 6.

35. *Disorders Inquiry Committee*, III, p. 114. Collett, *The Butcher of Amritsar*, pp. 240–1.

36. *Disorders Inquiry Committee*, III, p. 202.

37. Collett, *The Butcher of Amritsar*, pp. 247–9.

38. *Disorders Inquiry Committee*, II, p. 15.

Chapter 9: Protest and Response in Lahore

1. TNA: CAB 27/92 & 27/93, *Evidence Taken Before the Disorders Inquiry Committee* (7 vols, Calcutta, 1920) [Hereafter *Disorders Inquiry Committee*], IV, p. 20.

2. See R. Kumar, 'The Rowlatt Satyagraha in Lahore', in R. Kumar (ed.), *Essays on Gandhian Politics. The Rowlatt Satyagraha of 1919* (Oxford, 1971), pp. 237–75.

3. Kumar, 'The Rowlatt Satyagraha in Lahore', p. 276.

4. *The Congress Punjab Inquiry 1919–1920: Evidence* (Delhi, 1996; first published 1920), p. 629.

5. Kumar, 'The Rowlatt Satyagraha in Lahore', pp. 255–9, 277.

6. *Disorders Inquiry Committee*, IV, p. 314.

7. Command 681, *Report of the Committee Appointed by the Government of India to Investigate the Disturbances in the Punjab, etc.* (London, 1920) [Hereafter *Hunter Report*], p. 35.

8. *Disorders Inquiry Committee*, IV, pp. 2, 315. 40 men were at the Telegraph Office, 45 men were at the Gymkhana Club (where many European ladies were also present), 50 men were at Government House, 25 men were at the Club, and between 25 to 30 were at Faletti's Hotel.

9. Kumar, 'The Rowlatt Satyagraha in Lahore', pp. 282–3; *The Congress Punjab Inquiry 1919–1920: Evidence*, p. 183.

10. Frank Johnson to Adjutant-General in India, 30 July 1919, contained in *Disorders Inquiry Committee*, IV, p. 279. Nationalists dispute the number of people that gathered on 10 April. See *The Congress Punjab Inquiry 1919–1920: Evidence*, pp. 658–9.

11. *Disorders Inquiry Committee*, IV, p. 97.
12. *Hunter Report*, p. 36.
13. *Disorders Inquiry Committee*, IV, p. 316.
14. Dutt was 'commanding of presence, impetuous of temperament, and flamboyant of person'. Kumar, 'The Rowlatt Satyagraha in Lahore', p. 285.
15. *Disorders Inquiry Committee*, IV, pp. 77, 79, 316, 339.
16. For references to students in the crowds see Kumar, 'The Rowlatt Satyagraha in Lahore', p. 284; *Disorders Inquiry Committee*, IV, p. 120. One student was wounded in the firing at the mall on 10 April (p. 124). *Report of the Commissioners Appointed by the Punjab Sub-Committee of the Indian National Congress* [hereafter *Congress Punjab Inquiry*] in *The Collected Works of Mahatma Gandhi* (Electronic Book), New Delhi, Publications Division Government of India, 1999, 98 vols *http://www.gandhiserve.org/cwmg/cwmg.html* [hereafter *CWMG*], XX, pp. 85–6.
17. Kumar, 'The Rowlatt Satyagraha in Lahore', pp. 285–6.
18. *Disorders Inquiry Committee*, IV, pp. 95, 316, 339.
19. Sir M. O'Dwyer, *India as I Knew it 1885–1925* (London, 1925), p. 275.
20. *Disorders Inquiry Committee*, IV, p. 8, 280.
21. Kumar, 'The Rowlatt Satyagraha in Lahore', p. 286. Original emphasis.
22. *The Congress Punjab Inquiry 1919–1920: Evidence*, p. 160.
23. O'Dwyer, *India as I Knew it*, pp. 277–8.
24. *Disorders Inquiry Committee*, IV, pp. 83, 148.
25. Kumar, 'The Rowlatt Satyagraha in Lahore', p. 251.
26. *Disorders Inquiry Committee*, IV, pp. 113, 119, 339.
27. *Disorders Inquiry Committee*, IV, p. 142.
28. Details of meeting taken from 'Annexure', contained in *Disorders Inquiry Committee*, IV, pp. 145–8. See also *Disorders Inquiry Committee*, III, pp. 196–7.
29. *The Congress Punjab Inquiry 1919* Mughal *1920: Evidence*, pp. 161, 640.
30. *Disorders Inquiry Committee*, III, p. 197.
31. Kumar, 'The Rowlatt Satyagraha in Lahore', p. 290.
32. O'Dwyer, *India as I Knew it*, p. 279.
33. *Disorders Inquiry Committee*, IV, pp. 2, 3, 8, 22, 280. His insistence on taking such precautions seems to have stemmed from an incident six months prior to the disturbances when two men were wounded and another two were killed by a bomb in Anarkali Bazaar.
34. *Hunter Report*, p. 38.
35. *The Congress Punjab Inquiry 1919–1920: Evidence*, pp. 187, 200, 210, 230.
36. Mr W.G. Clarke (Deputy Superintendent of Police) claimed that while Fyson was ordering the crowd to disperse, another crowd came from the mosque, got behind the cavalry and began to throw stones. *Disorders Inquiry Committee*, IV, p. 78.
37. *Disorders Inquiry Committee*, IV, p. 3, 20, 280. He estimated that one person was killed and three or four were wounded.
38. Kumar, 'The Rowlatt Satyagraha in Lahore', p. 294.

Chapter 10: A 'Serious Rising' at Kasur

1. TNA: CAB 27/92 & 27/93, *Evidence Taken Before the Disorders Inquiry Committee* (7 vols, Calcutta, 1920) [Hereafter *Disorders Inquiry Committee*], IV, p. 263. Original emphasis.

2. The passengers were Mr Sherbourn (Signal and Interlocking Inspector, North Western Railway), Mrs Sherbourn and their three children, Captain Limby, Lieutenant Munro, Conductor Selby, Sergeant Mallett, Corporal Battson, Lance Corporal Gringham, Mr Khair-ud-Din (Travelling Inspector of Railway Accounts), Mr Gupta (Inspector of Works, North Western Railway) and Sheikh Din Muhammad (Extra Assistant Commissioner). *Disorders Inquiry Committee*, IV, p. 363.

3. The people on the bank were the Indian passengers from the train, some of whom had heard rumours of disturbances in Delhi and Amritsar and were expecting trouble at Kasur. *Disorders Inquiry Committee*, IV, pp. 244, 247.

4. *Disorders Inquiry Committee*, IV, pp. 244–5, 247, 249, 250.

5. Both men miraculously survived the mob after being helped by several bystanders. Battson was carried onto the Lahore train (at the other end of the station) and Gringham managed to escape onto the Ferozepore Road.

6. McRae, 'Report on the Administration of the Kasur Civil Area during the Punjab Riots, April 12th to May 8th, 1919', contained in *Disorders Inquiry Committee*, IV, p. 373.

7. *Disorders Inquiry Committee*, IV, p. 269.

8. Command 681, *Report of the Committee Appointed by the Government of India to Investigate the Disturbances in the Punjab, etc.* (London, 1920) [Hereafter *Hunter Report*], p. 41.

9. *Disorders Inquiry Committee*, IV, p. 259.

10. Sir M. O'Dwyer, *India as I Knew it 1885–1925* (London, 1925), p. 279.

11. *Disorders Inquiry Committee*, IV, p. 362.

12. *Disorders Inquiry Committee*, IV, pp. 236, 384.

13. McRae, 'Report on the Administration of the Kasur Civil Area during the Punjab Riots, April 12th to May 8th, 1919', contained in *Disorders Inquiry Committee*, IV, p. 377. See also pp. 263, 364. Sweeping and the dyeing of skin are traditionally lower-caste occupations.

14. *Disorders Inquiry Committee*, IV, pp. 261, 264.

15. See for example *Disorders Inquiry Committee*, IV, pp. 183, 237, 239, 259, 269, 384. *Census of India, 1921, Volume XV, Punjab and Delhi* (2 parts, Lahore, 1923), Part II, Tables, Table V.

16. *Disorders Inquiry Committee*, IV, p. 270.

17. When the *tahsil* was attacked, the mob apparently shouted '*Gandhi ki jai*', '*Kitchlew ki jai*' and '*Satyapal ki jai*', testifying to the influence of Amritsar on the town. *Disorders Inquiry Committee*, IV, p. 263.

18. *The Congress Punjab Inquiry 1919–1920: Evidence* (Delhi, 1996; first published 1920), p. 289.

19. *Disorders Inquiry Committee*, IV, pp. 186, 187, 260, 268.

20. *Disorders Inquiry Committee*, IV, p. 257.

21. *Disorders Inquiry Committee*, IV, pp. 244, 256, 372, 383. See also McRae, 'Report on the Administration of the Kasur Civil Area during the Punjab Riots, April 12th to May 8th, 1919', contained in *Disorders Inquiry Committee*, IV, p. 373.

22. *Disorders Inquiry Committee*, IV, pp. 251, 254, 255, 257.

23. *Disorders Inquiry Committee*, IV, pp. 258, 384.

24. McRae, 'Report on the Administration of the Kasur Civil Area during the Punjab Riots, April 12th to May 8th, 1919', contained in *Disorders Inquiry Committee*, IV, p. 373.

25. *Hunter Report*, pp. 26, 28.

26. O'Dwyer, *India as I Knew it*, pp. 282–3.

27. O'Dwyer, *India as I Knew it*, pp. 285–6.

28. When speaking at a packed meeting of the East India Association on 13 March 1940, Sir Michael had been shot and killed by a man named Udham Singh. At his trial Singh would claim that 'He deserved it. He was the real culprit, he wanted to crush the spirit of my people, so I have crushed him.' Udham Singh, cited in A. Draper, *The Amritsar Massacre. Twilight of the Raj* (London, 1985; first published 1981), p. 282.

29. *Disorders Inquiry Committee*, III, pp. 165, 181; O'Dwyer, *India as I Knew it*, p. 285.

30. O'Dwyer, *India as I Knew it*, p. 286.

31. Mr J.M. Coode (Director, Central Telegraph Engineering, Northern Circle) cited in *Hunter Report*, p. 55.

32. N. Collett, *The Butcher of Amritsar. General Reginald Dyer* (London, 2005), pp. 272–3. See also P.G. Robb, *The Government of India and Reform. Policies Towards Politics and the Constitution 1916–1921* (New Delhi, 1989), p. 177.

33. *Disorders Inquiry Committee*, V, p. 225.

34. O'Dwyer, *India as I Knew it*, p. 285.

Chapter 11: The 'High-Water Mark'

1. TNA: CAB 27/92 & 27/93, *Evidence Taken Before the Disorders Inquiry Committee* (7 vols, Calcutta, 1920) [Hereafter *Disorders Inquiry Committee*], IV, p. 59.

2. *Disorders Inquiry Committee*, VI, pp. 56, 57.

3. *Disorders Inquiry Committee*, V, pp. 3, 57, 185.

4. *Disorders Inquiry Committee*, V, pp. 34, 48.

5. *Disorders Inquiry Committee*, V, pp. 189–90.

6. Command 681, *Report of the Committee Appointed by the Government of India to Investigate the Disturbances in the Punjab, etc.* (London, 1920) [Hereafter *Hunter Report*], p. 43.

7. *The Congress Punjab Inquiry 1919–1920: Evidence* (Delhi, 1996; first published 1920), p. 317.

8. *Disorders Inquiry Committee*, V, p. 4.

9. *Disorders Inquiry Committee*, V, p. 61.

10. *The Congress Punjab Inquiry 1919–1920: Evidence*, pp. 317, 670, 671.
11. It remains a mystery who hung up the calf. See *Disorders Inquiry Committee*, V, p. 49.
12. See *Hunter Report*, pp. 44–5.
13. IOC: MSS EUR F394, Account of F.B. Wace.
14. *Disorders Inquiry Committee*, V, p. 62.
15. *Disorders Inquiry Committee*, V, p. 62.
16. *The Congress Punjab Inquiry 1919–1920: Evidence*, p. 326.
17. *Disorders Inquiry Committee*, V, pp. 65, 67; *Hunter Report*, p. 44.
18. *The Congress Punjab Inquiry 1919–1920: Evidence*, pp. 318–9.
19. *The Congress Punjab Inquiry 1919–1920: Evidence*, p. 684. See also *Disorders Inquiry Committee*, V, p. 68.
20. *Disorders Inquiry Committee*, V, p. 199. There were six sub-inspectors, 22 head constables and 119 constables available on 14 April.
21. *Hunter Report*, p. 45. Ahmad seems to have been concerned about the presence of boys in the crowd. See *Disorders Inquiry Committee*, V, p. 34. It was also alleged that some of the police officers were in league with the mobs, although it is difficult to state with any certainty whether this was true. *The Congress Punjab Inquiry 1919–1920: Evidence*, p. 328.
22. This appears in numerous works including S. Raghaven, 'Protecting the Raj: The Army in India and Internal Security, c. 1919–39', *Small Wars and Insurgencies*, 16/3 (December 2005), pp. 266–7. For a detailed, if more critical, examination see S. Shoul, 'Soldiers, Riot Control, and Aid to the Civil Power in India, Egypt and Palestine 1919–1939', Ph.D., University College London, 2006, pp. 64–6.
23. *The Congress Punjab Inquiry 1919–1920: Evidence*, pp. 320, 341, 343.
24. *Report of the Commissioners Appointed by the Punjab Sub-Committee of the Indian National Congress* [hereafter *Congress Punjab Inquiry*] in *The Collected Works of Mahatma Gandhi* (Electronic Book), New Delhi, Publications Division Government of India, 1999, 98 vols *http://www.gandhiserve.org/cwmg/cwmg.html* [hereafter *CWMG*], XX, pp. 122–3. The Congress claimed that 12 people were killed and 24 wounded (p. 123).
25. M. Misra, *Vishnu's Crowded Temple. India Since the Great Rebellion* (London, 2008; first published 2007), p. 152. Carpet bombing did not exist in 1919 and it was impossible to inflict such damage with a handful of 20-pound bombs thrown from an aircraft.
26. *Disorders Inquiry Committee*, V, p. 38.
27. *Hunter Report*, p. 46.
28. Shoul, 'Soldiers, Riot Control, and Aid to the Civil Power in India, Egypt and Palestine 1919–1939', p. 75.
29. Sir M. O'Dwyer, *India as I Knew it 1885–1925* (London: Constable, 1925), p. 287.
30. *Disorders Inquiry Committee*, VI, pp. 7, 56.
31. *Hunter Report*, pp. 48–9.
32. For the effect of aircraft see *Disorders Inquiry Committee*, V, pp. 50, 53, 54, 67, 69.

234   THE AMRITSAR MASSACRE

33. IOC: MSS EUR F394, Account of F.B. Wace.
34. *Disorders Inquiry Committee*, V, p. 53.
35. *Disorders Inquiry Committee*, V, p. 117.
36. *Disorders Inquiry Committee*, V, p. 226.
37. One of the more notable incidents occurred in the early hours of 16 April when an armoured train pulled up to Chuharkana station near Sheikhupura and fired upon a crowd. The railway lines in this area had been heavily damaged and the British and Indian officers in command evidently regarded the village of Chuharkana as being responsible. When they sighted large numbers of people out in the fields around the village, they fired and the crowd scattered into the night. *Hunter Report* [Minority], pp. 128–31.
38. *Report on the Administration of the Punjab and its Dependencies for 1919–20* (Lahore, 1921), pp. 146–7. In April the Government set up the Punjab Publicity Commission to explain the scope of the Rowlatt Bills and counter the spread of *satyagraha*. Over 125,000 copies of Rowlatt Act (in Urdu and Gurmukhi) were distributed throughout the province. NAI: Home Political (B) August 1919, pp. 447–448, 'Note on the work done by the Punjab Publicity Commission, regarding the Rowlatt Act propaganda and its effect'.
39. *Disorders Inquiry Committee*, IV, p. 323.
40. S. David, *The Indian Mutiny* (London, 2003; first published 2002), pp. 139-41.
41. *Disorders Inquiry Committee*, V, p. 212.

Chapter 12: Causes and Conspiracies

1. TNA: CAB 27/92 & 27/93, *Evidence Taken Before the Disorders Inquiry Committee* (7 vols, Calcutta, 1920) [Hereafter *Disorders Inquiry Committee*], VII, p. 107.
2. E.S. Montagu, *An Indian Diary*, V. Montagu (ed.) (London, 1930), p. 351.
3. IWM: 72/22/1, 'The Truth About Amritsar' by Lieutenant-Colonel H.M.L. Morgan, p. 6.
4. Gandhi to Devdas Gandhi, on or after 5 March 1919, in *The Collected Works of Mahatma Gandhi* (Electronic Book), New Delhi, Publications Division Government of India, 1999, 98 vols *http://www.gandhiserve.org/cwmg/cwmg.html* [hereafter *CWMG*], XVII, p. 323.
5. Gandhi to Private Secretary of the Viceroy, 11 March 1919, in *CWMG*, XVII, p. 327. This telegram was drafted on 11 March, but received the following day.
6. IOC: MSS EUR E264/5, Chelmsford to Montagu, 30 March 1919.
7. IOC: MSS EUR E264/5, Chelmsford to Montagu, 9 April 1919.
8. IOC: MSS EUR E264/5, Chelmsford to Montagu, 16 April 1919.
9. IOC: MSS EUR E264/5, Montagu to Chelmsford, 22 April 1919.
10. *Disorders Inquiry Committee*, VI, pp. 44, 60.
11. Sir M. O'Dwyer, *India as I Knew it 1885–1925* (London, 1925), pp. 263–317.
12. See *Disorders Inquiry Committee*, III, p. 135, 138; *Disorders Inquiry Committee*, IV, pp. 4, 24.
13. See Command 681, *Report of the Committee Appointed by the Government of India to Investigate the Disturbances in the Punjab, etc.* (London, 1920)

[Hereafter *Hunter Report*], Appendix II, 'List of Offences committed on the Railways in the Punjab', pp.153–4.

14. *Disorders Inquiry Committee*, V, p. 186.
15. *Disorders Inquiry Committee*, VII, p. 99.
16. O'Dwyer, *India as I Knew it*, pp. 272–3. Original emphasis.
17. B. Robson, *Crisis on the Frontier. The Third Afghan War and the Campaign in Waziristan 1919–1920* (Staplehurst, 2004), pp. 5–18.
18. See J.W. Cell, *Hailey. A Study in British Imperialism, 1872–1969* (Cambridge, 1992), p. 64; IOC: MSS EUR E220/57, Hailey Papers, Note, 1965, pp. 2, 3.
19. *Disorders Inquiry Committee*, VI, pp. 45, 62. See also p. 28.
20. *Disorders Inquiry Committee*, IV, p. 98. Admittedly there were some worrying incidents such as the arrival of an unusually large number of Malacca canes at Amritsar station in March and April 1919. This tempted many British officials to conclude that they were destined for rebel groups, but no further evidence on the mysterious arrivals was ever found. *Disorders Inquiry Committee*, III, p. 132. Similarly, in Lahore, the appearance of threatening posters helped to underline belief in a mysterious, hidden danger. See 'Specimens of Posters published in the Punjab during the Disorders' in V.N. Datta (ed.), *New Light on the Punjab Disturbances in 1919* (2 vols, Simla,1975), II, pp. 1008–14.
21. See *Hunter Report*, pp. 91–7.
22. *Hunter Report* [Minority], pp. 91–4.
23. See *Report of the Commissioners Appointed by the Punjab Sub-Committee of the Indian National Congress* [hereafter *Congress Punjab Inquiry*], in *CWMG*, XX, pp. 4–25.
24. *Congress Punjab Inquiry*, pp. 25, 38. This continues to influence nationalist discourse. See for example, K. Mohan, *Militant Nationalism in the Punjab 1919–1935* (New Delhi, 1985), p. 30.
25. *Hunter Report*, pp. 57, 68.
26. J.M. Brown, *Modern India. The Origins of an Asian Democracy*, 2nd edn (Oxford, 1994; first published 1985), p. 92.
27. *Disorders Inquiry Committee*, VI, p. 272.
28. British intelligence did, however, note that throughout April 1919, 'A considerable number of Sadhus have been noticed to be moving about.' See NAI: Foreign & Political General (B) Proceedings, May 1919, nos 142–150, 'Disturbances in India Arising out of the Agitation Against the Anarchical and Revolutionary Crimes Act (Commonly Called the Rowlatt Act)'.
29. *Hunter Report*, pp. 66, 68.

Chapter 13: The Introduction of Martial Law

1. Cited in CSAS: Sir J. Penny Papers, 'Punjab Memories 1910–1945', p. 94.
2. J. Nehru, *An Autobiography* (London, 2004; first published 1936), pp. 46–7.
3. M.K. Gandhi, 'General Dyer', in *Young India*, 14 July 1920, in *The Collected Works of Mahatma Gandhi* (Electronic Book), New Delhi, Publications Division

Government of India, 1999, 98 vols *http://www.gandhiserve.org/cwmg/cwmg.html* [hereafter *CWMG*], XXI, p. 47.

4. Useful accounts are contained in A. Draper, *The Amritsar Massacre. Twilight of the Raj* (London, 1985; first published 1981), pp. 106–23; H. Fein, *Imperial Crime and Punishment. The Massacre at Jallianwala Bagh and British Judgment, 1919–1920* (Honolulu, 1977), pp. 35–48; R. Furneaux, *Massacre at Amritsar* (London, 1963), pp. 99–104.

5. B.G. Horniman, *Amritsar and Our Duty to India* (Delhi, 1997; first published 1920), p. 112.

6. See *Report of the Commissioners Appointed by the Punjab Sub-Committee of the Indian National Congress* [hereafter *Congress Punjab Inquiry*] in *CWMG*, XX, pp. 176, 180.

7. See Draper, *The Amritsar Massacre*, p. 106 and Fein, *Imperial Crime and Punishment*, pp. 37, 41.

8. Sir M. O'Dwyer, *India as I Knew it 1885–1925* (London, 1925), pp. 302–3. For a discussion of O'Dwyer's role in this period see my 'Sir Michael O'Dwyer and "Imperial Terrorism" in the Punjab, 1919', *South Asia*, 33/3 (2010), pp. 363–80.

9. Ordinance No. 1 of 1919, contained in V.N. Datta (ed.), *New Light on the Punjab Disturbances in 1919* (2 vols., Simla,1975), II, p. 1038.

10. Command 681, *Report of the Committee Appointed by the Government of India to Investigate the Disturbances in the Punjab, etc.* (London, 1920) [Hereafter *Hunter Report*], p. 64.

11. Martial Law was withdrawn from railways on 25 August 1919.

12. *Hunter Report*, p. 65. The sentences ranged from the death penalty to transportation and various terms of imprisonment. Most of these were commuted by a Royal Proclamation of December 1919. Fein, *Imperial Crime and Punishment*, p. 37.

13. TNA: CAB 27/92 & 27/93, *Evidence Taken Before the Disorders Inquiry Committee* (7 vols, Calcutta, 1920) [Hereafter *Disorders Inquiry Committee*], VI, p. 49.

14. IOC: MSS EUR E264/5, Chelmsford to Montagu, 16 April 1919.

15. IOC: MSS EUR E264/22, Chelmsford to O'Dwyer, 30 April 1919.

16. S. Shoul, 'Soldiers, Riot Control, and Aid to the Civil Power in India, Egypt and Palestine 1919–1939', Ph.D., University College London, 2006, p. 17.

17. S. Shoul, 'Soldiers, Riot Control, and Aid to the Civil Power in India, Egypt and Palestine 1919–1939', Ph.D., University College London, 2006, p. 17.

18. *Disorders Inquiry Committee*, VI, pp. 39, 50. In his memoirs, Sir Michael O'Dwyer included a telegram from the Government of India (dated 18 April 1919) to Lahore insisting that it was impossible to place an officer with 'executive military authority' under his orders. O'Dwyer, *India as I Knew it*, pp. 298–9. O'Dwyer arranged with the government that the powers of martial law would only be given to officers of the rank of major or above. See IOC: MSS EUR E 264/5, Chelmsford to Montagu, 16 April 1919, in which Chelmsford states, 'I asserted ... that in place of Courts-Martial composed of young officers, inexperience and possibly prone to "see red", I gave him tribunals of Defence of India standing with Courts-Martial powers.'

19. P.G. Robb, *The Government of India and Reform. Policies Towards Politics and the Constitution 1916–1921* (New Delhi, 1989), pp. 180–1.
20. See IOC: MSS EUR E264/22, Chelmsford to O'Dwyer, 26 April 1919.
21. See O'Dwyer, *India as I Knew it*, pp. 298–306.
22. *Disorders Inquiry Committee*, VI, p. 59. O'Dwyer, *India as I Knew it*, p. 314.
23. IOC: MSS EUR E264/22, O'Dwyer to Chelmsford, 16 April 1919. On 16 April he noticed 'an improvement in the demeanour of the city rabble', but a large section was 'still hostile or sullen'.
24. IOC: MSS EUR E264/22, O'Dwyer to Chelmsford, 16 April 1919.
25. *Disorders Inquiry Committee*, IV, pp. 323–4.
26. Appendix XV, Instructions for Guidance of Officers Administering Martial Law, contained in *Disorders Inquiry Committee*, IV, p. 335.
27. IOC: MSS EUR E264/22, O'Dwyer to Chelmsford, 16 April 1919. Frank Johnson attended conferences at Government House on 15, 19, 20, 22, 23, 24, 26 April and 5 May 1919, usually at 7 p.m. TNA: PRO WO 95/5403, War Diary of Lahore (Civil) Area from 15 April 1919 to 30 April 1919.
28. *Disorders Inquiry Committee*, VI, p. 17.
29. IOC: MSS EUR E264/22, O'Dwyer to Chelmsford, 21 April 1919.
30. IOC: MSS EUR E264/5, Chelmsford to Montagu, 30 April 1919.
31. IOC: MSS EUR E264/22, Chelmsford to O'Dwyer, 30 April 1919.
32. See *Congress Punjab Inquiry*, pp. 65–9; N. Collett, *The Butcher of Amritsar. General Reginald Dyer* (London, 2005), pp. 269–93.
33. *Hunter Report*, p. 83.
34. *Congress Punjab Inquiry*, p. 181.
35. I. Colvin, *The Life of General Dyer* (Edinburgh & London, 1929), pp. 196–7; A. Swinson, *Six Minutes to Sunset. The Story of General Dyer and the Amritsar Affair* (London, 1964), p. 63.
36. See IWM: 83/31/1, Account of Brigadier F. McCallum, June 1975. For a discussion of this see Collett, *The Butcher of Amritsar*, pp. 282–5. Ian Colvin suggests that the assault on Miss Sherwood 'had infuriated the British troops in Amritsar to such an extent that General Dyer, for the sake of discipline, warned them against any attempt at reprisals of that account'. Colvin, *The Life of General Dyer*, p. 196. In Dyer's statement he refers to an unnamed NCO who made a number of prisoners pass along the street on all fours before he had issued his order. Command 771, *Disturbances in the Punjab. Statement by Brig-General R.E.H. Dyer, C.B.* (London, 1920), p. 17.
37. Brigadier-General R.E.H. Dyer to General Staff, 16th (Indian) Division, 25 August 1919, contained in *Disorders Inquiry Committee*, III, p. 205.
38. Command 771, *Disturbances in the Punjab*, p. 17.
39. *Hunter Report*, p. 83.
40. IOC: MSS EUR E264/22, O'Dwyer to Chelmsford, 1 May 1919.
41. See Gandhi, 'General Dyer', in *Young India*, 14 July 1920, in *CWMG*, XXI, p. 47.
42. *Hunter Report*, p. 84; *Disorders Inquiry Committee*, IV, pp. 1, 9, 26. The average number of lashes was 12.6.

43. Fein, *Imperial Crime and Punishment*, p. 42.
44. He would justify his orders against students on the grounds that they had not been loyal to the British Raj and that they had been 'insulting white ladies'. *Disorders Inquiry Committee*, IV, pp. 13, 14.
45. *Disorders Inquiry Committee*, IV, pp. 17, 285.
46. *Disorders Inquiry Committee*, IV, pp. 115, 116. Original emphasis.
47. A. Thomas, *Rhodes. The Race for Africa* (London, 1996), p. 214. See F.W.F. Johnson, *Great Days: The Autobiography of an Empire Pioneer* (London, 1940).
48. IOC: MSS EUR F137/13, J.P. Thompson Diary, 24 November 1919.
49. See Order No. 12 (16 April 1919), which deemed it unlawful for more than two people to walk abreast on any pavement (*Disorders Inquiry Committee*, IV, p. 293). Order No. 21 (21 April 1919) stated that all pedal-driven cycles not owned by Europeans were to be delivered to the authorities (p. 295). Order No. 24 (23 April 1919) allowed troops to enter any building and remove fans or electric lights (p. 296). Order No. 30 stated that defacing pictures of British subjects would be deemed a breach of martial law (p. 297).
50. *Disorders Inquiry Committee*, IV, pp. 3, 7, 26.
51. *Disorders Inquiry Committee*, IV, p. 60. Emphasis added.
52. *Disorders Inquiry Committee*, VI, pp. 23, 91.

Chapter 14: 'Fancy Punishments' and 'Erratic Acts'

1. TNA: CAB 27/92 & 27/93, *Evidence Taken Before the Disorders Inquiry Committee* (7 vols, Calcutta, 1920) [Hereafter *Disorders Inquiry Committee*], V, p. 16.
2. IOC: MSS EUR E264/22, Chelmsford to O'Dwyer, 12 May 1919.
3. IOC: MSS EUR E264/22, O'Dwyer to Chelmsford, 15 May 1919.
4. IOC: MSS EUR E264/22, O'Dwyer to Chelmsford, 27 May 1919. Chelmsford offered O'Dwyer his 'warm appreciation' of his service, in which he had shown his 'indomitable courage and untiring energy'. MSS EUR E264/23, Chelmsford to O'Dwyer, 27 May 1919.
5. IOC: MSS EUR E264/22, Maclagan to Chelmsford, 21 May 1919.
6. Command 681, *Report of the Committee Appointed by the Government of India to Investigate the Disturbances in the Punjab, etc.* (London, 1920) [Hereafter *Hunter Report*], p. 77. See NAI: Home Political (A) Proceedings, March 1920, nos 323–334 & K.W., 'Report by Reviewing Judges on Punjab Disturbances'.
7. IOC: MSS EUR E264/22, O'Dwyer to Chelmsford, 21 May 1919.
8. *Disorders Inquiry Committee*, IV, p. 67. Beynon would later remark that there were plenty of lawyers in Lahore anyway (p. 71).
9. See *Hunter Report*, p. 72 and *Report of the Commissioners Appointed by the Punjab Sub-Committee of the Indian National Congress* [hereafter *Congress Punjab Inquiry*] in *The Collected Works of Mahatma Gandhi* (Electronic Book), New Delhi, Publications Division Government of India, 1999, 98 vols *http://www.gandhiserve.org/cwmg/cwmg.html* [hereafter *CWMG*], XX, Chapter 5.
10. *Disorders Inquiry Committee*, VI, p. 10.
11. *Disorders Inquiry Committee*, IV, p. 61.
12. *Disorders Inquiry Committee*, VI, p. 102.

13. Details taken from McRae, 'Report on the Administration of the Kasur Civil Area during the Punjab Riots, April 12th to May 8th, 1919', contained in *Disorders Inquiry Committee*, IV, pp. 373–6.
14. *Disorders Inquiry Committee*, IV, pp. 384–5.
15. *Hunter Report*, p. 85.
16. *Congress Punjab Inquiry*, p. 111.
17. *Disorders Inquiry Committee*, IV, p. 207.
18. *Hunter Report* [Minority], pp. 123–7.
19. See H. Fein, *Imperial Crime and Punishment. The Massacre at Jallianwala Bagh and British Judgment, 1919–1920* (Honolulu, 1977), pp. 39–41.
20. *Disorders Inquiry Committee*, V, p. 208.
21. It has also alleged that Bosworth-Smith wanted to build a 'repentance house' at Sheikhupura in commemoration of the events of 1919. Like much of the criticism of the British authorities in this period, it goes too far. The 'repentance house' was never a realistic proposal and was never put before the Government. *Disorders Inquiry Committee*, V, p. 97.
22. P.G. Robb, *The Government of India and Reform. Policies Towards Politics and the Constitution 1916–1921* (New Delhi, 1989), p. 212. The others included Brigadier-General L.W.Y. Campbell (GOC Sialkot Brigade) and S.M. Jacob (Director of Agriculture and commander of a mobile column).
23. *Disorders Inquiry Committee*, IV, p. 211.
24. *Disorders Inquiry Committee*, V, pp. 5, 208.
25. B.G. Horniman, *Amritsar and Our Duty to India* (Delhi, 1997; first published 1920), p. 126.
26. *Hunter Report*, p. 84.
27. IOC: MSS EUR E264/22, Gandhi to Maffey, 21 April 1919.
28. *Disorders Inquiry Committee*, IV, pp. 6, 8, 286. See also *Disorders Inquiry Committee*, III, p. 124.
29. *Disorders Inquiry Committee*, IV, pp. 80, 81, 83.
30. CSAS: Sir J. Penny Papers, 'Punjab Memories 1910–1945', p. 96.
31. *Disorders Inquiry Committee*, VI, p. 24.
32. *Disorders Inquiry Committee*, IV, pp. 162, 226.
33. *Disorders Inquiry Committee*, IV, pp. 180, 181.
34. *Disorders Inquiry Committee*, IV, p. 287.
35. *Disorders Inquiry Committee*, V, p. 211.
36. See *Disorders Inquiry Committee*, VI, pp. 48–9, 50, 78 and *Disorders Inquiry Committee*, IV, p. 5.
37. *Disorders Inquiry Committee*, VI, pp. 49, 92.
38. *Disorders Inquiry Committee*, VII, p. 104.
39. Major-General Beynon believed that there was only one type of martial law, but there could be modifications to it. *Disorders Inquiry Committee*, IV, p. 70. Frank Johnson thought that there were three types of martial law. These were the 'will of the individual commanders', statutory martial law (a) (in which troops assisted the civil power) and statutory martial law (b) (which was concerned with forts and fortresses), p. 28. There were in fact three types of martial law: *de facto*

(once normal law had collapsed); *de jure* (formally proclaimed by civilian author-ities); and *statutory* (which enabled the military to take exceptional measures but without relinquishing all civilian authority). S. Shoul, 'Soldiers, Riot Control, and Aid to the Civil Power in India, Egypt and Palestine 1919–1939', Ph.D., University College London, 2006, p. 17.

40. *Disorders Inquiry Committee*, VI, p. 104.
41. *Disorders Inquiry Committee*, VI, p. 54.
42. *Disorders Inquiry Committee*, V, pp. 15, 91.
43. Fein, *Imperial Crime and Punishment*, pp. 45, 47.
44. See T.R. Metcalf, *Ideologies of the Raj* (Cambridge, 1994); C. Dewey, *Anglo-Indian Attitudes. The Mind of the Indian Civil Service* (London, 1993).

Chapter 15: Lord Hunter and the Disorders Inquiry Committee

1. IOC: MSS EUR E264/5, Montagu to Hunter, 29 August 1919.
2. Gandhi, 'Press Statement on Suspension of Civil Disobedience', 18 April 1919, in *The Collected Works of Mahatma Gandhi* (Electronic Book), New Delhi, Publications Division Government of India, 1999, 98 vols *http://www.gandhiserve.org/cwmg/cwmg.html* [hereafter *CWMG*], XVII, p. 443.
3. See J.M. Brown, *Gandhi's Rise to Power. Indian Politics 1915–1922* (Cambridge, 1972), pp. 175–89.
4. For the Third Afghan War see B. Robson, *Crisis on the Frontier. The Third Afghan War and the Campaign in Waziristan 1919–1920* (Staplehurst, 2004). Of those involved was Brigadier-General Dyer who led an exhausting relief march to the garrison at Thal on the Kurram River in Waziristan. See I. Colvin, *The Life of General Dyer* (Edinburgh & London, 1929), pp. 218, 228–9.
5. IOC: MSS EUR E264/22, Tagore to Chelmsford, 31 May 1919.
6. Brown, *Gandhi's Rise to Power*, p. 234.
7. 'Viceroy's Speech', cited in P. Mohan, *The Punjab "Rebellion" of 1919 and How It Was Suppressed*, R.M. Bakaya (ed.) (New Delhi, 1999; first published 1920), pp. 569–70.
8. IOC: MSS EUR E264/5, Montagu to Chelmsford, 1 May 1919.
9. V.N. Datta, 'Introduction', in V.N. Datta (ed.), *New Light on the Punjab Disturbances in 1919* (2 vols., Simla,1975), I, pp. 4–5.
10. IOC: MSS EUR E264/5, Montagu to Chelmsford, 15 August 1919.
11. IOC: MSS EUR E264/5, Chelmsford to Montagu, 20 August 1919.
12. IOC: MSS EUR E264/5, Montagu to Chelmsford, 29 August 1919.
13. IOC: MSS EUR E264/5, Montagu to Hunter, 29 August 1919.
14. IOC: MSS EUR E264/5, Montagu to Chelmsford, 29 August 1919.
15. TNA: CAB 27/92 & 27/93, *Evidence Taken Before the Disorders Inquiry Committee* (7 vols, Calcutta, 1920) [Hereafter *Disorders Inquiry Committee*], III, p. 39.
16. IOC: MSS EUR E264/5, Montagu to Chelmsford, 29 August 1919.
17. C.H. Setalvad, *Recollections and Reflections. An Autobiography* (Bombay, 1946), p. 311.
18. Criticism taken from A. Swinson, *Six Minutes to Sunset. The Story of General Dyer and the Amritsar Affair* (London, 1964), p. 95. Sir George Barrow, who served on

the Hunter Committee, denied that Hunter's lack of Indian languages mattered because the inquiry was held in English and many of those who came before the committee spoke English. Nevertheless, this did become a problem when Hunter tried to control the crowd, because he could not understand what they were saying. Sir G. Barrow, *The Life of General Sir Charles Carmichael Monro* (London, 1931), p. 210.

19. Sir G. Barrow, *The Fire of Life* (London, 1942), p. 227; IOC: MSS EUR E264/5, Montagu to Chelmsford, 28 November 1919.

20. Gandhi cited in N. Collett, *The Butcher of Amritsar. General Reginald Dyer* (London, 2005), p. 334.

21. *Disorders Inquiry Committee*, IV, pp. 65, 67.

22. *Disorders Inquiry Committee*, IV, p. 27.

23. Briggs died on the operating table three days after Dyer had appeared before the Hunter Committee. Contained in Swinson, *Six Minutes to Sunset*, pp. 125–6 is a claim that Briggs was murdered by having ground glass put in his food. Whether or not this was the case is impossible to say, but his sudden (and untimely) death is strange given that he had previously been in good health and was only 29 years old. Having ground glass in food was a recurring fear of Anglo-India.

24. IOC: MSS EUR D830/12, T.L. Hughes, *Man of Iron. A Biography of Major General Sir William Beynon*, p. 138. See also MSS EUR F161/110, Note by Sir Alexander Brebner (Chief Engineer, Public Works Department), 9 December 1969.

25. Details taken from *Disorders Inquiry Committee*, III, pp. 117, 118, 123.

26. Dyer would later deny that he had said that he wanted to 'do all men to death', but George Barrow maintained that these words had been uttered because he was listening intently and was immediately struck by the peculiarity of the phrase. Barrow, *The Life of General Sir Charles Carmichael Monro*, p. 211.

27. *Disorders Inquiry Committee*, III, p. 126.

28. Setalvad, *Recollections and Reflections*, pp. 310–1.

29. *Hunter Report*, pp. 29–31, 57–63, 66–75, 82–86.

30. *Hunter Report* [Minority], pp. 87–140.

31. Command 771, *Disturbances in the Punjab. Statement by Brig-General R.E.H. Dyer, C.B.* (London, 1920), pp. 4–5.

32. Swinson, *Six Minutes to Sunset*, p. 96.

33. *Disorders Inquiry Committee*, V, p. 11.

Chapter 16: Debates and Disagreements

1. Command 771, *Disturbances in the Punjab. Statement by Brig-General R.E.H. Dyer, C.B.* (London, 1920), pp. 16–17.

2. For Dyer's final years see I. Colvin, *The Life of General Dyer* (Edinburgh & London, 1929), Chapter 26.

3. For a discussion of the speeches see N. Collett, *The Butcher of Amritsar. General Reginald Dyer* (London, 2005), Chapter 22.

4. For the debate see *The Parliamentary Debates, Fifth Series, Volume 131, House of Commons* (London, 1920), cols 1705–1822.

5. Sir M. O'Dwyer, *India as I Knew it 1885–1925* (London, 1925), p. 325.

6. *The Parliamentary Debates, Fifth Series, Volume XLI, House of Lords* (London, 1920), cols 222–378. In the vote 129 members were for the motion and 86 against. In 1924 the Dyer affair briefly came to life again during a libel action between Sir Michael O'Dwyer and a former member of the Government of India, Sir Sankaran Nair. Nair had criticised O'Dwyer's handling of martial law in the Punjab in his book, *Gandhi and Anarchy* (1922). Affronted by this, O'Dwyer successfully sued Nair for libel and received a ringing endorsement of not only his actions, but also those of General Dyer from the judge who presided over the trial, Mr Justice McCardie. O'Dwyer, *India as I Knew it*, p. 355.

7. G. Rudé, *The Crowd in the French Revolution* (Oxford, 1959), p. 1.

8. Colvin, *The Life of General Dyer*, p. 172. See also A. Swinson, *Six Minutes to Sunset. The Story of General Dyer and the Amritsar Affair* (London, 1964), p. 47.

9. *Report of the Commissioners Appointed by the Punjab Sub-Committee of the Indian National Congress* [hereafter *Congress Punjab Inquiry*] in *The Collected Works of Mahatma Gandhi* (Electronic Book), New Delhi, Publications Division Government of India, 1999, 98 vols *http://www.gandhiserve.org/cwmg/cwmg.html* [hereafter *CWMG*], XX, pp. 58, 59, 64, 180. See also B.G. Horniman, *Amritsar and Our Duty to India* (Delhi, 1997; first published 1920), p. 96.

10. TNA: CAB 27/92 & 27/93, *Evidence Taken Before the Disorders Inquiry Committee* (7 vols, Calcutta, 1920) [Hereafter *Disorders Inquiry Committee*], III, pp. 40, 68. The Minority Report concluded that about 8 to 10,000 people heard the proclamation. Command 681, *Report of the Committee Appointed by the Government of India to Investigate the Disturbances in the Punjab, etc.* (London, 1920) [Hereafter *Hunter Report*], p. 111.

11. *Census of India, 1921, Volume XV, Punjab and Delhi* (2 parts, Lahore, 1923), Part II, Tables, Table V.

12. 'Rumours spread very rapidly in India'. *Disorders Inquiry Committee*, III, p. 2; A. Gauba, *Amritsar. A Study in Urban History (1840–1947)* (Jalandhar, 1988), p. 254.

13. *Congress Punjab Inquiry*, p. 58. See also V.N. Datta, *Jallianwala Bagh* (Ludhiana, 1969), pp. 95–6. Dyer would claim that the crowd 'must have received ample warning of my coming' and given the slow pace of his march, it is likely that boys ran alongside or ahead of them and spread word of his approach. Brigadier-General R.E.H. Dyer to General Staff, 16th (Indian) Division, 25 August 1919, contained in *Disorders Inquiry Committee*, III, p. 203.

14. V.N. Datta, 'Perceptions of the Jallianwala Bagh Massacre', in V.N. Datta & S. Settar (eds), *Jallianwala Bagh Massacre* (Delhi, 2000), p. 10.

15. *The Congress Punjab Inquiry 1919–1920: Evidence* (Delhi, 1996; first published 1920), p. 56.

16. P. Mohan, *The Punjab "Rebellion" of 1919 and How It Was Suppressed*, R.M. Bakaya (ed.) (New Delhi, 1999; first published 1920), pp. 131–3.

17. See A. Draper, *The Amritsar Massacre. Twilight of the Raj* (London, 1985; first published 1981), pp. 84, 86–7, Chapter 7.
18. Datta, *Jallianwala Bagh*, p. 166; H. Fein, *Imperial Crime and Punishment. The Massacre at Jallianwala Bagh and British Judgment, 1919–1920* (Honolulu, 1977), p. 34. See R. Ram, *The Jallianwala Bagh Massacre. A Premeditated Plan* (Chandigarh, 1978; first published 1969), p. 109. Ram believed that Raj was probably one of a number of police informants. See also Datta, 'Perceptions of the Jallianwala Bagh Massacre', pp. 12–13.
19. *The Congress Punjab Inquiry 1919–1920: Evidence*, pp. 47, 53–4, 62. Pearay Mohan also noticed this and claimed – rather tenuously – that he did this in order to keep the crowd in the Bagh. He also argued that Hans Raj had built a wooden platform so that when Dyer's troops arrived and began to fire at the crowd, he would have somewhere to hide. Mohan, *The Punjab "Rebellion" of 1919 and How It Was Suppressed*, pp. 137, 140.
20. NAI: Amritsar Conspiracy Case 1919 (Acc No. 1829), Dr S.D. Kitchlew, Dr Satyapal and 13 others, p. 84.
21. For Hans Raj's recollections of the gathering see NAI: Amritsar Conspiracy Case 1919 (Acc No. 1829), Dr S.D. Kitchlew, Dr Satyapal and 13 others, pp. 36, 83. Some of the spelling of the names of those present differs slightly.
22. *Hunter Report*, p. 29.
23. NAI: Amritsar Conspiracy Case 1919 (Acc No. 1829), Dr S.D. Kitchlew, Dr Satyapal and 13 others, p. 36.
24. It was also alleged that he led the mob during the attack on the National Bank. Swinson, *Six Minutes to Sunset*, p. 47. See also Colvin, *The Life of General Dyer*, p. 176; Datta, *Jallianwala Bagh*, p. 98. One of Brij Gopi Nath's poems, 'Bekal', included the following lines: 'Adieu to thee, O, patience! Now I have no strength to entertain you / Self-control is now out of question / Why should we not lament and wish for the death of the hunter? / He has indicated a pain for which there is no remedy / Oppression has passed its limit and power of endurance is gone / O, inventor of oppression! More than this cannot be born / I wish that I should have a sigh raining sparks of fire … Let me at least destroy the evil natured enemy / I will at least show the effects of the sigh of the oppressed.' NAI: Amritsar Conspiracy Case 1919 (Acc No. 1829), Dr S.D. Kitchlew, Dr Satyapal and 13 others, p. 170.
25. PSA: Punjab Government Civil Secretariat, 1920. Home Judicial (C) Proceedings, June, nos 61–7, 'Petitions and Orders in Amritsar Conspiracy Case – Defence of India Tribunal (case no. 8)', pp. 1–2.
26. Datta, 'Perceptions of the Jallianwala Bagh Massacre', p. 11.
27. It was on 13 April that the Goddess Ganga is reputed to have descended to earth.
28. Datta, *Jallianwala Bagh*, p. 98.
29. *Hunter Report* [Minority], p. 114.
30. S. Hans, 'Jallianwala Bagh: The Construction of a Nationalist Symbol', in Datta & Settar (eds), *Jallianwala Bagh Massacre*, p. 127.
31. *Disorders Inquiry Committee*, III, pp. 7, 16, 37, 41, 158.

32. Command 771, *Disturbances in the Punjab*, pp. 7, 16.

33. *Disorders Inquiry Committee*, III, p. 51.

34. Hans, 'Jallianwala Bagh: The Construction of a Nationalist Symbol', pp 130–1.

35. Gauba, *Amritsar. A Study in Urban History*, p. 26.

36. *The Congress Punjab Inquiry 1919–1920: Evidence*, pp. 62, 63.

37. See S.M. Rai, 'The Jallianwala Bagh Tragedy: Its Impact on the Political Awakening and Thinking in India' in Datta & Settar (eds), *Jallianwala Bagh Massacre*, p. 28; Ram, *The Jallianwala Bagh Massacre*, p. 87.

38. 'Report of Captain F.C. Briggs, D.S.O.' contained as Appendix A in Command 771, *Disturbances in the Punjab*, p. 25.

39. Brigadier-General R.E.H. Dyer to General Staff, 16th (Indian) Division, 25 August 1919, contained in *Disorders Inquiry Committee*, III, p. 203.

40. Hans, 'Jallianwala Bagh: The Construction of a Nationalist Symbol', p. 131.

41. P. Bose, *Organizing Empire. Individualism, Collective Agency, and India* (London & Durham, 2003), p. 39.

42. Gauba, *Amritsar. A Study in Urban History*, p. 265. Amritsar had a population of 95,106 men and 65,112 women in 1921. *Census of India, 1921, Volume XV, Punjab and Delhi* (2 parts, Lahore, 1923), Part II, Tables, Table V.

43. *Hunter Report*, p. 29. The Minority Report gives a figure of between 15,000 and 20,000. *Congress Punjab Inquiry*, pp. 49, 59.

Chapter 17: Dyer and the Jallianwala Bagh

1. E. Thompson, *A Letter From India* (London, 1932), p. 101.

2. I. Colvin, *The Life of General Dyer* (Edinburgh & London, 1929), p. 316.

3. See S.M. Rai, 'The Jallianwala Bagh Tragedy: Its Impact on the Political Awakening and Thinking in India' in V.N. Datta & S. Settar (eds), *Jallianwala Bagh Massacre* (Delhi, 2000), p. 28. See also P. Bose, *Organizing Empire. Individualism, Collective Agency, and India* (London & Durham, 2003), Chapter 1. Stanley Wolpert's (admittedly fictional) description of Dyer as a hysterical Christian bigot, full of racial hatred and suppressed sexual energy, defines his action within these terms. S. Wolpert, *An Error of Judgment* (Boston & Toronto, 1970), pp. 5–6, 17, 212–5, 220–3. V. N. Datta argues that Dyer was 'primarily motivated by revenge', *Jallianwala Bagh* (Ludhiana, 1969), p. 168. The American sociologist, Helen Fein, supports this interpretation. H. Fein, *Imperial Crime and Punishment. The Massacre at Jallianwala Bagh and British Judgment, 1919–1920* (Honolulu, 1977), p. 34. Nigel Collett argues that contrary to his reputation, Dyer fired at Amritsar not because he was 'callous or bloodthirsty', but because he believed what faced him, 'was a challenge to his way of life and everything he stood for'; the settled life of Anglo-India, the British Raj and the ideal of untainted English womanhood. N. Collett, *The Butcher of Amritsar. General Reginald Dyer* (London, 2005), pp. 422–3.

4. Brigadier-General R.E.H. Dyer, 'Report of Operations 21-00, 11th April 1919 to Genstaff Division', 14 April 1919, contained in TNA: CAB 27/92 & 27/93,

Evidence Taken Before the Disorders Inquiry Committee (7 vols, Calcutta, 1920) [Hereafter *Disorders Inquiry Committee*], III, p. 216.

5. Brigadier-General R.E.H. Dyer to General Staff, 16th (Indian) Division, 25 August 1919, contained in *Disorders Inquiry Committee*, III, p. 203.

6. Dyer to General Staff, 16th (Indian) Division, 25 August 1919, contained in *Disorders Inquiry Committee*, III, p. 202. For Dyer's time of arrival back at the Ram Bagh see p. 116. Swinson disputes this and claims that Dyer decided to return from the city at 2.30 p.m. Swinson, *Six Minutes to Sunset*, p. 45. Irving believed that it was just before 4 p.m. *Disorders Inquiry Committee*, III, p. 181. In any case both these claims highlight the very limited time available to Dyer.

7. According to Dyer's wife, before going to the Jallianwala Bagh Dyer had said to his Brigade Major, 'Briggs, I shall be cashiered for this probably, but I've got to do it.' LHCMA: Edmonds Papers, II/2/171, Mrs F. Dyer to Brigadier-General Sir James Edmonds, 9 June 1927.

8. Collett, *The Butcher of Amritsar*, p. 256.

9. Datta, *Jallianwala Bagh*, p. 164.

10. Collett, *The Butcher of Amritsar*, p. 257.

11. *Disorders Inquiry Committee*, III, pp. 7, 116.

12. *Disorders Inquiry Committee*, III, p. 122.

13. Dyer, 'Report of Operations 21-00, 11th April 1919 to Genstaff Division', 14 April 1919, contained in *Disorders Inquiry Committee*, III, p. 216.

14. Nigel Collett disagrees. In *The Butcher of Amritsar* (p. 255) he writes: 'As he had sent an aeroplane to seek out and assess the size of the meeting, and had information and advice being fed to him by local police throughout the afternoon, he was not unaware of the fact that he faced a crowd of considerable size in an enclosed space.' Unfortunately, Collett presents no evidence to support these statements. Before the Hunter Inquiry, Dyer admitted that an aircraft had been used for reconnaissance purposes on 12 April (it had come from Lahore), but what role it played the following day is unclear. He was at pains to stress that he only received *definite information* about the gathering at the Jallianwala Bagh at 4 p.m. from Rehill. *Disorders Inquiry Committee*, III, pp. 115, 116.

15. 'Report of Captain F.C. Briggs, D.S.O.' contained as Appendix A in Command 771, *Disturbances in the Punjab. Statement by Brig-General R.E.H. Dyer, C.B.* (London, 1920), p. 25.

16. *Disorders Inquiry Committee*, III, pp. 115, 198. Mr Lewis, the Manager of the Crown Cinema, seems to have been operating as an intelligence officer in Amritsar. See 'Report of Captain F.C. Briggs, D.S.O.', p. 25.

17. See Collett, *The Butcher of Amritsar*, p. 337.

18. It is likely that the armoured cars in Amritsar came from the garrisons at either Lahore or Ambala. Both garrisons were the bases for three armoured cars, all of which were the basic 'open box' India Pattern conversions of commercial automobiles. One vehicle in each India Pattern battery was fitted with a pintle-mounted machine gun, which would have been expected to fight dismounted if required. Many thanks to Dr Guy Finch for providing this information and for discussing the employment of armoured cars with me.

19. *Disorders Inquiry Committee*, III, p. 126. According to John Smyth, an officer who was in Lahore in 1919 and knew Dyer's Brigade Major, Briggs told him that they had worked out the following procedure. Dyer would 'enter the Bagh with an armoured car, from the top of which he would address the crowd and warn them that if they did not disperse immediately they would be fired upon'. CSAS: Sir J. Smyth Papers, 1, Sir John Smyth to *The Observer*, 13 April 1975 (unedited version), p. 3.

20. Collett, *The Butcher of Amritsar*, pp. 440–2.

21. An insurrection 'differs from a riot in this – that a riot has in view some enterprise *of a private nature*, while an insurrection savours of high treason, and contemplates some enterprise of a *general and public nature*'. See *Manual of Military Law* (London, 1914), pp. 216–7.

22. Collett, *The Butcher of Amritsar*, p. 441.

23. Command 681, *Report of the Committee Appointed by the Government of India to Investigate the Disturbances in the Punjab, etc.* (London, 1920) [Hereafter *Hunter Report*], pp. 66, 68.

24. For a discussion of minimum force in the Jallianwala Bagh see my 'The Amritsar Massacre and the Minimum Force Debate', *Small Wars & Insurgencies*, 21/2 (June 2010), pp. 382–403.

25. *Disorders Inquiry Committee*, III, pp. 117, 123, 131. See also Dyer to General Staff, 16th (Indian) Division, 25 August 1919 (p. 203). Dyer's calculated brutality was apparently given further credence in a widely-quoted piece in Jawaharlal Nehru's autobiography, in which he claims that while travelling by train he overhead Dyer talking to a group of army officers about his actions and saying that he could have reduced the city to ashes, but that he showed mercy. J. Nehru, *An Autobiography* (London, 2004; first published 1936), pp. 47–8. While many commentators have taken Nehru's word for this, it is very debatable. Nehru recorded this incident as happening at the end of 1919, but Dyer did not go to Delhi until March 1920. Collett, *The Butcher of Amritsar*, p. 503n.

26. Wathen Diary, 18 April 1919, cited in Collett, *The Butcher of Amritsar*, p. 264.

27. Collett, *The Butcher of Amritsar*, p. 442.

28. IWM: 72/22/1, 'The Truth About Amritsar' by Lieutenant-Colonel H.M.L. Morgan, p. 5.

29. Dyer to General Staff, 16th (Indian) Division, 25 August 1919, contained in *Disorders Inquiry Committee*, III, p. 203; Command 771, *Disturbances in the Punjab*, p. 8.

30. For a recent examination of this see S. Shoul, 'Soldiers, Riot Control, and Aid to the Civil Power in India, Egypt and Palestine 1919-1939', Ph.D., University College London, 2006, pp. 64–6.

31. CSAS: Sir J. Smyth Papers, 1, Sir John Smyth to *The Observer*, 13 April 1975 (unedited version), p. 3.

32. *Disorders Inquiry Committee*, III, pp. 7, 118, 135.

33. *Hunter Report*, p. 29.

34. *Report of the Commissioners Appointed by the Punjab Sub-Committee of the Indian National Congress* [hereafter *Congress Punjab Inquiry*] in *The Collected Works of Mahatma Gandhi* (Electronic Book), New Delhi, Publications Division Government of India, 1999, 98 vols *http://www.gandhiserve.org/cwmg/cwmg.html* [hereafter *CWMG*], XX, p. 62.

35. IOC: MSS EUR E264/5, Chelmsford to Montagu, 24 December 1919.

36. *Disorders Inquiry Committee*, III, p. 63.

37. *Disorders Inquiry Committee*, III, pp. 62–3.

38. PSA: Home Military B Proceedings, 10495/132 (No. 58, May 1922), 'Grant of Compensation to the Families of those Killed and those Injured at the Jallianwala Bagh and other places during the disturbances of 1919'.

39. Wathen Diary, 18 April 1919, cited in Collett, *The Butcher of Amritsar*, p. 264. Irving's quote can be found in Thompson, *A Letter From India*, p. 102.

40. *Disorders Inquiry Committee*, VI, p. 68; see also p. 34.

41. Thompson, *A Letter From India*, pp. 102–4.

42. Sir C.W. Gwynn, *Imperial Policing* (London, 1934), p. 55.

43. Collett, *The Butcher of Amritsar*, pp. 141–205. See R.E.H. Dyer, *Raiders of the Sarhadd: Being an Account of a Campaign of Arms and Bluff against the Brigands of the Persian-Baluchi Border During the Great War* (London, 1921). Dyer would later give public lectures on his experiences in the Sarhadd, the proceeds of which were 'distributed among the relatives of the Indians who fell during the Amritsar rebellion'. Such a gesture may well have reflected doubts over his actions in Amritsar and whether he had made a mistake in firing for so long. He would hardly have given money to the relatives of those killed in the Jallianwala Bagh if he was convinced that they were 'rebels' who deserved their punishment. See *The Times*, 27 January 1921, p. 7.

44. Dyer, 'Report of Operations 21-00, 11th April 1919 to Genstaff Division', 14 April 1919, contained in *Disorders Inquiry Committee*, III, p. 216. Three days later Dyer was in Lahore and saw J.P. Thompson (Chief Secretary to the Punjab Government). Thompson's diary recorded that 'General Dyer came in from Amritsar to see H.H. [presumably Havelock Hudson, the Adjutant-General]. Said he thought crowd was going to rush his men.' IOC: MSS EUR F137/13, J.P. Thompson Diary, 16 April 1919.

45. Thompson, *A Letter From India*, p. 101.

Chapter 18: Shadows of Amritsar

1. Cited in C. Barnett, *The Collapse of British Power* (London, 2002; first published 1972), p. 153.

2. Royal Proclamation cited in *Statement Exhibiting the Moral and Material Progress and Condition of India During the Year 1919* (London, 1920), pp. 49–52.

3. *Report on the Administration of the Punjab and its Dependencies for 1919–20* (Lahore, 1921), p. 5.

4. *Statement Exhibiting the Moral and Material Progress and Condition of India During the Year 1919*, pp. 52–3.

5. D.A. Low, 'The Government of India and the First Non-Co-operation Movement – 1920–1922', *Journal of Asian Studies*, 25/2 (February 1966), pp. 241–2.

6. IOC: MSS EUR E264/5, Montagu to Chelmsford, 22 April 1919.

7. Gandhi to Lord Chelmsford, 1 August 1920, in *The Collected Works of Mahatma Gandhi* (Electronic Book), New Delhi, Publications Division Government of India, 1999, 98 vols *http://www.gandhiserve.org/cwmg/cwmg.html* [hereafter *CWMG*], XXI, pp. 105–7.

8. See Gandhi, 'Boycott of Councils', 18 July 1920, in *CWMG*, XXI, pp. 56–8.

9. Low, 'The Government of India and the First Non-Co-operation Movement – 1920–1922', p. 242.

10. J.M. Brown, *Gandhi's Rise to Power. Indian Politics 1915–1922* (Cambridge, 1972), p. 327.

11. Sir P. Griffiths, *To Guard My People. A History of the Indian Police* (London, 1971), pp. 245–6.

12. See Low, 'The Government of India and the First Non-Co-operation Movement – 1920–1922', p. 245.

13. Account of Chauri Chaura taken from Griffiths, *To Guard My People*, pp. 246–7.

14. Gandhi, 'Speech to Congress Workers, Bardoli', 10 February 1922, in *CWMG*, XXVI, p. 137.

15. Low, 'The Government of India and the First Non-Co-operation Movement – 1920–1922', p. 255.

16. IOC: MSS EUR E264/3, Austen Chamberlain to Lord Chelmsford, 5 July 1917.

17. P.G. Robb, *The Government of India and Reform. Policies Towards Politics and the Constitution 1916–1921* (New Delhi, 1989), p. 268.

18. C. Dewey, *Anglo-Indian Attitudes. The Mind of the Indian Civil Service* (London, 1993), p. 58.

19. L.F. Rushbrook-Williams, *India in 1924–25* (Delhi, 1985; first published 1925), pp. 49, 51, 53, 55.

20. Robb, *The Government of India and Reform*, pp. 282–4. The repeal of Rowlatt Act 'gave an immediate stimulus to the revival of revolutionary movements in the Punjab and in Bengal'. Sir M. O'Dwyer, *India as I Knew it 1885–1925* (London, 1925), p. 395.

21. Brown, *Modern India*, p. 284.

22. Griffiths, *To Guard My People*, p. 297.

23. NAI: Home Political (Deposit), Proceedings, August 1919, no. 56, 'Proposal to Start a Government Party and to Concert Means to get Government's Measures and Policy Exhibited in a Better Light'.

24. NAI: Home Department Political (A): Proceedings, July 1920, nos 192–203, 'Proposals for the Inauguration of Cinematograph Propaganda in India'.

25. Emphasis added.

26. NAI: Home Political (Deposit), Proceedings, August 1919, no. 56, 'Proposal to Start a Government Party and to Concert Means to get Government's Measures and Policy Exhibited in a Better Light'.

Conclusion: Amritsar and the British in India

1. Sir S. Reed, *The India I Knew 1897–1947* (London, 1952), p. 193.
2. P. Woodruff [Philip Mason], *The Men Who Ruled India. The Guardians* (London, 1971; first published 1954), p. 13.
3. Norah Burke cited in M.M. Kaye, *The Sun in the Morning* (London, 1990), p. 450. Thanks to Susan Lloyd for bringing this to my attention.
4. J. Morris, *Farewell the Trumpets. An Imperial Retreat* (London, 1998; first published 1978), p. 273. See also K. Mohan, 'The Jallianwala Bagh Tragedy: A Catalyst of Indian Consciousness', in V.N. Datta & S. Settar (eds), *Jallianwala Bagh Massacre* (Delhi, 2000), pp. 52–3.
5. Sir M. O' Dwyer, *India as I Knew it 1885–1925* (London, 1925), pp. 306–8.
6. Sir C.W. Gwynn, *Imperial Policing* (London, 1934), p. 63.
7. P.G. Robb, *The Government of India and Reform. Policies Towards Politics and the Constitution 1916–1921* (New Delhi, 1989), pp. 192–3.
8. S. Shoul, 'Soldiers, Riot Control and Aid to the Civil Power in India, Egypt and Palestine, 1919–39', *Journal of the Society for Army Historical Research*, 86/346 (Summer 2008), p. 124.
9. D. Arnold, 'The Armed Police and Colonial Rule in South India, 1914–1947', *Modern Asian Studies*, 11/1 (1977), p. 105.
10. See R.L. Hardgrave, Jr., 'The Mappila Rebellion, 1921: Peasant Revolt in Malabar', *Modern Asian Studies*, 11/1 (1977), pp. 57–99.
11. LHCMA: General Sir John Burnett-Stuart Papers (2/3/1 – 2/3/3), 'Moplah Rebellion Memoir', p. 101. Burnett-Stuart later wrote, 'The Government of India were still shaken, I think, by General Dyer's actions less than two years before when he had opened fire prematurely on a troublesome mob and killed many people including women and children. An incident which brought down coals of fire on the heads of the government and made them loth to put too much power in the hands of any soldiers.' (pp. 101–2).
12. Shoul, 'Soldiers, Riot Control and Aid to the Civil Power in India, Egypt and Palestine, 1919–39', p. 128.
13. N. Collett, *The Butcher of Amritsar. General Reginald Dyer* (London, 2005), pp. 420–3; The last chapter of O'Dwyer, *India as I Knew it* is entitled 'Is India a Lost Dominion?' O'Dwyer concluded, defiantly, that India was not.
14. Details taken from C. Kaul, 'Montagu, Edwin Samuel (1879–1924)', *Oxford Dictionary of National Biography*, Oxford University Press, Sept 2004; online edn, Jan 2008 [http://www.oxforddnb.com/view/article/35074, accessed 4 June 2008].
15. IOC: MSS EUR E264/4, Montagu to Chelmsford, 1 January 1918.
16. IOC: MSS EUR E264/5, Montagu to Chelmsford, 1 May 1919.
17. Gandhi to Agatha Harrison, 15 August 1947, in *The Collected Works of Mahatma Gandhi* (Electronic Book), New Delhi, Publications Division Government of India, 1999, 98 vols *http://www.gandhiserve.org/cwmg/cwmg.html* [hereafter *CWMG*], LXXXVI, pp. 230–1; 'Talk with Communist Party Members', 15 August 1947, in *CWMG*, LXXXVI, p. 234.
18. D. Arnold, *Gandhi* (London, 2001), p. 111.

Epilogue: Operation Blue Star

1. M. Tully, *No Full Stops in India* (London, 1992; first published 1991), p. 154.
2. M. Tully & S. Jacob, *Amritsar. Mrs Gandhi's Last Battle* (London, 1985), pp. 159–61, 166–7.
3. R.L. Hardgrave, Jr., 'India in 1984: Confrontation, Assassination, and Succession', *Asian Survey*, 25/2 (February 1985), p. 133.
4. See the testimony of Lieutenant-General K. Sunderji, cited in Tully & Jacob, *Amritsar. Mrs Gandhi's Last Battle*, pp. 188–9.
5. Tully & Jacob, *Amritsar. Mrs Gandhi's Last Battle*, pp. 200–5.
6. Hardgrave, Jr., 'India in 1984: Confrontation, Assassination, and Succession', p. 132.
7. See I. Talbot, *Khizr Tiwana, the Punjab Unionist Party and the Partition of India* (Richmond, Surrey, 1996).
8. A. Kundu, 'The Indian Armed Forces' Sikh and Non-Sikh Officers' Opinions of Operation Blue Star', *Pacific Affairs*, 67/1 (Spring, 1994), pp. 49–52.
9. These included the National Security Act (1980), the Punjab Disturbed Areas Ordinance (1983), the Terrorist Areas (Special Courts) Act (1984), the Terrorist and Disruptive Activities (Prevention) Act (1985).
10. *India: Torture, Rape and Deaths in Custody* (London, 1992), pp. 29–31.
11. G. Singh, 'Punjab Since 1984: Disorder, Order, and Legitimacy', *Asian Survey*, 36/4 (April 1996), pp. 413–14.
12. S.J. Singh, *Operation Black Thunder. An Eyewitness Account of Terrorism in the Punjab* (New Delhi, 2002), p. 325.

Glossary of Selected Indian Words

ahimsa	non-violence
anna	the sixteenth of a rupee
Arja Samaj	Hindu reform movement founded in 1875
atta	wheat
baboo (or babu)	disparaging term for a petty government official
badmash	villain, immoral person
bagh	garden
Baisakhi	Sikh new year
Baluchi	nomadic people from southern Afghanistan
bania	merchant, shopkeeper
bazaar	market
bhadralok	middle-class, often higher-caste person from Bengal
bhisti	water-carrier
Brahmin	priestly caste in Hinduism
cantonment	permanent military station (in India)
chowky	police station or outpost
dak bungalow	travellers' rest house
danda fauj	'rebel army'
dhoti	piece of cloth worn around the lower body
durbar	royal court, hall of audience
Ghadr	*Revolt* (revolutionary group founded in the US and Canada and also the name of their newspaper)
godown	warehouse
Gurkha	Nepalese soldier
hartal	strike
jai	victory, triumph, long live!
jatha	armed band

Jihad	Islamic term for holy war
kacheri	court house
khadi	Indian hand-spun cloth that would become the uniform of Indian politicians
khalsa	Sikh brotherhood
Khalifat	Islamic political movement dedicated to protecting the Ottoman Caliphate
kotwali	police station
kukri	traditional curved knife of the Gurkhas
lakh	one hundred thousand
lathi	stick, made from bamboo, often bound with iron rings
maharaja	Indian prince
Mahatma	Sanskrit word for 'great soul'
memsahib	wife of British official
pandit	learned, wise, a clever scholar
raj	rule
Ram Naumi	Hindu festival celebrating the birthday of Lord Rama
sabha	association or political assembly
sadhu	Hindu holy man
sahib	title given to Europeans (equivalent to 'master')
sarkar	government
satyagraha	'truth-force' or 'love-force'
satyagrahi	signatory of Gandhi's *satyagraha* pledge
sepoy	Indian soldier
Seva Samiti	Indian charitable organisation
sowar	Indian cavalry soldier
swadeshi	locally made goods ('own country')
tahsil	local revenue office
tonga	horse-drawn carriage
topee	helmet worn by many British officials
vakil	lawyer, agent, representative
Waqt	*Time* (nationalist newspaper in Amritsar)

Bibliography

PRIMARY SOURCES

Archive sources

India Office Collections, British Library, London
    Major-General Sir William Beynon (MSS EUR D830)
    Viscount Chelmsford (MSS EUR E264)
    Indian Police Collection (MSS EUR F161/110)
    E.S. Montagu (MSS EUR D523)
    Sir J.P. Thompson (MSS EUR F137)
    F.B. Wace (MSS EUR F394)
    MSS EUR E264/43, *Sedition Committee, 1918 Report* (Calcutta, 1918)

Centre for South Asian Studies, University of Cambridge
    Sir J.C. Curry papers (Box 1)
    Sir James Penny papers
    Sir John Smyth papers

Liddell Hart Centre for Military Archives, Kings College, London
    Sir James Edmonds papers
    Sir John Burnett-Stuart papers

National Archives of India, New Delhi
    Home Political (A) Proceedings
    Home Political (B) Proceedings
    Home Political (Deposit) Proceedings
    Home Military
    Foreign & Political General (B) Proceedings
    Foreign & Political (Deposit) Internal, Proceedings

Report on Native Newspaper, Punjab, Jan–Dec 1920

Microfilm: Amritsar Conspiracy Case 1919 (Acc No. 1829)

The National Archives of the UK, Kew, London

CAB 27/92: *Evidence Taken Before the Disorders Inquiry Committee* (7 vols, Calcutta, 1920) [Vol. I *Delhi*; Vol. II *Bombay Presidency*; Vol. III *Amritsar*]

CAB 27/93: *Evidence Taken Before the Disorders Inquiry Committee* (7 vols, Calcutta: Government of India, 1920) [Vol. IV *Lahore & Kasur*; Vol. V *Gujranwala, Gujrat, Lyallpur and Punjab Provincial*; Vol. VI *Punjab Government and Sir Umar Hayat Khan*; Vol. VII *Government of India*]

PRO 30/30/18: Government of India. Home Department. Resolution, April 1920

PRO WO 95/5403: War Diary of Lahore (Civil) Area from 15 April 1919 to 30 April 1919

Punjab State Archives, Chandigarh

Home Judicial (B) Proceedings

Home Judicial (C) Proceedings

Home Military B Proceedings

Unpublished Letters and Memoirs in the Collections of the Imperial War Museum, London

Account of Brigadier F. McCallum (83/31/1)

Lieutenant-Colonel M.H.L. Morgan, 'The Truth About Amritsar' (72/22/1)

Online sources

The Collected Works of Mahatma Gandhi (Electronic Book), New Delhi, Publications Division Government of India, 1999, 98 volumes *http://www.gandhiserve.org/cwmg/cwmg.html*

Official publications

1. Government publications

Census of India, 1921, Volume XV, Punjab and Delhi (2 parts, Lahore, 1923)

India's Contribution to the Great War (Calcutta, 1923)

Report on the Administration of the Punjab and its Dependencies for 1919–20 (Lahore, 1921)

Statement Exhibiting the Moral and Material Progress and Condition of India During the Year 1917–18 (London, 1919)

Statement Exhibiting the Moral and Material Progress and Condition of India During the Year 1919 (London, 1920)

2. Parliamentary papers

Command 534, *Reports on the Punjab Disturbances April 1919* (London, 1920)

Command 681, *Report of the Committee Appointed by the Government of India to Investigate the Disturbances in the Punjab, etc.* (London, 1920)

Command 771, *Disturbances in the Punjab. Statement by Brig-General R.E.H. Dyer, C.B.* (London, 1920)

3. Congress reports

Report of the Special Session of the Indian National Congress Held at Bombay on 29th, 30th, 31st August and 1st September 1918 (Bombay: Bombay Chronicle Press, 1918)

The Congress Punjab Inquiry 1919–1920: Evidence (Delhi, 1996; first published 1920)

Memoirs and personal accounts

Barrow, Gen. Sir G., *The Fire of Life* (London, 1942)

Gandhi, M.K., *An Autobiography or the Story of my Experiments with Truth,* M. Desai (trans.) (London, 2001; first published, 1927 & 1929)

Montagu, E.S., *An Indian Diary*, V. Montagu (ed.) (London, 1930)

Nehru, J., *An Autobiography* (London, 1941; first published 1936)

O'Dwyer, Sir M., *India as I Knew it 1885–1925* (London, 1925)

Setalvad, C.H., *Recollections and Reflections. An Autobiography* (Bombay, 1946)

General works

Horniman, B.G., *Amritsar and Our Duty to India* (Delhi, 1997; first published 1920)

Mohan, P., *The Punjab "Rebellion" of 1919 and How It Was Suppressed*, R.M. Bakaya (ed.) (New Delhi, 1999; first published 1920)

SECONDARY SOURCES

Biographical sources

Arnold, D., *Gandhi* (London, 2001)

Barrow, Sir G., *The Life of General Sir Charles Carmichael Monro* (London, 1931)

Brown, J.M., *Gandhi's Rise to Power. Indian Politics 1915–1922* (Cambridge, 1972)

—, *Gandhi. Prisoner of Hope* (New Haven & London, 1998; first published 1989)

Collett, N., *The Butcher of Amritsar. General Reginald Dyer* (London, 2005)

Colvin, I., *The Life of General Dyer* (Edinburgh & London, 1929)

Fischer, L., *The Life of Mahatma Gandhi* (London, 1997; first published 1951)

Kitchlew, T., *Saifuddin Kitchlew. Hero of Jallianwala Bagh* (India, 1987)

Woodruff, P., *The Men Who Ruled India. The Guardians* (London, 1971; first published 1954)

General works

Allen, C. (ed.), *Plain Tales From the Raj. Images of British India in the Twentieth Century* (London, 1975)

Bakshi, S.R., *Jallianwala Bagh Tragedy* (New Delhi, 1982)

Barnett, C., *The Collapse of British Power* (London, 2002; first published 1972)

Bose, P., *Organizing Empire. Individualism, Collective Agency, and India* (London & Durham, 2003)

Brown, J.M., *Modern India. The Origins of an Asian Democracy*, 2nd edn (Oxford, 1994; first published 1985)

Das, M.N., *India Under Morley and Minto. Politics Behind Revolution, Repression and Reforms* (London, 1964)

Datta, V.N., *Jallianwala Bagh* (Ludhiana, 1969)

Datta, V.N. & Settar, S. (eds), *Jallianwala Bagh Massacre* (Delhi, 2000)

Dewey, C., *Anglo-Indian Attitudes. The Mind of the Indian Civil Service* (London, 1993)

Draper, A., *The Amritsar Massacre. Twilight of the Raj* (London: Buchan & Enright, 1985; first published 1981)

Edwardes, M., *The Myth of the Mahatma. Gandhi, the British and the Raj* (London, 1986)

Fein, H., *Imperial Crime and Punishment. The Massacre at Jallianwala Bagh and British Judgment, 1919–1920* (Honolulu, 1977)

Ferguson, N., *Empire. How Britain Made the Modern World* (London, 2003)

Furneaux, R., *Massacre at Amritsar* (London, 1963)

Gauba, A., *Amritsar. A Study in Urban History (1840–1947)* (Jalandhar, 1988)

Gilmour, D., *The Ruling Caste. Imperial Lives in the Victorian Raj* (London, 2005)

Griffiths, Sir P., *To Guard My People. A History of the Indian Police* (London, 1971)

Gwynn, Sir C.W., *Imperial Policing* (London: Macmillan & Co, 1934)

James, L., *Raj. The Making and Unmaking of British India* (London, 1998; first published 1997)

Judd, D., *The Lion and the Tiger. The Rise and Fall of the British Raj* (Oxford, 2005; first published 2004)

Kaul, C., *Reporting the Raj. The British Press and India, c. 1880–1922* (Manchester, 2003)

Keith, A.B., *A Constitutional History of India 1600–1935* (London, 1936)

Kumar, R. (ed.), *Essays on Gandhian Politics. The Rowlatt Satyagraha of 1919* (Oxford, 1971)

Low, D.A. (ed.), *Soundings in Modern South Asian History* (London, 1968)

—, *Congress and the Raj. Facets of the Indian Struggle 1917–47* (London, 1977)

Metcalf, T.R., *Ideologies of the Raj* (Cambridge, 1994)

Mohan, K., *Militant Nationalism in the Punjab 1919–1935* (New Delhi, 1985)

Narain, S., *The Historiography of the Jallianwala Bagh Massacre, 1919* (Surrey: South Godstone, 1998)

Perkins, R., *The Amritsar Legacy. Golden Temple to Caxton Hall, the Story of a Killing* (Chippenham, 1989)

Popplewell, R.J., *Intelligence and Imperial Defence. British Intelligence and the Defence of the Indian Empire 1904–1924* (London, 1995)

Ram, R., *The Jallianwala Bagh Massacre. A Premeditated Plan* (Chandigarh, 1978; first published 1969)

Robb, P.G., *The Government of India and Reform. Policies Towards Politics and the Constitution 1916–1921* (New Delhi, 1989)

Rumbold, A., *Watershed in India 1914–1922* (London, 1979)

Seal, A., *The Emergence of Indian Nationalism. Competition and Collaboration in the Later Nineteenth Century* (Cambridge, 1971; first published 1968)

Swinson, A., *Six Minutes to Sunset. The Story of General Dyer and the Amritsar Affair* (London, 1964)

Tai-Yong, T., *The Garrison State. The Military, Government and Society in Colonial Punjab, 1849–1947* (New Delhi & London, 2005)

Talbot, I., *Punjab and the Raj 1849–1947* (New Delhi, 1988)

Thompson, E., *A Letter From India* (London, 1932)

Wasti, S.R., *Lord Minto and the Indian Nationalist Movement 1905 to 1910* (Oxford, 1964)

Articles

Arnold, D., 'The Armed Police and Colonial Rule in South India, 1914–1947', *Modern Asian Studies*, 11/1 (1977), pp. 101–25

Bond, B., 'Amritsar 1919', *History Today*, 13/10 (1963), pp. 666–76

Campion, D.A., 'Authority, Accountability and Representation: the United Provinces Police and the Dilemmas of the Colonial Policeman in British India, 1902–39', *Historical Research*, 76/192 (May 2003), pp. 217–37

Danzig, R., 'The Announcement of August 20th, 1917', *Journal of Asian Studies*, 28/1 (November 1968), pp. 19–37

Ewing, A., 'The Indian Civil Service 1919–1924: Service Discontent and the Response in London and Delhi', *Modern Asian Studies*, 18/1 (1984), pp. 33–53

Fraser, T.G., 'Germany and Indian Revolution, 1914–18', *Journal of Contemporary History*, 12/2 (April 1977), pp. 255–72

George Boyce, D., 'From Assaye to the Assaye: Reflections on British Government, Force and Moral Authority in India', *Journal of Military History*, 63/3 (July 1999), pp. 643–68

Gerald Barrier, N., 'The Punjab Disturbances of 1907: The Response of the British Government in India to Agrarian Unrest', *Modern Asian Studies*, 1/4 (1967), pp. 353–83

Gordon, R., 'Non-Co-operation and Council Entry, 1919 to 1920', *Modern Asian Studies*, 7/3 (1973), pp. 443–73

Hardgrave Jr., R.L., 'The Mappila Rebellion, 1921: Peasant Revolt in Malabar', *Modern Asian Studies*, 11/1 (1977), pp. 57–99

Johnson, G., 'Partition, Agitation and Congress: Bengal 1904 to 1908', *Modern Asian Studies*, 7/3 (1973), pp. 533–88

Lloyd, N., 'Sir Michael O'Dwyer and "Imperial Terrorism" in the Punjab, 1919', *South Asia*, 33/3 (2010), pp. 363–80

—, 'The Amritsar Massacre and the Minimum Force Debate', *Small Wars & Insurgencies*, 21/2 (June 2010), pp. 382–403

—, 'The Errors of Amritsar', *BBC History Magazine*, 10/4 (April 2009), pp. 51–4

Low, D.A., 'The Government of India and the First Non-Co-operation Movement – 1920–1922', *Journal of Asian Studies*, 25/2 (February 1966), pp. 241–59

Raghaven, S., 'Protecting the Raj: The Army in India and Internal Security, c. 1919–39', *Small Wars & Insurgencies*, 16/3 (December 2005), pp. 253–79

Robb, P., 'The Government of India and Annie Besant', *Modern Asian Studies*, 10/1 (1976), pp. 107–30

Sayer, D., 'British Reaction to the Amritsar Massacre 1919–1920', *Past & Present*, 131 (May 1991), pp. 130–64

Shoul, S., 'Soldiers, Riot Control and Aid to the Civil Power in India, Egypt and Palestine, 1919–39', *Journal of the Society for Army Historical Research*, 86/346 (Summer 2008), pp. 120–39

Tai-Yong, T., 'An Imperial Home-Front: Punjab and the First World War', *Journal of Military History*, 64/2 (April 2000), pp. 371–410

Talbot, I., 'British Rule in the Punjab, 1849–1947: Characteristics and Consequences', *Journal of Imperial and Commonwealth History*, 19/2 (May 1991), pp. 203–21

Fictional works

Forster, E.M., *A Passage to India* (London, 1988; first published 1924)
Scott, P., *The Jewel in the Crown* (London, 2005; first published 1966)
Wolpert, S., *An Error of Judgment* (Boston & Toronto, 1970)

Unpublished theses

Shoul, S., 'Soldiers, Riot Control, and Aid to the Civil Power in India, Egypt and Palestine 1919–1939', Ph.D., University College London, 2006

Index